3 Books in 1

Mastering Data Analytics

Visualization and Communicating Data

2025

Complete Guidebook with Tips and Tricks and Strategies on Coding

Table of Contents

Book 1

Essential Data Analytics

Quick-Start Guide to Data Literacy for Beginners

Dr. Alex Harper

Chapter 1: Introduction to Data Literacy

Importance of Data Literacy in Today's World

In a world where every swipe, click, and transaction generates data, the ability to understand and interpret this data has become essential. Data literacy is not just a skill for data scientists or IT professionals; it's a critical competency for nearly everyone. From making informed personal decisions to succeeding in a data-driven job market, data literacy empowers individuals to navigate the complexities of modern life with confidence.

This chapter will explore why data literacy is vital in today's world, shedding light on the role data plays in every industry, its impact on society, and the benefits that individuals and organizations gain from becoming data-literate. By the end of this chapter, you'll understand why data literacy is a foundational skill that can boost your effectiveness and decision-making, setting you up for success throughout this book and beyond.

What is Data Literacy?

Before diving into its importance, let's clarify what data literacy actually means. Data literacy is the ability to read, interpret, understand, and communicate data. A data-literate person can critically analyze data to make informed decisions. They know how to interpret graphs, charts, and tables, and they can recognize patterns, trends, and outliers. Data literacy goes beyond simply understanding numbers; it involves asking the right questions, understanding data sources, and assessing the quality and reliability of data.

Why Data Literacy Matters

1. **Informed Decision-Making** Data literacy enables people to make more informed choices, whether for personal finances, health, career development, or business strategies. For instance, when buying a car, understanding data about fuel efficiency, safety ratings, and resale value can help you make a more informed decision. In the business world, data literacy allows managers and employees to base their decisions on solid evidence rather than guesswork.

2. **Navigating the Information Age** We live in an era defined by the constant flow of information. News, social media posts, and marketing content bombard us daily, often loaded with data or statistics. A data-literate individual can critically evaluate this information, spotting biased or misleading data and differentiating between reputable and unreliable sources. This skill is essential for making sound judgments and staying well-informed.

3. **Increasing Workplace Relevance** Data literacy is increasingly a key asset in the

workplace. As businesses strive to be more data-driven, employers are actively seeking employees who can understand and work with data. Regardless of industry—whether in healthcare, finance, education, or marketing—data literacy enhances an employee's ability to analyze trends, measure success, and provide insights that drive organizational success.

4. **Empowerment through Knowledge** Data literacy empowers individuals to harness the potential of data. It's a transformative skill that allows you to take control of the information around you, identifying insights that might otherwise go unnoticed. For example, a basic understanding of data can help you track and improve your fitness, budget, or even identify trends in your productivity.

How Data Shapes Our World

The importance of data literacy becomes even more apparent when considering the influence data has on global decisions, public policy, and the economy. Governments use data to make decisions about public health, education, transportation, and environmental protection. Corporations analyze data to create products, design services, and innovate. Even nonprofits rely on data to allocate resources effectively and measure the impact of their initiatives.

Consider some real-world scenarios:

- **Healthcare**: Data analysis helps doctors make accurate diagnoses, track disease trends, and provide better patient care. In the case of the COVID-19 pandemic, data literacy was crucial for understanding infection rates, hospital capacity, and vaccine efficacy.
- **Environmental Sustainability**: Data literacy is also essential in addressing global issues like climate change. Understanding data on carbon emissions, deforestation, and temperature increases informs policies and behaviors that contribute to sustainable practices.
- **Education**: In education, data is used to personalize learning, improve teaching strategies, and track student progress. Schools increasingly rely on data to understand and address learning gaps, enhancing outcomes for students.

These examples illustrate that data isn't just a corporate or governmental tool—it's at the core of almost every decision that impacts society.

The Benefits of Becoming Data-Literate

Becoming data-literate comes with a range of benefits:

- **Enhanced Personal Decision-Making**: Data literacy empowers you to make well-informed choices, whether it's in your personal or professional life. By understanding data, you can weigh options more objectively, saving time, money, and effort.
- **Improved Critical Thinking**: Data literacy sharpens your critical thinking skills. It encourages you to ask the right questions, consider multiple perspectives, and avoid common cognitive biases. With these skills, you can approach problems methodically and make logical, evidence-based decisions.
- **Increased Job Market Competitiveness**: A data-literate professional is a valuable asset in today's job market. Data skills, even at a foundational level, make you more competitive in nearly every field. You'll be able to back up your opinions with data, impressing employers with your ability to contribute to data-driven projects.
- **Ability to Spot Misinformation**: Data literacy helps you spot "fake news" or misinformation by evaluating data critically. You'll be better equipped to challenge questionable statistics, understand data context, and protect yourself from being swayed by misleading claims.

Common Misconceptions About Data Literacy

1. **"Data Literacy is Only for Data Scientists"** Many people believe that data literacy is only for technical professionals, but that's far from true. While data scientists dive deeply into complex algorithms and machine learning, data literacy is about having the foundational skills needed to work with data at any level.
2. **"You Need to Be Good at Math"** Another misconception is that data literacy requires advanced math skills. While some familiarity with numbers is helpful, data literacy focuses more on understanding, interpreting, and using data. You don't need to be a math whiz to gain insights from data.
3. **"Data Literacy Requires Expensive Tools"** Many people think that data analysis requires specialized software or costly tools. In reality, you can start developing data literacy using free or accessible tools, like spreadsheets or open-source data visualization software.

The Future of Data Literacy

With the world increasingly turning towards data-driven decision-making, data literacy will only become more important. Schools, businesses, and governments are beginning to prioritize data literacy as an essential skill, just like reading or writing. In the future, data literacy might become a standard part of education, ensuring that everyone has the ability to understand and work with data effectively.

As you continue reading this book, you'll start to see that data literacy is not only an accessible skill but also one that will give you a significant advantage in navigating both personal and professional landscapes.

Real-World Applications and Examples of Data Use

Data isn't just a collection of numbers and facts; it's a powerful tool that drives decisions, shapes strategies, and influences outcomes across various fields. From healthcare to marketing, and education to environmental science, data literacy allows individuals and organizations to make more informed, effective, and strategic choices. In this section, we'll explore some real-world applications of data to illustrate how data literacy transforms the way we live, work, and solve problems.

1. Healthcare: Enhancing Patient Care and Public Health

Healthcare is one of the most data-rich industries, with massive amounts of information generated daily. Medical data, from patient records to lab results, allows doctors and researchers to understand diseases, develop treatments, and improve patient care.

- **Predicting Disease Outbreaks**: During the COVID-19 pandemic, data analysis was essential in predicting hotspots, tracking the virus's spread, and managing healthcare resources. Data from hospitals, governments, and mobile devices helped authorities identify at-risk areas, set travel restrictions, and allocate resources efficiently.

- **Personalized Medicine**: Data has led to significant advancements in personalized medicine, where treatments are tailored based on individual characteristics, like genetics and lifestyle. For instance, analyzing genetic data can help doctors determine which cancer treatments are most likely to work for specific patients, resulting in higher success rates and fewer side effects.
- **Preventive Care and Early Diagnosis**: Data also plays a crucial role in preventive care. Wearable devices, such as fitness trackers and smartwatches, collect data on heart rate, sleep patterns, and physical activity. This information can alert users and healthcare providers to early signs of potential health issues, allowing for timely intervention and improved patient outcomes.

2. Retail and E-commerce: Understanding Consumer Behavior

In retail, data is invaluable for understanding customer preferences, predicting demand, and optimizing inventory. Through data literacy, retailers can turn raw data into insights that drive profits and improve customer satisfaction.

- **Personalized Recommendations**: E-commerce platforms, like Amazon and Netflix, use algorithms to analyze user behavior and recommend products or content that align with individual preferences. This personalization, powered by data on browsing history, past purchases, and demographics, enhances the customer experience and increases sales.
- **Inventory Management and Demand Forecasting**: Data analytics enables retailers to forecast demand accurately, ensuring that popular items are always in stock while avoiding overstocking slower-moving products. For example, by analyzing past sales data and trends, a fashion retailer can predict which clothing items will be in high demand for the upcoming season, allowing them to adjust their inventory accordingly.
- **Pricing Strategies**: Retailers also use data to set competitive prices. Dynamic pricing, for example, adjusts prices based on factors such as time of day, competitor pricing, and demand. Airlines and ride-sharing services, like Uber, frequently use this strategy to maximize profits during peak times while offering discounts during slower periods.

3. Education: Improving Learning Outcomes

In education, data literacy allows educators, students, and administrators to make better decisions about teaching methods, curricula, and resources. Educational institutions increasingly rely on data to improve learning experiences and boost student success rates.

- **Personalized Learning**: Schools and online learning platforms use data to tailor lessons to individual learning styles and abilities. For instance, by tracking a student's progress on assignments, teachers can identify areas where the student struggles and provide targeted support, ensuring a more personalized learning experience.
- **Tracking Student Engagement**: Data analytics can reveal trends in student engagement and participation, helping educators understand what teaching methods work best. For example, if data shows that students engage more with visual materials than with text-based resources, teachers might incorporate more videos and interactive content into their lessons.
- **Predicting Academic Success**: Schools use data to identify students who may be at risk of falling behind, allowing for timely interventions. Early warning systems, based on attendance, grades, and participation data, help schools provide the necessary resources and support to ensure students stay on track.

4. Environmental Science: Tackling Climate Change

Data plays an essential role in addressing environmental challenges, from climate change to biodiversity loss. By analyzing data on natural patterns, scientists and policymakers can make informed decisions to protect the planet.

- **Climate Modeling and Forecasting**: Climate scientists use data from satellite images, weather stations, and historical records to create models that predict climate trends. These models help governments and organizations prepare for climate-related challenges, such as rising sea levels, extreme weather, and changing ecosystems.
- **Conservation Efforts**: Data helps track the populations of endangered species, enabling conservationists to protect habitats and ensure biodiversity. For example, by analyzing data on animal migration patterns, scientists can identify critical areas that need protection, ensuring that species have safe migration routes.
- **Sustainable Resource Management**: Data is also vital for managing natural resources responsibly. By monitoring water usage, deforestation rates, and pollution levels, governments and organizations can develop policies that promote sustainability and minimize environmental impact.

5. Finance: Mitigating Risks and Maximizing Profits

In the finance industry, data literacy is crucial for managing risks, optimizing investments, and understanding market trends. Financial institutions use data to drive their strategies, ensuring both profitability and security.

- **Fraud Detection**: Financial institutions use data to detect unusual patterns and identify potential fraud. Machine learning algorithms analyze transactions in real time, flagging activities that deviate from a customer's typical behavior, such as large international purchases or sudden account withdrawals.
- **Investment Decisions**: Data analysis informs investment decisions, helping investors understand trends and assess the potential risks and rewards of different options. By analyzing market trends, historical performance, and economic indicators, investors can make data-driven choices to maximize returns.
- **Credit Scoring**: Credit agencies use data to determine individuals' creditworthiness, assessing factors like payment history, outstanding debts, and income. This information helps lenders make informed decisions about whether to approve loan applications, minimizing the risk of defaults.

6. Marketing and Advertising: Reaching the Right Audience

In marketing, data is indispensable for understanding audience demographics, optimizing ad campaigns, and measuring return on investment. Data literacy enables marketers to reach their target audience more effectively and maximize the impact of their efforts.

- **Targeted Advertising**: Marketers use data to segment audiences based on factors like age, location, and interests, allowing them to deliver more relevant ads. For instance, a travel agency may use data to show ads for tropical vacations to users who frequently search for beach destinations.
- **Measuring Campaign Effectiveness**: Data analytics allows marketers to measure the success of campaigns by tracking metrics such as click-through rates, conversion rates, and customer engagement. This information helps them refine their strategies and allocate resources to the most effective channels.
- **Customer Sentiment Analysis**: By analyzing data from social media and customer feedback, companies can gauge public sentiment about their brand or products. This information allows marketers to address concerns, improve products, and build stronger customer relationships.

7. Sports: Improving Performance and Fan Engagement

Data has become a key element in professional sports, where teams, coaches, and players use it to gain a competitive edge and enhance fan engagement.

- **Player Performance Analytics**: Coaches and sports analysts use data to assess player performance, track improvement, and identify areas for growth. For example, in basketball, data on shooting accuracy, speed, and endurance allows coaches to develop training programs tailored to each player's needs.
- **Game Strategy and Tactics**: Data analysis provides insights into team performance, enabling coaches to make strategic adjustments. In soccer, for instance, data on players' positioning and movement patterns can help coaches devise more effective game plans and improve teamwork.
- **Fan Engagement**: Sports teams also use data to improve the fan experience, offering personalized content, promotions, and merchandise. For instance, analyzing data on fan preferences helps teams create engaging experiences, from tailored social media posts to targeted offers.

The Power of Data Literacy in Everyday Life

As these examples demonstrate, data literacy is transforming diverse sectors and impacting people's daily lives. Understanding how data informs these fields can inspire you to see the potential of data in your own life, whether for personal decision-making, career advancement, or contributing to global challenges. As you continue through this book, you'll learn the skills to become more data-literate, empowering you to use data effectively in both professional and personal contexts.

Overview of Data Analytics as a Skill

Data analytics is the process of examining datasets to draw conclusions and make decisions based on evidence rather than intuition or assumptions. In today's world, where data is generated at an astonishing rate, the ability to interpret and analyze data is a powerful and highly sought-after skill. This section will delve into what data analytics involves, the key skills required, and why mastering data analytics is essential for individuals in a variety of roles.

By understanding the scope of data analytics and its applications, you'll gain a foundation for the practical skills you'll learn in the following chapters.

What is Data Analytics?

Data analytics encompasses a range of activities, from data collection and cleaning to statistical analysis and visualization. At its core, data analytics is about transforming raw data into meaningful insights that can guide decision-making. Data analytics is not a single process but rather a collection of skills and methods that work together to achieve specific goals, such as predicting future trends, identifying correlations, or uncovering patterns.

Here's a basic framework of the data analytics process:

1. **Data Collection**: The first step is gathering data from various sources. This could include surveys, databases, logs, or even web-scraped information. Effective data collection ensures you have reliable data to work with and a solid foundation for further analysis.
2. **Data Cleaning and Preparation**: Raw data is often messy, with duplicates, errors, or missing values. Data cleaning involves processing the data to make it usable, which might include removing irrelevant information, filling in missing values, and standardizing formats.
3. **Exploratory Data Analysis (EDA)**: EDA is the stage where analysts look at the data to uncover initial insights, visualize patterns, and formulate hypotheses. This often involves generating summary statistics and creating simple charts to understand the data's structure.
4. **Data Analysis and Modeling**: This is where analysts apply statistical methods or machine learning algorithms to extract deeper insights from the data. Depending on the goal, this

could involve predictive analytics, correlation analysis, or clustering.

5. **Data Visualization**: Presenting data in a visual format—such as graphs, charts, or dashboards—helps make complex information more understandable and actionable for stakeholders.

6. **Reporting and Decision-Making**: Finally, the insights from data analysis are communicated in reports or presentations, guiding decision-makers on the best actions to take based on the data.

By following these steps, data analytics allows professionals to gain meaningful insights and make data-driven decisions that lead to better outcomes.

Key Skills in Data Analytics

Mastering data analytics requires a combination of technical skills, critical thinking, and communication abilities. Here's an overview of some of the key skills involved:

1. **Data Collection and Management Skills**
   o Knowing where and how to gather data is essential for analytics. Skills in SQL (Structured Query Language) or data scraping tools are useful for retrieving data from databases or the web.

- Data management, which includes organizing and storing data efficiently, is crucial for ensuring that datasets are accessible, reliable, and ready for analysis.

2. **Statistical Analysis and Critical Thinking**
   - Understanding basic statistics is fundamental in data analytics. Skills in measures of central tendency (like mean and median), variability (such as standard deviation), and probability help analysts interpret data accurately.
   - Critical thinking allows analysts to question assumptions, identify biases, and avoid jumping to conclusions. This skill is invaluable for ensuring that insights are accurate and meaningful.

3. **Programming Skills**
   - Familiarity with programming languages like Python or R is highly beneficial for data analytics. These languages offer powerful libraries (such as Pandas for Python) that simplify data manipulation, analysis, and visualization.
   - Programming allows analysts to automate repetitive tasks, handle large datasets, and apply complex algorithms that would be challenging to execute manually.

4. **Data Visualization**
   - Effective data visualization is essential for communicating insights. This skill involves creating graphs, charts, and infographics that make data easy to interpret and highlight key findings.
   - Tools like Tableau, Power BI, or even Excel can be used to create visualizations that tell a story and help stakeholders understand the data's implications.
5. **Domain Knowledge**
   - Knowing the industry or field in which the data is being analyzed is also beneficial. For example, data analytics in healthcare may involve understanding medical terminology and health metrics, while analytics in finance requires knowledge of economic indicators and financial principles.
   - Domain knowledge allows analysts to ask the right questions, understand the context of the data, and provide insights that are relevant and valuable to the organization.

Why Data Analytics is an Essential Skill

1. **Enhanced Decision-Making** Data analytics enables individuals and organizations to make better decisions by providing evidence-based

insights. For example, in business, analytics can help determine which products to stock based on past sales trends or which marketing strategies lead to the highest engagement. Data-driven decisions are often more accurate and effective, minimizing risks and maximizing returns.

2. **Problem Solving and Innovation** Data analytics is a powerful tool for problem-solving. By analyzing data, individuals can identify issues that may not be apparent at first glance. For instance, in manufacturing, data analysis can uncover inefficiencies in production processes, allowing companies to make improvements and reduce costs. Analytics also fosters innovation by revealing new opportunities or potential market segments.

3. **Competitive Advantage** For businesses, data analytics provides a competitive edge by revealing insights that drive strategic initiatives. Companies that leverage data can better understand their customers, predict market trends, and stay ahead of competitors. For individuals, data analytics skills can enhance employability, as many employers seek professionals who can interpret and use data effectively.

4. **Efficiency and Automation** Data analytics also enables automation, making processes more efficient. For instance, retail companies

can use data to automate inventory restocking based on sales forecasts, or financial firms can use data analytics to automate fraud detection. These efficiencies save time, reduce manual labor, and allow employees to focus on more strategic tasks.

5. **Adaptability in a Data-Driven World** The ability to work with data makes individuals more adaptable in an increasingly data-driven world. As data becomes more integral to every aspect of business and daily life, individuals with data analytics skills will be better prepared to adapt to new roles, technologies, and challenges. This skill set is not only valuable now but will continue to grow in importance as technology advances.

Examples of Data Analytics in Action

1. **Marketing Campaign Optimization** Data analytics allows marketers to measure the performance of campaigns in real-time. By analyzing metrics such as click-through rates, engagement, and conversion rates, marketers can adjust their strategies on the fly, allocate budgets more effectively, and target specific demographics with precision.

2. **Customer Segmentation** In retail, data analytics helps businesses understand their customers better. By segmenting customers based on purchase history, demographics, and behavior, companies can create targeted

marketing campaigns that cater to specific customer needs, increasing satisfaction and loyalty.

3. **Operational Efficiency** Manufacturing and logistics companies use data analytics to optimize their supply chains. By analyzing data on production times, shipping costs, and inventory levels, these companies can identify bottlenecks, reduce waste, and streamline their operations, ultimately saving costs and improving delivery times.

4. **Risk Management in Finance** Financial institutions rely on data analytics for risk management. By analyzing transaction histories and patterns, banks can identify unusual activity, flag potential fraud, and assess the creditworthiness of loan applicants. Data analytics thus plays a key role in minimizing financial risks.

5. **Public Health Surveillance** Data analytics is essential in public health for tracking and controlling diseases. By analyzing data from hospitals, labs, and even social media, health organizations can monitor outbreaks, identify high-risk areas, and allocate resources to the communities that need them most.

Developing Your Data Analytics Skillset

Learning data analytics is like learning a new language. It takes time, practice, and patience, but it's an investment with immense rewards. This book is designed to guide you through the key components of data analytics, from understanding basic statistics to creating impactful visualizations. Each chapter will build on the concepts introduced here, equipping you with the knowledge to use data confidently and effectively.

Chapter 2: Understanding Basic Data Concepts

Definitions: Data, Information, and Knowledge

At the heart of data literacy lies an understanding of the fundamental concepts of data, information, and knowledge. These three terms are often used interchangeably, but each has a distinct meaning and plays a unique role in the process of gaining insights and making decisions. By differentiating between data, information, and knowledge, we set the stage for more effective data analysis and interpretation.

In this chapter, we'll explore what these terms mean, how they relate to each other, and how they form a hierarchy of understanding—from raw data to actionable insights. By understanding the distinctions, you'll be better prepared to work with data in meaningful ways, ultimately turning it into valuable knowledge.

What is Data?

Data is the raw, unprocessed facts and figures that are collected from various sources. It lacks context and meaning on its own and is often presented as numbers, text, or symbols. Data can be anything from sales figures to temperatures, survey responses, or even website traffic statistics. When we first encounter data, it is typically in its most basic form, without any interpretation or structure.

For example:

- A spreadsheet containing monthly sales figures, but without any analysis or explanation.
- The number of likes a post receives on social media, isolated from other engagement metrics.
- Results from a survey, such as a list of ages or geographic locations of respondents.

Data can be **qualitative** or **quantitative**:

- **Qualitative data** describes qualities or characteristics and is often non-numeric (e.g., colors, types of products, names, or locations).
- **Quantitative data** involves numbers and can be measured, counted, or expressed in numeric form (e.g., number of products sold, temperature, or revenue figures).

Data can also be categorized as **structured** or **unstructured**:

- **Structured data** is organized in a specific format, often in tables or spreadsheets, making it easy to search, organize, and analyze. For instance, a database of customer information with columns for names, emails, and purchase history is structured data.

- **Unstructured data** lacks a predefined format and can include text, images, videos, and audio files. Social media posts, emails, and customer feedback are common examples of unstructured data.

What is Information?

Information is data that has been processed, organized, or structured in a way that adds context and meaning. When data is put into a specific format or analyzed in a way that answers questions or provides context, it becomes information. Information allows us to understand "what happened" and provides the foundation for decision-making.

For example:

- When monthly sales data is summarized to show total sales by product category, it becomes information that can reveal popular and underperforming products.
- A chart displaying the number of website visitors by day provides information on traffic patterns, helping website owners understand peak times.
- Survey results that have been categorized to show the percentage of customers who prefer certain features add insight into customer preferences.

Data vs. Information Example: Let's say you have data on daily temperatures for a city over a month. The raw temperature values are simply data. However, if you calculate the average temperature for each week and then create a report on how temperatures have fluctuated, you've converted that data into information. Now, the temperature trends provide more context, helping us understand weather patterns over that month.

In essence, information is **data interpreted to answer specific questions** and often has a defined purpose. While data is the raw material, information is the processed output that can guide decision-making and further analysis.

What is Knowledge?

Knowledge is the culmination of data and information, combined with insights and expertise. Knowledge involves understanding the relationships and patterns within the information and knowing how to apply this understanding to make informed decisions. In other words, knowledge is information that has been synthesized, contextualized, and internalized to solve problems or predict outcomes.

Knowledge typically involves:

- **Applying insights** gained from information to understand why something happened or to predict what might happen in the future.

- **Leveraging experience** and expertise to interpret information within a broader context, making it more meaningful.
- **Using judgement** to draw conclusions, identify patterns, and make strategic decisions.

For example:

- A manager with knowledge of past sales trends and customer preferences might use current sales information to forecast demand and set inventory levels.
- A healthcare provider uses knowledge derived from patient data and medical research to diagnose and treat patients more effectively.
- A financial analyst with knowledge of market trends uses stock performance data and other economic indicators to make investment recommendations.

Information vs. Knowledge Example: Consider a retailer analyzing customer feedback. The feedback data, when summarized and categorized (information), may show that customers are frequently complaining about delayed deliveries. However, by combining this information with knowledge of the company's shipping process and market demand, the retailer gains knowledge about why delays are happening, allowing them to make informed changes to improve the delivery experience.

In the transition from data to knowledge, context and expertise play a crucial role. While information tells us what happened, knowledge tells us why it happened and what we can do about it. Knowledge enables actionable insights, bridging the gap between understanding data and making impactful decisions.

The Data-Information-Knowledge Hierarchy

To further illustrate the relationship between data, information, and knowledge, let's consider them as steps in a hierarchy:

1. **Data**: Raw, unprocessed facts that lack context. Example: Daily sales figures.
2. **Information**: Data that has been processed, organized, or analyzed to answer specific questions. Example: Monthly sales totals per product category.
3. **Knowledge**: Insights and understanding derived from information, often combined with expertise, to guide decisions. Example: Understanding which product categories are seasonal bestsellers and planning inventory accordingly.

This hierarchy represents the **flow of understanding** in data analytics. Data is the foundation that feeds into information; information, in turn, is refined into knowledge that supports strategic decisions.

Why Understanding This Hierarchy is Important

Each level of the data-information-knowledge hierarchy has its own value and purpose, and understanding these differences is key to data literacy. When you know where a piece of information falls within this hierarchy, you can better understand how to use it effectively.

- **Recognizing Data's Limitations**: Data alone is not enough to make decisions. Without analysis and context, raw data lacks meaning and could lead to misinterpretations if used prematurely. Recognizing this limitation helps ensure that you don't jump to conclusions based on incomplete information.
- **Turning Information into Actionable Insights**: Information, while valuable, still requires interpretation and understanding to guide decisions effectively. By advancing from data to information to knowledge, you ensure that your actions are based on sound, evidence-based insights.
- **Building Decision-Making Confidence**: Knowledge is what ultimately informs confident decision-making. By moving beyond data and information, you gain a comprehensive understanding that allows you to act strategically, not just reactively.

Practical Examples: Turning Data into Knowledge

Let's walk through a practical example to see how data becomes information and then knowledge.

Scenario: A Retail Store's Monthly Sales Analysis

1. **Data**: The store collects daily sales data on each product sold, including the date, product ID, quantity sold, and sales amount.
2. **Information**: The store organizes the data to show total sales per product category each week. This analysis reveals trends, such as which product categories are popular on weekends versus weekdays.
3. **Knowledge**: By combining this information with knowledge of local events and customer demographics, the store manager realizes that certain products sell better when local schools are on break. This knowledge allows the manager to adjust inventory and marketing strategies around school holidays, maximizing sales.

In this example, the raw data (daily sales figures) alone does not reveal much about customer behavior. When structured into weekly sales information, patterns start to emerge. Finally, by interpreting this information within the context of local events and demographics, the manager gains knowledge that can guide business decisions.

Key Takeaways

- **Data**: The raw, unprocessed facts and figures collected from various sources. It is the building block for information but lacks context or interpretation.

- **Information**: Processed data that has been organized or structured to provide context, answer questions, and reveal trends. It helps in understanding what happened.
- **Knowledge**: Information that has been synthesized, contextualized, and combined with expertise to provide deeper understanding and guide decision-making.

Understanding these distinctions is the first step to becoming proficient in data analytics. As we move forward in this book, we'll explore how to work with data, transform it into meaningful information, and leverage it to build actionable knowledge. With this foundation, you'll be well-prepared to harness the power of data effectively in any field or context.

Types of Data: Qualitative vs. Quantitative, Structured vs. Unstructured

Data can take many forms, each with unique characteristics, uses, and analytical methods. Understanding the types of data you encounter— qualitative vs. quantitative and structured vs. unstructured—is essential for determining how to process, analyze, and interpret it effectively. Knowing these distinctions will allow you to choose the right tools and methods for working with different data sets, ultimately helping you gain more accurate insights.

In this section, we'll break down these fundamental types of data, explain the differences, and discuss examples of each. By the end, you'll have a clearer understanding of how to classify data, which is an important first step in any data analysis process.

Qualitative vs. Quantitative Data

Data is often categorized as either qualitative or quantitative based on its nature and how it is measured. Let's explore the characteristics and applications of each type.

1. Qualitative Data

Qualitative data describes qualities, characteristics, or non-numeric attributes. This type of data is often used to understand opinions, motivations, and experiences, providing a more nuanced view of a subject. Qualitative data can be collected through interviews, observations, open-ended surveys, and even images or videos.

Characteristics of qualitative data:

- **Descriptive**: Qualitative data describes qualities or attributes, such as colors, textures, emotions, or preferences.

- **Non-numeric**: It usually consists of words or categories, making it harder to measure in a traditional sense.
- **Subjective**: This type of data is often open to interpretation, as it reflects personal opinions or perceptions.

Examples of Qualitative Data:

- **Customer Feedback**: Textual responses from a survey asking customers about their satisfaction with a product or service.
- **Observational Notes**: Notes taken during a research study observing participants' reactions or behaviors.
- **Social Media Comments**: User comments on social media platforms that provide insight into customer sentiment.

Uses of Qualitative Data: Qualitative data is commonly used in fields like psychology, marketing, and sociology, where understanding the "why" behind behaviors and choices is essential. For example, companies may analyze customer feedback to identify recurring themes in customer complaints, allowing them to improve products or services.

2. Quantitative Data

Quantitative data is numeric data that can be measured and quantified. This type of data answers questions such as "how many," "how much," or "how often." Quantitative data is essential for statistical analysis because it provides concrete, measurable values.

Characteristics of quantitative data:

- **Numeric**: Quantitative data is expressed in numbers, making it easy to analyze using mathematical and statistical methods.
- **Objective**: Since it is measurable, quantitative data is generally more objective and less open to interpretation.
- **Structured**: It often follows a set structure, like values recorded in tables, making it suitable for statistical tests and trend analysis.

Examples of Quantitative Data:

- **Sales Figures**: Monthly revenue figures for a business, including the total number of items sold.
- **Survey Ratings**: Responses from a survey where participants rate their satisfaction on a scale from 1 to 10.
- **Temperature Readings**: Daily temperature measurements recorded over time.

Uses of Quantitative Data: Quantitative data is widely used in scientific research, finance, healthcare, and business. For instance, a company might analyze sales figures to identify trends over time, allowing them to forecast future demand and adjust inventory levels accordingly.

Structured vs. Unstructured Data

In addition to being classified as qualitative or quantitative, data can also be categorized as structured or unstructured based on its organization. Structured data is highly organized and easy to analyze, while unstructured data is more complex and requires additional processing to extract meaningful information.

1. Structured Data

Structured data is organized into a defined format, typically in rows and columns, making it easily searchable and analyzable. This type of data often resides in databases or spreadsheets, where it can be quickly queried and processed using standard tools like SQL or Excel.

Characteristics of structured data:

- **Organized and Easily Accessible**: Structured data is organized in a way that makes it easy to locate, sort, and analyze.
- **Standard Format**: It is typically stored in databases, with clearly defined fields, making it compatible with traditional data analysis tools.

- **Easily Searchable**: Structured data is formatted for easy retrieval using queries, making it well-suited for real-time analysis.

Examples of Structured Data:

- **Customer Database**: A table containing customer names, addresses, purchase history, and contact information.
- **Inventory List**: A spreadsheet with columns for product ID, name, quantity in stock, and price.
- **Transaction Records**: Bank records listing each transaction with details like date, amount, type (debit or credit), and account balance.

Uses of Structured Data: Structured data is commonly used in business and financial analysis because it's easy to sort, filter, and analyze. For example, a retail company might use structured sales data to calculate monthly revenue, analyze purchase patterns, and create sales forecasts.

2. Unstructured Data

Unstructured data lacks a predefined format or organization, making it more challenging to process and analyze. This type of data often includes text, images, videos, and other formats that do not fit neatly into tables. Unstructured data represents a large portion of the data generated today, particularly with the rise of social media and digital content.

Characteristics of unstructured data:

- **Lacks a Standard Structure**: Unstructured data doesn't follow a uniform format, making it difficult to organize and analyze using traditional methods.
- **Complex and Varied Formats**: It can include text, images, audio, video, and more, often requiring specialized tools for analysis.
- **Challenging to Search**: Due to its lack of structure, unstructured data is harder to search and query without advanced tools like natural language processing (NLP) and machine learning.

Examples of Unstructured Data:

- **Social Media Posts**: User comments, tweets, and posts on platforms like Facebook, Twitter, and Instagram.
- **Emails**: The text in emails, which may include both relevant and irrelevant information, attachments, and images.
- **Customer Reviews**: Written reviews on websites like Amazon, Yelp, or TripAdvisor that express customer opinions and experiences.

Uses of Unstructured Data: Although unstructured data is harder to analyze, it contains valuable insights, particularly in understanding customer sentiment, market trends, and user behavior. For instance, companies often use sentiment analysis on social media posts to gauge public opinion about their brand or products. This analysis can reveal trends in customer satisfaction, identify common complaints, and help improve customer service strategies.

Comparing the Types: How They Work Together

Both structured and unstructured data, as well as qualitative and quantitative data, offer unique insights and are often used in combination to provide a comprehensive view. Let's examine some ways these data types complement each other:

1. **Customer Feedback Analysis**
   - **Structured, Quantitative Data**: A survey where customers rate their satisfaction on a scale of 1 to 5 provides structured, quantitative data that can be easily summarized to show the average satisfaction rating.
   - **Unstructured, Qualitative Data**: Open-ended survey responses or social media comments allow customers to explain their ratings and share specific

experiences, providing unstructured, qualitative data.

Combining both types allows companies to quantify customer satisfaction while also understanding the specific reasons behind those ratings, enabling a more holistic approach to customer service improvements.

2. **Market Research**
   o **Structured, Quantitative Data**: Sales figures, demographic information, and purchase histories provide structured, quantitative data that can reveal purchase trends and customer demographics.
   o **Unstructured, Qualitative Data**: Customer reviews, product feedback, and social media posts offer unstructured, qualitative insights into customer preferences and motivations.

By analyzing both types, companies can not only identify popular products and trends but also understand customer sentiments, enabling them to tailor marketing efforts more effectively.

3. **Medical Research**
   o **Structured, Quantitative Data**: Patient records, lab test results, and medication dosage are examples of

structured, quantitative data that researchers can use to identify patterns and correlations in health outcomes.

- ○ **Unstructured, Qualitative Data**: Doctor's notes, patient interviews, and case studies offer unstructured, qualitative insights into symptoms, treatment experiences, and lifestyle factors.

Together, these data types enable medical professionals to study not only statistical trends but also the personal experiences of patients, leading to more personalized and effective healthcare strategies.

Key Takeaways

- **Qualitative vs. Quantitative**: Qualitative data describes characteristics and is often text-based, while quantitative data involves measurable, numeric values.
- **Structured vs. Unstructured**: Structured data is organized into a specific format, like rows and columns, making it easy to analyze. Unstructured data lacks a predefined format and requires specialized tools to interpret.
- **Combining Data Types**: Many analyses benefit from combining structured and unstructured, qualitative and quantitative data, providing a richer understanding of the subject.

Understanding these types of data equips you with the knowledge to classify data correctly, an essential skill in data literacy. As you progress through this book, you'll learn how to work with each type of data, extracting valuable insights and transforming data into meaningful knowledge.

Introduction to Datasets, Variables, and Data Sources

A crucial part of data literacy is knowing where data comes from, how it's structured, and how to interpret the variables within it. Datasets, variables, and data sources are fundamental components of data analysis, allowing analysts to identify patterns, make comparisons, and draw insights. In this section, we'll break down these concepts, providing definitions, examples, and insights on how they interconnect and contribute to meaningful data analysis.

What is a Dataset?

A **dataset** is a structured collection of data, typically organized in rows and columns. Each dataset contains observations or entries that are recorded on specific variables, providing a comprehensive set of information related to a particular topic. Think of a dataset as a table where each row represents an individual observation (e.g., a customer, product, or transaction), and each column represents a variable describing attributes of those observations.

Characteristics of Datasets

- **Organized Structure**: Datasets are commonly formatted in tables, with each row representing a unique observation and each column representing a variable.
- **Consistency**: Datasets generally maintain a consistent structure, allowing for easy comparison and analysis of observations.
- **Defined Scope**: A dataset often focuses on a specific topic or subject, such as customer demographics, sales data, or scientific measurements.

Types of Datasets

1. **Tabular Datasets**: These are the most common and are arranged in rows and columns, as in a spreadsheet or database table.
2. **Time Series Datasets**: Datasets that track information over time, often used in economics and finance to observe changes in metrics like stock prices or sales volume.
3. **Spatial Datasets**: These include data tied to specific geographic locations, used in fields like geography, urban planning, and environmental science.
4. **Hierarchical Datasets**: These datasets contain nested structures, such as organizational data where each department contains multiple teams, each with several employees.

Examples of Datasets

- **Customer Database**: A dataset containing information on customers, with each row representing a unique customer and columns for attributes like age, location, and purchase history.
- **Financial Transactions**: A dataset that records every transaction made by a business, with rows for each transaction and columns for transaction date, amount, and payment method.
- **Weather Data**: A dataset with daily records of temperature, humidity, and precipitation levels for a specific location, with each row representing a single day.

Understanding Variables

A **variable** is a characteristic or attribute that can be measured or categorized, providing specific information about each observation in a dataset. Variables are the individual columns in a dataset and are essential for analysis, as they allow us to compare, correlate, and assess data in meaningful ways.

Types of Variables

Variables can be classified in different ways based on their properties:

1. **Categorical Variables** (also known as qualitative or nominal variables)
    o Represent categories or groups.
    o Values do not have a numerical significance and cannot be meaningfully added or subtracted.
    o Examples: Gender (Male, Female, Other), Product Category (Electronics, Clothing, Food).
2. **Ordinal Variables**
    o Similar to categorical variables but with an inherent order or ranking.
    o Examples: Education Level (High School, Bachelor's, Master's), Customer Satisfaction (Poor, Fair, Good, Excellent).
3. **Numerical Variables** (also known as quantitative variables)
    o Represent measurable quantities and can be further classified into two types:
        ▪ **Continuous Variables**: Can take any value within a range and are often measured, such as height, weight, or temperature.
        ▪ **Discrete Variables**: Represent countable values, often integers, such as number of products sold, number of employees, or customer age.

4. **Binary Variables**
   - ○ Represent two possible states, typically "yes" or "no," "true" or "false."
   - ○ Examples: Customer Subscription Status (Subscribed/Not Subscribed), Employee Attendance (Present/Absent).

Examples of Variables in a Dataset

Let's say we have a dataset of customer purchases. Here are some examples of variables we might find:

- **Customer Age**: A numerical variable (discrete) representing the customer's age.
- **Product Type**: A categorical variable indicating the type of product purchased.
- **Purchase Date**: A temporal variable representing the date of purchase, often useful in time series analysis.
- **Purchase Amount**: A numerical variable (continuous) showing the total amount spent on each purchase.

Data Sources: Where Does Data Come From?

Data sources refer to the origin of data. Data can be collected from a wide range of sources, including internal company records, government databases, sensors, surveys, and social media. Understanding the data source is crucial for determining data quality, reliability, and relevance for a specific analysis.

Types of Data Sources

1. **Primary Data Sources**
   - Primary data is collected firsthand by the researcher or organization for a specific purpose.
   - Examples: Surveys, interviews, observations, and experiments.
   - **Advantages**: Data is specific to the research needs, providing a high level of control and relevance.
   - **Disadvantages**: Collecting primary data can be time-consuming and costly.
2. **Secondary Data Sources**
   - Secondary data is data that was collected by someone else for a different purpose but can be reused for new analysis.
   - Examples: Government reports, industry publications, scientific research papers, and publicly available databases.
   - **Advantages**: Access to a large amount of data without needing to collect it from scratch, saving time and resources.

- o **Disadvantages**: Data may not be tailored to specific research needs and could be outdated or incomplete.
3. **Internal Data Sources**
   - o Data generated and stored within an organization, often as a result of day-to-day operations.
   - o Examples: Sales records, customer databases, inventory management systems.
   - o **Advantages**: Relevant to the organization and often real-time or recent.
   - o **Disadvantages**: Limited in scope to the organization's activities and may not provide a comprehensive view.
4. **External Data Sources**
   - o Data obtained from outside the organization, providing broader insights into the market or industry.
   - o Examples: Market research reports, social media data, government databases.
   - o **Advantages**: Can provide context to internal data, helping to benchmark against industry trends.
   - o **Disadvantages**: Access may require subscriptions or fees, and external data may not align perfectly with the organization's specific needs.

Examples of Common Data Sources

1. **Publicly Available Databases**
   o Examples: U.S. Census Bureau, World Bank, World Health Organization.
   o Uses: Demographic analysis, economic studies, health research.
2. **Social Media Platforms**
   o Examples: Twitter, Facebook, Instagram.
   o Uses: Sentiment analysis, brand monitoring, social trend analysis.
3. **Transactional Data**
   o Examples: Online purchases, in-store transactions, financial transactions.
   o Uses: Sales analysis, customer behavior studies, inventory management.
4. **Sensor and IoT Data**
   o Examples: Data from weather sensors, traffic cameras, and fitness trackers.
   o Uses: Real-time monitoring, predictive maintenance, environmental studies.

Putting It All Together: The Role of Datasets, Variables, and Data Sources in Analysis

Understanding datasets, variables, and data sources is essential for effective data analysis. Here's a summary of how these components work together:

1. **Datasets**: The structured compilation of data relevant to a particular question or study. Datasets are the foundation of data analysis and provide the organized framework within which variables are studied.
2. **Variables**: The specific attributes or characteristics within a dataset that are measured and analyzed. Variables allow us to make comparisons, identify patterns, and extract insights from data.
3. **Data Sources**: The origin of the data, whether collected firsthand or sourced from external repositories. Understanding the source of data is crucial for assessing its reliability, context, and potential limitations.

Practical Example: Analyzing Customer Feedback Data

To illustrate how datasets, variables, and data sources interact, let's consider an example involving customer feedback analysis.

Scenario: A company wants to analyze customer feedback to improve its services.

1. **Dataset**: The company collects data from a survey sent to customers who recently made a purchase. The dataset includes rows representing individual customer responses.
2. **Variables**: The dataset might include the following variables:

- Customer Age (numerical)
  - **Customer Age** (numerical)
  - **Product Purchased** (categorical)
  - **Satisfaction Rating** (ordinal, on a scale of 1 to 5)
  - **Open-ended Feedback** (textual)
3. **Data Source**: The data is collected directly from customers (primary data) using an online survey. This data source provides first-hand insights into customer opinions, ensuring that the feedback is specific to the company's products.

By analyzing this dataset, the company can extract valuable insights. For instance, they may find that satisfaction ratings are lower for a specific product category or identify common themes in the open-ended feedback, such as complaints about delivery time. With this information, the company can make targeted improvements to enhance customer satisfaction.

Key Takeaways

- **Datasets**: Structured collections of data, typically organized in rows and columns, that provide a framework for analysis.
- **Variables**: Attributes or characteristics within a dataset, used to measure and compare observations.
- **Data Sources**: Origins of data that influence its reliability and relevance. Data can come

from primary, secondary, internal, or external sources.

Understanding datasets, variables, and data sources is a foundational skill in data analysis, helping analysts organize, interpret, and make informed decisions. In the chapters to follow, we'll dive deeper into working with datasets and manipulating variables to gain meaningful insights.

Chapter 3: Tools of the Trade: Essential Software for Data Analytics

Overview of Commonly Used Tools: Excel, Google Sheets, and Basic SQL

When it comes to data analytics, having the right tools is essential for managing, processing, and analyzing data effectively. While data analytics includes advanced software and specialized programming languages, many powerful analyses can be performed using accessible, commonly used tools like Microsoft Excel, Google Sheets, and SQL. These tools provide a strong foundation, enabling you to perform data manipulation, visualization, and basic statistical analysis, even if you're new to data analytics.

In this chapter, we'll explore how Excel, Google Sheets, and SQL can be used in data analytics, discussing their key features, functionalities, and best practices. By the end, you'll have a clear understanding of how each tool contributes to data analysis, empowering you to choose the best one for your needs.

Microsoft Excel

Microsoft Excel is one of the most widely used tools in data analytics, known for its flexibility, user-friendly interface, and extensive range of functions. Excel is ideal for managing small to medium-sized datasets, performing calculations, and creating visualizations. Excel's versatility makes it a valuable tool for both beginners and experienced analysts.

Key Features of Excel for Data Analytics

1. **Data Organization and Management**
   - Excel allows users to organize data in rows and columns, providing a straightforward structure for managing datasets.
   - Users can sort and filter data to quickly locate specific information or view subsets of data.
2. **Formulas and Functions**
   - Excel includes hundreds of built-in functions for mathematical, statistical, and logical operations. Functions like SUM, AVERAGE, COUNT, and IF make it easy to perform calculations.
   - More advanced functions, such as VLOOKUP, INDEX, and MATCH, allow you to search for specific values and perform complex lookups within the dataset.
3. **Pivot Tables**
   - Pivot tables are one of Excel's most powerful features, enabling users to summarize and aggregate data efficiently.
   - With pivot tables, you can quickly calculate totals, averages, and counts,

organize data by categories, and analyze data trends without manually creating complex formulas.

4. **Data Visualization**
   o Excel offers a variety of chart options, including bar charts, line graphs, pie charts, and scatter plots, allowing users to visualize data effectively.
   o Users can customize charts by adding titles, labels, and formatting options, making it easy to communicate insights visually.

5. **Data Analysis ToolPak**
   o Excel's Data Analysis ToolPak is an add-in that provides additional statistical tools, including regression analysis, histograms, and descriptive statistics.
   o These tools are especially helpful for users interested in more advanced analytics, such as hypothesis testing and correlation analysis.

Practical Uses of Excel in Data Analytics

- **Budget Tracking and Financial Analysis**: Excel is widely used for financial planning, budgeting, and forecasting. Analysts can use Excel to track expenses, calculate financial ratios, and project future revenues.
- **Sales and Marketing Analysis**: Marketing teams use Excel to track campaign

performance, calculate conversion rates, and analyze customer data to improve strategies.

- **Data Cleaning**: Excel provides various tools for cleaning data, such as removing duplicates, trimming spaces, and converting text to columns. Clean data is crucial for accurate analysis and ensures consistency.

Google Sheets

Google Sheets is a cloud-based spreadsheet tool that offers similar functionality to Excel but with the added advantage of real-time collaboration. It's accessible, easy to use, and provides many of the same formulas and functions found in Excel. Google Sheets is a popular choice for small teams or individuals who need to work on data collaboratively and have access to it from anywhere.

Key Features of Google Sheets for Data Analytics

1. **Real-Time Collaboration**
   - Google Sheets allows multiple users to work on the same spreadsheet simultaneously, making it ideal for team projects and collaborative data analysis.
   - Users can leave comments, suggest edits, and track changes, promoting efficient teamwork.
2. **Formulas and Functions**

- Like Excel, Google Sheets offers a wide range of formulas and functions, including basic mathematical operations (SUM, AVERAGE) and more advanced functions (VLOOKUP, FILTER).
- Google Sheets also has unique functions, such as IMPORTRANGE (for pulling data from other Google Sheets) and GOOGLEFINANCE (for real-time financial data).

3. **Data Visualization**
   - Google Sheets includes built-in charting tools, allowing users to create bar graphs, line charts, and pie charts to visualize data.
   - While the charting options are somewhat limited compared to Excel, Google Sheets is continuously expanding its visualization capabilities.

4. **Add-Ons and Integrations**
   - Google Sheets offers add-ons that expand its functionality, such as tools for data analysis, automation, and integration with other Google products like Google Forms.
   - It integrates seamlessly with Google's ecosystem, making it easy to collect data from Google Forms and import it directly into Sheets.

5. **Automatic Backups and Cloud Storage**
   - As a cloud-based tool, Google Sheets automatically saves changes in real-time, ensuring data is never lost.
   - Users can access their data from any device with an internet connection, making it highly convenient.

Practical Uses of Google Sheets in Data Analytics

- **Survey Data Collection and Analysis**: Google Sheets integrates with Google Forms, allowing survey responses to be automatically recorded in a spreadsheet for easy analysis.
- **Project Tracking and Collaboration**: Google Sheets is commonly used by project teams to track progress, manage tasks, and collaborate on data analysis.
- **Data Sharing and Accessibility**: Because it's cloud-based, Google Sheets is often preferred when data needs to be accessed by multiple users or shared with external partners.

SQL (Structured Query Language)

SQL, or Structured Query Language, is a programming language designed specifically for managing and querying data in relational databases. While Excel and Google Sheets are effective for smaller datasets, SQL is ideal for working with large datasets and more complex data structures. SQL is widely used by data analysts, data scientists, and database administrators to extract, manipulate, and analyze data stored in databases.

Key Features of SQL for Data Analytics

1. **Data Querying**
   - SQL allows users to query data from databases efficiently. The SELECT statement, for example, enables users to retrieve specific columns or rows based on defined criteria.
   - Common SQL statements like WHERE, ORDER BY, and GROUP BY allow for filtering, sorting, and grouping data, making it easy to perform focused analysis.

2. **Data Manipulation**
   - SQL includes commands for modifying data within the database. The INSERT, UPDATE, and DELETE commands allow users to add, change, or remove records, maintaining data accuracy.
   - Analysts can use SQL to clean and preprocess data directly within the database, ensuring that it's in the proper format for analysis.

3. **Aggregations and Calculations**
   - SQL includes powerful aggregation functions such as SUM, AVG, COUNT, and MAX/MIN, allowing users to calculate

totals, averages, and other summary statistics quickly.

- o By combining these functions with GROUP BY, analysts can calculate aggregated values for different categories within the dataset (e.g., total sales per product category).

4. **Joins for Combining Data**
   - o SQL supports various types of joins (INNER JOIN, LEFT JOIN, RIGHT JOIN) that allow users to combine data from multiple tables based on common fields.
   - o Joins are essential for relational databases, as they enable analysts to integrate data from different tables, enriching the dataset with additional context.

5. **Data Integrity and Security**
   - o SQL databases are designed with built-in mechanisms for data integrity and security. Primary keys, foreign keys, and constraints ensure that data remains consistent and accurate.
   - o Access control features in SQL databases allow administrators to grant or restrict user permissions, maintaining data security.

Practical Uses of SQL in Data Analytics

- **Customer Segmentation**: Analysts use SQL to filter and group customer data by various attributes (e.g., location, age, purchase history) to create targeted marketing campaigns.
- **Financial Analysis**: SQL is used to query and aggregate financial data, allowing analysts to calculate key metrics such as revenue growth, profit margins, and customer lifetime value.
- **Inventory Management**: SQL enables companies to monitor inventory levels, track shipments, and manage stock across multiple locations, ensuring efficient operations.

Comparing the Tools: Choosing the Right One

Each of these tools—Excel, Google Sheets, and SQL—has unique strengths, making them suitable for different tasks within data analytics:

1. **Excel**: Best for small to medium-sized datasets, financial modeling, and data visualization. Excel is ideal for tasks that require flexibility, such as budgeting, project planning, and creating charts.
2. **Google Sheets**: Best for collaborative projects and cloud-based data access. Google Sheets is especially useful for data collection, team collaboration, and tasks that require accessibility from multiple devices.

3. **SQL**: Best for large datasets, complex queries, and relational database management. SQL is ideal for tasks that involve combining data from multiple tables, performing large-scale aggregations, and managing data in a structured database.

Practical Example: Analyzing Sales Data Across the Tools

Let's consider a scenario where a company wants to analyze monthly sales data across different regions:

1. **Using Excel**: The company's analyst downloads a CSV file of sales data and imports it into Excel. Using pivot tables, they quickly summarize total sales by region and month, creating charts to visualize trends.
2. **Using Google Sheets**: The analyst shares the sales data with their team in Google Sheets, allowing team members from different departments to view, comment, and edit collaboratively. They use conditional formatting to highlight top-performing regions.
3. **Using SQL**: The company's database stores several years of sales data. Using SQL, the analyst queries the database to retrieve monthly sales data by region, calculates average sales per region, and joins tables to add customer demographics. The query

results can then be exported for further analysis or reporting.

By understanding these tools and their strengths, analysts can choose the right tool for each task, ensuring efficient and effective analysis.

Key Takeaways

- **Excel**: A versatile tool for data organization, calculations, and visualization, suitable for small to medium-sized datasets.
- **Google Sheets**: A cloud-based spreadsheet with collaboration features, ideal for projects requiring real-time teamwork and accessibility.
- **SQL**: A powerful language for querying and managing large datasets in relational databases, essential for handling complex data structures and large volumes of data.

Each of these tools is foundational for data analysis. As you progress, you'll learn how to leverage their features to extract insights, create visualizations, and make data-driven decisions effectively.

Introduction to Data Visualization Tools: Tableau and Power BI

Data visualization is an essential skill in data analytics, allowing analysts to present complex data in a way that's easy to understand and interpret.

While tools like Excel and Google Sheets have basic charting capabilities, specialized data visualization tools like Tableau and Power BI take visual storytelling to a new level. These tools enable users to create dynamic, interactive dashboards that provide insights at a glance, making it easier to communicate data findings to decision-makers.

In this section, we'll explore Tableau and Power BI— two of the most popular data visualization tools in the industry. We'll discuss the unique features of each, how they support data analysis, and why they're invaluable for making data accessible and actionable.

Tableau

Tableau is a data visualization tool known for its intuitive interface, powerful visual capabilities, and ability to handle large datasets. It is widely used by data professionals and organizations to create interactive, visually engaging dashboards that reveal data patterns, trends, and insights.

Key Features of Tableau for Data Visualization

1. **Drag-and-Drop Interface**
   o Tableau's drag-and-drop interface makes it easy to create visualizations without needing extensive technical skills. Users can quickly connect data, choose variables, and build charts by

simply dragging fields onto the workspace.

- o This interface allows for fast prototyping of visualizations, making it accessible for beginners while still powerful enough for advanced users.

2. **Wide Range of Visualizations**
   - o Tableau supports a variety of visualization types, including bar charts, line charts, scatter plots, heat maps, and geographic maps, enabling users to represent data in diverse ways.
   - o The tool allows users to customize visualizations extensively, giving them control over colors, labels, legends, and tooltips, ensuring that the visuals are both informative and visually appealing.

3. **Data Blending and Integration**
   - o Tableau can connect to multiple data sources simultaneously, allowing users to blend data from different platforms, such as Excel files, SQL databases, Google Sheets, and online APIs.
   - o Data blending is particularly useful for combining information from various departments or sources, providing a comprehensive view of the data.

4. **Interactive Dashboards**
   - o Tableau enables users to create interactive dashboards that allow

viewers to explore data on their own by clicking on filters, hovering over data points, and drilling down into details.

- o Interactive dashboards are particularly valuable for presentations, as they allow stakeholders to explore specific insights relevant to their interests, creating a more engaging data experience.

5. **Geographic Mapping**
   - o Tableau has robust geographic mapping capabilities, allowing users to visualize data on maps and analyze patterns based on location. Users can create heat maps, color-coded regions, and pinpoint locations based on geographic variables.
   - o This feature is especially useful for industries like retail, logistics, and urban planning, where location-based insights can drive strategic decisions.

6. **Advanced Analytics**
   - o Tableau offers advanced analytics features, including trend lines, forecasting, and clustering, which provide deeper insights into the data.
   - o With features like calculated fields and statistical modeling, users can go beyond basic visualizations to perform more sophisticated analysis.

Practical Uses of Tableau in Data Analytics

- **Sales Performance Analysis**: Tableau can be used to create dashboards showing sales metrics by region, product category, or sales representative, helping companies track performance and identify high- or low-performing areas.
- **Customer Demographics**: Using geographic mapping and demographic data, analysts can visualize customer distribution, preferences, and purchasing patterns across different regions.
- **Healthcare Data Analysis**: Tableau's interactive dashboards allow healthcare providers to analyze patient data, monitor trends in treatments, and visualize disease prevalence by region, supporting data-driven healthcare decisions.

Power BI

Power BI is a data visualization and business intelligence tool developed by Microsoft. Known for its integration with other Microsoft products, Power BI is popular among organizations that use the Microsoft ecosystem. It provides powerful data visualization capabilities along with tools for data preparation, modeling, and reporting, making it a comprehensive solution for data-driven decision-making.

Key Features of Power BI for Data Visualization

1. **Integration with Microsoft Ecosystem**
   - o Power BI integrates seamlessly with other Microsoft applications, including Excel, SQL Server, and Azure, making it ideal for organizations already using these platforms.
   - o This integration allows users to import data from various sources within the Microsoft environment easily and link Power BI reports to existing workflows.

2. **Data Modeling and Transformation**
   - o Power BI includes tools for transforming and cleaning data before creating visualizations. The Power Query Editor allows users to filter, sort, merge, and modify data directly within Power BI, ensuring that the dataset is ready for analysis.
   - o Users can create data models that define relationships between tables, allowing for multi-dimensional analysis and complex reporting.

3. **Customizable Visualizations**
   - o Power BI supports a wide array of visualizations, such as line graphs, pie charts, scatter plots, and treemaps. Users can also download custom visualizations from the Power BI marketplace or create their own

visuals using the Power BI Developer
tool.

- This flexibility makes Power BI highly
  customizable, enabling users to tailor
  visuals to fit their specific analytical
  needs.

4. **Interactive and Shareable Dashboards**
   - Power BI dashboards are highly
     interactive, allowing users to explore
     data by selecting filters, highlighting
     trends, and drilling down into details.
   - Power BI also offers robust sharing
     capabilities, allowing users to publish
     and share dashboards across teams.
     This feature is valuable for
     organizations that want to ensure all
     team members have access to the
     latest insights.

5. **Natural Language Query (Q&A)**
   - Power BI's Q&A feature allows users
     to ask questions in natural language
     (e.g., "What was the total revenue last
     quarter?"), and Power BI will generate
     relevant visuals based on the question.
   - This feature is particularly helpful for
     non-technical users, as it makes it easy
     to generate insights without needing to
     create complex queries manually.

6. **Data Connectivity**
   - Power BI supports connections to a
     wide range of data sources, including

SQL databases, cloud storage platforms, web-based applications, and flat files. Users can pull in data from services like Google Analytics, Salesforce, and Azure, providing a broad view of an organization's data.

o Real-time data connectivity also allows users to update dashboards automatically, ensuring they always display the latest data.

Practical Uses of Power BI in Data Analytics

- **Financial Reporting**: Power BI's data modeling and aggregation features allow finance teams to track key financial metrics like revenue, expenses, and profit margins, helping them manage budgets and forecast future financial performance.
- **Human Resources Analytics**: HR teams can use Power BI to visualize employee data, monitor turnover rates, and analyze recruitment metrics, helping them optimize hiring strategies and improve employee retention.
- **Supply Chain Management**: Power BI enables supply chain teams to monitor inventory levels, track supplier performance, and analyze logistics costs, ensuring efficient and cost-effective operations.

Comparing Tableau and Power BI: Choosing the Right Tool

While Tableau and Power BI share many similarities, each tool has its strengths. Here's a comparison to help you decide which tool is best for specific needs:

Feature	Tableau	Power BI
Ease of Use	Intuitive, user-friendly drag-and-drop	User-friendly, especially for Excel users
Integration	Connects with multiple data sources	Strong integration with Microsoft products
Customization	Extensive customization for visuals	Custom visuals available in marketplace
Data Modeling	Limited data transformation capabilities	Robust data modeling and transformation tools
Cost	Generally higher subscription costs	Cost-effective, with a free version available
Best For	Data visualization and interactive dashboards	Comprehensive BI solutions, particularly for Microsoft users

Choosing between Tableau and Power BI depends on factors such as budget, the scale of analysis, data integration requirements, and the tool's compatibility with other software used in the organization.

- **Tableau** is ideal for organizations that prioritize high-quality visualizations, need to connect to a diverse range of data sources, and have larger budgets.
- **Power BI** is an excellent choice for Microsoft-based organizations, as it offers strong integration with Excel and Azure, is more affordable, and has robust data modeling capabilities.

Practical Example: Analyzing Marketing Data with Tableau and Power BI

Let's explore how a marketing team might use these tools to analyze campaign performance:

1. **Using Tableau**: The marketing team imports data from Google Analytics and social media platforms into Tableau. They create an interactive dashboard showing website traffic, conversion rates, and social media engagement metrics by campaign. With Tableau's geographic maps, they visualize engagement by region, helping them identify areas with the highest response.
2. **Using Power BI**: The team imports the same data into Power BI, linking it with internal

sales data stored in SQL Server. They use Power Query to clean and transform the data, ensuring consistency across sources. The team then builds a dashboard that combines engagement metrics with revenue figures, allowing them to measure each campaign's impact on sales. They share the dashboard with the sales team, who can view real-time updates.

Both tools provide valuable insights but in slightly different ways. Tableau focuses on visual appeal and user interaction, while Power BI emphasizes data modeling and integration within the Microsoft ecosystem.

Key Takeaways

- **Tableau**: Known for its powerful visualization capabilities and ease of use, Tableau is ideal for creating visually appealing, interactive dashboards. It's best suited for organizations needing to connect to multiple data sources and prioritize high-quality visuals.
- **Power BI**: A comprehensive BI tool with strong integration within the Microsoft ecosystem, Power BI offers advanced data modeling and transformation features. It's a cost-effective option for organizations using Microsoft products and those needing robust data preparation capabilities.

Both Tableau and Power BI are valuable tools for data analytics, each catering to different needs and preferences. By mastering these tools, you'll be able to create impactful visualizations that make complex data accessible and actionable for decision-makers.

How to Choose the Right Tool for the Task

With so many tools available for data analytics, knowing which one to use for a specific task can be challenging. Each tool—Excel, Google Sheets, SQL, Tableau, and Power BI—has unique strengths, making it more suited to certain types of analysis, data sizes, and reporting needs. This section will provide a guide to selecting the right tool, helping you optimize your workflow, maximize efficiency, and produce the most accurate results.

By understanding the strengths and limitations of each tool, you'll be better equipped to make informed decisions that align with your data analysis goals.

Factors to Consider When Choosing a Tool

Before diving into specific recommendations, it's helpful to consider some key factors that influence tool selection:

1. **Data Size and Complexity**
   - Small datasets with basic calculations and visualizations can often be

handled in tools like Excel or Google Sheets.

- o For larger, more complex datasets, SQL is better suited for querying and managing data, while Tableau and Power BI offer strong visualization capabilities for large data.

2. **Data Source and Integration**
   - o If your data resides in multiple sources or needs to be integrated from different platforms, a tool with strong data connectivity (like Tableau or Power BI) may be ideal.
   - o SQL is also useful for data integration if you're working directly from a relational database.

3. **Type of Analysis**
   - o Simple calculations and basic visualizations are easily handled in Excel or Google Sheets.
   - o For more advanced analysis, such as statistical modeling, trend analysis, and multi-dimensional analysis, SQL, Tableau, or Power BI may be better options.

4. **Collaboration Needs**
   - o For collaborative projects where multiple users need real-time access to data, Google Sheets or Power BI (for Microsoft users) provide the best options.

- Excel and SQL are more limited in terms of real-time collaboration but can still be effective for smaller teams.

5. **Budget and Accessibility**
   - Budget constraints can play a significant role, as some tools require paid licenses (e.g., Tableau, Power BI Pro).
   - Google Sheets and Excel offer accessible, budget-friendly options, while SQL, if used with open-source databases, can be highly cost-effective.

6. **Skill Level and Training**
   - Tools like Excel and Google Sheets are generally easier to learn and widely accessible.
   - SQL, Tableau, and Power BI may require some training, especially for users new to data analytics or programming.

Tool Selection by Task

Let's examine some common data analytics tasks and recommend the best tools for each.

1. Data Entry, Cleaning, and Basic Analysis

Recommended Tools: **Excel** and **Google Sheets**

- **Why**: Excel and Google Sheets are both excellent for simple data entry, quick cleaning tasks, and basic calculations. Their interfaces are user-friendly, and they offer functions for sorting, filtering, and basic formatting.
- **Features**:
  - **Excel**: Offers tools like the Data Analysis ToolPak, pivot tables, and conditional formatting for data exploration and cleaning.
  - **Google Sheets**: Provides similar functionalities to Excel, with the added advantage of real-time collaboration.

Use Case Example: A marketing analyst is tasked with cleaning and categorizing customer responses from a recent survey. They use Excel to remove duplicates, sort responses, and apply conditional formatting to categorize answers by sentiment.

Limitations: While Excel and Google Sheets are powerful, they are limited when handling very large datasets or complex data transformation tasks.

2. Querying Large Datasets and Data Preparation

Recommended Tool: SQL

- **Why**: SQL is designed for querying large datasets and extracting data from relational databases. It's highly efficient for data retrieval, filtering, and data manipulation.

- **Features**:
    - SQL can handle complex data extraction with commands like `SELECT`, `JOIN`, and `GROUP BY`, making it ideal for combining tables and creating customized data views.
    - SQL is also effective for data cleaning tasks directly within the database, allowing for efficient data preparation before analysis.

Use Case Example: A sales analyst needs to retrieve sales data from a large database, filtering it by region and product type. Using SQL, they execute a query to extract only the necessary data, reducing the amount of data they need to process and analyze.

Limitations: SQL is less effective for visualization. After querying and preparing data, users may export it to another tool like Tableau or Power BI for visualization.

3. Data Visualization and Dashboard Creation

Recommended Tools: **Tableau** and **Power BI**

- **Why**: Both Tableau and Power BI specialize in data visualization and dashboard creation, enabling users to create dynamic, interactive visuals that support data storytelling and presentation.

- **Features**:
  - ○ **Tableau**: Known for its advanced visualization capabilities and user-friendly drag-and-drop interface, Tableau is ideal for creating high-quality, interactive dashboards.
  - ○ **Power BI**: Power BI offers strong data connectivity and integration with Microsoft products, making it effective for reporting within the Microsoft ecosystem. It's also cost-effective and provides powerful data modeling capabilities.

Use Case Example: An HR team wants to create a dashboard to visualize employee turnover rates, demographics, and department-specific metrics. Using Power BI, they connect to their HR database, transform the data, and build an interactive dashboard accessible to managers across the company.

Limitations: Tableau and Power BI require licenses for full functionality, which may not be cost-effective for small organizations or users with minimal visualization needs.

4. Advanced Data Analysis and Modeling

Recommended Tools: **Excel** (for moderate analysis) and **SQL** (for complex analysis and modeling)

- **Why**: For advanced analysis, such as regression, trend analysis, and clustering, SQL can efficiently handle large datasets and perform complex aggregations. For moderate data analysis, Excel's Data Analysis ToolPak offers tools for regression analysis, ANOVA, and other statistical functions.
- **Features**:
  - **Excel**: The Data Analysis ToolPak includes tools for advanced statistical analysis, while functions like FORECAST and TREND allow for predictive analytics.
  - **SQL**: With advanced SQL functions and stored procedures, SQL can execute large-scale analysis and manipulate data directly within the database.

Use Case Example: A finance team is tasked with performing trend analysis on monthly revenue data. Using SQL, they group the data by year and month, calculate average revenue growth, and identify seasonal trends over several years.

Limitations: SQL is not ideal for data visualization, and Excel's performance may be limited when working with very large datasets. For large-scale visualization of analysis results, Tableau or Power BI may be necessary.

5. Real-Time Data Analysis and Collaboration

Recommended Tool: **Google Sheets** and **Power BI**

- **Why**: Google Sheets is cloud-based, allowing multiple users to collaborate on data analysis in real-time. Power BI's sharing and collaboration features are particularly strong within the Microsoft ecosystem, and it allows for real-time updates if connected to live data sources.
- **Features**:
  - **Google Sheets**: Provides real-time collaboration, making it suitable for teams that need to work on data together from different locations.
  - **Power BI**: Allows users to publish reports and dashboards to the Power BI service, enabling real-time data access and collaboration across teams.

Use Case Example: A product development team is tracking feedback from beta testers in Google Sheets, allowing everyone on the team to access, edit, and comment on the data as responses come in. For high-level summaries, the data can be exported to Power BI, where the team creates a real-time dashboard that updates as new feedback is entered.

Limitations: Google Sheets may struggle with large datasets or advanced analytics, while Power BI's real-time data capabilities may require additional setup and permissions.

Tool Comparison Table

Here's a summary table to help you quickly identify the best tool for common data analytics tasks:

Task	Recommended Tool(s)	Why
Data Entry, Cleaning, and Basic Analysis	Excel, Google Sheets	Simple calculations and data cleaning tasks
Querying Large Datasets	SQL	Efficient data retrieval and filtering for large datasets
Data Visualization and Dashboard Creation	Tableau, Power BI	Advanced visualizations and interactive dashboards
Advanced Data Analysis and Modeling	Excel (moderate), SQL (complex)	Statistical analysis, trend analysis, data modeling
Real-Time Analysis and Collaboration	Google Sheets, Power BI	Real-time collaboration and access to live data

Practical Example: Choosing the Right Tool for a Multi-Stage Analysis

Let's consider a scenario where a retail company wants to analyze customer purchasing behavior across multiple regions:

1. **Data Preparation**: The company has a large database with customer and transaction data. They start by using **SQL** to query and clean the data, filtering for customers who made purchases within the past year.
2. **Exploratory Analysis**: After extracting relevant data, the analyst imports it into **Excel** for exploratory analysis, using pivot tables to understand purchase trends by region and product category.
3. **Visualization**: For presenting the findings, they choose **Tableau** to create an interactive dashboard that shows customer demographics, purchasing behavior, and regional differences. Managers can click on filters to view data by specific regions.
4. **Real-Time Updates**: To keep the dashboard updated, they later shift to **Power BI** and connect it to their SQL database. This setup allows the team to access real-time customer insights and track purchasing patterns as they evolve.

By using each tool where it performs best, the company gains a comprehensive view of customer behavior, benefiting from SQL's data management, Excel's analytical flexibility, and Tableau and Power BI's visualization strengths.

Key Takeaways

- **Excel** and **Google Sheets** are best for simple data entry, cleaning, and calculations.
- **SQL** is ideal for querying and managing large datasets, especially within relational databases.
- **Tableau** and **Power BI** excel at data visualization, creating dynamic and interactive dashboards that present complex data in an accessible way.
- Choosing the right tool depends on factors like data size, complexity, collaboration needs, and budget.

Selecting the appropriate tool for each stage of analysis ensures efficiency and accuracy, allowing you to leverage each tool's strengths to achieve your data analysis goals effectively.

Chapter 4: Collecting and Cleaning Data

Methods of Data Collection

Data collection is the first step in any data analysis process, as the quality and relevance of the data directly impact the insights that can be gained. Different methods of data collection are used based on the type of analysis, available resources, and specific goals of a project. Understanding these methods helps analysts choose the most effective way to gather accurate and relevant data, setting a solid foundation for subsequent analysis.

In this section, we'll explore the primary methods of data collection, discussing how each works, when to use them, and their advantages and limitations.

1. Surveys

Surveys are one of the most common methods of data collection, particularly for gathering qualitative and quantitative data directly from respondents. Surveys can be conducted online, over the phone, in person, or via mail, making them versatile and widely applicable.

How Surveys Work

- Surveys consist of a series of questions designed to gather information about

opinions, behaviors, preferences, or demographic information.
- Questions can be closed-ended (multiple choice, yes/no) or open-ended, depending on the depth of information needed.
- Surveys are typically distributed to a targeted group to ensure that responses represent the desired population or demographic.

Types of Surveys

- **Questionnaires**: Usually self-administered and designed for a wide audience, they can be completed online or in print.
- **Interviews**: One-on-one or group interviews conducted face-to-face, over the phone, or virtually, allowing for more in-depth responses.

Advantages of Surveys

- **Wide Reach**: Surveys can reach large populations quickly, particularly when conducted online.
- **Quantitative and Qualitative Data**: They can gather both numeric data and detailed feedback, providing a balanced view of respondents' opinions or behaviors.
- **Cost-Effective**: Online surveys are relatively inexpensive, especially when compared to in-person interviews or focus groups.

Limitations of Surveys

- **Response Bias**: Respondents may not answer honestly, especially on sensitive topics.
- **Question Design**: Poorly designed questions can lead to misinterpretation or unreliable results.
- **Low Response Rates**: Surveys, particularly online ones, may suffer from low response rates, potentially skewing results.

Example Use Case: A retail company conducts an online survey to understand customer satisfaction with recent purchases, gathering feedback on product quality, service, and delivery speed.

2. Observations

Observation involves collecting data by watching and recording behaviors or events as they occur. This method is particularly valuable in settings where understanding natural behavior is essential, such as in product usability studies, customer behavior analysis, or social research.

How Observations Work

- Observers typically document behaviors, events, or environmental conditions without interfering or interacting with subjects.
- Observations can be structured (using checklists or predefined categories) or

unstructured (recording events as they naturally unfold).

Types of Observation

- **Direct Observation**: The observer is present in the environment and watches behaviors firsthand.
- **Participant Observation**: The observer interacts with subjects, often blending into the environment to observe natural behaviors.
- **Remote Observation**: Using video recording or remote monitoring, allowing for later analysis without the observer's physical presence.

Advantages of Observations

- **Real-Time Data**: Captures behaviors and events as they happen, providing immediate, accurate data.
- **Reduced Response Bias**: Observations record natural behavior, reducing the risk of respondents altering their behavior as they might in surveys.
- **Contextual Understanding**: Observation provides insight into the context of behavior, allowing for a deeper understanding of underlying motivations or influences.

Limitations of Observations

- **Time-Consuming**: Observations require a significant amount of time and resources, particularly for long-term studies.
- **Limited Scope**: Observational data is often qualitative, making it difficult to quantify or analyze statistically.
- **Observer Bias**: Observers may unintentionally influence or misinterpret behaviors, especially in unstructured observation.

Example Use Case: A grocery store conducts an observation study to see how customers navigate aisles, revealing insights about product placement and store layout effectiveness.

3. Experiments

Experiments are a method of data collection that involve manipulating one or more variables to observe their effect on another variable. Experiments are often used in scientific, marketing, and psychological research to test hypotheses in a controlled environment.

How Experiments Work

- Experiments consist of a controlled setting where researchers manipulate independent variables to observe their effect on dependent variables.

- They typically involve at least two groups: an experimental group (exposed to the variable) and a control group (not exposed).
- By controlling other factors, researchers can isolate the effect of the independent variable and determine causation.

Types of Experiments

- **Laboratory Experiments**: Conducted in controlled environments where variables can be tightly managed.
- **Field Experiments**: Conducted in real-world settings, where environmental factors are less controlled but results may have higher external validity.

Advantages of Experiments

- **Causal Relationships**: Experiments can establish causation, not just correlation, which is essential for testing specific hypotheses.
- **Control over Variables**: Researchers can isolate variables, reducing the risk of confounding factors.
- **Replicable**: Experiments can be repeated to validate findings, especially in lab settings.

Limitations of Experiments

- **Artificial Environment**: Laboratory experiments may not reflect real-world conditions, limiting external validity.
- **Resource Intensive**: Experiments often require significant resources, including time, personnel, and funding.
- **Ethical Concerns**: Experiments on sensitive topics or vulnerable populations must be designed carefully to avoid ethical issues.

Example Use Case: A skincare brand conducts an experiment to test the effectiveness of a new product. Participants are divided into two groups, with one group using the product and the other using a placebo, allowing researchers to observe differences in skin improvement.

4. Transactional Data

Transactional data refers to data automatically recorded as part of an individual's or organization's daily transactions. This type of data is commonly used in retail, finance, and e-commerce for analyzing trends, customer behaviors, and operational efficiency.

How Transactional Data Works

- Transactional data is automatically generated and recorded whenever a transaction occurs, such as purchases, website clicks, or financial transfers.

- It often includes timestamps, item descriptions, amounts, locations, and customer IDs, providing detailed records for analysis.

Advantages of Transactional Data

- **Automated Collection**: Transactional data is collected automatically, reducing the risk of human error.
- **Large Volumes**: Organizations can collect massive amounts of transactional data, enabling trend analysis and pattern identification.
- **Accurate and Timely**: Recorded in real-time, transactional data provides up-to-date information for immediate analysis.

Limitations of Transactional Data

- **Unstructured**: Transactional data may require significant cleaning and preprocessing to make it suitable for analysis.
- **Privacy Concerns**: Sensitive data may require strict privacy and security measures to protect against unauthorized access.
- **Limited Context**: Transactional data often lacks contextual information, making it difficult to understand the "why" behind behaviors.

Example Use Case: An online retailer analyzes transactional data to understand customer purchase patterns, tracking variables such as purchase frequency, product preferences, and spending habits.

5. Social Media and Web Scraping

Social media and web scraping involve collecting publicly available data from social media platforms, websites, and online forums. This method is increasingly popular for sentiment analysis, trend tracking, and competitive analysis.

How Social Media and Web Scraping Work

- Social media data is gathered from platforms like Twitter, Facebook, and Instagram, where users share opinions, reviews, and preferences.
- Web scraping involves using automated tools to extract data from websites, such as product prices, customer reviews, and blog comments.

Advantages of Social Media and Web Scraping

- **Real-Time Insights**: Social media data offers real-time insights into customer opinions, preferences, and trends.
- **Publicly Accessible**: Web scraping allows analysts to access large volumes of data without needing permissions or direct interaction with respondents.

- **Broad Reach**: Social media and online platforms capture opinions and trends across diverse user demographics.

Limitations of Social Media and Web Scraping

- **Data Quality**: Social media data is often unstructured, requiring significant cleaning and processing.
- **Ethical and Legal Concerns**: Web scraping may violate terms of service for some websites, and privacy concerns must be addressed.
- **Bias**: Social media users may not represent the broader population, leading to skewed insights.

Example Use Case: A company uses social media data to analyze customer sentiment around a recent product launch, identifying common themes in positive and negative feedback.

6. Sensor Data and Internet of Things (IoT)

Sensor data is collected through devices that monitor environmental conditions, machine performance, or human activity. This data collection method is prevalent in manufacturing, healthcare, and environmental science.

How Sensor Data Works

- Sensors detect and measure specific variables, such as temperature, humidity, or movement, and record the data in real time.
- Data is often transmitted through IoT networks, where it can be monitored and analyzed remotely.

Advantages of Sensor Data

- **Real-Time Monitoring**: Sensors provide real-time data, enabling immediate responses to changes or anomalies.
- **Automated Collection**: Data is collected automatically and continuously, reducing human intervention and error.
- **High Volume and Precision**: Sensors generate large datasets with precise measurements, suitable for complex analyses.

Limitations of Sensor Data

- **High Costs**: Installing and maintaining sensors can be expensive.
- **Data Overload**: Sensors produce large volumes of data, requiring advanced storage, processing, and analysis capabilities.
- **Privacy Concerns**: Sensor data in healthcare or personal devices must be managed with strict privacy protections.

Example Use Case: A smart home system collects data on energy usage from various appliances, allowing homeowners to track consumption patterns and reduce energy costs.

Key Takeaways

- **Surveys** are effective for gathering opinions and demographic data directly from respondents.
- **Observations** capture real-time behavior, ideal for studying natural, in-the-moment actions.
- **Experiments** enable researchers to establish causal relationships by controlling variables.
- **Transactional Data** provides accurate, automated records of daily operations.
- **Social Media and Web Scraping** offer real-time insights into public opinion and online trends.
- **Sensor Data** enables continuous monitoring, particularly useful in fields that require precise measurements.

Selecting the right data collection method depends on the type of data needed, the context of the study, and the resources available. Each method has unique advantages and limitations, making it essential to choose the most appropriate method based on your data analysis goals.

Common Data Quality Issues and How to Fix Them

Data quality is critical in data analysis, as inaccurate or inconsistent data can lead to flawed conclusions and misguided decisions. However, raw data often contains errors, inconsistencies, and gaps that must be addressed before analysis. In this section, we'll explore some of the most common data quality issues encountered in analytics, along with practical techniques for identifying and fixing them.

Effective data cleaning is a foundational skill in data analytics and is essential for transforming raw data into a reliable resource for insights.

1. Missing Data

Missing data occurs when values for certain variables are absent in one or more records, which can happen due to human error, data entry issues, or system malfunctions. Missing data can compromise the accuracy of analysis, particularly if the missing values are frequent or concentrated in specific variables.

Types of Missing Data

- **Missing Completely at Random (MCAR):** The missing values have no pattern and are unrelated to any other variable in the dataset.

- **Missing at Random (MAR)**: The missing values are related to other observed variables but not to the missing values themselves.
- **Missing Not at Random (MNAR)**: The missing values have a specific pattern and are related to the missing variable itself, potentially indicating bias.

Solutions for Missing Data

1. **Deletion**:
   - **Listwise Deletion**: Remove entire rows with missing values. This is appropriate if the missing data is minimal and spread across the dataset.
   - **Pairwise Deletion**: Remove only the specific cells with missing values and analyze the available data. Useful for correlation analysis, as it allows retaining as much data as possible.
2. **Imputation**:
   - **Mean/Median Imputation**: Replace missing values with the mean or median of the variable. This works well for numeric data without extreme outliers.
   - **Mode Imputation**: For categorical data, replace missing values with the mode (most frequent value) of the variable.
   - **Predictive Imputation**: Use a model, such as regression, to predict and fill

in missing values based on
relationships with other variables.

Example: A dataset has missing values in the "Age"
column. You could replace the missing values with
the mean age of the dataset or use regression
imputation if age correlates with other variables like
income or education level.

2. Duplicate Data

Duplicate data refers to records that appear more
than once in the dataset, often due to data entry errors
or multiple data sources. Duplicates can skew results
by overrepresenting certain entries and should be
identified and removed during data cleaning.

Solutions for Duplicate Data

1. **Identify Duplicates**:
    o Use built-in functions in tools like
      Excel or SQL to detect duplicates
      based on key identifiers, such as
      names, emails, or unique IDs.
    o In SQL, the DISTINCT function can be
      used to remove duplicates in query
      results.
2. **Remove Duplicates**:
    o **Manual Removal**: For small datasets,
      manually review and delete duplicate
      rows.

- **Automated Removal**: Use data cleaning tools in Excel, Google Sheets, or data management software to identify and remove duplicates quickly.

Example: A customer database has multiple entries for the same customer due to repeat purchases. By filtering for duplicate customer IDs, you can delete duplicate rows, keeping only unique customer entries.

3. Inconsistent Data Formats

Inconsistent data formats occur when data is recorded in different formats across the dataset, making it challenging to analyze. For example, dates might be entered in multiple formats (e.g., "MM/DD/YYYY" vs. "DD-MM-YYYY"), or phone numbers might include varying country codes and delimiters.

Solutions for Inconsistent Data Formats

1. **Standardization**:
   - Convert data to a common format. For example, reformat all dates to "YYYY-MM-DD" or phone numbers to include the country code and consistent separators.
   - Use built-in functions to reformat data. In Excel, the TEXT function can convert dates and numbers to consistent formats, while in SQL, date

and string functions like FORMAT or CAST can standardize formats.

2. **Validation Rules**:
   - Set up validation rules to ensure that new data entries follow the correct format. This is especially useful for recurring data collection or automated data entry systems.

Example: A dataset includes dates recorded as both "01/05/2024" and "2024-05-01." By applying a consistent format (e.g., "YYYY-MM-DD"), you ensure that all dates are uniformly represented, enabling accurate time-series analysis.

4. Outliers

Outliers are data points that deviate significantly from the rest of the dataset. They can occur due to measurement errors, data entry mistakes, or natural variability. Outliers can heavily influence statistical analysis, leading to skewed results or inaccurate conclusions.

Solutions for Outliers

1. **Identify Outliers**:
   - Use visualizations, such as box plots or scatter plots, to detect unusual values.
   - Calculate statistical measures like the interquartile range (IQR) or standard

deviation. Values that fall outside 1.5 times the IQR or 3 standard deviations from the mean may be considered outliers.

2. **Handle Outliers**:
   o **Removal**: If the outliers result from data entry errors or measurement issues, consider removing them.
   o **Transformation**: Apply log transformations or normalization techniques to reduce the impact of outliers.
   o **Winsorizing**: Cap outliers to a specified percentile, such as the 5th and 95th percentiles, to reduce their influence without removing them entirely.

Example: In a dataset of annual incomes, one entry shows an income of $5,000,000, which is significantly higher than the typical values. After verifying that it's not a data entry error, you might cap it to the 95th percentile to prevent it from skewing the analysis.

5. Inaccurate Data Entry

Inaccurate data entry occurs when values are incorrectly recorded, often due to human error. Common issues include misspelled names, incorrect numerical values, and misplaced decimals. Inaccurate entries can reduce data reliability and lead to misleading results.

Solutions for Inaccurate Data Entry

1. **Data Validation**:
   - Use validation rules in Excel or Google Sheets to limit values to specific ranges, formats, or lists, reducing the likelihood of incorrect entries.
   - For numeric data, set logical constraints (e.g., a minimum and maximum range) to prevent impossible values.
2. **Automated Tools**:
   - Use data cleaning software or programming languages like Python and R to identify anomalies in numeric fields or unusual strings in text fields.
   - Spell-checkers or natural language processing (NLP) techniques can help correct misspelled text entries.

Example: A survey dataset includes entries for "United States," "USA," and "U.S." as country names. To ensure consistency, you can replace all variations with a single standardized value, such as "USA."

6. Inconsistent Categorical Values

Inconsistent categorical values occur when data in categorical fields (e.g., gender, department, product category) is recorded with slight variations, such as typos or abbreviations. This can lead to redundant categories and unreliable summaries.

Solutions for Inconsistent Categorical Values

1. **Data Standardization**:
   - Standardize categorical values by choosing a single term for each category. For example, replace all instances of "M" and "Male" with "Male."
   - Use lookup tables or conditional formatting to quickly identify and replace inconsistent values.
2. **Automated Matching**:
   - For large datasets, use automated matching algorithms or data-cleaning tools to detect and merge similar categorical values.

Example: In an employee database, the department field includes entries such as "HR," "Human Resources," and "human resources." Standardizing all variations to "HR" ensures consistency, enabling accurate reporting and analysis.

7. Data Redundancy

Data redundancy occurs when the same data is repeated unnecessarily, often due to merging datasets from different sources or duplicate entries. Redundant data can lead to larger file sizes and potential inaccuracies in analysis.

Solutions for Data Redundancy

1. **Database Normalization**:
   - If working within a relational database, normalize the data by dividing it into related tables. This minimizes redundancy while preserving data integrity.
2. **De-Duplication Tools**:
   - Use de-duplication functions in software tools like Excel, Google Sheets, or SQL to remove redundant entries.
   - In SQL, use the DISTINCT function or GROUP BY clause to filter out repeated data entries.

Example: A CRM system has duplicate customer records due to importing data from multiple sources. By running a de-duplication process, the company removes redundant entries, reducing storage costs and improving data accuracy.

8. Non-Standard Units and Measurement Scales

Data often contains values recorded in different units (e.g., kilograms vs. pounds) or measurement scales (e.g., Celsius vs. Fahrenheit). Non-standard units make it challenging to compare or aggregate data accurately.

Solutions for Non-Standard Units and Measurement Scales

1. **Unit Conversion**:
   o Convert all values to a single standard unit. For instance, convert all weights to kilograms or all temperatures to Celsius.
   o Use formulas in Excel or conversion functions in programming languages like Python to standardize units across the dataset.
2. **Add Metadata for Units**:
   o Clearly label units within the dataset to avoid confusion. For example, include "(kg)" or "(lbs)" in column headers to indicate measurement units.

Example: A dataset records temperatures in both Celsius and Fahrenheit, creating inconsistencies. Converting all temperatures to Celsius provides a uniform basis for analysis, enabling accurate calculations and comparisons.

Key Takeaways

- **Missing Data**: Addressed through deletion or imputation methods, depending on the extent and type of missing values.
- **Duplicate Data**: Detected and removed using automated functions or manual review to prevent overrepresentation.
- **Inconsistent Data Formats**: Standardized to ensure uniformity, especially for dates, phone numbers, and text fields.
- **Outliers**: Identified through statistical measures or visualizations, then handled through removal, transformation, or capping.
- **Inaccurate Data Entry**: Reduced through data validation rules, spell-checking, and automated error detection.
- **Inconsistent Categorical Values**: Standardized to ensure uniformity in categories, reducing redundancies and improving accuracy.
- **Data Redundancy**: Minimized through normalization, de-duplication, or data matching algorithms.
- **Non-Standard Units**: Standardized through unit conversions, ensuring consistency in analysis.

By addressing these common data quality issues, you create a reliable, clean dataset that supports accurate and meaningful analysis, improving the overall integrity of your insights.

Data Cleaning Basics: Removing Duplicates, Handling Missing Values, and Formatting

Data cleaning is an essential step in data analysis, as raw data often contains inconsistencies, errors, and missing values that can compromise the accuracy of insights. Effective data cleaning transforms raw data into a reliable resource, improving its quality and ensuring that subsequent analysis produces valid results. In this section, we'll cover the basics of data cleaning, focusing on three fundamental tasks: removing duplicates, handling missing values, and standardizing data formatting.

1. Removing Duplicates

Duplicate data refers to repeated entries in a dataset, which can lead to overrepresentation and skewed analysis. Duplicates often occur due to data entry errors, merging datasets from different sources, or system glitches. Identifying and removing duplicates is an important step in ensuring data accuracy.

How to Identify Duplicates

1. **Using Excel**: Excel provides a built-in tool to detect duplicates.
    - Select the range of cells, then go to **Data > Remove Duplicates**. You can specify which columns to consider for duplication.

- o Excel will highlight duplicate entries or remove them directly, depending on your preference.
2. **Using Google Sheets**: Google Sheets offers a similar tool to remove duplicates.
   - o Select the data range, then go to **Data > Data cleanup > Remove duplicates**. Check the columns you want to use for duplicate detection.
3. **Using SQL**: SQL is effective for identifying duplicates in large datasets.
   - o Use the GROUP BY and COUNT functions to find duplicate entries based on specific columns.
   - o For example, the query below identifies duplicate records based on the "customer_id" field:

```sql
Copy code
SELECT customer_id, COUNT(*)
FROM customers
GROUP BY customer_id
HAVING COUNT(*) > 1;
```

How to Remove Duplicates

1. **Listwise Removal**: Delete all rows that contain duplicate values. This method is straightforward but may remove useful data if duplicates are present in only one column.
2. **Partial Removal**: If only certain columns contain duplicates, remove duplicates

selectively, retaining unique rows based on a key identifier like a customer ID.

Example: In a customer dataset with multiple entries for the same customer ID, you can filter for unique customer IDs, keeping only one record per customer.

2. Handling Missing Values

Missing data is a common issue in raw datasets, resulting from incomplete entries, system errors, or data collection problems. Ignoring missing values can lead to inaccurate results, so it's essential to handle them effectively. The approach to handling missing values depends on the extent of the missing data and its significance to the analysis.

How to Identify Missing Values

1. **Using Excel**: In Excel, you can filter cells to find blanks or use conditional formatting to highlight cells with missing values.
2. **Using Google Sheets**: Apply filters to columns and select the "Blanks" option to locate missing values.
3. **Using SQL**: Use the IS NULL condition to identify rows with missing values in specific columns.
    o For example:

    ```sql
    sql
    Copy code
    ```

```
SELECT *
FROM orders
WHERE customer_id IS NULL;
```

Strategies for Handling Missing Values

1. **Deletion**:
   - **Listwise Deletion**: Remove rows with missing values entirely. This is suitable if missing data is minimal and does not significantly affect the dataset.
   - **Pairwise Deletion**: Remove missing values only for specific analyses, retaining as much data as possible. This approach is useful when performing correlation analysis.
2. **Imputation**:
   - **Mean/Median Imputation**: For numeric data, replace missing values with the mean or median of the column. This is effective for data without outliers.
   - **Mode Imputation**: For categorical data, replace missing values with the mode (most common value) in the column.
   - **Predictive Imputation**: Use a regression or machine learning model to estimate and replace missing values based on relationships with other variables.

- **Forward or Backward Fill**: In time series data, fill missing values with the previous or next valid entry. This approach is useful for datasets where continuity is important.

Example: A sales dataset has missing values in the "quantity_sold" column. You can replace missing values with the mean sales quantity for more accurate reporting, or use predictive imputation if there's a strong correlation with other variables.

3. Standardizing Data Formatting

Inconsistent data formats are common in datasets, especially when data comes from multiple sources or manual entry. Inconsistent formatting complicates analysis, as data may be recorded in various styles or units. Standardizing data ensures uniformity, making it easier to manipulate, analyze, and interpret.

Common Formatting Issues and Solutions

1. **Dates**:
   - **Issue**: Dates may be recorded in multiple formats (e.g., "MM/DD/YYYY," "DD-MM-YYYY").
   - **Solution**: Convert all dates to a single format, such as "YYYY-MM-DD," to ensure consistency. In Excel, you can use the TEXT function to reformat

dates, while in SQL, functions like FORMAT or CAST standardize dates.

- o **Example in Excel**:

```excel
Copy code
=TEXT(A2, "YYYY-MM-DD")
```

2. **Text Case Consistency**:
   - o **Issue**: Text values, such as city names or product categories, may appear in different cases (e.g., "new york," "New York," "NEW YORK").
   - o **Solution**: Standardize text to a single case, such as proper case or uppercase. In Excel, you can use the UPPER, LOWER, or PROPER functions to convert text case.

3. **Numerical Formatting**:
   - o **Issue**: Numerical data may include inconsistent units (e.g., currency symbols, commas as thousand separators).
   - o **Solution**: Remove non-numeric characters (e.g., "$") and ensure all numbers are formatted correctly. In Excel, use the VALUE function to convert text to a numeric format.
   - o **Example**: For a column containing values with commas, such as "1,000," use Excel's "Find and Replace" tool to

remove commas and convert values to a consistent numeric format.

4. **Phone Numbers and Addresses**:
   - **Issue**: Contact information often contains variations in format, including parentheses, dashes, and spaces.
   - **Solution**: Standardize formats by removing extra characters or adding country codes. In Excel, use custom formatting options or the SUBSTITUTE function to clean up phone numbers.
   - **Example in Excel**:

```excel
Copy code
=SUBSTITUTE(SUBSTITUTE(A2, "-",
""), "(", "")
```

Automated Formatting Tools

- **Data Validation**: Set up validation rules in Excel or Google Sheets to enforce specific formats during data entry, helping prevent inconsistencies from the start.
- **Conditional Formatting**: Apply conditional formatting to identify cells that do not match the desired format, allowing for quick corrections.

Example: In an employee database, names are inconsistently recorded as "First Last" or "Last, First." Using text functions, you can standardize all names to "First Last" format, ensuring consistency in the dataset.

Practical Example: Cleaning a Customer Dataset

Let's walk through a practical example where a customer service team needs to clean a dataset containing customer information:

1. **Removing Duplicates**: The team uses Excel's "Remove Duplicates" function to eliminate repeated entries based on unique customer IDs. This ensures that each customer appears only once in the dataset, preventing overrepresentation.

2. **Handling Missing Values**: Some customers are missing contact information. The team fills in missing values for "phone number" with "Not Available" (using mode imputation) and uses listwise deletion to remove rows missing critical data, such as "customer ID" or "email."

3. **Standardizing Formatting**:
   - **Date Format**: All date entries are converted to "YYYY-MM-DD" for uniformity.
   - **Text Consistency**: The "City" column is converted to proper case, ensuring entries are consistently formatted as

"New York" instead of "new york" or
"NEW YORK."

- o **Phone Numbers**: All phone numbers
  are formatted with country codes and
  standardized spacing for easier
  readability.

After cleaning the data, the customer service team has
a reliable, consistent dataset ready for analysis,
enabling them to accurately track and evaluate
customer interactions.

Key Takeaways

- **Removing Duplicates**: Duplicate entries are
  identified and removed using functions in
  Excel, Google Sheets, or SQL to ensure each
  record is unique.
- **Handling Missing Values**: Missing data is
  handled through deletion or imputation
  techniques, with approaches varying based on
  the type of data and analysis requirements.
- **Standardizing Formatting**: Uniform formats
  for dates, text, and numerical values are
  applied to ensure consistency and simplify
  analysis.

By following these data cleaning basics, you'll
improve data quality and accuracy, laying a strong
foundation for meaningful analysis. Effective data
cleaning minimizes errors, enhances reliability, and

ensures your dataset is ready for insightful and impactful analysis.

Chapter 5: Exploring and Analyzing Data

Descriptive Analytics: Measures of Central Tendency and Variability

Descriptive analytics is the process of summarizing and interpreting data to gain insights into its main characteristics. It helps you understand the general patterns and distribution of data, laying the groundwork for more advanced analysis. In this section, we'll focus on two core aspects of descriptive analytics: measures of central tendency and measures of variability.

Measures of central tendency—mean, median, and mode—help describe the "center" of the data, or where most values cluster. Measures of variability—such as range and standard deviation—reveal how spread out the data points are, indicating the extent to which values differ from each other. Together, these measures provide a balanced view of the data, helping you understand both typical values and the overall diversity within the dataset.

Measures of Central Tendency: Mean, Median, and Mode

Measures of central tendency are used to find the central point around which data values are distributed. Each measure of central tendency provides a unique perspective on the "average" or typical value within a dataset, helping you summarize the data in meaningful ways.

1. Mean (Average)

The mean, often referred to as the average, represents the central value of a dataset by taking into account all values. It provides an overall summary by balancing the values on either side of it. The mean is particularly useful when values are evenly distributed, as it gives a straightforward sense of the "center" of the data.

- **When to Use**: The mean is ideal when you want a quick summary of the data and when values are distributed evenly, without extreme outliers.
- **Example**: In a dataset of test scores, calculating the mean gives you an idea of the average performance of the group. If the mean score is 75 out of 100, you know that, on average, the group performed around this level.
- **Limitations**: The mean can be affected by outliers—values that are significantly higher or lower than the rest of the data. If a dataset contains extreme values, they can pull the mean away from the true center, giving a misleading impression of the "average" value.

2. Median

The median is the middle value in a dataset when all values are ordered from lowest to highest. The median gives a sense of the central point in the data, especially when values are not evenly distributed. Since it isn't affected by extreme values, the median is often used when the dataset has outliers or a skewed distribution.

- **When to Use**: The median is ideal for datasets with outliers or skewed distributions, as it gives a more accurate representation of the "typical" value without being influenced by extremes.
- **Example**: If you have data on household incomes in a neighborhood, the median income will give you a better sense of the typical income than the mean, especially if a few very high incomes skew the data.
- **Limitations**: The median may not fully capture the influence of all data points, as it focuses only on the middle position. This can make it less effective for understanding overall trends when there are no extreme values.

3. Mode

The mode is the most frequently occurring value in a dataset. Unlike the mean and median, which focus on central values, the mode shows which value appears most often. It's especially useful for categorical data, where values represent categories rather than numbers.

- **When to Use**: The mode is helpful when you want to understand the most common value in a dataset, particularly for categorical data (such as color preferences or product types).
- **Example**: In a survey where respondents indicate their favorite fruit, the mode will reveal the most popular choice, such as "apple," providing insight into preferences.
- **Limitations**: The mode may not always provide a meaningful summary, especially if the dataset has many unique values with similar frequencies or if there's no repeating value. Additionally, some datasets may have more than one mode, which can make interpretation more complex.

Measures of Variability: Range and Standard Deviation

While measures of central tendency describe the "center" of the data, measures of variability show how spread out the data points are. Variability provides insights into the consistency or diversity of the data, helping you understand the extent of differences among values.

1. Range

The range is the simplest measure of variability, representing the difference between the highest and lowest values in a dataset. It provides a quick overview of the spread, showing the extent to which values vary.

- **When to Use**: The range is helpful when you need a basic understanding of the spread of values, as it gives you the difference between the maximum and minimum points.
- **Example**: If you're looking at daily temperatures over a month, the range will tell you the difference between the hottest and coldest days, giving a sense of temperature variability.
- **Limitations**: The range can be influenced by outliers, as it only considers the highest and lowest values. This may give a misleading impression of variability if the majority of data points are closer to the mean.

2. Standard Deviation

Standard deviation is a more comprehensive measure of variability, showing how much the values in a dataset differ from the mean. A high standard deviation indicates that values are spread out from the mean, while a low standard deviation means they are clustered closely around it. Standard deviation provides a sense of how "typical" values vary from the central point, making it useful for understanding data consistency.

- **When to Use**: Standard deviation is useful when you want a more detailed understanding of how data points differ from the mean. It's especially valuable in comparing datasets with similar means to see if they vary in terms of consistency.
- **Example**: If you're analyzing the test scores of two classes with the same mean score, the class with the lower standard deviation has scores that are more consistent, while the other class has a wider range of scores.
- **Limitations**: Standard deviation assumes data is symmetrically distributed around the mean, so it may not accurately describe variability in highly skewed datasets. It also doesn't convey the exact range of values, focusing instead on typical deviations from the mean.

Practical Examples of Central Tendency and Variability in Action

Let's consider some real-world examples to see how measures of central tendency and variability work together to provide a full picture of data.

1. **Employee Salaries**: Imagine you're analyzing the salaries within a company.
   o **Mean**: The average salary gives a general sense of employee earnings.
   o **Median**: The median salary might be more informative if there are a few

executives with very high salaries, which could skew the mean.

- o **Range**: The range reveals the salary gap between the highest and lowest earners, giving insight into pay equity.
- o **Standard Deviation**: A low standard deviation would indicate that salaries are relatively uniform across employees, while a high standard deviation suggests a wide variation in earnings.

2. **Product Review Scores**: Consider a dataset of product review scores, rated from 1 to 5 stars.

- o **Mean**: The average score helps summarize overall customer satisfaction.
- o **Mode**: The mode shows the most common score, indicating the typical rating customers give.
- o **Range**: The range tells you the gap between the best and worst ratings, providing insight into the consistency of customer experiences.
- o **Standard Deviation**: A low standard deviation means most customers have similar views, while a high standard deviation indicates mixed reviews.

3. **School Test Scores**: Suppose a teacher wants to understand her class's performance on a recent exam.

- Mean: The average score gives her a sense of overall class performance.
- Median: The median score shows the middle point, useful if some students scored unusually high or low.
- Range: The range highlights the difference between the top and bottom scores, showing the spread of performance.
- Standard Deviation: A low standard deviation indicates that most students performed similarly, while a high standard deviation suggests diverse performance levels.

Summary of Central Tendency and Variability Measures

Measure	Description	Best Used When
Mean	The average of all values, showing overall level	Values are evenly distributed
Median	The middle value, useful for skewed data	Data has outliers or skewed values
Mode	The most frequent value, ideal for categories	Identifying common categories

Measure	Description	Best Used When
Range	Difference between highest and lowest values	Quick sense of data spread
Standard Deviation	Typical deviation from the mean, shows consistency	Detailed view of data consistency

Key Takeaways

- **Mean, Median, and Mode**: Each measure of central tendency offers a different way to understand the typical or average value in a dataset, depending on its distribution and presence of outliers.
- **Range and Standard Deviation**: These measures of variability reveal the extent of differences among values, helping you gauge data consistency and spread.

Understanding these measures equips you to explore datasets effectively, highlighting both typical values and overall diversity. With these insights, you'll be ready to dive deeper into your data, armed with a foundational understanding of its core characteristics.

Visualizing Data Insights with Charts and Graphs

Data visualization is a powerful way to communicate insights, patterns, and trends within a dataset. While tables of numbers provide detailed information, charts and graphs translate this information into visuals that are easier to interpret, enabling viewers to quickly grasp key findings. In this section, we'll cover essential chart types, explaining the purpose of each and the types of data they best represent. Whether you're presenting sales trends, customer demographics, or survey results, choosing the right visualization can make your data more compelling and accessible.

Why Visualize Data?

The goal of data visualization is to simplify complex information, making it understandable and impactful. By transforming data into visual formats, you can highlight important insights, illustrate relationships, and support data-driven decisions. Visualizations can help answer questions such as:

- **How has a metric changed over time?** (e.g., sales growth)
- **How do categories compare to one another?** (e.g., product popularity)
- **What's the relationship between two variables?** (e.g., advertising spend vs. sales)

- **How is data distributed?** (e.g., income levels within a population)

Good visualizations make data insights accessible and engaging, providing context at a glance. Let's look at some common chart types and how they help reveal these insights.

1. Line Charts

Line charts are used to display trends over time, making them ideal for tracking changes, such as monthly sales, website traffic, or stock prices. They plot data points on a continuous line, showing whether values have increased, decreased, or remained stable over time.

When to Use Line Charts

- **Trends Over Time**: Use line charts when you want to show how data changes over time, highlighting peaks, valleys, and trends.
- **Comparison of Multiple Series**: Line charts are also effective for comparing trends across multiple groups. For example, you could compare monthly revenue trends across different product lines.

Example

A business tracks monthly sales over the past year, showing a clear upward trend during the holiday season. The line chart highlights these seasonal fluctuations, allowing managers to plan inventory more effectively.

Key Takeaway

Line charts are straightforward and effective for visualizing time-based data, making them essential for trend analysis.

2. Bar Charts

Bar charts represent categorical data with rectangular bars. Each bar's length corresponds to the value of the category it represents, making it easy to compare quantities across categories. Bar charts can be displayed horizontally or vertically, depending on the preference or context.

When to Use Bar Charts

- **Category Comparisons**: Bar charts are ideal for comparing the size of different categories, such as the number of units sold by product type or customer demographics by age group.
- **Ranked Data**: They're useful for ranking data, as it's easy to see which categories have the highest or lowest values.

Example

A marketing team analyzes social media engagement across platforms. By visualizing the data with a bar chart, they can see that Instagram has the highest engagement, followed by Facebook and Twitter, helping them prioritize their social media efforts.

Key Takeaway

Bar charts are versatile and easy to interpret, making them suitable for comparing categories and ranking data.

3. Pie Charts

Pie charts show proportions within a whole, dividing a circle into segments that represent different categories. Each segment's size reflects the proportion of each category, allowing viewers to quickly see the relative size of each part.

When to Use Pie Charts

- **Showing Parts of a Whole**: Pie charts work best for visualizing data that represents parts of a whole, such as budget allocations or market share percentages.
- **Limited Categories**: They are most effective when the dataset has only a few categories; too many categories can make a pie chart hard to read.

Example

A nonprofit organization displays its budget allocation using a pie chart, showing that 50% goes to programs, 30% to outreach, and 20% to administration. The pie chart provides a clear view of how funds are distributed.

Key Takeaway

Pie charts are useful for representing proportions, but they are best suited for small datasets where categories add up to 100%.

4. Histograms

Histograms are used to visualize the distribution of numerical data by grouping data points into bins (or intervals). They look similar to bar charts but show frequency distributions, helping you see where values cluster and where gaps occur.

When to Use Histograms

- **Distribution Analysis**: Use histograms to understand the distribution of data points, such as the frequency of test scores or income levels within a group.
- **Continuous Data**: Histograms are effective for continuous data, where values are not discrete but fall within a range.

Example

An instructor analyzes the distribution of student test scores using a histogram. The chart reveals that most students scored between 70 and 80, while fewer scored above 90 or below 60, helping the instructor understand the range and average of class performance.

Key Takeaway

Histograms provide insight into the distribution of values in a dataset, allowing you to observe trends, clusters, and outliers within a range.

5. Scatter Plots

Scatter plots show the relationship between two variables by plotting data points on a two-dimensional grid. Each point represents one observation, with its position determined by its values on both the horizontal (x-axis) and vertical (y-axis) axes.

When to Use Scatter Plots

- **Identifying Relationships**: Scatter plots are useful for examining relationships or correlations between two variables, such as income and education level.
- **Spotting Patterns or Outliers**: They are effective for identifying patterns, clusters, and outliers, which can suggest potential trends or anomalies.

Example

A company plots advertising spend against sales revenue, using a scatter plot to see if higher advertising spending correlates with higher sales. The points generally follow an upward trend, suggesting a positive relationship between the two variables.

Key Takeaway

Scatter plots are valuable for visualizing relationships between two variables, helping to identify correlations, clusters, and outliers.

6. Box Plots

Box plots (or box-and-whisker plots) summarize data distribution and highlight data spread, showing the range, median, and variability. They are particularly helpful for identifying outliers and understanding the overall distribution of values within a dataset.

When to Use Box Plots

- **Comparing Distributions**: Box plots are ideal for comparing distributions across multiple groups, such as test scores by class.
- **Outlier Detection**: They are effective for identifying outliers, as any values falling outside the "whiskers" of the box plot are considered unusual.

Example

A researcher compares income levels across different regions using a box plot. Each region's income distribution is represented by a box plot, showing that one region has significantly higher variability and a few outliers.

Key Takeaway

Box plots offer a comprehensive view of data distribution, making them suitable for comparing multiple groups and identifying outliers.

7. Heatmaps

Heatmaps display data in a matrix format, with colors representing values. Darker or more intense colors often indicate higher values, making it easy to identify patterns, trends, or concentrations within a grid.

When to Use Heatmaps

- **Showing Intensity or Density**: Heatmaps are useful when you want to illustrate intensity or density, such as customer activity by day and hour.
- **Correlation Matrices**: Heatmaps are also common for showing correlation matrices, where each cell represents the correlation between two variables.

Example

A website analyzes user activity, using a heatmap to display visit frequency by day and time. The heatmap shows peak activity times with darker colors, helping the team identify when users are most active.

Key Takeaway

Heatmaps are effective for visualizing intensity and patterns within a grid, making them ideal for dense data, correlations, and time-based activity.

Choosing the Right Chart: Summary Table

Here's a summary of each chart type and its best uses, to help you select the right chart for your data insights:

Chart Type	Best For	Key Insights
Line Chart	Trends over time	Highlights changes over time
Bar Chart	Comparing categories	Shows category rankings
Pie Chart	Parts of a whole	Illustrates proportions
Histogram	Distribution analysis	Reveals frequency distribution

Chart Type	Best For	Key Insights
Scatter Plot	Relationships between two variables	Identifies correlations and patterns
Box Plot	Comparing distributions, outliers	Shows data spread and outliers
Heatmap	Intensity, dense data patterns	Highlights activity or density

Practical Example: Creating a Sales Dashboard

Suppose a sales team wants to create a dashboard to track monthly sales performance, compare product category popularity, and analyze customer purchase patterns. Here's how they could use different charts:

1. **Line Chart**: Tracks total monthly sales over the past year, revealing seasonal trends.
2. **Bar Chart**: Compares sales across product categories, identifying the best and worst-selling items.
3. **Scatter Plot**: Analyzes the relationship between marketing spend and sales revenue, helping determine if higher marketing budgets lead to increased sales.

4. **Pie Chart**: Shows market share by region, allowing the team to visualize regional contributions to total sales.

By combining these charts, the sales team creates a comprehensive dashboard that provides actionable insights, helping them make informed decisions on inventory, marketing, and sales strategies.

Key Takeaways

- **Line Charts** and **Bar Charts** are versatile, widely used tools for tracking trends and comparing categories.
- **Pie Charts** work well for visualizing parts of a whole but are best for datasets with few categories.
- **Histograms** and **Box Plots** provide insights into data distribution, highlighting clusters, outliers, and spread.
- **Scatter Plots** help identify relationships between variables, while **Heatmaps** are useful for visualizing intensity and dense data patterns.

Choosing the right chart type is essential for effectively communicating your insights. By matching your data to the appropriate visualization, you can create clear, compelling representations that make complex data accessible and informative.

Recognizing Patterns, Trends, and Outliers

Data exploration often involves identifying patterns, trends, and outliers—elements that reveal essential characteristics about the data. Recognizing these elements helps analysts uncover insights, predict future outcomes, and make informed decisions. This section covers the fundamentals of detecting patterns, understanding trends, and spotting outliers, each of which offers unique insights into the data's structure and behavior.

Why Recognize Patterns, Trends, and Outliers?

Recognizing patterns, trends, and outliers is critical because they offer different perspectives on the data:

- **Patterns** reveal repeated sequences, behaviors, or structures that can provide insights into underlying relationships.
- **Trends** show the direction of data movement over time, helping predict future outcomes and understand past changes.
- **Outliers** indicate unusual data points that may signify errors, anomalies, or unique insights into rare occurrences.

By understanding these elements, you can create a richer narrative around your data, helping stakeholders make decisions that are both informed and proactive.

Recognizing Patterns

Patterns are recurring sequences or structures within data that can suggest relationships or dependencies among variables. Recognizing patterns is particularly useful for understanding the general behavior of a dataset, detecting seasonality, or discovering associations between variables.

Types of Patterns

1. **Sequential Patterns**: Patterns where data follows a predictable sequence or order.
   - Example: An e-commerce website observes that visits peak during specific hours every day, showing a sequential pattern in user behavior.
2. **Cyclical Patterns**: Patterns that repeat over regular intervals, often related to natural cycles or seasonal events.
   - Example: Retailers often see higher sales during holiday seasons, indicating a cyclical pattern that repeats annually.
3. **Spatial Patterns**: Patterns that reveal relationships based on location or geographic data.
   - Example: Real estate prices in a city may show spatial patterns, with higher prices in certain neighborhoods compared to others.

How to Recognize Patterns

- **Visual Analysis**: Charts and graphs, such as line charts, scatter plots, and heatmaps, make it easier to observe recurring behaviors.
- **Cross-Tabulation**: Creating tables that categorize data can help identify associations and co-occurrences among variables.
- **Clustering**: Clustering algorithms group similar data points, making patterns among groups more visible.

Example: A restaurant notices a pattern of increased bookings every Friday and Saturday, indicating a predictable sequence in customer behavior that helps with staffing and inventory planning.

Why Patterns Matter

Identifying patterns provides insights into predictable behavior, allowing you to anticipate future occurrences. This can be especially useful in sectors like retail, finance, and manufacturing, where understanding customer or market behavior leads to better planning and resource allocation.

Analyzing Trends

Trends represent the general direction of data points over time, showing how values increase, decrease, or remain stable. Trend analysis is valuable for understanding changes, forecasting future outcomes, and tracking the progress of key metrics.

Types of Trends

1. **Upward Trend**: When data points generally increase over time, indicating growth or improvement.
    - o **Example**: A company's revenue shows an upward trend over several quarters, signaling business growth.
2. **Downward Trend**: When data points decrease over time, suggesting a decline or negative performance.
    - o **Example**: A reduction in product sales over several months might indicate decreased demand or increased competition.
3. **Stable Trend**: When data points fluctuate minimally, suggesting consistency.
    - o **Example**: Monthly customer satisfaction scores that remain consistently high show a stable trend in service quality.

How to Recognize Trends

- **Line Charts**: Plotting data over time on a line chart helps reveal upward, downward, or stable trends.

- **Moving Averages**: Calculating moving averages smooths out short-term fluctuations, making long-term trends more visible.
- **Time Series Analysis**: Advanced statistical methods in time series analysis, such as exponential smoothing, can help forecast trends by considering seasonality and randomness.

Example: A business tracks its website traffic, noticing an upward trend that coincides with a new marketing campaign, indicating that the campaign is likely driving more visitors to the site.

Why Trends Matter

Trends help you understand long-term changes and anticipate future movements, which is essential for strategic planning. Identifying trends allows organizations to capitalize on positive changes, address declines, and monitor the effectiveness of ongoing initiatives.

Spotting Outliers

Outliers are data points that deviate significantly from other observations, either much higher or lower than typical values. Outliers can result from errors, natural variation, or unique occurrences. Identifying outliers is crucial because they can skew analysis results, influence averages, and highlight unusual phenomena that may warrant further investigation.

Types of Outliers

1. **Extreme Values**: Outliers that are exceptionally high or low compared to the rest of the data.
   - Example: In a dataset of exam scores, most students score between 60 and 80, but one student scores 100, making it an extreme outlier.
2. **Errors or Data Entry Mistakes**: Outliers caused by incorrect data entry, such as an extra zero added to a number.
   - Example: An inventory dataset mistakenly records 1,000 units instead of 100, creating a misleadingly high outlier.
3. **Natural Variations**: Outliers that result from genuine but rare events.
   - Example: An unusually high sales spike on Black Friday is a natural outlier driven by the holiday season.

How to Spot Outliers

- **Box Plots**: Box plots display the data spread and highlight outliers, making them ideal for identifying unusual values.
- **Scatter Plots**: Scatter plots can reveal outliers that deviate significantly from the main data cluster.
- **Standard Deviation**: If a value is far from the mean and outside the normal range, it is likely

an outlier. Standard deviation is a common measure used to determine what counts as a "normal" distance from the mean.

Example: An HR team notices that one employee's annual leave days are significantly higher than the rest of the team. This outlier prompts further investigation, revealing an error in leave recording.

Why Outliers Matter

Outliers can provide meaningful insights or distort analysis, depending on their cause. Identifying outliers helps you decide whether to investigate or exclude them from analysis, ensuring accuracy in trends and averages.

Practical Approaches for Recognizing Patterns, Trends, and Outliers

Let's go through some practical examples of how you might recognize patterns, trends, and outliers in real-world datasets.

1. **Sales Data**: A company tracks monthly sales data across product lines.
   - **Pattern**: Sales tend to increase every November and December, indicating a seasonal pattern around the holiday season.
   - **Trend**: Over the past two years, the company sees a gradual upward trend

in annual sales, suggesting business growth.

- o **Outliers**: One month has unusually high sales due to a major promotional event, which stands out as an outlier from regular sales figures.

2. **Website Analytics**: A marketing team monitors weekly website traffic to assess the effectiveness of a new ad campaign.
   - o **Pattern**: Traffic spikes every Friday, suggesting a pattern in user behavior.
   - o **Trend**: There's a steady upward trend in overall traffic, indicating that the campaign is successfully attracting more visitors.
   - o **Outliers**: One week shows an unexpected drop in traffic due to a technical issue, which is easily identified as an outlier.

3. **Customer Feedback Scores**: A company tracks customer feedback scores to monitor service quality.
   - o **Pattern**: Higher scores are consistently reported during certain times of the year, such as the holiday season.
   - o **Trend**: The average customer satisfaction score has gradually improved over time, showing a positive trend.

- o **Outliers**: A few exceptionally low scores suggest isolated incidents of customer dissatisfaction, prompting further investigation.

Tools for Identifying Patterns, Trends, and Outliers

1. **Excel and Google Sheets**:
   - o Use line charts, scatter plots, and conditional formatting to highlight patterns and trends.
   - o Box plots and conditional formatting can help flag outliers visually.
2. **Tableau and Power BI**:
   - o Create interactive dashboards that reveal patterns and trends across different categories and time periods.
   - o Use filters and sorting options to isolate outliers and observe their impact on overall data.
3. **SQL**:
   - o SQL queries can help identify outliers by filtering values that are above or below specific thresholds.
   - o SQL's aggregation functions can reveal patterns, such as peak times for transactions or high-frequency behaviors.
4. **Python and R**:

- o Python's libraries like Pandas and Seaborn, and R's ggplot2, provide tools for plotting trends, detecting patterns, and spotting outliers.
- o Statistical libraries help automate calculations for measures like standard deviation to detect potential outliers.

Key Takeaways

- **Patterns**: Repeated sequences or behaviors within data that reveal consistent associations, making it easier to anticipate future occurrences.
- **Trends**: General directions of data change over time, showing upward, downward, or stable movement, essential for forecasting.
- **Outliers**: Unusual data points that differ significantly from others, often signaling errors, anomalies, or rare events.

Recognizing patterns, trends, and outliers allows analysts to gain a deep understanding of their data, providing context, predicting future behavior, and identifying areas that require further investigation. By developing these skills, you'll be able to draw richer insights and support data-driven decision-making in a wide range of scenarios.

Chapter 6: Introduction to Data Visualization

Importance of Data Visualization in Storytelling

Data visualization is a crucial tool for transforming raw data into visuals that are accessible, engaging, and informative. In today's data-driven world, information is abundant but often complex. Data visualization enables us to present this information in ways that are easy to understand, allowing viewers to quickly grasp insights and make informed decisions. Effective data visualization is more than just graphs and charts—it is a storytelling technique that gives data meaning, creating a narrative that resonates with audiences and drives action.

In this chapter, we'll explore why data visualization is so important in storytelling, how it enhances communication, and the ways it makes data more compelling, relatable, and impactful.

Why Data Visualization Matters in Storytelling

The human brain processes visual information far more effectively than text or numbers alone. Visualization transforms complex datasets into visuals that are easier to interpret and understand, bridging the gap between data and insight. By visualizing data, we create a form of storytelling that can communicate trends, patterns, and relationships in a way that resonates emotionally and intellectually with the audience. In business, research, and public communication, the ability to tell stories with data can lead to better decision-making, increase audience engagement, and make an impact.

Key benefits of data visualization in storytelling include:

1. **Enhanced Comprehension**: Visuals help audiences understand data faster and with less cognitive load than text or tables.
2. **Emotional Engagement**: Well-designed visuals evoke emotional responses, helping viewers connect with the message on a personal level.
3. **Improved Retention**: People remember visual information more effectively, which makes visual storytelling memorable and persuasive.
4. **Increased Accessibility**: Visuals make complex data accessible to a broader audience, regardless of technical background.

Let's dive deeper into how data visualization brings storytelling to life.

Creating a Narrative with Data Visualization

Data storytelling combines data, visuals, and narrative elements to communicate insights. While raw data is often overwhelming and abstract, data storytelling helps contextualize information, transforming facts and figures into a coherent message. Effective data visualization provides the backbone for this narrative, helping to structure the story in a way that flows logically and keeps the audience engaged.

Steps to Building a Data Story

1. **Identify the Central Message**: The first step is identifying the main message or insight you want to convey. Rather than overwhelming your audience with numbers, focus on the one key point that you want them to remember.

2. **Organize Data to Support the Story**: Structure your data to reveal patterns, trends, or comparisons that emphasize your main point. The way data is organized and presented directly affects how easily the story unfolds for the audience.

3. **Select Appropriate Visuals**: Different types of data and messages require different visual formats. For example, line charts are ideal for trends, bar charts for comparisons, and pie charts for showing proportions. Choosing the right type of chart or graph is essential to effectively telling the story.

4. **Add Context and Narrative**: Providing context helps the audience understand why

the data matters. Adding a narrative element, such as annotations or captions, guides viewers through the story, emphasizing important points and explaining complex information.

5. **Highlight Key Takeaways**: A successful data story should leave the audience with clear takeaways. Use visual cues, like color and font size, to emphasize critical points, ensuring the message is both memorable and actionable.

Example

Imagine you're analyzing customer satisfaction survey results over the past year. You might start by showing a line chart that illustrates the trend in satisfaction scores. Adding annotations about specific events—like a new product launch or a change in customer service policies—helps to connect the data with real-world actions. This context transforms a simple trend line into a story about how company initiatives impact customer satisfaction.

How Visualization Enhances Audience Engagement

Data visualization engages audiences by transforming abstract numbers into tangible, relatable stories. Here's how visualization helps enhance audience engagement:

1. **Immediate Impact**: Visuals capture attention instantly, making it easier for audiences to focus on the story. A well-designed visualization can convey the essence of the message at a glance, allowing audiences to grasp complex information quickly.
2. **Simplification of Complex Data**: Visualizations distill complex datasets into clear, understandable insights, reducing the cognitive load on the audience. This simplification allows viewers to focus on the message without being overwhelmed by details.
3. **Emotional Resonance**: Colors, shapes, and design elements can evoke emotions, which helps to create a deeper connection with the audience. For example, a red color in a chart showing declining sales may trigger a sense of urgency, while a green line indicating upward trends can evoke optimism.
4. **Interactivity and Exploration**: Interactive visualizations, such as those in Tableau or Power BI, allow users to explore the data for themselves. By interacting with filters or drilling down into details, users can personalize their experience, making the data story more relevant and engaging.

Example

Consider a company presenting its annual performance to stakeholders. A static chart showing annual revenue can quickly summarize overall growth, but adding interactive filters for different regions or product lines allows stakeholders to explore specific areas of interest, making the presentation more engaging and informative.

Types of Visualizations that Enhance Storytelling

Choosing the right type of visualization is essential for effective storytelling. Different visualizations are suited to different types of insights, so selecting the most appropriate format helps to communicate your message clearly. Here are some common types of visualizations used in storytelling:

1. **Line Charts**: Ideal for showing trends over time, such as growth in monthly sales or changes in market share.
2. **Bar Charts**: Effective for comparing categories, like sales by product or customer satisfaction by region.
3. **Scatter Plots**: Useful for showing relationships between variables, such as advertising spend versus sales revenue.
4. **Heatmaps**: Great for illustrating intensity or density, such as peak website traffic times.
5. **Pie Charts**: Used for showing proportions within a whole, such as market share or budget allocation.

Each type of visualization has unique strengths, so choosing the right one for your data and message enhances the story you're trying to tell.

Example of Choosing the Right Visualization

If you're telling the story of a successful product launch, a line chart showing sales over time might illustrate the initial boost in revenue. To add depth, a bar chart comparing sales by region can show where the launch was most successful, giving stakeholders a clearer picture of the campaign's impact.

Building Credibility and Trust with Visualization

Data storytelling is not only about engaging the audience but also about building credibility. Visualizations that are clear, accurate, and honest help establish trust with the audience, demonstrating transparency and integrity in reporting.

Key Practices for Building Trust

1. **Avoid Misleading Visuals**: Ensure that charts and graphs accurately represent the data. For example, avoid truncating axes or using overly complex visuals that could confuse or mislead the audience.
2. **Use Consistent Scales**: Consistency in scales across multiple charts allows for accurate

comparison, making the story more cohesive and credible.

3. **Provide Context**: Including contextual information, such as timeframes, data sources, or explanations for unusual data points, helps the audience understand the full story and trust the findings.

4. **Be Transparent about Limitations**: If the data has limitations, such as sample size or data collection constraints, openly communicate these limitations to ensure transparency.

Example

A government agency reporting on unemployment rates can use clear, consistent visuals with full context about how data was collected. Including information on the sample size, collection method, and limitations (like seasonal adjustments) helps the public trust the accuracy of the report.

The Role of Visual Storytelling in Decision-Making

Data visualization aids decision-making by providing stakeholders with actionable insights. When data is presented clearly, decision-makers can quickly interpret key metrics, assess performance, and evaluate options. Visual storytelling turns abstract metrics into specific narratives that guide strategy and action.

How Visualization Supports Decisions

- **Clarity of Key Insights**: Well-crafted visuals highlight critical insights, enabling stakeholders to make informed decisions based on clear evidence.
- **Rapid Comparisons**: Visualizations like bar charts and scatter plots allow decision-makers to compare options quickly, facilitating faster, more accurate decisions.
- **Reinforcement of Recommendations**: Visual storytelling supports recommendations by showing the underlying data, making it easier for decision-makers to understand and accept the suggested actions.

Example

A marketing manager presents data on campaign performance using bar charts and line graphs. The visuals reveal which channels performed best, supporting the recommendation to allocate more budget to high-performing channels. The clarity of the visual story gives stakeholders confidence in the recommendation, facilitating data-driven decisions.

The Future of Data Visualization in Storytelling

As technology advances, data visualization continues to evolve, incorporating new tools and techniques that enhance storytelling. From interactive dashboards to augmented reality and virtual reality visualizations, the future of data visualization promises even more engaging, immersive, and insightful ways to communicate data stories.

Emerging Trends in Data Visualization

1. **Real-Time Data Visualization**: Increasingly, businesses rely on real-time data to make agile decisions. Interactive dashboards with live data updates allow stakeholders to track metrics in real time, enhancing responsiveness.
2. **Augmented and Virtual Reality (AR/VR)**: These technologies enable immersive data experiences, allowing users to interact with data in three-dimensional spaces. AR and VR hold promise for industries like architecture, healthcare, and education.
3. **Data Storytelling with AI**: AI-powered data visualization tools can automatically generate narratives, charts, and insights from raw data, making it easier for analysts to build compelling stories without extensive design skills.
4. **Personalized Visualizations**: As more data becomes available, visualizations can be personalized to show relevant insights to different audience segments, making data stories more relevant and actionable.

Key Takeaways

- **Data Visualization as a Storytelling Tool**: Visuals transform complex data into narratives that audiences can understand, connect with, and act on.
- **Engagement and Accessibility**: Visuals simplify data interpretation, increasing audience engagement and making insights accessible to a wider audience.
- **Trust and Credibility**: Clear, honest visualizations build trust with audiences, establishing data storytelling as a credible source of information.
- **Enhanced Decision-Making**: Data visualization supports decision-making by clarifying options, highlighting key insights, and reinforcing recommendations.

The ability to tell stories with data is an invaluable skill in today's information-rich world. Effective data visualization not only makes data more understandable but also empowers audiences to draw meaningful conclusions, make informed decisions, and drive positive change.

Types of Charts and When to Use Each

Data visualization transforms raw data into accessible, engaging visuals that communicate key insights. Choosing the right type of chart is essential for conveying your message effectively. Different charts are suited to different kinds of data and storytelling goals, so understanding their strengths and limitations will help you make the best choice. In this section, we'll review common chart types—bar charts, pie charts, line charts, and more—exploring when and why to use each.

1. Bar Charts

Bar charts use rectangular bars to represent data, with the length of each bar corresponding to the value of the category it represents. Bar charts are versatile, making it easy to compare values across categories.

When to Use Bar Charts

- **Category Comparison**: Bar charts are ideal for comparing values across discrete categories, such as sales by product type, customer satisfaction by region, or survey responses.
- **Ranking Data**: They are effective for ranking data, as it's easy to see which categories have the highest or lowest values.
- **Horizontal or Vertical**: Use vertical bars (column charts) for limited categories and horizontal bars when there are many categories or when labels need more space.

Example

A retail company uses a bar chart to compare monthly sales for different product lines. The chart quickly shows which product lines are performing best, allowing managers to make inventory decisions accordingly.

Variations

- **Stacked Bar Chart**: Useful for showing subtotals within categories, allowing you to see contributions of different sub-categories within each bar.
- **Grouped Bar Chart**: Effective for comparing multiple sub-categories across main categories, such as product sales by month for each region.

Key Takeaway

Bar charts are straightforward and effective for comparing values across categories, making them one of the most commonly used chart types in data analysis.

2. Pie Charts

Pie charts display data as slices of a circle, with each slice representing a category's proportion within a whole. They are often used to show percentages and relative sizes.

When to Use Pie Charts

- **Showing Parts of a Whole**: Pie charts work well for visualizing proportions and illustrating how each category contributes to a total.

- **Limited Categories**: They are most effective when the dataset has only a few categories (ideally less than six), as too many categories make the chart difficult to read.
- **Quick Overview**: Pie charts are best for simple visuals where exact values are not as important as the general distribution.

Example

A nonprofit organization uses a pie chart to show its budget distribution, with segments for programs, outreach, and administrative costs. The pie chart makes it easy for donors to see where their contributions go.

Key Takeaway

Pie charts are useful for illustrating proportions within a whole, but they are best suited for small datasets where categories add up to 100%.

3. Line Charts

Line charts use points connected by lines to display changes over time, making them ideal for tracking trends and patterns in time-series data.

When to Use Line Charts

- **Trends Over Time**: Line charts are ideal for showing data trends across time periods, such as monthly revenue, daily temperatures, or annual growth rates.
- **Multiple Series Comparison**: They are effective for comparing trends across multiple groups. For example, you could compare sales trends for different products over the same time period.
- **Highlighting Change**: Line charts make it easy to see when values increase, decrease, or remain stable, making them useful for tracking progress.

Example

A finance team uses a line chart to track monthly expenses over the past year. The chart shows a gradual upward trend, helping the team spot patterns and adjust budgets.

Key Takeaway

Line charts are essential for visualizing trends and changes over time, making them popular in financial, sales, and performance tracking.

4. Scatter Plots

Scatter plots display individual data points plotted on a two-dimensional grid, with one variable on each axis. This chart type is used to show relationships or correlations between variables.

When to Use Scatter Plots

- **Exploring Relationships**: Scatter plots are useful for examining relationships between two variables, such as age and income, or advertising spend and sales revenue.
- **Spotting Patterns or Clusters**: Scatter plots can help identify patterns, clusters, and outliers within the data, providing insights into potential trends or anomalies.
- **Large Datasets**: Scatter plots are particularly useful for large datasets with numerous data points, as they reveal density and spread.

Example

A company uses a scatter plot to examine the relationship between customer satisfaction scores and loyalty program participation. The scatter plot shows a positive correlation, suggesting that customers in the loyalty program are generally more satisfied.

Key Takeaway

Scatter plots are ideal for showing correlations and relationships between two variables, as well as spotting patterns and outliers.

5. Histograms

Histograms look similar to bar charts but are used to show the distribution of a continuous variable by grouping data points into intervals or "bins." They're commonly used to understand the shape of the data distribution.

When to Use Histograms

- **Distribution Analysis**: Histograms are ideal for understanding the distribution of values, such as age ranges, income levels, or exam scores.
- **Identifying Skewness**: Histograms reveal whether data is skewed to one side (left or right), which can inform data interpretation.
- **Spotting Clusters and Gaps**: They help identify clusters or gaps in data, showing where values are concentrated and where they are sparse.

Example

An instructor uses a histogram to analyze student test scores, revealing that most students scored between 70 and 85. This insight helps the instructor assess overall class performance and identify students who may need extra help.

Key Takeaway

Histograms are valuable for visualizing data distributions, making them useful for identifying patterns, skewness, and clusters in continuous data.

6. Box Plots

Box plots (or box-and-whisker plots) display the distribution and spread of data by dividing values into quartiles. They show the median, range, and variability, making them useful for comparing distributions across different categories.

When to Use Box Plots

- **Comparing Distributions**: Box plots are ideal for comparing distributions across multiple groups, such as test scores across different classrooms or income levels by region.
- **Identifying Outliers**: Box plots highlight outliers, as any points outside the "whiskers" are considered unusual values.
- **Analyzing Spread and Symmetry**: They provide a quick summary of data spread and whether data is symmetrical or skewed.

Example

A healthcare analyst uses box plots to compare patient recovery times across different hospitals. The box plots reveal variations in recovery times, showing which hospitals have shorter recovery periods.

Key Takeaway

Box plots provide a comprehensive view of data spread, making them ideal for comparing distributions, spotting outliers, and understanding data variability.

7. Heatmaps

Heatmaps display data in a matrix format with colors representing values. Darker or more intense colors often indicate higher values, making it easy to identify patterns or clusters within the data.

When to Use Heatmaps

- **Showing Intensity or Density**: Heatmaps are useful for visualizing intensity or density, such as frequency of website visits by hour and day.
- **Correlation Matrices**: Heatmaps are commonly used to show correlation matrices, where each cell represents the correlation between two variables.
- **Large Data Grids**: They are effective for showing large datasets, where each cell's color represents a different value.

Example

A website analyzes user activity, using a heatmap to display visit frequency by day and hour. The heatmap shows peak activity times with darker colors, helping the team identify when users are most active.

Key Takeaway

Heatmaps are effective for visualizing density and intensity within a grid format, making them ideal for time-based data, correlation matrices, and high-density datasets.

8. Area Charts

Area charts are similar to line charts but fill the space below the line with color, emphasizing the magnitude of the trend. They are useful for showing cumulative data or comparing multiple trends over time.

When to Use Area Charts

- **Cumulative Totals**: Use area charts to show cumulative totals over time, such as total sales or revenue.
- **Comparing Multiple Trends**: Area charts are effective for showing multiple data series, with each area representing a different category.
- **Highlighting Proportions Over Time**: They help show how different parts contribute to a

total over time, especially when categories stack on each other.

Example

A company uses an area chart to illustrate revenue from various product lines over the past year. The chart highlights how each product line contributes to the overall revenue, with clear distinctions between categories.

Key Takeaway

Area charts are ideal for illustrating cumulative totals and comparing multiple series, especially when showing contributions over time.

Choosing the Right Chart: Summary Table

Here's a summary of each chart type and its best uses, to help you select the right chart for your data insights:

Chart Type	Best For	Key Insights
Bar Chart	Comparing categories	Shows category rankings and differences
Pie Chart	Parts of a whole	Illustrates proportions

Chart Type	Best For	Key Insights
Line Chart	Trends over time	Highlights changes over time
Scatter Plot	Relationships between two variables	Identifies correlations and patterns
Histogram	Distribution analysis	Reveals frequency distribution
Box Plot	Comparing distributions, outliers	Shows data spread and outliers
Heatmap	Intensity, dense data patterns	Highlights activity or density
Area Chart	Cumulative totals over time	Shows contribution trends

Practical Example: Creating a Dashboard with Multiple Chart Types

Let's say a company wants to create a dashboard to monitor monthly sales performance, compare product line popularity, and analyze customer behavior. Here's how they might use different charts:

1. **Line Chart**: Tracks monthly sales, showing the overall trend in revenue.

2. **Bar Chart**: Compares sales across product categories, helping to identify top-performing products.
3. **Scatter Plot**: Shows the relationship between marketing spend and sales, helping assess the impact of advertising.
4. **Heatmap**: Displays customer activity by time and day, highlighting peak shopping hours.

By combining these charts, the company creates a comprehensive dashboard that provides a clear, multi-dimensional view of business performance.

Key Takeaways

- **Choosing the Right Chart**: Selecting the correct chart type enhances understanding and effectively communicates insights.
- **Bar Charts and Pie Charts**: Ideal for comparing categories and showing proportions, respectively.
- **Line Charts and Scatter Plots**: Best for trends and relationships between variables.
- **Histograms and Box Plots**: Useful for distribution and variability analysis.
- **Heatmaps and Area Charts**: Effective for visualizing intensity, density, and cumulative totals over time.

Understanding the purpose and strengths of each chart type helps you create visuals that tell a clear, compelling story. By mastering these fundamentals, you can select the best visual for your data, ensuring it resonates with your audience and supports informed decision-making.

Tips for Creating Effective Visuals

Creating effective visuals is key to successful data communication. A well-designed visualization can make complex data easy to understand, highlight key insights, and support decision-making. However, not all visuals achieve these goals—some may confuse or mislead if not designed thoughtfully. In this section, we'll explore essential tips for creating effective data visuals, covering design principles, color choices, layout, and more to ensure your visuals communicate insights clearly and impactfully.

1. Define the Purpose of the Visualization

Before starting any visualization, clarify its purpose. Ask yourself:

- **What insight or message do I want to communicate?**
- **Who is my audience, and what's important to them?**
- **What action do I want viewers to take based on this information?**

Having a clear purpose will guide your design choices, ensuring that each element contributes to the overall message.

Example

If you're creating a visualization for a sales team, your purpose might be to highlight quarterly revenue growth. In this case, you'd focus on a line chart showing trends over time rather than a detailed breakdown of individual sales, which could distract from the main message.

2. Choose the Right Chart Type

Selecting the appropriate chart type is crucial for accurately conveying your data. Each chart type has unique strengths:

- **Bar charts** are ideal for comparing categories.
- **Line charts** work well for showing trends over time.
- **Pie charts** illustrate proportions within a whole.
- **Scatter plots** highlight relationships between variables.

Consider what you're trying to show—comparisons, trends, parts of a whole, or relationships—and choose a chart type that best suits the message.

Example

To show the market share of different product lines, a pie chart would clearly illustrate each line's contribution to total sales. For monthly sales trends, a line chart would be more effective.

3. Simplify and Remove Clutter

When it comes to data visualization, less is often more. Cluttered visuals can overwhelm the audience and obscure the message. Focus on essential information by removing unnecessary elements like gridlines, excessive labels, and decorative graphics that don't add value.

Tips for Simplifying Visuals

- **Limit Color Use**: Use only a few colors to avoid visual noise. Reserve bright colors to highlight key data points.
- **Reduce Labels**: Label only essential elements and use concise titles and annotations.
- **Avoid Excessive Data**: Focus on the most relevant data points, and avoid overcrowding the chart with too much information.

Example

A bar chart comparing sales performance across regions can become cluttered if each bar is labeled with exact values. Simplifying the chart by labeling only the top-performing regions and using a clean title can make the chart easier to interpret.

4. Use Color Purposefully

Color can make visuals engaging, highlight important data, and convey information quickly. However, using color effectively requires careful consideration to avoid confusion or misinterpretation.

Best Practices for Using Color

- **Highlight Key Points**: Use a bold or contrasting color to draw attention to specific data points or categories.
- **Use Consistent Color Schemes**: Choose a color scheme that aligns with your brand or the context of your data. Avoid using too many colors, as this can create visual clutter.
- **Consider Color Blindness**: Use color palettes that are accessible to all viewers. Avoid relying solely on color to convey information—use patterns, labels, or icons to reinforce key points.

Example

In a line chart showing revenue over time, use a neutral color for the baseline trend and a bold color to highlight a period of significant growth. This approach draws attention to the specific period while maintaining a clear overall view.

5. Add Clear Labels and Titles

Effective labels and titles guide the viewer through the visualization, helping them understand the data quickly. Each element—titles, labels, legends, and annotations—should be clear, concise, and placed strategically to enhance readability.

Best Practices for Labels and Titles

- **Use Descriptive Titles**: A good title tells the viewer what the chart represents. Instead of a vague title like "Quarterly Sales," a more descriptive title like "Quarterly Sales Growth by Region" provides context.
- **Label Key Data Points**: If certain data points are particularly important, label them directly on the chart to ensure they stand out.
- **Use Legends Wisely**: Place legends close to the chart and keep them simple. If possible, label data directly to avoid relying on legends, which can make the viewer work harder to understand the chart.

Example

A scatter plot showing advertising spend vs. sales could benefit from a title like "Correlation Between Advertising Spend and Sales Revenue." Adding direct labels to outliers or notable points will also help viewers focus on the most important parts of the data.

6. Use Consistent Scales and Axes

Inconsistent scales and axes can lead to misinterpretation and bias. To ensure clarity, use scales that accurately represent your data and avoid unnecessary manipulation of axis ranges.

Tips for Consistent Scales

- **Start at Zero**: Where possible, start your axis at zero to prevent visual distortion. This is especially important for bar charts, as truncating the axis can exaggerate differences.
- **Use Even Intervals**: Consistent intervals on both axes make comparisons straightforward and prevent misleading impressions.
- **Avoid Overcrowding the Axis**: Keep axis labels readable, using abbreviations or fewer tick marks if necessary.

Example

In a line chart tracking monthly revenue, starting the y-axis at zero will provide a realistic view of growth. If the axis starts at a higher value, the growth could appear more dramatic than it actually is, potentially misleading the viewer.

7. Highlight Key Insights

To emphasize the most critical information, highlight key insights in your visual. This helps guide viewers' attention to the points that matter most, ensuring they leave with a clear understanding of the main takeaways.

Techniques for Highlighting Insights

- **Use Annotations**: Adding text boxes or arrows to highlight significant events, such as peaks, dips, or anomalies, directs the viewer's focus.
- **Adjust Color and Opacity**: Use a distinct color or make other elements more transparent to highlight specific data points.
- **Focus on Key Data Points**: In some cases, you can grey out less relevant data to emphasize the most important insights.

Example

A line chart showing monthly website traffic may have a notable spike during a marketing campaign. By adding a label indicating "Campaign Launch" on that data point, you emphasize the correlation between the marketing effort and traffic increase.

8. Provide Context with Annotations

Annotations are brief notes added to visuals to provide context, explain anomalies, or highlight trends. They help viewers interpret data by connecting it to real-world events, making the visualization more informative.

When to Use Annotations

- **Explain Anomalies**: Use annotations to clarify outliers or unusual data points, such as a sudden drop in sales due to an external event.
- **Highlight Trends and Changes**: Add notes that explain significant trends, such as the introduction of a new product or a seasonal effect.
- **Add Insights**: Annotations can also be used to add commentary, helping viewers understand why certain data points are important.

Example

In a bar chart comparing quarterly revenue, a note like "Seasonal Increase" next to a peak in Q4 helps viewers understand that this spike is part of an annual pattern, not a permanent increase.

9. Maintain a Balanced Layout

A well-organized layout enhances readability and flow. Balanced visuals avoid overwhelming viewers, presenting information in a logical order that guides them through the data story.

Best Practices for Layout

- **Group Related Information**: Place similar elements together. For example, if you're displaying sales by region, put all regional data visuals in one area.
- **Use White Space**: White space improves readability, giving viewers a break between elements and helping each part of the visual stand out.
- **Establish a Visual Hierarchy**: Prioritize the most important data and place it in a prominent location. Secondary information should be smaller or placed around the main insights.

Example

In a dashboard showing monthly sales, arrange the main revenue chart in the top center. Place secondary charts, such as sales by product or region, around it, creating a clear focal point while still presenting additional context.

10. Test Your Visuals with Others

Finally, testing your visuals with colleagues or stakeholders can help identify potential improvements. Feedback allows you to ensure that your message is clear, relevant, and engaging.

Tips for Testing

- **Gather Feedback from Non-Experts**: Ask someone unfamiliar with the data to interpret the visual. If they struggle, consider simplifying the design or adding more context.
- **Check for Misinterpretations**: Ensure that viewers interpret key points correctly and that there's no ambiguity in your message.
- **Refine Based on Input**: Use feedback to refine color schemes, labels, and layout, improving clarity and effectiveness.

Example

Before presenting a new product sales report, a marketing team shows the visualization to a few team members. Their feedback leads to improvements in label placement and color choice, making the final presentation more polished and effective.

Summary of Tips for Creating Effective Visuals

Tip	Key Insight
Define the Purpose	Focus on the main message
Choose the Right Chart	Match the chart type to the data
Simplify and Remove Clutter	Focus on essential elements

Tip	Key Insight
Use Color Purposefully	Highlight important data points with color
Add Clear Labels and Titles	Guide viewers with descriptive labels
Use Consistent Scales	Ensure accurate data representation
Highlight Key Insights	Emphasize the most important points
Provide Context with Annotations	Add notes to clarify data trends and anomalies
Maintain a Balanced Layout	Organize visuals for readability
Test with Others	Get feedback to refine visuals

Key Takeaways

Creating effective visuals is both a science and an art, requiring attention to design principles, clarity, and purpose. By following these tips, you can ensure that your data visuals are clear, engaging, and impactful. Thoughtful visual design enables audiences to understand key insights quickly, supporting informed decisions and meaningful discussions.

Effective data visualization is not just about presenting numbers but about crafting a visual narrative that resonates with audiences and encourages action. With these strategies, you'll be well-equipped to create visuals that communicate your data's story in the most effective way.

Chapter 7: Basics of Data Interpretation and Decision-Making

Understanding the Story Behind the Numbers

Data by itself is just a collection of numbers; the true value of data lies in its interpretation. Data interpretation involves analyzing data in a way that reveals patterns, trends, and relationships that drive understanding and decision-making. By understanding the story behind the numbers, analysts and decision-makers can transform raw data into meaningful insights that tell a story about past events, current conditions, and potential future outcomes.

In this chapter, we'll explore the basics of data interpretation, focusing on techniques for uncovering insights, making informed decisions, and drawing actionable conclusions from data.

Why Data Interpretation Matters

Effective data interpretation is essential because it turns complex information into clear, actionable insights. Raw numbers rarely provide meaning on their own, but interpretation provides context, connects the data to real-world scenarios, and uncovers the narrative hidden in the numbers.

Benefits of Effective Data Interpretation

1. **Informed Decision-Making**: Interpretation provides insights that support data-driven decisions, helping organizations act based on evidence rather than intuition.
2. **Pattern and Trend Recognition**: By interpreting data, we can identify recurring patterns and long-term trends that provide insight into ongoing dynamics.
3. **Risk Management**: Interpreting data helps identify risks and opportunities early, allowing decision-makers to mitigate potential issues before they escalate.
4. **Clear Communication**: Interpretation allows data to be communicated in ways that are accessible and relatable, supporting collaboration and alignment across teams.

Understanding the story behind the numbers brings clarity, which is crucial for effective action and strategy development.

Key Steps in Data Interpretation

Data interpretation is both an art and a science. It involves reviewing the data, identifying relationships, and translating these relationships into a story that answers questions and guides decisions.

Step 1: Define the Goal and Ask the Right Questions

Before diving into data interpretation, it's important to clarify the goal. Understanding what you're looking to achieve or understand will shape how you approach the data and what insights you seek to uncover.

- **What business question am I trying to answer?**
- **What decision will be made based on this data?**
- **What information does my audience need to make this decision?**

These questions help focus your analysis, ensuring you're interpreting the data in ways that are relevant and meaningful.

Example

Suppose you're examining customer satisfaction scores to improve service. Defining the goal as "identifying factors that impact customer satisfaction" helps narrow your focus to specific data points—such as response times or issue resolution rates—that directly relate to the goal.

Step 2: Organize and Clean the Data

Interpretation becomes challenging if data is messy or disorganized. Cleaning and organizing data ensures accuracy and clarity, enabling a clear view of patterns and relationships.

- **Remove Duplicates and Outliers**: Identify and address any duplicate records or outliers that could distort insights.
- **Check for Missing Data**: Handle missing values through imputation or by acknowledging gaps in data.
- **Standardize Formats**: Ensure consistency in units, categories, and date formats to make comparisons valid.

Example

In analyzing monthly sales data, missing entries or incorrect product categories can misrepresent the overall trend. Cleaning and organizing data helps ensure accurate interpretation, reducing the risk of drawing incorrect conclusions.

Step 3: Look for Patterns and Trends

Patterns and trends often tell the clearest stories. Trends show changes over time, while patterns reveal recurring behaviors. Identifying these elements can provide insight into underlying causes, helping you predict future outcomes and make proactive decisions.

- **Analyze Trends Over Time**: Look for upward or downward trends in time-series data, which indicate growth, decline, or stability.

- **Identify Seasonal Patterns**: In certain industries, data may show seasonal patterns, such as higher sales during holidays or peaks in website traffic at certain times of day.
- **Compare Categories**: For categorical data, compare groups to see if there are any recurring patterns among them, such as higher performance in a specific region or among certain demographics.

Example

If customer complaints spike every December, this pattern could suggest seasonal service issues. Recognizing this allows management to investigate and potentially allocate additional resources during peak times.

Step 4: Interpret Relationships and Correlations

Relationships between variables, such as correlations, can provide deeper insights into cause and effect, revealing factors that might influence performance, behavior, or outcomes.

- **Correlations**: A positive or negative correlation between two variables, such as advertising spend and sales, can indicate potential causal relationships.
- **Comparative Analysis**: Examining relationships between groups (e.g., demographics or regions) helps uncover

factors contributing to differences in outcomes.

- **Causal Links**: While correlation doesn't equal causation, understanding potential causal links helps generate hypotheses that can be tested further.

Example

If data shows a strong correlation between customer satisfaction and issue resolution time, it may indicate that faster response times contribute to higher satisfaction, suggesting that improving response efficiency could enhance customer experience.

Common Pitfalls in Data Interpretation

Misinterpreting data can lead to misguided decisions and incorrect conclusions. Recognizing common pitfalls ensures your interpretation remains accurate and reliable.

1. Confusing Correlation with Causation

Just because two variables move together doesn't mean one causes the other. While correlations can suggest potential relationships, further investigation is needed to establish causation.

2. Ignoring Context

Data points don't exist in isolation—they're part of a broader context. Ignoring external factors, such as economic changes or seasonal effects, can lead to oversimplified conclusions.

3. Overlooking Outliers

Outliers can sometimes reveal important insights. Ignoring them may cause you to miss unusual but significant patterns. However, outliers should be carefully examined to determine if they're meaningful or simply errors.

Example

A company might observe a spike in sales in a particular month and assume it's due to a marketing campaign, overlooking the fact that the spike coincided with a major holiday season. Failing to account for this context could lead to misattributing success to the wrong factor.

Telling the Story Behind the Data

Once patterns, trends, and relationships have been identified, the next step is to communicate the insights clearly and effectively. Storytelling with data is about connecting numbers to real-world outcomes, translating data into a narrative that resonates with stakeholders.

Elements of Effective Data Storytelling

1. **Start with the Big Picture**: Begin by summarizing the main insight or message. This helps set the stage for deeper analysis and clarifies the focus of your story.
2. **Provide Context**: Explain the data's background and relevance. Describe the data source, the period covered, and any external factors influencing the numbers.
3. **Highlight Key Insights**: Point out significant findings, such as trends, patterns, or correlations. Emphasize insights that answer the original business question and support decision-making.
4. **Draw Conclusions and Recommendations**: Conclude with specific takeaways and, if possible, actionable recommendations. Tying insights to concrete actions gives the story purpose and helps move stakeholders toward informed decisions.

Example

A company analyzing customer churn might tell the following story: "Over the past year, customer churn rates have increased, especially among younger customers. Analysis shows that these customers are less engaged with the loyalty program. We recommend enhancing the loyalty program to appeal more to younger demographics, which could improve retention."

This storytelling approach not only highlights the main finding (higher churn among younger customers) but also provides context, insight, and an actionable recommendation.

Using Data for Decision-Making

After interpreting the data and telling its story, the final step is using these insights to make informed decisions. Data-driven decision-making ensures that actions are based on evidence rather than assumptions.

Steps for Data-Driven Decision-Making

1. **Evaluate the Insights**: Assess the validity and significance of the insights. Consider whether additional data or further analysis is needed to confirm the findings.
2. **Assess Options and Scenarios**: Based on the data, evaluate possible options or strategies. Consider how each scenario aligns with business goals and constraints.
3. **Implement Decisions and Monitor Outcomes**: Once a decision is made, track its impact and adjust as necessary. Monitoring results ensures that actions are effective and allows for quick responses to unforeseen changes.
4. **Review and Reflect**: Regularly review data to evaluate the ongoing effectiveness of decisions. Reflection supports continuous

improvement and allows for proactive adjustments.

Example

An e-commerce company observes a trend of high cart abandonment rates on mobile devices. After reviewing the data, the team decides to optimize the mobile checkout process. Post-implementation monitoring shows a 15% reduction in abandonment rates, validating the decision to improve the mobile experience.

Case Study: Data-Driven Decision-Making in Action

Imagine a healthcare provider wants to improve patient satisfaction. The team collects data from patient feedback surveys and identifies key factors affecting satisfaction, such as wait times, staff interactions, and facility cleanliness.

Interpreting the Data

1. **Identify Trends**: Survey responses reveal that satisfaction rates are generally lower during peak hours.
2. **Analyze Correlations**: Data shows a strong negative correlation between wait times and satisfaction scores.

3. **Recognize Patterns**: Patterns indicate that staff interaction quality has the highest impact on satisfaction among all factors.

Making the Decision

Based on the data, the provider decides to:

- Increase staffing during peak hours to reduce wait times.
- Implement staff training programs focused on enhancing patient interaction.

Monitoring the Impact

After implementing these changes, the provider tracks satisfaction scores. Within three months, scores improve by 20%, confirming that the data-driven decision was effective in enhancing patient satisfaction.

Key Takeaways

Interpreting data effectively requires moving beyond raw numbers to uncover the underlying story. By understanding patterns, relationships, and trends within data, decision-makers can make informed, evidence-based choices. The key elements of successful data interpretation and decision-making include:

- **Defining the Goal**: Start with a clear question or purpose to guide your interpretation.
- **Identifying Patterns and Trends**: Look for recurring behaviors and changes over time to understand underlying dynamics.
- **Recognizing Relationships**: Correlations and comparisons reveal important connections between variables.
- **Communicating Insights**: Use data storytelling to convey findings in a clear, engaging way.
- **Making Informed Decisions**: Apply insights to drive actions that align with business goals.

Interpreting the story behind the numbers ensures that data is not just a series of values but a valuable resource for understanding the past, managing the present, and planning for the future. With strong data interpretation skills, you can transform complex data into actionable insights that make a real impact.

Avoiding Common Pitfalls in Data Interpretation

Data interpretation is a critical step in deriving insights, but even skilled analysts can fall into common traps that distort findings and lead to misleading conclusions. Avoiding these pitfalls ensures that insights are accurate, that patterns and trends are correctly identified, and that decisions are based on solid evidence rather than misconceptions or errors. In this section, we'll examine some of the most common pitfalls in data interpretation and provide strategies for avoiding them.

1. Confusing Correlation with Causation

One of the most common pitfalls in data interpretation is assuming that correlation implies causation. Just because two variables appear to move together doesn't mean one causes the other. Correlation simply indicates a relationship, not that one variable is responsible for changes in the other.

Example

Suppose a company notices that ice cream sales and sunscreen purchases increase at the same time every year. While these variables are correlated, buying sunscreen doesn't cause ice cream sales to rise. Both trends are driven by a third factor: warmer weather.

How to Avoid This Pitfall

- **Look for Other Influencing Factors**: Consider external or underlying factors that may be influencing both variables.
- **Use Causal Analysis Techniques**: To establish causation, use experimental or causal analysis methods, such as A/B testing, where you control for variables to isolate effects.
- **Avoid Overinterpretation**: When reporting correlated variables, clearly indicate that

correlation does not imply causation unless further evidence supports it.

2. Ignoring Outliers

Outliers are data points that deviate significantly from other observations. While some analysts remove outliers to simplify their analysis, ignoring them entirely can lead to a loss of important insights. Outliers can sometimes reveal unique cases, errors, or extreme events that are worth investigating.

Example

A delivery service company finds an outlier in delivery times—one order took significantly longer than average. On investigation, they discover it was due to an unexpected weather delay. Ignoring this outlier would miss the insight that extreme weather events can significantly impact delivery performance.

How to Avoid This Pitfall

- **Investigate Outliers**: Always investigate outliers to understand whether they are data entry errors, natural variations, or indicative of underlying issues.
- **Document Decisions**: If you decide to remove outliers, document the rationale and ensure that it is consistent across analyses.
- **Use Robust Measures**: Use statistical measures that are less sensitive to outliers,

such as the median or interquartile range, to supplement mean and standard deviation.

3. Overgeneralizing Findings

Overgeneralizing occurs when conclusions from a specific dataset or population are applied too broadly. This pitfall can lead to inaccurate conclusions if the sample is not representative or if the findings are interpreted as universally applicable without sufficient evidence.

Example

A survey conducted among college students shows a preference for digital textbooks. Overgeneralizing this finding to all age groups could lead to incorrect assumptions about general textbook preferences, as older populations may have different preferences.

How to Avoid This Pitfall

- **Understand Sample Limitations**: Consider the demographics and characteristics of your sample and recognize any limitations in how representative it is of the broader population.
- **Use Multiple Data Sources**: Whenever possible, cross-validate findings with data from other sources to ensure broader applicability.
- **Clearly Define Scope**: Clearly state the scope of your findings and avoid making broad

claims unless they are supported by additional evidence.

4. Cherry-Picking Data

Cherry-picking involves selectively using data points that support a particular conclusion while ignoring data that doesn't. This can lead to biased interpretations and distort findings, often resulting in confirmation bias—where you see only what you expect or want to see.

Example

A company analyzing sales growth focuses only on months with high sales to demonstrate consistent growth, ignoring months with lower sales. This cherry-picking creates an incomplete picture and could mislead stakeholders about actual performance trends.

How to Avoid This Pitfall

- **Examine All Relevant Data**: Avoid filtering data in ways that exclude relevant information. Include both supporting and contradicting data in your analysis.
- **Use Transparent Analysis Methods**: Make your methodology transparent so that others can see which data points were included and excluded.

- **Challenge Your Assumptions**: Actively seek out data that challenges your assumptions to reduce the likelihood of confirmation bias.

5. Misinterpreting Averages

Averages, such as the mean, provide a useful summary but can be misleading if not interpreted carefully. Averages can hide important variations or create a skewed impression if there are significant outliers or if data is distributed unevenly.

Example

An employer looks at the average salary in a department and assumes all employees earn around this amount. However, high salaries among senior managers may raise the average, masking lower salaries among entry-level employees.

How to Avoid This Pitfall

- **Use Multiple Measures of Central Tendency**: Consider using the median or mode along with the mean to get a more accurate picture, especially if the data is skewed.
- **Examine the Distribution**: Look at data distribution to see if there are significant deviations from the average or clusters around certain values.

- **Consider Variability**: Use measures like standard deviation or range to understand the spread of data around the average.

6. Failing to Provide Context

Numbers and statistics rarely speak for themselves; without context, they can easily be misinterpreted. Context includes factors like the time period, geographic scope, industry trends, and external influences that may affect data.

Example

A sudden increase in website traffic may seem positive at first glance. However, without the context that this increase was due to a temporary marketing campaign, stakeholders might overestimate the long-term trend.

How to Avoid This Pitfall

- **Provide Background Information**: Explain the context of the data, including any relevant events, timeframes, or market conditions.
- **Use Annotations**: In visuals, add annotations to explain notable data points, like campaign launches or policy changes, that may impact interpretation.
- **Compare to Benchmarks**: Compare data to industry benchmarks or historical trends to give stakeholders a more realistic view.

7. Misleading with Data Visualizations

Visualizations can enhance understanding, but poor design choices can also mislead viewers. Common pitfalls in data visualization include manipulating axis scales, using overly complex charts, or choosing inappropriate colors, all of which can distort interpretation.

Example

A bar chart with a truncated y-axis exaggerates differences between values, making changes seem more dramatic than they are. This can lead to incorrect assumptions about the significance of those changes.

How to Avoid This Pitfall

- **Use Consistent Scales**: Start axes at zero whenever possible, especially for bar charts, to avoid exaggerating differences.
- **Choose the Right Visualization**: Select chart types that accurately represent the data, such as using line charts for trends over time and bar charts for category comparisons.
- **Simplify and Avoid Clutter**: Avoid overly complex visuals and focus on clarity. Use colors and labels sparingly to avoid overwhelming viewers.

8. Ignoring Small Sample Sizes

When interpreting data, it's essential to consider sample size. Small sample sizes can lead to unreliable results and increase the risk of drawing incorrect conclusions due to random variations.

Example

A company tests a new feature with a sample of only 10 users and concludes that it's popular based on a high approval rate. With such a small sample, the results are unlikely to represent the larger customer base accurately.

How to Avoid This Pitfall

- **Use Larger Samples When Possible**: Ensure your sample size is adequate to draw statistically significant conclusions. Larger samples reduce the likelihood of random error.
- **Acknowledge Limitations**: If you must work with a small sample, acknowledge this limitation in your interpretation and be cautious about generalizing findings.
- **Consider Statistical Confidence**: Use statistical tests to measure confidence levels and margins of error, especially in decision-making.

9. Neglecting Time-Series Analysis for Temporal Data

For data that changes over time, such as sales figures or website traffic, failing to consider time-series trends can result in missing key patterns. Without time-based analysis, it's easy to overlook seasonality or trends that affect long-term performance.

Example

An analyst looks at monthly sales figures without recognizing that sales tend to peak every December due to holiday shopping. Without time-series analysis, this seasonal trend goes unnoticed, and forecasts may underestimate expected sales.

How to Avoid This Pitfall

- **Analyze Trends Over Time**: Use time-series analysis methods to identify trends, seasonality, and cyclical patterns in data.
- **Compare Year-Over-Year**: When relevant, compare data to the same period in previous years to identify consistent seasonal patterns.
- **Use Moving Averages**: Moving averages help smooth out short-term fluctuations and reveal long-term trends.

10. Making Assumptions Based on Initial Impressions

Data interpretation can be influenced by first impressions or assumptions, leading analysts to overlook deeper insights or alternative explanations.

It's easy to fall into this trap, especially when findings seem to confirm pre-existing beliefs or expectations.

Example

A company sees a drop in customer satisfaction and immediately attributes it to recent policy changes. However, a deeper analysis reveals that the decline was driven by seasonal factors unrelated to the policy change.

How to Avoid This Pitfall

- **Take a Comprehensive View**: Look beyond initial impressions and explore multiple potential explanations for observed trends or patterns.
- **Challenge Initial Assumptions**: Test hypotheses with additional data and consider alternative explanations to avoid confirmation bias.
- **Collaborate with Others**: Involve other team members or stakeholders to get diverse perspectives and reduce the risk of one-sided interpretation.

Key Takeaways

Avoiding pitfalls in data interpretation ensures accuracy, reliability, and objectivity in decision-making. Key strategies include:

- **Recognizing Correlation vs. Causation**: Avoid assuming that relationships between variables imply causation.
- **Providing Context and Clarity**: Interpret data with a clear understanding of its context and limitations.
- **Ensuring Data Representativeness**: Consider sample size, distribution, and relevance when generalizing findings.
- **Using Visuals Responsibly**: Design visualizations that enhance understanding without distorting insights.
- **Looking Beyond First Impressions**: Keep an open mind and seek diverse perspectives to validate interpretations.

By being mindful of these pitfalls, analysts and decision-makers can interpret data more accurately, leading to insights that genuinely reflect reality and support informed decisions.

Applying Data Insights to Real-Life Decision-Making

Data insights are only as valuable as the actions they inspire. In today's data-driven world, businesses, governments, and individuals rely on data to inform decisions, predict trends, and solve problems. However, translating insights from raw data into real-life decisions requires a structured approach, thoughtful interpretation, and a keen understanding of context. In this chapter, we'll explore how to effectively apply data insights to real-life decision-making, moving from numbers to actionable strategies.

Why Applying Data Insights Matters

The ultimate purpose of data analysis is to enable informed decision-making. Insights alone are not enough; they must be actionable, relevant, and applied effectively to make a real impact. Applying data insights helps organizations:

1. **Reduce Uncertainty**: Data-driven insights provide concrete evidence that can replace guesswork, enabling decision-makers to proceed with confidence.
2. **Improve Efficiency**: By identifying areas for improvement or optimization, data insights can streamline processes, reduce costs, and increase productivity.
3. **Identify Opportunities and Risks**: Insights reveal trends and potential risks, allowing proactive responses to market shifts, emerging threats, or new growth areas.
4. **Drive Strategic Goals**: Effective data-driven decision-making ensures that daily operations align with long-term strategic goals.

Let's dive into how to turn insights into action and apply them in various real-life scenarios.

Key Steps for Applying Data Insights to Decisions

Applying data insights to decision-making involves a structured process that ensures insights are both relevant and actionable.

Step 1: Define the Objective

Start by defining the objective. Clear objectives ensure that data interpretation aligns with the organization's needs, guiding the analysis toward actionable insights. Consider what you're trying to achieve, the problem you're solving, or the decision that needs to be made.

Example

An e-commerce company wants to improve its customer retention rate. Defining the objective as "increasing customer retention by 10% in the next quarter" provides a specific goal that guides analysis.

Step 2: Gather Relevant Data

Collect the data most relevant to your objective. This could involve customer data, market trends, historical performance, or survey results. Using data that directly relates to your goal ensures that insights are actionable.

Example

For the customer retention goal, relevant data might include purchase frequency, product satisfaction ratings, customer support interactions, and loyalty program participation. These data points can reveal what influences retention.

Step 3: Identify Key Insights and Patterns

Once the data is prepared, analyze it to identify key insights. Look for trends, correlations, and patterns that can inform your decision. Use visualization tools like bar charts, line charts, and scatter plots to make patterns more apparent.

Example

The analysis shows that customers who engage with the company's loyalty program are 20% more likely to make repeat purchases. Additionally, customers who have positive experiences with customer support are more likely to remain loyal.

Step 4: Develop Actionable Recommendations

Based on the insights, create specific, actionable recommendations that address the objective. Recommendations should be clear, practical, and directly linked to the data insights.

Example

To increase retention, the company could:

1. **Enhance the Loyalty Program**: Offer more rewards and personalized incentives to encourage repeat purchases.
2. **Improve Customer Support**: Implement training to improve customer support interactions and introduce follow-up messages after support cases are resolved.

Step 5: Implement Decisions and Monitor Outcomes

Put the recommended actions into practice. Implementation should include clear timelines, responsibilities, and measurable milestones. Once actions are in place, monitor outcomes closely to measure success and make adjustments as needed.

Example

The company launches an improved loyalty program and sets a quarterly review process to track retention rates. Weekly check-ins on customer support metrics help ensure that improvements are having the intended effect on customer satisfaction.

Real-Life Applications of Data-Driven Decision-Making

Let's explore practical examples of how different industries apply data insights to real-life decisions.

1. Retail: Optimizing Inventory Management

Retail businesses rely heavily on data to manage inventory levels, predict demand, and reduce waste. Data-driven inventory management uses sales trends, seasonality, and customer preferences to make stocking decisions.

Example

A clothing retailer analyzes historical sales data to identify peak demand seasons for specific products, such as winter coats in the colder months. The retailer uses this data to optimize inventory orders, reducing overstocking and preventing stockouts. As a result, the store minimizes storage costs and increases sales by ensuring products are available when customers want them.

Key Insights

- **Seasonality**: Winter coats peak in sales from November through February.
- **Customer Preferences**: Certain styles and colors sell faster, suggesting high demand and guiding stocking decisions.

Decision

Based on these insights, the retailer adjusts inventory orders to stock more winter coats in November, reducing excess inventory during warmer months and boosting profit margins.

2. Healthcare: Improving Patient Care

In healthcare, data analysis helps providers identify patient needs, track outcomes, and improve treatment protocols. Healthcare data insights can reveal trends in patient visits, common health conditions, and areas for service improvement.

Example

A hospital uses data from patient surveys and electronic health records to identify factors influencing patient satisfaction. The data shows that wait times for appointments significantly impact patient satisfaction. By addressing this, the hospital reduces patient churn and enhances care quality.

Key Insights

- **Wait Time Impact**: Long wait times are correlated with lower patient satisfaction scores.
- **Patient Preferences**: Patients prefer earlier appointment slots, suggesting potential adjustments in scheduling.

Decision

The hospital decides to hire additional staff during peak hours and implement a scheduling system that prioritizes shorter wait times, resulting in higher patient satisfaction and improved retention.

3. Marketing: Increasing Campaign Effectiveness

Marketing teams use data insights to optimize campaigns, target the right audiences, and maximize return on investment (ROI). Analysis of metrics like click-through rates, conversion rates, and engagement can reveal which strategies are most effective.

Example

A marketing team analyzes past campaigns and finds that social media ads targeting specific age groups yield higher engagement and conversions than general ads. They also discover that video ads are 40% more effective than static images.

Key Insights

- **Audience Segmentation**: Ads targeting younger demographics have a higher conversion rate.
- **Content Type**: Video ads outperform static ads, suggesting a preference for dynamic content.

Decision

Based on these insights, the team allocates more budget to social media ads targeting younger demographics and produces more video content. This data-driven adjustment results in higher engagement and conversion rates, optimizing marketing ROI.

4. Manufacturing: Enhancing Production Efficiency

In manufacturing, data insights help optimize production processes, reduce downtime, and improve quality. Analyzing data from sensors, production logs, and maintenance records can reveal bottlenecks and inefficiencies.

Example

A manufacturing company analyzes production line data and finds that one machine frequently malfunctions, leading to production delays. By identifying patterns in downtime and repair records, the company decides to replace the aging machine, improving overall efficiency.

Key Insights

- **Frequent Downtime**: The machine has more frequent breakdowns during peak production periods.
- **Repair Costs**: Maintenance costs for this machine exceed those of other machines, making it a candidate for replacement.

Decision

The company invests in a new machine and establishes a preventive maintenance schedule, reducing downtime and boosting production efficiency.

5. Human Resources: Improving Employee Retention

HR departments use data to monitor employee satisfaction, track turnover, and identify retention strategies. Analyzing engagement survey results, performance data, and turnover trends helps HR teams address issues that impact employee morale.

Example

An HR team reviews engagement survey data and exit interview feedback, finding that employees in specific departments feel undervalued due to a lack of growth opportunities. The data suggests that offering development programs could improve retention in these departments.

Key Insights

- **Growth Opportunities**: Employees cite career advancement as a key factor in job satisfaction.

- **Departmental Differences**: Certain departments have higher turnover rates, suggesting targeted interventions.

Decision

The HR team implements a development program for employees in high-turnover departments, including training workshops and clear paths for advancement. Retention rates improve as employees feel more invested in their roles.

Best Practices for Applying Data Insights in Real Life

To effectively apply data insights in decision-making, consider these best practices:

1. **Ensure Data Quality**: Accurate data is the foundation of reliable insights. Verify data quality by checking for accuracy, consistency, and completeness.
2. **Communicate Insights Clearly**: Use visuals, summaries, and clear language to present insights in an accessible way. Effective communication ensures that stakeholders understand the findings and can act on them.
3. **Involve Stakeholders in Interpretation**: Engage stakeholders early to ensure insights are relevant and actionable. Involving team members from different departments also

brings diverse perspectives that enhance decision-making.

4. **Consider Long-Term Implications**: When applying insights, think about long-term impacts as well as short-term gains. This approach ensures that decisions align with strategic goals and sustainability.

5. **Be Open to Iteration**: Data-driven decisions should be revisited as new data becomes available. Be prepared to adapt strategies as circumstances change and new insights emerge.

Key Takeaways

Applying data insights effectively requires thoughtful planning, clear objectives, and a structured approach. By moving from insight to action, organizations can make data-driven decisions that:

- **Align with Goals**: Ensure decisions support broader strategic objectives, from customer retention to operational efficiency.
- **Address Real Needs**: Use data to solve specific problems or seize opportunities, creating value and addressing pressing needs.
- **Drive Continuous Improvement**: Data-driven decision-making is iterative, allowing teams to adjust strategies based on ongoing analysis.

When applied thoughtfully, data insights become powerful tools for real-life decision-making, transforming raw data into practical solutions that drive success. By following these steps and best practices, you'll be able to leverage data to make informed decisions that have a lasting impact.

Chapter 8: Hands-On Analytics: Sample Projects

Project 1: Analyzing a Simple Dataset with Excel

Excel is one of the most widely used tools for data analysis due to its accessibility, flexibility, and powerful set of functions. For beginners, Excel provides an excellent introduction to hands-on analytics, enabling users to manipulate data, create visualizations, and draw insights from simple datasets. In this project, we'll work with a sample sales dataset to demonstrate fundamental analytical techniques. By the end of this exercise, you'll be comfortable using basic Excel functions, creating charts, and interpreting key insights.

Project Overview

In this project, we'll analyze a sample dataset containing sales information for an imaginary retail company. The dataset includes details such as product category, sales amount, region, and date. Our goal is to explore the dataset, perform calculations to summarize sales performance, and create visualizations to uncover trends and insights.

Project Objectives:

1. Summarize and interpret key metrics, such as total sales and sales by category.

2. Identify top-performing products and regions.
3. Visualize trends over time using charts.
4. Present findings in a clear, organized format.

Step 1: Importing and Exploring the Dataset

1.1 Import the Dataset

To begin, open Excel and import the dataset. If the data is in a .csv file:

1. Go to **File > Open** and select the .csv file to load it in Excel.
2. Alternatively, go to **Data > Get External Data > From Text/CSV** and select the file.

Once imported, your dataset should appear in a table format, with headers such as **Date**, **Region**, **Product Category**, **Product Name**, **Units Sold**, and **Sales Amount**.

1.2 Explore the Dataset

Start by taking a moment to review the dataset and understand its structure. Familiarize yourself with the columns:

- **Date**: The transaction date.
- **Region**: The geographical location where the sale occurred.
- **Product Category**: Type of product sold (e.g., Electronics, Clothing, Home Goods).

- **Product Name**: Name of the product.
- **Units Sold**: Quantity of the product sold.
- **Sales Amount**: Total revenue from the sale.

Exploring the dataset helps you identify any inconsistencies or data issues, such as missing values, that need to be addressed.

Step 2: Cleaning and Preparing the Data

Before analyzing the data, ensure it's clean and formatted correctly.

2.1 Check for Duplicates

- Go to **Data > Remove Duplicates** and select all columns to ensure that there are no duplicate entries. This step prevents overcounting sales.

2.2 Handle Missing Values

- Look for any blank cells, especially in key columns like **Sales Amount** or **Units Sold**. If there are any, fill in missing values with "0" or use Excel's **Filter** tool to filter out incomplete rows.

2.3 Format Data Correctly

- Ensure that **Date** is in the correct date format, and **Sales Amount** is formatted as currency.

Highlight the column, right-click, select **Format Cells**, and choose **Currency** or **Date**.

With a clean and formatted dataset, you're ready to start analyzing.

Step 3: Calculating Key Metrics

Excel provides several functions to quickly calculate metrics like total sales, average sales, and sales by category.

3.1 Calculate Total Sales

- In a new cell, use the **SUM** function to calculate total sales:

```excel
Copy code
=SUM(F2:F1000)
```

This formula calculates the total revenue across all sales records.

3.2 Calculate Average Sales per Transaction

- In another cell, use the **AVERAGE** function to calculate the average sales amount:

```excel
Copy code
=AVERAGE(F2:F1000)
```

This gives an idea of the average transaction value.

3.3 Summarize Sales by Product Category

- To see total sales by category, use a **PivotTable**:
  - Select your data range.
  - Go to **Insert > PivotTable** and select a new worksheet.
  - Drag **Product Category** to the **Rows** area and **Sales Amount** to the **Values** area.
  - Set the **Values** field to show the **Sum** of Sales Amount.

The PivotTable summarizes sales by each category, showing which categories generate the most revenue.

3.4 Find the Top-Performing Product

- Within the same PivotTable, add **Product Name** under **Product Category** to see sales totals for each product.
- Sort the **Sales Amount** column in descending order to easily identify the top-performing product in each category.

These calculations provide a snapshot of the company's sales performance, identifying which categories and products drive the most revenue.

Step 4: Visualizing Data Insights

Charts help communicate insights visually, making it easier to spot trends and patterns.

4.1 Create a Bar Chart for Sales by Category

- Select the **Product Category** and **Sales Amount** columns from your PivotTable.
- Go to **Insert > Chart** and select **Bar Chart**.
- Customize the chart title to "Sales by Product Category" and add data labels if needed.

This bar chart shows the sales contribution of each product category, making it easy to compare performance.

4.2 Create a Line Chart to Show Sales Trends Over Time

- To analyze monthly sales trends, first create a **PivotTable** with **Date** in the **Rows** area and **Sales Amount** in the **Values** area.
- Adjust the **Date** field settings to group data by **Months**.
- With the PivotTable results, go to **Insert > Line Chart** and select a simple line chart.
- Customize the chart title to "Monthly Sales Trends."

This line chart reveals seasonal trends, growth patterns, and any potential sales peaks or dips over the year.

4.3 Create a Pie Chart for Sales by Region

- In your PivotTable, drag **Region** to the **Rows** area and **Sales Amount** to the **Values** area to summarize sales by region.
- Select the region data and go to **Insert > Chart > Pie Chart** to create a pie chart.
- Label the chart as "Sales by Region" and add data labels to show the percentage of total sales for each region.

The pie chart provides a visual breakdown of sales distribution by region, helping identify top-performing regions.

Step 5: Interpreting the Results

Now that you've calculated key metrics and created visualizations, it's time to interpret the results. Consider the following questions as you analyze the charts and tables:

1. **Which Product Category Performs Best?**
   o From the bar chart, identify the category with the highest sales. For example, if Electronics leads, this may indicate high customer demand, and

the company might consider expanding the electronics product line.

2. **What are the Sales Trends Over Time?**
   - ○ Examine the line chart to see if there are any seasonal patterns. If sales peak during certain months, such as December, the company could increase inventory or offer promotions in anticipation of high demand.

3. **Which Regions Drive the Most Sales?**
   - ○ The pie chart shows sales distribution by region. If one region generates a disproportionately high amount of sales, the company might focus marketing efforts or inventory adjustments there to maximize revenue.

4. **Which Products Contribute Most to Revenue?**
   - ○ In the PivotTable, sort products by sales to find the top sellers. These popular items could be included in promotions or bundled with other products to boost revenue.

Step 6: Presenting Your Findings

To present the findings clearly and concisely, create a summary report with the following sections:

1. **Executive Summary**: Briefly outline the main findings, such as the best-performing

product category, overall sales trends, and top regions.

2. **Key Metrics**: Summarize total sales, average sales, and other key figures in a small table or as bullet points.

3. **Visualizations**: Include the bar chart, line chart, and pie chart in your report with descriptive titles.

4. **Recommendations**: Based on the insights, suggest actionable steps. For example:
   o Increase inventory in high-demand months.
   o Focus marketing efforts in top regions.
   o Expand the electronics category due to its high sales.

Example Summary Report

Executive Summary: "Sales for the year totaled $500,000, with Electronics as the top-performing category. Sales peak in December, likely due to holiday demand, and Region A contributes 40% of overall sales. To capitalize on these trends, we recommend expanding inventory during peak months and increasing marketing focus in Region A."

Key Takeaways

This project demonstrates how to analyze a simple dataset using basic Excel functions and tools. By calculating key metrics, creating visualizations, and interpreting insights, you can gain a comprehensive view of performance and make data-driven decisions. Key takeaways include:

- **Basic Calculations**: Use functions like SUM and AVERAGE to derive key metrics quickly.
- **PivotTables**: Summarize data and gain insights with ease.
- **Charts and Visuals**: Create bar charts, line charts, and pie charts to visualize insights.
- **Interpreting Results**: Translate findings into actionable recommendations that guide decision-making.

This hands-on project provides foundational skills for analyzing datasets in Excel, setting you up for more advanced analytics projects in the future.

Project 2: Creating a Visualization with a Free Tool (Google Data Studio)

Google Data Studio is a free, web-based tool that enables users to create interactive and visually appealing reports and dashboards. With its integration capabilities and customizable features, Google Data Studio is ideal for visualizing data in ways that are easy to understand and share with others. In this project, we'll walk through the steps to create a simple dashboard in Google Data Studio, using a sample dataset to showcase fundamental visualization techniques.

Project Overview

In this project, we'll use a sample dataset of website analytics for a fictional e-commerce company. The dataset includes metrics such as website traffic, user engagement, and conversions, which we'll use to create charts, tables, and a summary dashboard. By the end of this project, you'll have a solid understanding of how to use Google Data Studio's features to create effective data visualizations.

Project Objectives:

1. Connect a dataset to Google Data Studio and understand its interface.
2. Create visualizations such as line charts, bar charts, and scorecards.
3. Design an interactive dashboard that presents website analytics.
4. Interpret insights from the visualizations to make data-driven decisions.

Step 1: Setting Up Google Data Studio

1.1 Sign Up for Google Data Studio

To get started, you'll need a Google account. Visit Google Data Studio and sign in with your Google credentials. Google Data Studio is free, and using it requires no downloads as it operates entirely in the cloud.

1.2 Familiarize Yourself with the Interface

The Google Data Studio interface includes the following key areas:

- **Data Sources**: Where you connect to various data sources, such as Google Analytics, Google Sheets, or CSV files.
- **Report Canvas**: The main area where you design your report and place charts and visuals.
- **Toolbar**: Tools for adding elements like charts, scorecards, and images to your report.
- **Properties Panel**: Allows you to adjust settings, including chart types, data fields, and formatting options.

Step 2: Connecting Your Dataset

Google Data Studio can connect to multiple data sources. For this project, we'll use a Google Sheet containing our sample e-commerce analytics data, including fields like **Date**, **Sessions**, **Page Views**, **Conversions**, and **Revenue**.

2.1 Set Up Your Data Source

1. Open Google Sheets and create a new sheet with your sample data, or import a .csv file into Google Sheets. Be sure your data has a header row.
2. In Google Data Studio, click on **Create > Data Source**.

3. Select **Google Sheets** and choose your data file from Google Drive.
4. Confirm your data source settings, ensuring that each field (like Date, Sessions, Revenue) is recognized correctly. Adjust field types if necessary (e.g., make sure dates are recognized as **Date** and numeric fields as **Number** or **Currency**).

2.2 Connect Your Data Source to the Report

Once your data source is set up, click **Connect**. Your data is now available for use in creating visualizations on the report canvas.

Step 3: Creating Basic Visualizations

With your data connected, you can now add charts and visuals to your dashboard. We'll start by creating a few key visualizations, including a line chart for website traffic trends, a scorecard to display total revenue, and a bar chart for conversion rates by region.

3.1 Add a Scorecard for Total Revenue

Scorecards are a simple yet powerful way to display key metrics at a glance.

1. Go to the report canvas and click **Add a chart > Scorecard**.

2. Position the scorecard on the canvas where you want it to appear.
3. In the **Data** panel, select **Revenue** as the metric to display.
4. Customize the scorecard to display currency formatting in the **Style** tab.
5. Label the scorecard as "Total Revenue."

This scorecard provides an instant snapshot of total revenue, a key metric for any e-commerce business.

3.2 Create a Line Chart for Website Traffic Trends

A line chart is ideal for visualizing website sessions over time.

1. Click **Add a chart > Time series** and place it on the canvas.
2. In the **Data** panel, select **Date** as the **Dimension** and **Sessions** as the **Metric**.
3. Customize the date range in the **Date Range** section if needed (e.g., to show the last six months).
4. Use the **Style** tab to adjust colors, line thickness, and add data points for emphasis.

This line chart displays traffic trends, helping identify high-traffic periods and seasonal fluctuations.

3.3 Add a Bar Chart for Conversions by Region

Bar charts are useful for comparing categorical data, such as conversions by region.

1. Click **Add a chart > Bar chart** and place it on the canvas.
2. In the **Data** panel, select **Region** as the **Dimension** and **Conversions** as the **Metric**.
3. Adjust sorting options to show the highest converting regions at the top.
4. Use the **Style** tab to adjust the bar colors and add data labels for clarity.

This bar chart shows which regions drive the most conversions, highlighting where the business may focus additional marketing efforts.

3.4 Add a Pie Chart for Device Breakdown

A pie chart can show the distribution of sessions across different devices (e.g., mobile, desktop, tablet).

1. Click **Add a chart > Pie chart** and position it on the canvas.
2. Select **Device Type** as the **Dimension** and **Sessions** as the **Metric**.
3. Customize the chart's color scheme and add data labels to display percentages.

This pie chart reveals the proportion of sessions by device, indicating whether the website is more popular on mobile or desktop, which can inform responsive design decisions.

Step 4: Customizing the Dashboard Layout

Now that you have your key metrics and visualizations, it's time to arrange and style the dashboard to make it visually appealing and easy to interpret.

4.1 Arrange Charts Logically

Place scorecards at the top for quick reference, followed by charts in a logical order. For instance, start with traffic trends, then conversions by region, and finally device breakdown. This layout guides the viewer through the data in a logical flow.

4.2 Add Filters for Interactivity

Adding filters allows users to customize the view, such as by adjusting the date range or filtering by region.

1. Click **Add a control > Date range control** to add a date filter. Position it near the top of the dashboard so viewers can easily adjust the reporting period.
2. To add a region filter, click **Add a control > Filter control** and set **Region** as the dimension.

3. Position the filter controls at the top of the dashboard for easy access.

These interactive controls allow users to explore the data by different time periods or focus on specific regions.

4.3 Apply Styling for Visual Consistency

Use the **Style** tab to apply consistent colors, fonts, and borders. A clean, consistent design improves readability and ensures that the dashboard looks professional.

- **Color Scheme**: Choose a color scheme that aligns with the company's branding. For example, use a different color for each chart type (e.g., green for revenue, blue for sessions).
- **Text and Labels**: Use concise titles and descriptions for each chart. Labels should be clear and informative, such as "Monthly Sessions" or "Top Converting Regions."

Step 5: Interpreting Insights from the Dashboard

With your dashboard complete, you can now analyze and interpret the data insights provided by each visualization.

Insights and Analysis

1. **Website Traffic Trends**: The line chart may show a steady increase in sessions with a peak in certain months, such as during a holiday season or a recent marketing campaign.
2. **Total Revenue**: The scorecard provides an at-a-glance view of total revenue, helping assess overall performance.
3. **Conversions by Region**: The bar chart reveals which regions are converting at higher rates, suggesting areas for targeted marketing efforts or localized content.
4. **Device Breakdown**: The pie chart indicates which devices are most popular among users. If mobile sessions are high, investing in mobile optimization could improve user experience and conversions.

Example Summary

"Our analysis reveals that website traffic peaks during December, likely due to seasonal promotions, and Region A leads in conversions. Mobile users account for 60% of sessions, suggesting that further investment in mobile optimization could increase conversions."

Step 6: Sharing the Dashboard

One of the strengths of Google Data Studio is the ease with which you can share dashboards with others.

1. Click **Share** in the top-right corner of the report.
2. Choose to share via email or create a shareable link. You can set permissions to control who can view or edit the report.
3. For regular updates, set up automated data refresh options so the dashboard stays up-to-date without requiring manual updates.

Sharing the dashboard allows team members to access real-time insights and make data-driven decisions collaboratively.

Key Takeaways

This project demonstrates the basics of using Google Data Studio for data visualization. Key takeaways include:

- **Connecting Data**: Link data from various sources, including Google Sheets, to create a dynamic dashboard.
- **Creating Visuals**: Use different chart types— scorecards, line charts, bar charts, and pie charts—to present a comprehensive view of data.
- **Interactive Filters**: Add filters to enhance interactivity, allowing users to customize the data view.
- **Insights and Actions**: Translate data into actionable insights that inform decisions, such

as focusing on high-converting regions or optimizing for mobile users.

Google Data Studio's flexibility and ease of use make it an ideal tool for beginners and professionals alike. By completing this project, you'll be able to create insightful dashboards that visualize data effectively, making it accessible and actionable for decision-makers.

Guidance on How to Present Findings

Data analysis is valuable only when its insights are clearly and effectively communicated. Presenting findings involves more than displaying charts and graphs; it requires a structured approach that connects data-driven insights to specific objectives and actions. Whether you're presenting to stakeholders, team members, or clients, your goal is to ensure that your findings are understandable, relevant, and actionable. In this section, we'll explore best practices for structuring presentations, storytelling with data, and tailoring communication to your audience.

1. Know Your Audience

The first step in presenting findings is understanding your audience's needs, preferences, and technical familiarity with the data. Different audiences require different levels of detail, technicality, and focus. Knowing who you're speaking to enables you to customize the presentation to their level of understanding, ensuring your insights are relevant and clear.

Key Audience Considerations

- **Technical Expertise**: For a technical audience, include details on data sources, methodology, and analysis techniques. For a non-technical audience, focus more on key insights, actions, and results rather than technical specifics.
- **Goals and Interests**: Identify the goals of your audience. For example, an executive team may want insights into revenue growth, while a marketing team may be more interested in customer engagement metrics.
- **Decision-Making Authority**: Tailor recommendations to the decision-making power of your audience. If they can implement changes directly, your presentation can include tactical actions. If they are senior leaders, focus on strategic insights and broad implications.

2. Structure Your Presentation for Clarity

A well-structured presentation guides your audience through your analysis in a logical sequence, from background to insights to recommended actions. This approach keeps the audience engaged and helps them understand the progression from data collection to insights.

Suggested Presentation Outline

1. **Introduction**: Begin with the objective of the analysis. Briefly explain what you set out to understand or solve, providing context for the audience.
2. **Methodology and Data Overview** (optional): For a technical audience, provide an overview of your data sources, sample size, and methodology. Keep this section concise for non-technical audiences.
3. **Key Findings**: Present the main insights, supported by visuals and data points. Focus on findings that directly relate to your objectives.
4. **Analysis and Interpretation**: Explain what the findings mean and why they matter. Avoid jargon and simplify complex concepts.
5. **Recommendations**: Based on your findings, suggest specific, actionable steps. Recommendations should align with the goals and capabilities of your audience.
6. **Conclusion**: Summarize key takeaways and reinforce the next steps or actions the audience should consider.

3. Tell a Story with Your Data

Storytelling is an effective way to communicate data insights, making them more memorable and impactful. A good data story provides context, meaning, and relevance, helping your audience understand the "why" behind the numbers.

Elements of a Strong Data Story

- **Context**: Begin with background information that sets the stage, explaining why the analysis was conducted and what problem or question you aimed to address.
- **Insight**: Highlight key findings in a way that builds interest. Use charts and visual aids to show how data supports each insight, moving from simple observations to deeper analysis.
- **Impact**: Describe the implications of the insights. For instance, "An increase in website traffic during holiday promotions led to a 20% increase in conversions," linking data to business outcomes.
- **Next Steps**: Conclude with recommendations that flow naturally from your findings, guiding the audience on what to do next based on the insights.

Example of a Data Story

"Last quarter, we noticed a sharp increase in website traffic, particularly during our holiday sales campaign. Analyzing the data further, we found that the majority of this traffic came from mobile devices. However, mobile conversions were lower than desktop conversions, suggesting a potential friction in the mobile experience. By improving mobile site speed and optimizing the checkout process, we can likely boost mobile conversions and increase revenue during peak sales periods."

This narrative connects findings to practical recommendations and anticipated outcomes, making the data more relatable and actionable.

4. Use Visuals Effectively

Visuals are powerful tools for communicating data insights, but they must be carefully designed to avoid confusion or misinterpretation. Choosing the right chart type, simplifying visual elements, and using consistent formatting all contribute to clarity and impact.

Best Practices for Effective Visuals

- **Choose the Right Chart**: Use line charts for trends over time, bar charts for category comparisons, pie charts for proportions, and scatter plots for correlations. Selecting the right chart helps your audience understand the data more quickly.
- **Focus on Key Data Points**: Highlight important data points or trends with bold colors or annotations. This approach directs attention to the most significant insights.
- **Limit Colors**: Stick to a consistent color scheme, using bright colors only to highlight specific data points. Avoid using too many

colors, as this can distract from the main message.

- **Label Clearly**: Ensure that each chart has a clear title, axis labels, and data labels where needed. Labels provide context and prevent misinterpretation.

Example

A line chart showing monthly revenue over a year can be enhanced by highlighting the holiday season months in a different color. This highlights seasonal revenue peaks, making it easy for the audience to see the impact of holiday promotions.

5. Summarize Key Takeaways

After presenting your findings, summarize the key takeaways in a concise manner. Summaries reinforce the main points, helping the audience remember the most important insights and understand their implications.

Tips for Summarizing Key Takeaways

- **Be Concise**: Focus on the most impactful insights that are directly relevant to the audience's goals.
- **Use Bullet Points**: Bullet points or short phrases can make key takeaways easy to remember and visually accessible.

- **Emphasize Actionable Points**: Highlight any actions or recommendations that the audience should consider following the presentation.

Example Summary

"Key Takeaways:

- Holiday campaigns significantly boost website traffic and revenue, with a 30% increase in December.
- Mobile traffic outpaced desktop but had lower conversion rates, suggesting a need for mobile optimization.
- Focusing on high-converting regions can yield better returns from targeted marketing efforts."

6. Offer Actionable Recommendations

Data insights should lead to action. Providing clear, actionable recommendations based on your findings makes it easier for your audience to move from insight to implementation. Each recommendation should be specific, practical, and directly related to your analysis.

Crafting Effective Recommendations

- **Link to Findings**: Make sure each recommendation ties back to a specific insight from your analysis.

- **Be Specific**: Avoid vague recommendations. Instead of saying "improve marketing efforts," specify "increase ad spend in high-converting regions."
- **Prioritize**: Rank recommendations by importance or feasibility. If the audience has limited resources, focus on the actions with the highest potential impact.

Example Recommendations

Based on findings from a sales performance analysis:

1. **Enhance Mobile Experience**: Improve mobile site speed and streamline the checkout process to increase mobile conversions by an estimated 15%.
2. **Target High-Performing Regions**: Focus marketing efforts on regions with higher conversion rates to maximize ROI.
3. **Plan for Seasonal Demand**: Increase inventory and staffing levels during the holiday season to accommodate higher demand and boost sales.

7. Be Ready for Questions

Your audience may have questions that require clarification or additional detail. Being prepared to answer questions ensures that you can address any uncertainties, provide deeper insights, and reinforce the credibility of your findings.

Tips for Handling Questions

- **Anticipate Common Questions**: Think ahead about what questions may arise based on your analysis. Be prepared to discuss methodology, data sources, or deeper implications.
- **Use Data to Support Answers**: If possible, refer to specific data points or visuals in your presentation to support your answers.
- **Clarify Limitations**: If questions address areas outside the scope of your analysis, clarify any limitations and offer to investigate further if needed.

Example

If a stakeholder asks why mobile conversions are lower than desktop conversions, you might explain, "Our analysis suggests that checkout friction may be a factor, as mobile users experience slower load times. We recommend optimizing mobile site speed to improve the user experience and potentially increase conversions."

8. Follow Up with a Summary Report

After the presentation, provide a summary report that captures the key insights, visuals, and recommendations. A summary report reinforces your presentation's findings and serves as a reference for decision-makers as they consider next steps.

Elements of a Good Summary Report

- **Executive Summary**: A brief overview of the objectives, findings, and recommendations.
- **Key Insights and Visuals**: Include charts and graphs that were part of the presentation to illustrate main points.
- **Recommendations**: Outline actionable steps based on the insights, with any prioritization noted.
- **Contact Information**: Make it easy for readers to follow up with questions by including your contact details.

Example of a Summary Report

An executive summary might read, "This report provides insights into website traffic trends, with a focus on increasing conversions. Key findings include high traffic during the holiday season, lower mobile conversion rates, and strong performance in specific regions. We recommend optimizing the mobile experience and focusing marketing efforts in high-converting areas to drive future growth."

Key Takeaways

Presenting findings is a vital step in data analysis that bridges the gap between insights and action. By structuring your presentation, using effective storytelling, and focusing on actionable recommendations, you can ensure that your analysis is both understood and impactful. Key takeaways include:

- **Understand Your Audience**: Tailor your presentation to the audience's technical level and decision-making needs.
- **Use Storytelling Techniques**: Present data in a way that flows logically and engages your audience.
- **Emphasize Key Findings and Recommendations**: Highlight the most important insights and link them to clear, actionable steps.
- **Be Prepared for Follow-Up**: Address questions confidently and provide a summary report for future reference.

Effective presentation of data findings makes it easier for stakeholders to understand and act on insights, leading to more informed and successful decision-making. By mastering these skills, you'll enhance the value of your data analysis and ensure your insights lead to meaningful results.

Chapter 9: Pathways to Intermediate Data Skills

Databases, Programming, and Advanced Statistics

Once you have a solid foundation in data analysis, the next step is to develop more advanced skills that can help you handle larger datasets, automate processes, and perform sophisticated analyses. Mastering databases, programming, and advanced statistical techniques will enable you to work with complex data, enhance your analytical capabilities, and take on more challenging projects. In this chapter, we'll explore the essential intermediate skills in these areas, providing a pathway to expand your analytical toolkit.

1. Working with Databases

Databases are crucial for managing large datasets efficiently, enabling storage, retrieval, and manipulation of data at scale. As data grows in volume and complexity, understanding database structures and learning how to interact with databases using SQL (Structured Query Language) is essential for any data analyst.

Key Concepts in Databases

- **Relational Databases**: Relational databases store data in structured tables with defined relationships between them, which makes it easy to organize and query information. Examples include MySQL, PostgreSQL, and Microsoft SQL Server.

- **Database Schema**: The schema defines the structure of a database, including tables, fields, and relationships. Understanding schema design is important when working with multiple tables and joining data.
- **SQL**: SQL is the primary language used to interact with relational databases, allowing users to query, update, and manipulate data.

Essential SQL Skills

1. **Basic Queries**: Learn to select, filter, and sort data using commands like SELECT, WHERE, ORDER BY, and LIMIT.
2. **Joins**: Mastering JOIN operations is crucial, as it allows you to combine data from multiple tables. Common types of joins include INNER JOIN, LEFT JOIN, and RIGHT JOIN.
3. **Aggregation Functions**: Functions like SUM, COUNT, AVG, and GROUP BY enable you to calculate totals, averages, and other summary statistics.
4. **Subqueries**: Subqueries are queries within queries, allowing you to perform complex filtering and aggregations.

5. **Data Manipulation**: Learn commands like INSERT, UPDATE, and DELETE to modify data within the database.

Example: Querying Sales Data

Suppose you have a database with tables for **Customers**, **Orders**, and **Products**. You could use SQL to find the total sales by region, the top-selling products, or the most frequent customers.

```sql
Copy code
SELECT region, SUM(order_total) AS
total_sales
FROM Orders
JOIN Customers ON Orders.customer_id =
Customers.customer_id
GROUP BY region
ORDER BY total_sales DESC;
```

This query provides a summary of sales by region, helping the company identify its most profitable locations.

Learning Resources

- **Online Courses**: Platforms like Coursera, Udacity, and DataCamp offer SQL courses for beginners to advanced levels.
- **SQL Practice Websites**: Websites like SQLBolt and Mode Analytics provide interactive exercises to reinforce SQL skills.

- **Hands-On Projects**: Practice by setting up a database with sample data and running queries to answer business questions.

2. Introduction to Programming for Data Analysis

Programming adds power and flexibility to data analysis, enabling you to automate tasks, handle large datasets, and perform complex calculations. Python and R are two of the most popular languages for data analysis due to their extensive libraries, versatility, and supportive communities.

Why Learn Programming?

Programming allows you to:

- **Automate Repetitive Tasks**: Write scripts to automate data cleaning, transformations, and repetitive calculations.
- **Process Large Datasets**: Handle data too large for spreadsheet tools like Excel, especially with libraries that optimize data manipulation.
- **Create Custom Visualizations**: Build unique charts and dashboards tailored to specific needs.
- **Perform Advanced Analytics**: Use statistical and machine learning libraries to build predictive models and uncover deeper insights.

Getting Started with Python

Python is a beginner-friendly language with a broad ecosystem of libraries suited to data analysis. Here are some essential Python libraries for data analysts:

1. **Pandas**: Used for data manipulation and analysis. It provides functions for reading, cleaning, filtering, and aggregating data.
2. **NumPy**: Supports numerical calculations and is particularly useful for handling large datasets and performing mathematical operations.
3. **Matplotlib and Seaborn**: These libraries are commonly used for data visualization, enabling you to create line charts, bar charts, histograms, and more.
4. **Scikit-Learn**: A powerful machine learning library for predictive analysis, clustering, and regression.

Example: Analyzing Customer Data with Python

Suppose you have a dataset of customer purchases in a CSV file. You could use Python and Pandas to analyze customer spending patterns.

```python
Copy code
import pandas as pd

# Load data
```

```
data =
pd.read_csv("customer_purchases.csv")

# Calculate average spending by customer
average_spending =
data.groupby("customer_id")["purchase_amoun
t"].mean()

# Identify high-spending customers
high_spenders =
average_spending[average_spending > 100]
```

This script loads the data, calculates average spending per customer, and identifies customers with average spending over $100.

Learning Resources

- **Online Courses**: Websites like DataCamp, Coursera, and Codecademy offer introductory courses in Python and R for data analysis.
- **Documentation and Tutorials**: The official documentation for libraries like Pandas, Matplotlib, and Scikit-Learn is an excellent resource.
- **Practice Projects**: Try projects like analyzing a dataset with Pandas, building a visualization in Matplotlib, or creating a basic predictive model with Scikit-Learn.

3. Advanced Statistics and Data Analysis Techniques

Advanced statistical skills enable you to draw more robust insights from data and apply sophisticated analytical techniques. Proficiency in statistics is essential for building predictive models, conducting experiments, and making data-driven decisions based on probability and uncertainty.

Key Statistical Concepts for Intermediate Analysts

1. **Probability Distributions**: Understanding distributions like normal, binomial, and Poisson helps in interpreting data and calculating probabilities.
2. **Hypothesis Testing**: Hypothesis testing allows you to make inferences about data, such as determining whether observed differences are statistically significant. Key tests include t-tests, chi-square tests, and ANOVA.
3. **Regression Analysis**: Regression models describe relationships between variables. Common techniques include linear regression, logistic regression, and multiple regression.
4. **ANOVA (Analysis of Variance)**: ANOVA helps you compare means across multiple groups, useful for testing if group differences are statistically significant.
5. **Time Series Analysis**: Time series methods, like moving averages and exponential smoothing, are used to analyze data over time, identify trends, and make forecasts.

Example: Using Regression Analysis to Predict Sales

Suppose you want to predict future sales based on historical data, including advertising spend, seasonality, and product category.

1. Collect and clean your data, ensuring all variables are in a usable format.
2. Use linear regression to model the relationship between advertising spend and sales, incorporating other variables as needed.
3. Interpret the regression coefficients to understand the impact of each variable on sales.

In Python, you can use Scikit-Learn to perform linear regression:

```python
python
Copy code
from sklearn.linear_model import
LinearRegression

# Define predictors and target variable
X = data[["advertising_spend",
"seasonality", "product_category"]]
y = data["sales"]

# Fit the model
model = LinearRegression()
model.fit(X, y)

# Predict future sales
predicted_sales = model.predict(X)
```

This analysis provides insights into the factors driving sales and allows you to forecast future sales based on input variables.

Learning Resources

- **Online Courses**: Look for advanced statistics courses on websites like Udacity, Khan Academy, or Coursera.
- **Books**: Titles like *The Art of Statistics* by David Spiegelhalter and *Practical Statistics for Data Scientists* are valuable resources.
- **Statistical Software**: Explore software like R, which is widely used in academia and offers robust statistical packages.

Bringing It All Together: A Sample Project

To illustrate how databases, programming, and statistics can be combined in an analysis project, let's consider a real-life example:

Sample Project: Customer Segmentation Analysis

Objective: To identify and segment customers for targeted marketing.

Steps:

1. **Data Collection**: Gather customer data, including demographics, purchase history,

and engagement metrics. Store this data in a relational database (e.g., MySQL).

2. **Data Preparation**: Use SQL to clean and filter the data, removing duplicates and organizing it by key variables.

3. **Data Analysis in Python**: Use Python to analyze customer spending patterns, calculate average order values, and identify high-value customers. Employ clustering techniques, such as K-Means, to segment customers.

4. **Statistical Analysis**: Perform statistical tests to validate that the segments differ significantly in terms of spending, demographics, and engagement.

5. **Report Findings**: Present findings in a dashboard with charts that illustrate each segment's characteristics. Include actionable insights, such as personalized marketing strategies for each customer group.

Key Takeaways

Expanding your skills in databases, programming, and advanced statistics enables you to tackle more complex data challenges, create custom analyses, and draw deeper insights. Key takeaways include:

- **Database Skills with SQL**: Master SQL to efficiently manage and query large datasets stored in databases.

- **Programming Skills with Python or R**: Use programming to automate tasks, manipulate large datasets, and perform advanced analysis.
- **Advanced Statistical Techniques**: Apply statistical methods to validate findings, make predictions, and draw robust conclusions from data.

These intermediate skills will make you a more versatile analyst, capable of handling complex data scenarios and delivering high-impact insights.

Why Ongoing Learning is Essential in Data Analytics

Data analytics is a dynamic field, constantly evolving with new tools, techniques, and trends. Keeping your skills up to date is crucial for staying relevant, enhancing your career prospects, and improving the quality of your analyses. By committing to continuous learning, you'll be well-equipped to adapt to advancements in data science, explore new methodologies, and confidently tackle more complex data challenges.

1. Build a Continuous Learning Plan

A structured learning plan can help you prioritize skills and allocate time for development. Identify the skills you want to enhance and set specific, measurable goals to track your progress.

Steps to Build Your Learning Plan

1. **Identify Key Areas for Growth**: Reflect on your current skill set and consider which areas you'd like to improve. These might include advanced statistical techniques, programming languages, or specialized tools like Tableau or SQL.
2. **Set Learning Goals**: Create short- and long-term goals. For example, set a goal to learn the basics of machine learning within three months or master SQL in six months.
3. **Allocate Regular Time for Learning**: Designate a consistent time each week for learning. Even an hour or two can make a significant difference over time.
4. **Assess Your Progress**: Periodically review your progress, evaluate your understanding, and update your learning goals as needed.

Example Learning Plan

Goal: Improve Python programming skills.

- **Timeline**: Three months
- **Steps**:
  - Month 1: Complete a Python fundamentals course
  - Month 2: Practice data analysis with Pandas and NumPy

- Month 3: Complete a mini-project in Python, such as analyzing a dataset or building a simple visualization

A learning plan like this helps you stay focused and see steady progress in your skill development.

2. Take Advantage of Online Courses and Certifications

Online courses and certifications provide structured, comprehensive learning and help validate your skills to potential employers. Many reputable platforms offer high-quality content taught by industry experts.

Recommended Platforms for Data Analytics

- **Coursera**: Courses from top universities like Stanford, Johns Hopkins, and the University of Washington, covering topics from data science fundamentals to advanced machine learning.
- **Udacity**: Specialized nanodegree programs, including Data Analyst, Machine Learning Engineer, and SQL for Data Analysis.
- **DataCamp**: Interactive courses with a focus on Python, R, SQL, and other data science tools. DataCamp's short exercises and projects are ideal for hands-on learning.
- **edX**: Provides data science courses from institutions like MIT and Harvard, often with an option for certification.

- **Khan Academy and freeCodeCamp**: Excellent free resources for learning the basics of statistics, Python programming, and SQL.

How to Choose the Right Course

- **Evaluate the Syllabus**: Ensure the course covers relevant topics aligned with your learning goals.
- **Check Reviews and Ratings**: Look at reviews from past learners to gauge the course quality and effectiveness.
- **Consider Hands-On Projects**: Select courses that offer practical exercises, projects, or capstone tasks, as hands-on learning is essential in data analytics.

Suggested Certifications

- **Google Data Analytics Professional Certificate**: A beginner-friendly certification covering fundamental data analytics skills.
- **IBM Data Science Professional Certificate**: A comprehensive program that includes Python, SQL, and data visualization.
- **Microsoft Certified: Data Analyst Associate**: Ideal for those focusing on Power BI and data visualization.
- **Certified Analytics Professional (CAP)**: A rigorous, industry-recognized credential for experienced analysts.

These certifications can serve as milestones in your learning journey and enhance your professional credibility.

3. Stay Updated on Industry Trends and Tools

Staying current with industry trends, new tools, and emerging techniques is essential as the data field evolves. Following industry leaders, reading relevant content, and joining online communities can keep you informed and inspired.

Sources for Staying Updated

- **Blogs and News Sites**: Sites like KDnuggets, Towards Data Science, Analytics Vidhya, and Data Science Central regularly publish articles on the latest developments in data science.
- **Industry Reports**: Organizations like Gartner, McKinsey, and the International Institute for Analytics publish reports on trends and technologies impacting the data analytics field.
- **Newsletters**: Sign up for newsletters like Data Elixir, O'Reilly Data & AI Newsletter, and Analytics Weekly to receive curated content on data science and AI.
- **YouTube Channels**: Channels like StatQuest with Josh Starmer, Corey Schafer, and Sentdex offer tutorials and explanations on a range of data science topics, including

programming, statistics, and machine learning.

Tip: Set Up Google Alerts

Use Google Alerts to get notifications on topics like "data analytics trends," "machine learning tools," or "Python for data science." This will keep you up to date on developments that matter most to your career goals.

4. Join Data Science Communities and Networks

Communities provide a space to exchange ideas, seek help, and connect with other data enthusiasts. Networking within data science communities allows you to learn from others' experiences, gain insights into best practices, and even discover career opportunities.

Recommended Data Science Communities

- **Kaggle**: Kaggle is one of the largest data science communities, offering datasets, competitions, and discussion forums where members share solutions and collaborate.
- **Reddit**: Subreddits like r/datascience, r/statistics, and r/learnpython are active communities where users share resources, ask questions, and discuss industry trends.

- **Stack Overflow**: A valuable resource for troubleshooting coding issues and finding solutions to technical challenges in Python, SQL, and other languages.
- **LinkedIn Groups**: Join LinkedIn groups like Data Science Central, Big Data and Analytics, and Python Developers to stay updated on industry news, participate in discussions, and network with professionals.
- **Meetup.com**: Look for local data science or machine learning groups that host events, webinars, and networking opportunities. Meeting people in person or virtually can be an excellent way to expand your knowledge and connections.

Benefits of Community Engagement

- **Learning from Peers**: See how others approach data problems, and learn from their experiences.
- **Getting Feedback**: Share your work and get constructive feedback, which can help you improve.
- **Access to Resources**: Communities often share helpful resources like articles, tutorials, and code libraries.
- **Job Opportunities**: Networking can open doors to job referrals, freelance gigs, or project collaborations.

5. Practice with Real-World Data Projects

Applying your skills to real-world data projects is one of the best ways to deepen your knowledge. Projects give you hands-on experience, build your portfolio, and demonstrate your capabilities to potential employers.

Types of Projects to Consider

- **Data Cleaning and Transformation**: Work with messy, real-world datasets to practice data cleaning techniques like handling missing values, standardizing formats, and restructuring data.
- **Exploratory Data Analysis (EDA)**: Use a dataset from Kaggle or a public source to explore relationships, trends, and patterns. EDA projects showcase your ability to derive insights from data.
- **Predictive Modeling**: Build simple models using regression, classification, or clustering to predict outcomes or segment data. Predictive projects highlight your understanding of machine learning basics.
- **Data Visualization**: Create a dashboard in Tableau, Power BI, or Google Data Studio to display KPIs for a specific dataset. Visualization projects demonstrate your ability to communicate insights effectively.

Resources for Finding Project Datasets

- **Kaggle**: Offers thousands of datasets on topics from sports to healthcare, ideal for analysis, modeling, and visualization projects.
- **UCI Machine Learning Repository**: Provides free datasets frequently used in machine learning research.
- **Google Dataset Search**: A search engine that helps you find datasets across the web.
- **Government Databases**: Sites like Data.gov (US), Data.gov.uk (UK), and the World Bank provide public datasets on economics, health, environment, and more.

6. Keep a Portfolio of Your Work

Building a portfolio is essential for showcasing your skills to potential employers. A portfolio demonstrates your ability to analyze, visualize, and interpret data and serves as a record of your progress over time.

Elements of a Strong Data Portfolio

- **Project Descriptions**: Provide a brief summary of each project, including objectives, data sources, methods, and key insights.
- **Code and Documentation**: Include code snippets or links to code repositories (e.g., GitHub) to demonstrate your technical skills.
- **Visualizations and Reports**: Share charts, dashboards, or reports that illustrate your

ability to communicate data insights effectively.

- **Personal Website or GitHub**: Consider setting up a personal website or a GitHub profile to host your portfolio and make it accessible to recruiters.

Example Project for Portfolio

Project: Customer Segmentation Analysis

- **Objective**: Segment customers based on purchasing behavior to inform targeted marketing.
- **Methodology**: Used K-Means clustering to identify customer groups, performed EDA, and visualized findings in a Tableau dashboard.
- **Outcome**: Identified three main customer segments with distinct spending habits, leading to personalized marketing strategies.

7. Experiment with New Tools and Techniques

The data analytics field is continuously introducing new tools, libraries, and techniques. Experimenting with these innovations can expand your skills and keep you adaptable.

Tools and Techniques to Explore

- **New Programming Libraries**: Try libraries like Plotly for interactive visualizations, PyCaret for automated machine learning, or NLTK for natural language processing.
- **Cloud-Based Analytics**: Platforms like Google BigQuery, Amazon Redshift, and Microsoft Azure offer cloud-based data storage and analytics capabilities.
- **Automated Machine Learning (AutoML)**: Tools like H2O.ai, Google AutoML, and DataRobot simplify the model-building process, allowing you to experiment with predictive modeling without extensive coding.
- **Deep Learning**: If you're ready for advanced concepts, explore TensorFlow or PyTorch to experiment with neural networks and deep learning models.

Key Takeaways

To remain competitive in the data analytics field, continuous learning is essential. By following these strategies, you can stay updated, broaden your skills, and keep pace with industry advancements:

- **Build a Structured Learning Plan**: Set clear goals, dedicate regular time, and review your progress.
- **Leverage Online Resources**: Use courses, certifications, and tutorials to learn at your own pace.

- **Stay Updated with Industry News**: Follow blogs, reports, and newsletters to keep up with trends and developments.
- **Engage with Communities**: Participate in data science forums, meetups, and online groups to learn and network.
- **Practice with Real-World Projects**: Develop practical skills by working on projects and building a portfolio.
- **Experiment with New Tools**: Explore new libraries, platforms, and technologies to expand your capabilities.

By committing to ongoing learning, you'll be prepared to tackle future data challenges, stay ahead of industry trends, and achieve lasting success in your data analytics career.

Why Data Literacy is Essential Across All Careers

Data literacy—the ability to read, work with, interpret, and communicate data—is a valuable skill in virtually every profession today. Whether you're in business, healthcare, education, or marketing, understanding how to use data empowers you to make informed decisions, solve problems efficiently, and contribute to data-driven strategies. In this chapter, we'll explore how data literacy applies to a range of careers, offering specific tips and examples for leveraging data effectively in each field.

1. Data Literacy in Business and Management

In business and management, data literacy enables professionals to make strategic decisions, identify opportunities for growth, and optimize resources. Data-driven decision-making has become a cornerstone of competitive advantage, as it helps leaders understand customer behavior, market trends, and operational efficiency.

Tips for Applying Data Literacy in Business

- **Use Dashboards for Real-Time Monitoring**: Leverage dashboards in tools like Tableau or Power BI to monitor key performance indicators (KPIs) like sales, customer retention, and operational costs. Real-time data allows you to respond quickly to changes and make timely adjustments.
- **Analyze Financial Data for Budgeting and Forecasting**: Use historical financial data to identify spending trends and forecast future budgets. Analyzing expenses by category can help in making cost-cutting decisions without affecting essential operations.
- **Conduct Customer Analysis**: Use data from CRM (Customer Relationship Management) systems to analyze customer behavior, preferences, and purchasing patterns. Insights from customer segmentation can guide

marketing strategies and improve customer engagement.

Example

A sales manager might use data from a CRM system to identify high-value customers and focus sales efforts on these segments. Analyzing customer data by region, spending habits, and engagement history can help prioritize leads and tailor sales pitches to different groups.

2. Data Literacy in Healthcare

Healthcare professionals use data to improve patient outcomes, streamline hospital operations, and track treatment effectiveness. Data literacy enables healthcare providers to make evidence-based decisions and respond proactively to patient needs.

Tips for Applying Data Literacy in Healthcare

- **Monitor Patient Outcomes**: Use data on patient recovery rates, readmission statistics, and treatment effectiveness to adjust care protocols and improve outcomes.
- **Optimize Resource Allocation**: Analyze data on hospital occupancy, staffing levels, and equipment usage to optimize resource allocation and reduce wait times.
- **Conduct Predictive Analysis**: Use patient data to predict health outcomes and identify

at-risk patients. Predictive modeling can help in early intervention and preventive care planning.

Example

A hospital administrator might use data to track patient wait times in the emergency department. By analyzing peak times and average waiting durations, they can adjust staffing schedules to ensure adequate support during busy periods, improving patient satisfaction and reducing congestion.

3. Data Literacy in Marketing

Marketing professionals rely heavily on data to understand customer behavior, track campaign performance, and optimize advertising strategies. Data literacy allows marketers to make targeted decisions and improve ROI on campaigns by identifying which strategies work best.

Tips for Applying Data Literacy in Marketing

- **Track Campaign Performance Metrics**: Use tools like Google Analytics to track metrics such as click-through rates, conversions, and customer engagement. Regular analysis helps refine targeting and improve future campaigns.
- **Conduct A/B Testing**: Use data-driven experiments to test different ad creatives,

email headlines, or landing page designs. A/B testing allows you to determine which version performs better based on actual user behavior.

- **Segment Audiences for Personalized Campaigns**: Segment your customer base by demographics, purchasing history, or engagement level to create targeted campaigns. Audience segmentation enables marketers to tailor messages and improve relevance.

Example

A digital marketing team might analyze conversion data to find that certain demographics respond better to specific messaging. By segmenting their audience and personalizing content, they can increase engagement and optimize advertising spend for a better return on investment.

4. Data Literacy in Finance and Accounting

In finance, data literacy enables professionals to analyze financial health, detect fraud, and forecast future performance. Data-driven insights are crucial for managing risk, identifying growth opportunities, and ensuring regulatory compliance.

Tips for Applying Data Literacy in Finance

- **Analyze Financial Ratios**: Use financial ratios like profit margin, return on assets, and debt-to-equity ratio to assess company health and make comparisons with industry benchmarks.

- **Implement Risk Analysis Models**: Use statistical analysis to evaluate risk and model potential scenarios. For example, calculating Value at Risk (VaR) helps assess the probability of a financial loss.
- **Forecast with Historical Data**: Use historical data to project future performance, budget requirements, and cash flow. Forecasting enables proactive planning and investment decisions based on reliable trends.

Example

A financial analyst might use trend analysis on historical revenue data to predict next quarter's revenue. By identifying seasonal fluctuations, the analyst can create a more accurate forecast and inform strategic decisions, such as adjusting budget allocations for marketing during peak periods.

5. Data Literacy in Human Resources

HR departments use data to manage workforce performance, improve employee retention, and optimize recruitment strategies. Data literacy empowers HR professionals to make informed, people-centered decisions and improve organizational culture.

Tips for Applying Data Literacy in HR

- **Analyze Employee Turnover**: Use data on employee tenure, exit interviews, and department turnover rates to understand why employees leave and develop retention strategies.
- **Measure Employee Engagement**: Conduct and analyze employee engagement surveys to identify areas for improvement. Engagement data can reveal patterns related to job satisfaction, work-life balance, and organizational culture.
- **Optimize Recruitment Strategies**: Use data on time-to-hire, recruitment sources, and applicant demographics to improve hiring practices and reduce costs associated with employee turnover.

Example

An HR manager might analyze turnover data to find that a specific department has a higher-than-average turnover rate. After identifying potential causes, such as workload or lack of development opportunities, the manager can implement targeted retention strategies, such as training programs or work-life balance initiatives.

6. Data Literacy in Education

In education, data literacy helps educators improve student outcomes, track engagement, and make data-informed decisions about curriculum and teaching methods. Analyzing educational data supports student success and enhances learning experiences.

Tips for Applying Data Literacy in Education

- **Track Student Performance Metrics**: Analyze data on test scores, attendance, and engagement to identify areas where students may need additional support.
- **Conduct Curriculum Analysis**: Use feedback and performance data to evaluate curriculum effectiveness. Identifying which areas are challenging for students can inform curriculum adjustments.
- **Personalize Learning**: Use data on learning styles and progress to create personalized learning plans for students, improving their engagement and success rates.

Example

A teacher might analyze assessment data to identify topics where students consistently score lower. This data could suggest a need for additional resources, different teaching strategies, or one-on-one tutoring for students struggling with certain concepts.

7. Data Literacy in Supply Chain and Operations

In supply chain and operations, data literacy enables professionals to optimize inventory management, streamline logistics, and reduce costs. By analyzing data on production, transportation, and inventory, companies can improve efficiency and meet customer demands effectively.

Tips for Applying Data Literacy in Supply Chain

- **Monitor Inventory Levels**: Use data to track inventory turnover rates, reorder points, and demand patterns. Data-driven inventory management reduces costs associated with overstocking or stockouts.
- **Optimize Logistics**: Analyze transportation data to identify cost-saving opportunities, such as route optimization, fuel usage, and carrier performance.
- **Forecast Demand**: Use historical sales data to forecast demand accurately. Demand forecasting allows for better production planning and inventory control.

Example

An operations manager might analyze seasonal sales data to identify peak periods and adjust inventory accordingly. By aligning inventory with anticipated demand, the company can avoid stockouts during high-demand periods and minimize excess inventory in off-peak seasons.

8. Data Literacy in Product Development

Product development teams use data to understand customer needs, assess product performance, and guide innovation. Data literacy in this field supports product design, testing, and continuous improvement based on real-world usage patterns and feedback.

Tips for Applying Data Literacy in Product Development

- **Analyze User Feedback**: Collect and analyze customer feedback data to identify common issues and areas for improvement.
- **Conduct Usage Analysis**: Track user behavior data to understand how customers interact with a product, which features are most popular, and which are underutilized.
- **Perform A/B Testing**: Use data-driven experiments to test different product features or designs. A/B testing allows you to assess which options perform best with users.

Example

A product manager might analyze usage data to find that a specific feature is not being used as expected. This insight could lead to redesigning the feature or providing user education to enhance its usability and encourage adoption.

Key Takeaways

Data literacy is a versatile skill that enhances decision-making, problem-solving, and strategy in every field. By leveraging data effectively, professionals can drive improvements, anticipate challenges, and create value for their organizations. Key takeaways include:

- **Business and Management**: Use data to drive strategy, optimize resources, and understand customer behavior.
- **Healthcare**: Apply data to improve patient outcomes, optimize resource allocation, and plan preventive care.
- **Marketing**: Use data insights to refine targeting, personalize campaigns, and track campaign success.
- **Finance**: Conduct risk analysis, assess financial health, and forecast trends using data.
- **Human Resources**: Use data to analyze turnover, measure engagement, and improve recruitment.
- **Education**: Track student performance and personalize learning to improve educational outcomes.
- **Supply Chain and Operations**: Optimize inventory, streamline logistics, and accurately forecast demand.
- **Product Development**: Analyze user feedback and conduct testing to enhance product features and usability.

Data literacy empowers you to unlock insights and make informed decisions, no matter your field. By applying these tips, you'll be able to leverage data more effectively in your career, enhance your professional impact, and contribute to data-driven success in your organization.

Conclusion and Resources

Summary of Key Takeaways

As you reach the end of this journey into data literacy, it's worth reflecting on the key insights and skills you've gained. Mastering data literacy opens doors to new opportunities, enhances your decision-making, and allows you to drive positive changes in your field. Here's a summary of the core takeaways from each section:

1. **Understanding Data Basics**: Learning foundational concepts—such as the differences between data, information, and knowledge—forms the building blocks of data literacy. Knowing how to distinguish between data types (qualitative vs. quantitative, structured vs. unstructured) helps you work more effectively with various datasets.

2. **Data Collection and Cleaning**: Data cleaning is an essential step that ensures data accuracy and reliability. Removing duplicates, handling missing values, and standardizing formats prepares your data for meaningful analysis, making it easier to derive reliable insights.

3. **Data Analysis Techniques**: From calculating averages to visualizing trends, understanding data analysis techniques enables you to interpret data accurately. Exploring patterns, identifying correlations, and analyzing trends

are all vital skills that provide actionable insights.

4. **Data Visualization**: Visualizing data through charts and graphs allows you to communicate findings clearly. Selecting the right chart type, organizing information logically, and emphasizing key insights make your data accessible and impactful.

5. **Using Data for Decision-Making**: Applying data insights to real-life scenarios, from business to healthcare, empowers you to make informed decisions. By interpreting data in context and understanding its implications, you can drive better outcomes.

6. **Pathways to Advanced Skills**: Developing skills in databases, programming, and advanced statistics enables you to work with complex datasets, automate processes, and perform sophisticated analyses. Expanding your technical knowledge broadens your data capabilities and prepares you for more advanced challenges.

7. **Staying Updated and Lifelong Learning**: Data literacy is an evolving field, making continuous learning essential. By staying informed about industry trends, joining data communities, and setting learning goals, you ensure that your skills remain current and relevant.

8. **Applying Data Literacy Across Careers**: Data literacy enhances your impact in any

field, from business and healthcare to education and marketing. By applying data skills strategically, you can solve real-world problems, optimize performance, and contribute to data-driven decision-making in your career.

By mastering these fundamentals, you've gained a comprehensive toolkit to tackle data challenges confidently. Whether you're analyzing customer behavior, predicting financial trends, or personalizing learning experiences, data literacy equips you with the insights needed to make a meaningful impact.

Resources for Continued Learning

Data literacy is a lifelong journey, and there are numerous resources available to help you continue growing your skills. Here are some recommended resources for expanding your knowledge, keeping up with trends, and practicing hands-on data analysis:

1. **Online Learning Platforms**
   - **Coursera**: Offers courses from top universities on data science, machine learning, data analysis, and more.
   - **Udacity**: Known for its nanodegree programs, which offer comprehensive training in data analysis, machine learning, and artificial intelligence.

- o **DataCamp**: Provides interactive courses focused on Python, R, SQL, and data visualization.
- o **edX**: Partnered with universities and institutions to offer data science courses on a wide range of topics.

2. **Certification Programs**
   - o **Google Data Analytics Professional Certificate**: A beginner-friendly program covering data analysis fundamentals.
   - o **IBM Data Science Professional Certificate**: An in-depth program that includes Python, SQL, and data visualization.
   - o **Microsoft Certified: Data Analyst Associate**: Focused on Power BI and data visualization.
   - o **Certified Analytics Professional (CAP)**: A recognized certification for advanced analytics professionals.

3. **Books for Deeper Learning**
   - o *Storytelling with Data* by Cole Nussbaumer Knaflic: A guide to effective data visualization and data-driven storytelling.
   - o *Python for Data Analysis* by Wes McKinney: An essential guide for using Python, Pandas, and NumPy for data analysis.

- *The Art of Statistics* by David Spiegelhalter: A beginner-friendly introduction to statistical concepts and their applications.
- *Data Science for Business* by Foster Provost and Tom Fawcett: A book that explains data science concepts in the context of real-world business applications.

4. **Data Science Communities and Forums**
   - **Kaggle**: A platform that provides datasets, competitions, and a community of data science enthusiasts.
   - **Reddit**: Subreddits like r/datascience, r/learnpython, and r/statistics offer discussions, resources, and support for data professionals.
   - **LinkedIn Groups**: Groups like Data Science Central and Big Data & Analytics foster networking and knowledge sharing.
   - **Stack Overflow**: A valuable resource for troubleshooting coding issues, especially for Python, SQL, and R users.

5. **Practice Datasets and Project Ideas**
   - **Kaggle Datasets**: Thousands of datasets on diverse topics, from healthcare to finance, ideal for practice and projects.

- UCI Machine Learning Repository:
  A well-known source of datasets for
  machine learning research and
  practice.
- Google Dataset Search: A search
  engine that finds datasets across the
  web.
- Data.gov: A source of public
  government datasets on economics,
  health, environment, and more.

6. Professional Networking and Learning
   Events
   - Meetup.com: Search for local data
     science meetups and webinars to
     connect with other data professionals.
   - Conferences: Conferences like Strata
     Data, Data Science Summit, and KDD
     (Knowledge Discovery in Data) offer
     learning and networking opportunities.
   - Workshops and Hackathons:
     Participate in hackathons, like those
     hosted by Kaggle and DataHack, to
     apply your skills to real-world
     problems and compete with peers.

By engaging with these resources, you'll continue to
expand your data skills, stay updated with industry
changes, and connect with a network of data
professionals who can support your learning journey.

Encouragement and Call to Action

You've taken an important step toward data literacy by working through this book and acquiring the foundational skills necessary to read, interpret, and apply data in meaningful ways. Whether you're using data to make strategic decisions, optimize processes, or simply understand the world better, data literacy has empowered you with a new lens for thinking critically, questioning assumptions, and making evidence-based decisions.

As you move forward, remember that data literacy is a journey—one where there is always more to learn, new tools to explore, and deeper insights to uncover. Embrace a mindset of curiosity and growth. The more you practice and apply your skills, the more confident you will become in using data to solve complex problems and make a positive impact.

Here's how you can continue this journey:

1. **Stay Curious**: Ask questions, seek answers in data, and challenge yourself to go deeper. Curiosity is the driving force behind innovation and discovery.
2. **Practice Regularly**: Data skills are like any other skill—the more you use them, the stronger they become. Seek out opportunities to analyze new datasets, try different tools, and tackle real-world problems.
3. **Share Your Insights**: Communicating your findings with others reinforces your learning and adds value to your work. Share your

insights with your team, present your analyses confidently, and be open to feedback.

4. **Network and Collaborate**: Engage with the data community to exchange knowledge, find inspiration, and stay motivated. Collaboration with others will expose you to diverse perspectives and broaden your understanding of data applications.

The demand for data-literate professionals is growing in every industry, and by continuing to build your skills, you'll be well-prepared to thrive in a data-driven world. Your journey in data literacy not only enhances your career but also enables you to make a meaningful impact in your field.

Remember, the possibilities with data are limitless—your journey has just begun. Embrace the power of data literacy, and keep exploring, questioning, and growing. The future belongs to those who can turn data into insights, and now you are equipped to be part of that future.

References

1. **Anderson, C. (2015).** *Creating a Data-Driven Organization: Practical Advice from the Trenches.* O'Reilly Media.
   - This book offers practical strategies for building a data-driven culture within organizations, with real-world advice on implementing data literacy and driving analytics adoption.

2. **Camm, J. D., Cochran, J. J., Fry, M. J., & Ohlmann, J. W. (2020).** *Business Analytics.* Cengage Learning.
   - This comprehensive textbook covers foundational concepts in data analytics, including descriptive, predictive, and prescriptive analytics. It's widely used in business analytics courses and provides examples that are relevant across industries.

3. **Chen, C. C., Hardle, W. K., & Unwin, A. (2007).** *Handbook of Data Visualization.* Springer.
   - This handbook provides a thorough exploration of data visualization techniques and best practices, offering both theoretical and practical insights into visualizing complex datasets effectively.

4. **Few, S. (2012).** *Show Me the Numbers: Designing Tables and Graphs to Enlighten.* Analytics Press.

   o This book focuses on effective data visualization design, helping readers understand how to create clear and impactful visuals to support data interpretation and communication.

5. **Han, J., Pei, J., & Kamber, M. (2011).** *Data Mining: Concepts and Techniques.* Morgan Kaufmann.

   o An in-depth guide to data mining techniques, covering foundational and advanced concepts in extracting meaningful patterns from data. This text is especially useful for readers interested in the technical aspects of data analysis.

6. **Knaflic, C. N. (2015).** *Storytelling with Data: A Data Visualization Guide for Business Professionals.* Wiley.

   o Knaflic's book is a highly accessible guide to data visualization and storytelling, providing practical tips for creating visuals that effectively communicate insights to non-technical audiences.

7. **McKinney, W. (2017).** *Python for Data Analysis: Data Wrangling with Pandas, NumPy, and IPython.* O'Reilly Media.

- This book by the creator of the Pandas library offers a detailed introduction to data manipulation and analysis in Python, making it ideal for readers interested in using Python for data literacy.

8. **Provost, F., & Fawcett, T. (2013).** *Data Science for Business: What You Need to Know About Data Mining and Data-Analytic Thinking.* O'Reilly Media.
   - A foundational text that connects data science principles to business applications. It covers data-driven decision-making and is accessible for those new to data science.

9. **Siegel, E. (2013).** *Predictive Analytics: The Power to Predict Who Will Click, Buy, Lie, or Die.* Wiley.
   - Siegel's book explains predictive analytics in an engaging way, demonstrating the impact of predictive modeling across various industries and offering case studies on real-world applications.

10. **Spiegelhalter, D. (2019).** *The Art of Statistics: How to Learn from Data.* Basic Books.
    - Spiegelhalter's book is an approachable introduction to statistical thinking, helping readers develop the

foundational skills needed for interpreting data insights accurately.

11. **Tufte, E. R. (2001).** *The Visual Display of Quantitative Information.* Graphics Press.

    o A classic text on data visualization principles, Tufte's book provides guidance on creating clear and impactful data visuals, emphasizing design that enhances understanding without adding unnecessary complexity.

12. **Valli, C. (2021).** *Machine Learning with Python Cookbook: Practical Solutions from Preprocessing to Deep Learning.* O'Reilly Media.

    o This resource provides practical solutions and code snippets for data manipulation, feature engineering, and machine learning in Python, suitable for readers looking to build hands-on skills.

13. **Wickham, H., & Grolemund, G. (2016).** *R for Data Science: Import, Tidy, Transform, Visualize, and Model Data.* O'Reilly Media.

    o This book introduces readers to data science in R, focusing on the "tidyverse" approach to data analysis. It's an essential reference for those interested in data literacy through R programming.

14. **Yau, N. (2013).** *Data Points: Visualization That Means Something.* Wiley.

    o Yau's book explores the storytelling aspect of data visualization, with emphasis on creating visuals that reveal insights in meaningful ways. It covers the technical and creative sides of data storytelling.

15. **Zikmund, W. G., Babin, B. J., Carr, J. C., & Griffin, M. (2012).** *Business Research Methods.* South-Western College Publishing.

    o This textbook covers research methods and data collection techniques, offering insights into both qualitative and quantitative data analysis, which are applicable across fields.

16. **Khan Academy** *(n.d.).* Statistics and Probability. https://www.khanacademy.org

    o Khan Academy's free online courses on statistics and probability provide accessible resources for learning foundational concepts in data analysis and statistical reasoning.

17. **DataCamp** *(n.d.).* Data Science and Data Analysis Courses. https://www.datacamp.com

    o DataCamp offers interactive courses covering data analysis, programming, and machine learning, with hands-on projects and exercises that reinforce data literacy skills.

18. **Kaggle Datasets and Competitions** *(n.d.).*
    https://www.kaggle.com
    - o Kaggle provides a vast library of datasets and hosts data science competitions, making it a valuable platform for practice and learning with real-world data.

19. **Google Data Analytics Professional Certificate** *(2021)*. Coursera.
    https://www.coursera.org/professional-certificates/google-data-analytics
    - o This program, designed by Google, covers foundational data skills, including data cleaning, analysis, and visualization, making it ideal for those seeking a structured introduction to data literacy.

About the author

Dr. Alex Harper is a data scientist, educator, and industry consultant with over 15 years of experience in data analytics, data-driven decision-making, and business intelligence. With a Ph.D. in Information Systems from the University of California, Berkeley, Dr. Harper has held key roles in technology and finance, where they specialized in turning complex datasets into actionable insights that drive growth and innovation.

Throughout their career, Dr. Harper has been passionate about making data accessible to all, regardless of technical background. They have taught data analytics courses at several universities, mentored aspiring data professionals, and spoken at global conferences on topics ranging from data visualization to predictive modeling. Dr. Harper is known for their ability to demystify data concepts, making them relatable and practical for individuals in diverse fields.

Dr. Harper believes that data literacy is a skill everyone can master, and their latest book, *Data Literacy Essentials: From Basics to Practical Applications*, empowers readers to harness data in meaningful ways, no matter their profession. When not working with data, Dr. Harper enjoys hiking, traveling, and exploring culinary arts.

Disclaimer

The information presented in *Essential Data Analytics Quick-Start Guide to Data Literacy for Beginners* is for educational purposes only. While every effort has been made to ensure the accuracy and completeness of the information contained within this book, the author and publisher make no representations or warranties of any kind and assume no liability for any errors or omissions. The data concepts, techniques, and examples provided are intended as general guides and may not be suitable for all situations or applications.

This book does not constitute professional advice, and readers should seek the guidance of qualified professionals regarding any specific data analysis, business, or legal matters. The author and publisher disclaim any liability, personal or professional, for loss or risk incurred as a consequence, directly or indirectly, of the use or application of any of the contents in this book.

All product names, logos, and brands mentioned in this book are property of their respective owners.

Copyright and Legal Notice

Essential Data Analytics Quick-Start Guide to Data Literacy for Beginners

Book 2

Intermediate

Data Analytic Skills

*Databases, Programming, and
Advanced Statistics*

Dr. Alex Harper

Chapter 1: The Foundation of Intermediate Data Analytics

Why Intermediate Data Analytics Skills Matter

In the digital age, data is often referred to as the "new oil." But like oil, data in its raw form is not inherently valuable. It must be refined, processed, and analyzed to unlock insights that can drive better decisions. Intermediate data analytics skills bridge the gap between simple data observation and in-depth data-driven decision-making, equipping analysts to extract actionable insights from complex datasets. Let's explore how intermediate data analytics is transforming decision-making across some of the world's largest and most influential industries: healthcare, finance, and marketing.

1. Healthcare: Data Analytics for Precision Medicine and Operational Efficiency

Healthcare organizations generate enormous volumes of data every day, from patient records to clinical trial data and insurance claims. With intermediate data analytics skills, analysts can process this data to find trends that save lives, reduce costs, and improve patient outcomes.

Predictive Diagnostics: Intermediate analytics can help predict the likelihood of a disease by analyzing historical patient data and recognizing early signs of conditions. For instance, using regression analysis and machine learning algorithms, healthcare providers can identify patients at risk for chronic illnesses like diabetes or heart disease, enabling early intervention.

Optimizing Patient Care and Resource Allocation: By analyzing patterns in patient admissions and discharge data, hospitals can better allocate resources, predict peak times for specific departments, and streamline their staff scheduling to meet demand. Advanced data manipulation and statistical modeling help analysts interpret patient flow trends, ultimately improving efficiency and reducing waiting times.

Drug Development and Personalized Medicine: With vast amounts of genomic and clinical data, data analytics is helping to shape the field of precision medicine, tailoring treatments to individual patients. Clustering and classification techniques, applied at an intermediate level, are used to categorize patient data into meaningful groups, aiding in personalized treatment plans that align with each patient's unique medical profile.

2. Finance: Data Analytics for Risk Management and Fraud Detection

Finance is one of the most data-driven industries, where risk management, fraud prevention, and investment decision-making are heavily reliant on data insights. Intermediate data analytics plays a crucial role in ensuring the financial industry operates securely and profitably.

Risk Assessment and Management: Banks and financial institutions use intermediate-level analytics to evaluate the risk profiles of clients and potential investments. By employing logistic regression and other classification methods, analysts can assess which loans are likely to default or identify investments with a high risk of loss. This level of analytics provides insights that protect financial institutions from risky ventures.

Fraud Detection: Financial fraud detection is a priority across the industry, especially in the age of digital transactions. Data analysts use clustering and pattern recognition techniques to flag suspicious transactions, with advanced algorithms identifying anomalies that deviate from a customer's normal spending behavior. This proactive approach to fraud detection, which builds on foundational analytics, helps secure customer funds and maintain trust.

Portfolio Optimization and Market Analysis: Intermediate data analytics skills allow financial analysts to optimize investment portfolios by identifying trends and using predictive modeling. Time series analysis is particularly valuable for examining stock price trends and making informed predictions about market shifts. These insights support financial advisors and investors in making informed, data-backed decisions for wealth growth.

3. Marketing: Data Analytics for Customer Insights and Campaign Effectiveness

Marketing in the digital era is highly data-centric, with a focus on understanding customer behavior and optimizing campaign outcomes. Intermediate data analytics skills empower marketers to create targeted, impactful strategies based on deep insights.

Customer Segmentation and Personalization: Through clustering and advanced segmentation, marketers can divide their audience into distinct groups based on shared behaviors, demographics, or purchasing patterns. This enables personalized marketing that resonates more deeply with customers, increasing engagement and conversion rates. Intermediate skills allow analysts to run complex segmentation algorithms and identify meaningful patterns in large datasets, such as transaction history or website interaction data.

Campaign Performance Tracking and Optimization: Measuring the effectiveness of marketing campaigns is essential for budget allocation and strategy refinement. By applying intermediate-level statistical tests (e.g., A/B testing) and time series analysis, marketers can identify which aspects of a campaign are driving results and optimize their strategies accordingly. With these insights, companies can continually refine campaigns for maximum ROI.

Sentiment Analysis and Brand Reputation Management: In today's online landscape, customers often express their opinions about brands on social media and review platforms. Intermediate analytics enables sentiment analysis, a technique that uses text analysis and machine learning algorithms to gauge the public's perception of a brand. By identifying positive, negative, or neutral sentiment patterns, marketers can quickly adapt their strategies to protect or improve brand reputation.

Skill Advancement Pathway: How Databases, Programming, and Advanced Statistics Work Together

The journey from basic to intermediate data analytics involves mastering a set of complementary skills that transform data from mere numbers into meaningful insights. While beginner-level analytics often focuses on descriptive statistics and simple spreadsheet tools, intermediate analytics requires a deeper understanding of data management, programming for data manipulation, and statistical techniques for analyzing and interpreting complex datasets. By developing intermediate skills in databases, programming, and advanced statistics, analysts can bridge the gap between raw data and actionable insights, allowing for more impactful, real-world decision-making.

1. Databases: Efficiently Storing, Organizing, and Retrieving Data

Databases are essential for handling large volumes of data. As analysts move beyond basic analytics, they need to interact with databases to access and manage datasets too large or complex for typical spreadsheet software.

- **Understanding and Utilizing Relational Databases:** At an intermediate level, analysts must go beyond importing files and instead work with relational databases like SQL to store, retrieve, and organize data. Relational databases store information in structured tables, allowing for organized and efficient access to datasets through queries. Intermediate skills in SQL (Structured Query Language) enable analysts to perform complex data retrieval operations, such as joining tables and filtering datasets based on specific criteria.

- **Data Cleaning and Preprocessing in SQL:** Databases also support essential data-cleaning steps. Analysts learn to use SQL to preprocess data directly in the database by removing duplicates, handling missing values, and standardizing formats. This preprocessing stage ensures that data is ready for more advanced analysis, saving time and resources by minimizing the need for post-extraction cleaning.
- **Data Organization for Analysis:** With intermediate knowledge of databases, analysts can create views, indexes, and structured queries that organize data effectively. This preparation step is crucial, as it allows analysts to quickly access and pull data relevant to their analysis, making their work more efficient and reducing processing time.

2. Programming: Transforming and Manipulating Data

Programming skills, especially in languages like Python and R, allow analysts to go beyond what's possible in standard spreadsheet tools. Programming is key to handling large datasets, automating repetitive tasks, and performing complex data transformations.

- **Data Wrangling and Transformation with Python/R:** Intermediate programming skills enable analysts to use libraries such as Pandas in Python or dplyr in R to manipulate data. They can clean data by removing outliers, handling missing values, and performing transformations like normalizing and encoding categorical variables. This step is essential for preparing data for statistical analysis, making it more reliable and accurate.

- **Creating Reusable Code for Efficiency:** Programming also allows analysts to automate workflows by writing reusable code. For example, if an analyst is performing the same data cleaning steps for different datasets, they can create functions to apply these steps consistently, reducing the time and potential for error. Intermediate programming skills empower analysts to write these functions and scripts, streamlining their workflow and making complex analyses more manageable.

- **Combining Data from Multiple Sources:** Programming also enables analysts to integrate data from multiple sources, including databases, APIs, and flat files, into one cohesive dataset. This skill is especially valuable in intermediate analytics, where analysts often need to pull data from various sources, transform it, and merge it into a single file for analysis.

3. Advanced Statistics: Generating Deeper Insights from Data

Advanced statistical techniques allow analysts to move beyond descriptive analytics and make more sophisticated inferences and predictions based on the data. These skills are essential for tackling more complex questions, such as predicting future outcomes or identifying relationships within the data.

- **Regression and Predictive Modeling:** Intermediate statistics often begin with regression analysis, a powerful tool for understanding relationships between variables and predicting future outcomes. Linear and logistic regression are particularly useful for business contexts, where analysts can model relationships, like customer behavior or sales trends, and make predictions that inform decision-making. By mastering regression, analysts can add predictive power to their analyses, providing insights that go beyond what happened in the past.
- **Hypothesis Testing and Statistical Inference:** Intermediate analysts also learn to apply hypothesis testing and confidence intervals to test ideas and make data-driven conclusions. This skill is crucial for decision-making, as it allows analysts to validate assumptions and

quantify the likelihood of observed effects. With these techniques, analysts can assess the significance of their findings, leading to more confident, data-supported recommendations.

- **Clustering and Segmentation:** Clustering methods, such as k-means and hierarchical clustering, are valuable for identifying patterns and segmenting data into meaningful groups. In marketing, for example, clustering can help identify customer segments based on purchasing behavior, which can then inform targeted marketing strategies. This type of advanced statistical analysis allows analysts to uncover patterns in the data that aren't immediately apparent, revealing insights that can guide strategic decisions.

Integrating Databases, Programming, and Statistics: A Cohesive Analytical Workflow

The real power of intermediate data analytics lies in the ability to combine these three skill sets into a cohesive analytical workflow. Here's how they come together:

1. **Data Retrieval and Preparation (Databases):** Analysts start by accessing and cleaning data from databases,

ensuring that it's well-structured and ready for analysis.

2. **Data Transformation and Analysis (Programming):** Next, they use programming languages to transform and manipulate the data, creating new variables, standardizing values, and preparing datasets for analysis. This step also allows them to automate repetitive tasks and work with data that may come from multiple sources.

3. **Insight Generation (Advanced Statistics):** Finally, they apply statistical techniques to generate insights, such as predicting trends, testing hypotheses, or segmenting the data into meaningful groups. By using advanced statistical methods, analysts can move beyond surface-level insights to provide deeper, data-driven recommendations.

In combining these skills, analysts transition from simple data observations to an in-depth analytical approach that adds substantial value to their organizations. Intermediate data analytics skills equip professionals to make informed decisions that drive positive business outcomes, proving the value of their analytical expertise.

Databases as the Heart of Data Storage and Retrieval

Understanding Relational Databases: The Backbone of Data Storage

In the world of data analytics, storing and managing data efficiently is fundamental to obtaining accurate, actionable insights. Relational databases, such as those managed with SQL (Structured Query Language), provide the structure and flexibility needed to handle large volumes of complex data. Unlike flat files or spreadsheets, relational databases organize data into related tables, allowing for streamlined data retrieval and ensuring consistency across datasets. Mastering relational databases is essential for intermediate-level data analysts, as it enables them to work with data in ways that are both scalable and efficient.

The Structure of Relational Databases: Tables, Rows, and Columns

At the core of relational databases is the concept of tables. A relational database organizes data into tables (also called relations), where each table represents a specific type of entity (such as customers, products, or transactions) and contains rows and columns.

- **Tables as Data Entities:** Each table in a relational database is structured to represent a single entity type, such as "Customers," "Orders," or "Products." By organizing data into tables, databases enable analysts to efficiently store and retrieve information without redundancy. For example, in a retail database, the "Customers" table might include columns for customer ID, name, and contact information, while an "Orders" table could track individual purchases.
- **Rows and Columns for Structured Data Storage:** Rows represent individual records within a table (e.g., a single customer or transaction), while columns represent the attributes or fields associated with each record (e.g., customer name, date of purchase). By defining clear columns for each attribute, relational databases ensure that data is consistently structured, reducing the chance of errors and making it easier to analyze.
- **Primary and Foreign Keys:** Relational databases use unique identifiers called primary keys to differentiate records within a table. In addition, foreign keys link related records across tables, forming relationships between them. For example, in a customer-order database, the "CustomerID" in the "Orders" table may serve as a foreign key that connects each

order to a specific customer in the "Customers" table. These keys are essential for creating meaningful relationships between tables, allowing data to be connected and referenced efficiently.

The Importance of SQL in Data Management

SQL (Structured Query Language) is the standard language used for managing relational databases. SQL allows analysts to create, read, update, and delete data within a database, which is commonly referred to as CRUD operations. Intermediate SQL skills empower analysts to perform complex data retrievals, transformations, and analyses directly within the database environment.

- **Data Retrieval and Filtering:** One of SQL's most powerful features is its ability to retrieve data quickly and filter results based on specific criteria. Using SQL's SELECT statement, analysts can query specific columns and apply filters (using WHERE clauses) to retrieve only the data they need. For example, an analyst could use SQL to find all transactions over $1,000 within a specific date range, providing valuable insights without needing to process entire tables.

- **Data Aggregation and Summarization:** SQL's aggregation functions (e.g., SUM, AVG, COUNT) enable analysts to perform calculations directly within the database. For example, by grouping transactions by customer ID and using SUM, an analyst can quickly calculate each customer's total spending. This ability to summarize data within the database is highly efficient, especially for large datasets, as it reduces the amount of data that needs to be transferred for further analysis.

- **Complex Joins for Multi-Table Analysis:** Relational databases excel at handling complex data relationships through joins, which allow data to be combined from multiple tables. SQL join operations (INNER JOIN, LEFT JOIN, RIGHT JOIN, FULL OUTER JOIN) enable analysts to pull related information across tables, making it possible to analyze interconnected datasets. For example, an INNER JOIN between the "Customers" and "Orders" tables allows analysts to connect each customer with their corresponding orders, providing a complete view of customer behavior.

Benefits of Relational Databases for Intermediate Data Analytics

Relational databases offer a structured, flexible, and scalable solution for managing data, making them invaluable for intermediate data analytics. Here's how they contribute to data analysis:

1. **Consistency and Data Integrity:** By organizing data into structured tables, relational databases ensure that data remains consistent across records. Relationships between tables are enforced through constraints (such as foreign keys), preventing issues like duplicate records or orphaned entries. This consistency is essential for data accuracy, as errors in data integrity can lead to flawed analyses and poor decision-making.

2. **Efficient Data Retrieval and Processing:** SQL allows analysts to query only the data they need, reducing processing time and minimizing memory usage. For instance, rather than loading an entire dataset into a program like Python or R, analysts can use SQL to filter and retrieve only relevant data, making analysis faster and more manageable.

3. **Scalability for Large Datasets:** Relational databases are designed to handle large volumes of data. As companies generate more data, relational databases provide the scalability needed to store and retrieve information without compromising performance. This

scalability is crucial for intermediate analysts, who often work with larger datasets that would be unwieldy in traditional spreadsheets.

4. **Security and Access Control:** Many relational databases offer built-in security features, allowing administrators to control access and permissions for different users. This is important for maintaining data privacy and security, especially when handling sensitive information, such as customer data or financial records. Intermediate analysts benefit from this control as it ensures that data remains secure while allowing authorized access for analysis.

Relational Databases in Practice: An Example

To illustrate the role of relational databases in data analysis, consider a company that uses a relational database to track sales, customers, and inventory. This company might have separate tables for "Customers," "Orders," "OrderDetails," and "Products."

- **Step 1: Organizing Data into Tables:** Each table is structured with relevant columns. The "Orders" table contains information on each purchase, while the "OrderDetails" table lists individual items for each order. This structure ensures that data is organized and accessible.

- **Step 2: Joining Tables for Analysis:** To analyze customer purchasing behavior, an analyst can use SQL to perform a join between the "Customers," "Orders," and "OrderDetails" tables. This join would connect each customer to their orders and items within each order, enabling a complete view of purchasing patterns.

- **Step 3: Applying Filters and Aggregations:** Using SQL's filtering and aggregation features, the analyst can identify high-value customers, calculate total spending by customer, and determine the most popular products. By using SQL directly in the relational database, the analyst can obtain insights without needing to transfer large amounts of data to another tool.

Conclusion: The Role of Relational Databases in Intermediate Data Analytics

Relational databases are at the core of effective data storage and retrieval in intermediate data analytics. With a solid understanding of SQL and relational database structures, analysts can access, organize, and analyze complex data more efficiently, providing valuable insights that drive better business decisions. Mastering databases enables intermediate analysts to manage large datasets, work with interconnected data, and build a foundation for more advanced analytics skills.

Advanced SQL Queries for Intermediate Users

As you advance in data analytics, mastering SQL becomes essential, especially as your data grows larger and more complex. Advanced SQL skills enable you to move beyond simple SELECT queries and harness powerful techniques like joins, subqueries, and window functions. These features allow you to analyze relationships, retrieve insights from multiple tables, and work with grouped data in ways that transform raw data into actionable information. In this section, we'll explore some advanced SQL techniques, with practical examples and an explanation of how each is used in real-world data analysis.

Joins: Connecting Data Across Tables

In many databases, data is split across multiple tables. For example, a sales database might have one table for customer information and another for orders. To analyze a customer's purchasing behavior, you'll need to connect these tables to see which customers made which purchases. This is where joins come in.

There are several types of joins, but we'll focus on two common ones: INNER JOIN and LEFT JOIN.

INNER JOIN: Viewing Only Matching Records

Imagine you want to see only those customers who have placed an order. That's where an INNER JOIN comes in handy. By joining the "Customers" and "Orders" tables, SQL returns only the customers who have a corresponding order record in both tables. For example, when you join the two tables on the CustomerID, SQL connects matching records, allowing you to view customer names along with their order dates. INNER JOINs are especially helpful for cases where you only need data that exists in both tables, such as details of customers who actually made purchases.

LEFT JOIN: Including All Records from One Table

A LEFT JOIN, on the other hand, retrieves all records from the left table, regardless of whether there's a match in the right table. So, if you want a complete list of customers, including those who haven't made any purchases, LEFT JOIN is the tool you need. It pulls all customers into the results and fills in missing order details with NULL values for those who haven't placed any orders. This can be incredibly useful when identifying customers who haven't engaged recently, offering valuable insights for marketing campaigns.

Subqueries: Embedding Queries Within Queries

Subqueries, or "nested queries," are queries placed inside another SQL query. These are powerful tools for scenarios where you need to calculate something separately, then use it within a larger query. Subqueries let you handle complex data requirements in steps.

For example, imagine you want to identify customers who have spent more than the average amount. First, you calculate the average total spent, then pull only those customers who have spent more than this amount. In this case, a subquery calculates the average spending across all customers, while the outer query retrieves only those who exceed this average. Subqueries are particularly effective for comparisons, letting you retrieve values based on conditions you calculate on the fly.

Correlated Subqueries offer another layer of flexibility. Unlike standard subqueries, correlated subqueries reference columns from the outer query. They're useful when the inner query depends on values from the outer query to execute. For example, to find customers who have made an order over $500, the subquery references the CustomerID from the outer "Customers" query, allowing it to match criteria across related tables seamlessly.

Window Functions: Analyzing Data Across Rows

Window functions are SQL tools that allow you to perform calculations across a set of rows related to the current row, known as the "window." They're especially useful for tasks like ranking, running totals, and calculating moving averages. Unlike aggregate functions that collapse rows, window functions retain all rows and simply add calculations alongside them.

For instance, **ROW_NUMBER()** lets you assign a sequence number to each row. Imagine you have a sales table and want to rank each sale based on the highest order total. ROW_NUMBER() helps by creating a sequence for each row, ranking sales from highest to lowest. This function is especially useful for ordered lists or leaderboards.

When you need to rank but want to handle ties, **RANK()** and **DENSE_RANK()** are helpful alternatives. They assign the same rank to tied values but differ in handling the sequence gaps created by ties. If two orders have the same total, both will receive the same rank, but the next rank will skip a number. These functions are essential when you want to maintain relative positions, even with duplicate values.

Finally, for cumulative calculations like running totals, **SUM() OVER()** is an invaluable tool. Let's say you want to calculate a running total of sales over time. SUM() OVER() allows you to do this directly within your query, tracking total sales progression row by row.

This query produces a cumulative total for each order, showing the ongoing sum of sales by date. Running totals are often used in financial and sales data to track growth over time, and window functions make it easy to calculate these within SQL.

Applying Advanced SQL Techniques in Real-World Analysis

Advanced SQL queries are foundational tools for intermediate analysts, offering the flexibility to connect data across tables, filter results based on complex conditions, and generate calculations that reveal deeper insights. Here's a quick summary of how these advanced SQL techniques can be used:

1. **Joins** let you combine tables, bringing together related information that's stored separately for efficiency and organization.
2. **Subqueries** allow you to create conditions and comparisons that use values generated within the query, ideal for layered data requirements.
3. **Window functions** enable powerful row-by-row calculations that preserve the data's structure, allowing for rankings, cumulative totals, and more detailed analyses.

By mastering these SQL techniques, you're equipping yourself with the tools to analyze complex data structures, make faster data-driven decisions, and add significant value to your data analytics projects. These advanced queries bring efficiency, depth, and flexibility to your analysis, helping you tackle real-world data challenges with confidence.

Programming for Data Manipulation and Analysis

Python and R in Data Analysis: Versatile Tools for Data Manipulation and Insights

As you transition to intermediate data analytics, programming skills become invaluable for handling complex datasets and performing advanced analyses. Two programming languages dominate the data analytics landscape: Python and R. Both are versatile, powerful, and widely used, but each has its unique strengths that make it suited to different types of data tasks. Understanding the roles of Python and R in data analysis will help you choose the right tool for the job and maximize your analytical capabilities.

Python: A Multi-Purpose Language for Data Manipulation, Automation, and Machine Learning

Python is a general-purpose programming language that has gained immense popularity in data science and analytics due to its flexibility, readability, and extensive library support. It's a go-to choice for many data analysts because it can handle everything from data manipulation and statistical analysis to automation and machine learning. Let's explore some key reasons Python is an essential tool for data analytics:

1. **Data Manipulation with Pandas and NumPy:** Python's Pandas and NumPy libraries are foundational tools for data manipulation. Pandas offers a DataFrame structure, similar to a spreadsheet, that allows analysts to load, manipulate, and clean data with ease. This includes handling missing values, filtering data, merging tables, and applying complex transformations. NumPy, on the other

hand, is optimized for numerical calculations, providing the speed and efficiency needed for handling large datasets.

- o *Example:* If you have a dataset with missing values and need to fill those gaps based on specific criteria, Pandas allows you to quickly fill or replace values. For instance, you can use df.fillna() to replace missing data in a DataFrame.

2. **Automation and Workflow Efficiency:** Python's versatility allows you to automate repetitive tasks, streamlining your data workflow. By writing functions and scripts, analysts can automate data collection, data cleaning, and even report generation. This reduces manual effort and minimizes errors, especially when working with large, recurring datasets.

- o *Example:* You could write a Python script that connects to a database, extracts data, cleans it, performs analysis, and then exports the results, all in a single automated process. This is particularly useful for tasks that need to be repeated regularly, like weekly sales reporting.

3. **Machine Learning and Predictive Analytics:** Python is also highly regarded

for machine learning due to libraries like Scikit-Learn, TensorFlow, and PyTorch. For intermediate-level analysts, Scikit-Learn offers accessible tools for building basic predictive models, such as regression and classification, without needing extensive knowledge of machine learning. These models can provide valuable insights into trends, forecasts, and customer behavior.

- o *Example:* With Scikit-Learn, you can build a simple linear regression model to predict sales based on historical data, using only a few lines of code. Python's ecosystem allows you to quickly move from data manipulation to model building, all within the same environment.

4. **Visualization with Matplotlib and Seaborn:** Visualization is a critical component of data analysis, as it allows analysts to communicate findings effectively. Python's Matplotlib and Seaborn libraries offer a wide range of chart types, from basic line charts and bar plots to complex heatmaps and distribution plots, helping analysts to represent data visually.

- o *Example:* You might use Seaborn's sns.heatmap() to create a heatmap of correlation between variables, making it easier to spot relationships and patterns in your data.

In summary, Python is a powerful tool for data analysis because it combines flexibility, ease of use, and a comprehensive set of libraries. It's particularly useful for data manipulation, automation, machine learning, and visualization, making it a go-to language for analysts aiming to handle diverse tasks within one environment.

R: A Statistical Powerhouse for Data Analysis and Visualization

R is a language developed specifically for statistical analysis and data visualization, making it an excellent choice for analysts focused on data-driven insights, statistical modeling, and data exploration. While Python is more versatile across a range of applications, R excels in statistical analysis and is often preferred by statisticians and researchers. Here's how R supports intermediate-level data analysis:

1. **Data Wrangling with dplyr and tidyr:** R's dplyr and tidyr packages simplify data manipulation, allowing analysts to filter, arrange, group, and summarize data efficiently. Dplyr's syntax is straightforward and highly readable, using verbs like filter(), mutate(), and

summarize() to make data transformations easy to understand and implement. Tidyr complements dplyr by helping to clean and reshape data into a tidy format, essential for structured analysis.

- o *Example:* Using dplyr's group_by() and summarize() functions, you can quickly calculate average sales per region, making it easy to analyze grouped data.

2. **Advanced Statistical Analysis:** R was designed with statistics in mind, making it a natural choice for analysts focused on in-depth statistical modeling. Whether it's regression, hypothesis testing, or time series analysis, R has built-in functions and packages like stats, MASS, and forecast that make complex statistical tasks straightforward. R's statistical capabilities make it easier to perform advanced analyses, test hypotheses, and validate results with statistical rigor.

- o *Example:* R's lm() function allows you to run linear regression with just a line of code, making it quick and efficient for intermediate users to analyze relationships between variables.

3. **Data Visualization with ggplot2:** ggplot2 is one of the most powerful and flexible data visualization packages

available, allowing analysts to create high-quality, publication-ready visualizations. It's based on the grammar of graphics, which provides a structured approach to creating visualizations by layering components like axes, scales, and geometries.

- ○ *Example:* With ggplot2, you can create complex visualizations like layered line charts and customized scatter plots. Using just a few lines of code, ggplot2 lets you produce visualizations that are both visually appealing and informative, enhancing your ability to communicate findings.

4. **Handling Big Data with R:** While R is often associated with smaller datasets, it has packages like data.table and specialized libraries (such as bigmemory) for handling larger datasets. These packages allow R to process larger data efficiently, although Python is typically faster for extremely large datasets. However, with data.table, you can work on larger datasets in R with greater efficiency, leveraging its advanced functionality for filtering and aggregating data.

5. **Interactive Data Exploration with Shiny:** Shiny is a unique feature of R that allows you to create interactive web applications and dashboards. This is

particularly valuable for analysts who want to make their findings interactive and accessible to stakeholders. With Shiny, you can create web-based interfaces where users can explore data, adjust parameters, and view real-time results.

- *Example:* You could create a Shiny dashboard that allows managers to explore sales data across different regions and time frames, providing a user-friendly interface that helps decision-makers interact with the data directly.

In summary, R is an exceptional tool for statistical analysis, advanced data visualization, and interactive data exploration. Its built-in statistical functions and visualization capabilities make it ideal for tasks that require deep statistical analysis and graphical representation.

Python vs. R: Choosing the Right Tool for the Job

When to use Python or R often depends on the specific requirements of your analysis:

- **Choose Python** when you need a versatile tool that supports a range of tasks, from data manipulation and automation to machine learning. Python's extensive libraries and flexible syntax make it ideal for analysts who want an all-in-one solution that scales from data preparation to model deployment.

- **Choose R** when your work involves in-depth statistical analysis, high-quality visualizations, or interactive data presentations. R's specialized statistical functions and visualization packages make it perfect for research-heavy environments and data-driven reporting.

For many intermediate analysts, learning both languages can be highly beneficial. While each has its strengths, Python and R can complement each other, allowing you to choose the best tool for each task and maximize your efficiency in data analytics.

By understanding the roles of Python and R, you can select the most effective tool for each analytical task, improving both the quality and speed of your data analysis. Both languages are invaluable assets, each offering unique features that enhance the way you handle, analyze, and visualize data. As you continue to develop your programming skills, you'll be equipped to tackle increasingly complex data challenges and provide deeper insights to your organization.

Key Libraries and Functions for Intermediate Data Manipulation

To perform data analysis effectively, it's essential to be familiar with specialized libraries that simplify data manipulation, transformation, and visualization. Python and R offer powerful libraries designed specifically for handling and analyzing data, each providing a wide array of functions that reduce the amount of code you need to write and increase the efficiency of your workflow. In this section, we'll explore some key intermediate libraries—Pandas and NumPy for Python, and dplyr and ggplot2 for R—and provide some power-user tips to make the most of these tools.

Python Libraries: Pandas and NumPy

Python's Pandas and NumPy libraries are foundational tools in data analytics, enabling intermediate analysts to manipulate and analyze data with precision and efficiency.

Pandas: The Data Manipulation Powerhouse

Pandas provides the DataFrame structure, a two-dimensional, table-like data structure that makes it easy to manipulate, clean, and analyze data. Here are some key functions and power-user tips for getting the most out of Pandas.

Filtering and Selecting Data with loc and iloc

To start, let's talk about two powerful methods in Pandas: loc and iloc. These methods help you quickly filter and select data from a DataFrame, which is essential for working with large datasets. loc is label-based, so you can use it to select rows and columns by their names, while iloc is position-based, helping you access data by its position in the DataFrame. This flexibility is valuable when you need specific rows or columns based on certain criteria. For example, if you want to select rows where a customer's age is over 30, you can use loc to do just that. It's a simple and efficient way to filter data based on conditions without needing complex syntax.

Chaining Methods for Cleaner Code

One of Pandas' strengths is the ability to chain methods together, letting you perform multiple actions in a single, streamlined line. This approach makes your code cleaner and more efficient, which is a huge help when working with data. For instance, instead of breaking up operations, you could filter, sort, and reset the index of a DataFrame all in one line. By chaining these operations, you keep your code concise and readable, which is especially useful for anyone maintaining or reading your code later.

Using GroupBy for Aggregated Analysis

The groupby function in Pandas is an incredibly powerful tool. It lets you group data by specific columns and perform aggregations like sum, mean, and count. This is particularly useful for summarizing data by category. Say you want to find the average purchase amount per customer; groupby makes this easy, providing insights into customer spending behavior by creating a summary of their average purchases.

Pivot Tables for Multi-Dimensional Analysis

Pivot tables in Pandas work similarly to those in Excel, giving you the ability to summarize data in a multi-dimensional format. They're perfect for creating cross-tabulations and quickly analyzing large datasets. Imagine you want to see the total sales for each product across different regions. A pivot table organizes this data in a clear, comparative format, making it easy to understand regional sales performance at a glance.

NumPy: High-Performance Numerical Computation

Now let's dive into NumPy, a library that complements Pandas with high-performance array operations, ideal for handling large-scale numerical data.

Creating and Manipulating Arrays

NumPy's array function creates arrays that are faster and more memory-efficient than Python lists. For example, creating a two-dimensional array gives you a compact, structured way to store and manipulate data, which is especially useful for large datasets.

Applying Vectorized Operations

One of the best features of NumPy is vectorization, which lets you perform operations on entire arrays without writing loops. For instance, if you need to multiply each element in an array by 2, you can simply multiply the entire array. This speeds up computation significantly, especially with larger datasets.

Statistical Analysis with NumPy

NumPy also provides a range of functions for statistical analysis, such as mean, median, standard deviation, and sum. These functions are perfect for quick, on-the-fly statistical summaries, saving you time and effort when you need to get a general sense of your data.

R Libraries: dplyr and ggplot2

R's dplyr and ggplot2 libraries offer a powerful toolkit for data manipulation and visualization, making them valuable for intermediate-level analytics work.

dplyr: Data Wrangling Made Simple

With dplyr, you have access to functions like filter, select, and arrange, which allow you to manipulate data in a readable, almost English-like syntax. For example, filtering rows where sales are above a certain threshold, or selecting only specific columns, becomes straightforward and intuitive.

Summarizing Data with Group By

Combining group_by and summarize lets you perform quick aggregations, which is great for calculating statistics across different categories. For instance, you can group your data by region and calculate average sales, giving you a summary of regional performance with just a few lines of code.

Transforming Data with Mutate

The mutate function allows you to create new columns or modify existing ones on the fly. This is perfect for adding calculated fields, like showing a 10% discount on prices, directly in your DataFrame. It's incredibly useful in financial and sales analysis, where creating derived metrics is a common requirement.

ggplot2: Advanced Data Visualization

The ggplot2 library, built on the grammar of graphics, is highly flexible and lets you create publication-quality visualizations. Starting with ggplot to define your data and aesthetics, you can then add layers like geom_point for scatter plots or geom_bar for bar charts, giving you control over your visualizations.

Faceting for Multi-Panel Plots

Faceting allows you to split your data into multiple panels, making it easy to compare subsets within the same chart. For example, creating separate plots for each region helps you visually compare trends across categories, which is incredibly useful for exploratory data analysis.

Customizing Visuals with Themes and Colors

With ggplot2, you have extensive customization options to make your visuals truly stand out. This includes applying themes, colors, and custom labels. By adding theme() and scale_* functions, you can adjust the look and feel of your charts to better fit your style or presentation needs. For example, using a minimal theme and adding color by region makes your charts cleaner and more visually appealing. It's a straightforward way to give your graphics a polished look while making the data easier to interpret.

Summary of Key Libraries and Power-User Tips

For intermediate data analysts, mastering libraries in both Python and R can significantly boost productivity and depth in analysis:

- **Python's Pandas and NumPy:** These libraries are ideal for data manipulation, numerical analysis, and data cleaning.
    - Use **method chaining** in Pandas for more concise and readable code.
    - Take advantage of **vectorized operations** in NumPy for quicker calculations across large datasets.
- **R's dplyr and ggplot2:** These are perfect for streamlined data wrangling and sophisticated visualizations.
    - Apply **group_by** and **summarize** in dplyr for efficient aggregation and category-level insights.
    - Use **ggplot2** to create layered, customizable charts that enhance the clarity and impact of your data storytelling.

With these tools, Python and R provide a powerful combination for efficient, insightful analysis and compelling visual communication.

By incorporating these libraries into your workflow, you'll streamline data analysis tasks, reduce code complexity, and create more effective visualizations. These libraries empower intermediate analysts to handle larger datasets and conduct more sophisticated analyses, adding significant value to their data analytics toolkit.

Hands-On Example: Extracting and Manipulating Data Using SQL and Python/R

In this hands-on exercise, you'll learn how to extract data from a SQL database and then manipulate it in Python or R. By combining these two powerful tools, you'll gain a deeper understanding of how databases and programming work together to create a seamless, efficient data analysis process.

Imagine you're an analyst at an e-commerce company. You want to analyze customer purchasing behavior to identify high-value customers and uncover trends in product purchases. The data you need is stored in a SQL database, but analyzing it directly in SQL is challenging. Instead, you'll pull the data into Python or R, clean and transform it, and generate insights that can drive marketing and sales decisions.

Step 1: Extract Data from SQL Database

First, we need to connect to the SQL database and extract the data. Let's assume you have two tables in your SQL database:

1. **Customers**: Contains customer information (CustomerID, Name, Email, Country)
2. **Orders**: Contains order details (OrderID, CustomerID, OrderDate, TotalAmount)

We want to retrieve customer information along with their total spending across all orders, focusing on those who have spent more than $500.

SQL Query for Data Extraction

To begin, let's take a look at our SQL query. This query joins the Customers and Orders tables, calculates the total spending for each customer, and filters for those who spent more than $500. It first joins the two tables by CustomerID, groups the data by customer details like ID, Name, Email, and Country, then sums up the total amount each customer spent. Finally, it filters out only those customers whose total spending exceeds $500. This approach gives us a focused dataset for further analysis.

Step 2: Connect to the Database in Python or R

Now that we have our query, the next step is to connect to the database and pull the data into Python or R, where we can load it into a DataFrame for analysis.

In **Python**, you can connect using the sqlite3 or SQLAlchemy libraries. With SQLAlchemy, establish a connection, execute the query, and load the result into a DataFrame. This makes it easy to work with the data directly in Python.

In **R**, use the DBI and RSQLite packages to connect to the database and run the query. After loading the results into a DataFrame, disconnect from the database. Now, you have a DataFrame called customer_data containing each customer's total spending, ready for manipulation.

Step 3: Data Manipulation in Python or R

With our data in place, let's start transforming it. We'll use Python's Pandas or R's dplyr package to classify customers into spending tiers, calculate summary statistics, and even create some visualizations.

Data Manipulation in Python with Pandas

1. **Classify Customers by Spending Tier**
   Using a simple function, we can assign customers into three spending tiers based on their total spending. For instance, customers

spending over $1,000 might be classified as "High," over $750 as "Medium," and below that as "Low." By applying this function, we create a new column in the DataFrame labeled SpendingTier.

2. **Calculate Summary Statistics**
Next, group the data by spending tier to calculate the average, total, and count of spending within each tier. This summary provides a quick overview of customer behavior across different spending levels.

3. **Visualize Spending by Tier**
Finally, we can visualize the total spending by tier with a bar plot. Using Matplotlib, plot each spending tier along with its total spending, labeling the axes for clarity. This visualization makes it easy to see how spending compares across tiers.

Data Manipulation in R with dplyr

1. **Classify Customers by Spending Tier**
In R, the mutate() and case_when() functions allow us to create a new column for spending tiers. As in Python, we define thresholds for "High," "Medium," and "Low" tiers and apply them across the dataset.

2. **Calculate Summary Statistics**
Use group_by() and summarize() to calculate average spending, total

spending, and customer count by tier. This step provides the same summary statistics in a clean, easy-to-read format.

3. **Visualize Spending by Tier**
   For visualization, ggplot2 makes it easy to create a bar plot. Map the spending tiers to the x-axis and the total spending to the y-axis, and label the plot for clarity. This visual summary of spending by tier is a quick way to communicate customer behavior trends.

By following these steps, you'll have a clear, detailed breakdown of customer spending and behavior, and you'll be able to present these insights visually, making it easy to communicate your findings.

Step 4: Interpret and Analyze the Results

Now, let's analyze our results and see how combining SQL with Python or R enhances our insights:

- **Spending Tiers**: By categorizing customers into spending tiers, we gain a clearer picture of customer value segments, which is useful for targeted marketing. For example, "High" spending customers might be VIPs, while "Medium" spenders could be targeted for loyalty programs.

- **Summary Statistics**: The summary table provides insights into average and total spending for each tier, helping us understand the revenue contribution of each customer group.
- **Visualization**: The bar plot allows us to visually compare the spending across tiers, which is especially useful for sharing insights with stakeholders.

Conclusion: Combining SQL and Programming for Efficient Data Analysis

This example demonstrates how to extract data from a SQL database, manipulate it using Python or R, and visualize the results. Combining SQL and programming languages allows you to take advantage of SQL's power for data extraction and aggregation, along with Python or R's flexibility for data manipulation and visualization. This integrated workflow streamlines your analysis and provides a comprehensive approach to uncovering actionable insights.

By mastering these techniques, you can efficiently handle large datasets, perform sophisticated data transformations, and create impactful visualizations—all essential skills for intermediate-level data analytics.

Advanced Statistical Techniques for Insightful Analysis

Introduction to Key Techniques: Regression, Clustering, and Time Series Analysis

As you progress into intermediate data analytics, statistical techniques become essential tools for uncovering deeper insights and making data-driven predictions. This section introduces three foundational statistical methods—regression, clustering, and time series analysis—that are widely used across industries to understand patterns, segment data, and forecast future trends. Each of these techniques has unique applications and can provide powerful insights when applied appropriately.

1. Regression Analysis: Understanding Relationships and Making Predictions

Regression analysis is a statistical technique used to identify the relationship between one or more independent variables (predictors) and a dependent variable (outcome). It's particularly valuable for predictive modeling, as it allows analysts to understand how changes in predictor variables impact the outcome, helping in forecasting and decision-making.

Types of Regression

- **Linear Regression**: Linear regression is the simplest form of regression analysis, where the relationship between the independent variable(s) and the dependent variable is assumed to be linear. This method is widely used in business and economics for predictive analysis, such as forecasting sales or predicting housing prices based on factors like location and square footage.
- **Multiple Linear Regression**: Multiple linear regression is an extension of linear regression that involves multiple independent variables. For example, in predicting a house's price, factors like square footage, neighborhood, and age of the house can all be considered simultaneously. Multiple regression helps capture the impact of several predictors on the dependent variable, providing a more comprehensive model.
- **Logistic Regression**: Logistic regression is used when the dependent variable is binary or categorical, such as predicting whether a customer will churn (yes/no) based on their behavior. Logistic regression is commonly used in marketing and healthcare to predict outcomes where the response variable has two categories.

Practical Applications of Regression

- **Business Forecasting**: Regression is frequently used to forecast demand, sales, and revenue. For example, a company might use historical sales data to predict future sales based on factors such as seasonality, marketing spending, and economic indicators.
- **Healthcare Predictions**: In healthcare, regression models can help predict patient outcomes, such as the likelihood of readmission based on patient characteristics and medical history. This allows healthcare providers to allocate resources more efficiently.
- **Financial Risk Assessment**: Regression is also used in finance to assess risk, such as estimating credit risk based on income, debt, and credit history. This allows banks to make data-driven lending decisions.

Regression analysis provides a structured approach to understanding relationships within data and making informed predictions. By applying regression models, analysts can uncover trends, test hypotheses, and create predictive models that inform decision-making.

2. Clustering: Identifying Patterns and Segmentation

Clustering is an unsupervised learning technique that groups data into clusters, or segments, based on similarities among data points. Unlike regression, clustering doesn't predict an outcome but instead identifies natural groupings within the data. Clustering is highly valuable in exploratory data analysis, as it helps uncover hidden patterns, segment customers, and identify subgroups within a dataset.

Types of Clustering

- **K-Means Clustering**: K-means is one of the most popular clustering algorithms. It partitions data into K clusters based on the proximity of data points to cluster centroids. Analysts can define the number of clusters (K), and the algorithm assigns each data point to the nearest cluster. K-means is often used in customer segmentation and market research.
- **Hierarchical Clustering**: Hierarchical clustering builds a tree-like structure of clusters, where each data point is initially a single cluster, and similar clusters are merged iteratively. This method doesn't require specifying the number of clusters beforehand and is useful for exploring data hierarchies. Hierarchical clustering is used in fields like genomics to classify genetic data into meaningful categories.

- **DBSCAN (Density-Based Spatial Clustering of Applications with Noise)**: DBSCAN groups data points based on density, identifying clusters of various shapes and sizes. Unlike K-means, DBSCAN can identify outliers, which makes it suitable for datasets with noise or irregular patterns. It's commonly used in anomaly detection and geospatial analysis.

Practical Applications of Clustering

- **Customer Segmentation**: Clustering is widely used in marketing to segment customers based on purchasing behavior, demographics, and engagement. For example, customers can be grouped into segments like "high-value," "occasional," and "new" customers, allowing for targeted marketing strategies.
- **Image and Document Classification**: Clustering techniques are also used in machine learning for image and document classification. For instance, clustering can help organize large image databases by grouping similar images or classifying documents based on topics.
- **Fraud Detection**: In finance, clustering can help detect unusual behavior that may indicate fraud. By clustering transaction data, banks can identify outliers or unusual patterns that deviate from typical

customer behavior, flagging potential cases of fraud.

Clustering techniques provide a powerful way to explore data, identify patterns, and create targeted strategies based on natural groupings within the data. By segmenting data, analysts can gain insights that are not immediately apparent and create more personalized and effective strategies.

3. Time Series Analysis: Tracking Trends and Forecasting Over Time

Time series analysis is a statistical method used to analyze data points collected or recorded at specific time intervals. It's particularly valuable for identifying trends, seasonal patterns, and forecasting future values based on historical data. Time series analysis is widely used in fields that rely on trend data over time, such as economics, finance, and meteorology.

Key Components of Time Series Analysis

- **Trend**: A trend represents the long-term movement in a time series, showing the general direction of the data over time. For instance, sales data may exhibit an upward trend as a business grows.
- **Seasonality**: Seasonality refers to repeating patterns in the data at regular

intervals, such as quarterly sales spikes in retail or increased electricity usage in winter. Identifying seasonal patterns is critical for understanding cyclic behaviors in data.

- **Cyclic Patterns**: Cyclic patterns are fluctuations that occur over a longer period than seasonality, often due to economic or business cycles. Unlike seasonality, cyclic patterns do not have a fixed frequency.
- **Noise**: Noise represents random fluctuations in the data that don't follow any specific pattern. Removing noise is essential for creating accurate forecasts.

Types of Time Series Models

- **Moving Average (MA)**: Moving average models smooth out short-term fluctuations by averaging values over a specific time window. This is useful for identifying trends and seasonality without the influence of noise.
- **Autoregressive Integrated Moving Average (ARIMA)**: ARIMA models are commonly used for forecasting time series data. ARIMA combines autoregressive (AR) and moving average (MA) components and is particularly effective for data with trends or seasonal patterns.

- **Seasonal Decomposition of Time Series (STL)**: STL is used to separate a time series into seasonal, trend, and residual components. This decomposition helps identify the underlying patterns and cyclical behaviors in data, making it easier to forecast accurately.

Practical Applications of Time Series Analysis

- **Sales Forecasting**: Time series analysis is frequently used in retail to forecast demand and sales. By identifying trends and seasonal patterns, companies can optimize inventory and marketing strategies to align with anticipated demand.
- **Financial Market Analysis**: In finance, time series models are used to analyze stock prices, interest rates, and exchange rates over time. Time series analysis helps investors understand market trends, volatility, and economic cycles, aiding in investment decisions.
- **Weather and Environmental Forecasting**: Meteorologists use time series models to predict weather patterns, such as temperature and rainfall, based on historical data. These models also apply to environmental monitoring, such as tracking pollution levels over time.

Time series analysis enables analysts to gain insights into trends, patterns, and forecasts, allowing for data-driven decision-making that anticipates future events. This technique is invaluable for industries that depend on timely, accurate forecasts.

Conclusion: The Power of Advanced Statistical Techniques

Regression, clustering, and time series analysis are key techniques that elevate your ability to derive insights from data. By applying regression, you can understand relationships and make predictions. With clustering, you can identify natural groupings and segments, allowing for targeted actions based on patterns. Time series analysis lets you forecast trends, helping organizations prepare for future demand and changes. Together, these statistical methods form a powerful toolkit for intermediate data analysts, enabling you to analyze data in-depth and make impactful, data-driven decisions.

Choosing the Right Method: A Decision-Making Guide for Statistical Analysis

With a variety of statistical techniques available, choosing the right method for data analysis can be challenging. Each technique has specific strengths, requirements, and applications. To help you make informed decisions, this guide provides a structured approach for selecting the most appropriate method based on the nature of your data, the relationships you want to explore, and the outcomes you aim to predict.

This guide focuses on three main types of analysis techniques: regression, clustering, and time series analysis. We'll cover how to decide which method to use, when it's best suited, and what types of data each technique requires.

Step 1: Define Your Data Type and Analysis Goal

The first step in choosing the right statistical technique is to understand the type of data you have and the goal of your analysis. Answering the following questions can clarify your path:

1. **Is the data continuous or categorical?**
   - Continuous data includes variables that can take on a range of values, such as income, temperature, and age.
   - Categorical data includes variables that fall into distinct groups, such as gender, region, or product category.
2. **Do you want to understand relationships, make predictions, or segment the data?**

- o **Understand relationships**: If your goal is to understand how one variable influences another, regression might be the right choice.
- o **Make predictions**: If you aim to predict future outcomes based on historical data, regression and time series analysis are common choices.
- o **Segment the data**: If you want to group similar data points or create distinct segments, clustering is likely the best approach.

Once you've clarified your data type and analysis goal, you can proceed to select the most suitable technique.

Step 2: Determine When to Use Regression Analysis

Regression is appropriate when your primary goal is to understand relationships between variables or predict the value of a target variable based on one or more predictors.

Best Suited For:

- • **Continuous Outcome Variables**: Regression is ideal when the outcome you're trying to predict is continuous, like sales revenue, temperature, or customer spending.

- **Explaining Relationships**: Use regression when you want to quantify the relationship between predictor and outcome variables. For example, you may want to understand how marketing spend affects sales or how age impacts income levels.

Common Applications of Regression Analysis

- **Linear Regression**: Use linear regression if you're analyzing a single predictor variable with a linear relationship to the outcome, like predicting house prices based on square footage.
- **Multiple Linear Regression**: Choose multiple linear regression when you have multiple predictors. For instance, predicting a product's sales could consider factors such as advertising budget, season, and competitor pricing.
- **Logistic Regression**: Opt for logistic regression if your outcome variable is binary (e.g., yes/no or 0/1), such as predicting customer churn or email response likelihood.

Example Decision Scenarios

- **Sales Prediction**: If you want to predict next month's sales based on factors like past sales, advertising spend, and economic indicators, multiple linear regression is a good choice.
- **Customer Churn**: If you're predicting whether a customer will churn based on account activity and demographics, logistic regression is ideal due to the binary outcome.

Use regression analysis when your goal is to make predictions or understand linear relationships, especially when your outcome variable is continuous or binary.

Step 3: Decide If Clustering is Appropriate for Your Needs

Clustering is a type of unsupervised learning that's ideal when you want to segment data into groups without predefined categories. Clustering does not have a dependent variable; instead, it looks for patterns or similarities within the data.

Best Suited For:

- **Exploratory Data Analysis**: Clustering is highly effective for exploring data and discovering hidden patterns, such as grouping customers by purchasing behavior.

- **Segmentation Without Predefined Labels**: Use clustering when you want to categorize data points (e.g., customers, products, or transactions) into groups based on similarity, especially when you don't have predefined labels.

Common Applications of Clustering

- **K-Means Clustering**: Use K-means when you know the approximate number of clusters you want, such as customer segments in marketing.
- **Hierarchical Clustering**: Choose hierarchical clustering if you want a tree-like structure to visualize relationships, which can help you identify sub-clusters within larger groups.
- **DBSCAN**: Select DBSCAN for data with irregular cluster shapes or significant noise, as it can identify clusters of various densities.

Example Decision Scenarios

- **Customer Segmentation**: If your goal is to segment customers based on purchasing behavior, K-means clustering can group them into categories like "high spenders" or "infrequent buyers."
- **Anomaly Detection**: If you want to identify unusual transactions, DBSCAN

can help by separating common patterns from anomalies.

Use clustering when your analysis involves grouping data points without a dependent variable, especially when you need to explore and identify patterns in the data.

Step 4: Choose Time Series Analysis for Temporal Data

Time series analysis is designed for data that is collected over time. It's ideal for analyzing trends, seasonality, and cyclic patterns in data that changes at regular intervals, such as daily, monthly, or annually.

Best Suited For:

- **Forecasting Future Values**: Use time series analysis if your primary goal is to forecast future trends based on past data.
- **Analyzing Patterns Over Time**: Time series analysis is effective for identifying patterns, such as trends (long-term movement), seasonality (regular fluctuations), and cycles (longer, irregular patterns).

Common Applications of Time Series Analysis

- **Moving Averages**: Use moving averages to smooth out short-term fluctuations and reveal underlying trends in time series data.
- **ARIMA (Autoregressive Integrated Moving Average)**: Choose ARIMA when you need a comprehensive model for forecasting that can handle both trend and seasonality.
- **Exponential Smoothing**: Use exponential smoothing for data with a strong trend or seasonal component, especially when recent observations are more relevant to the forecast.

Example Decision Scenarios

- **Sales Forecasting**: If you want to predict future sales based on historical data, such as monthly sales figures, ARIMA or exponential smoothing is ideal.
- **Weather Forecasting**: If your data includes daily or monthly temperature readings, time series analysis can help identify seasonal trends and forecast future temperatures.

Use time series analysis when your data includes a time component and you need to analyze trends, seasonal patterns, or cycles over time.

Final Decision Guide: Putting It All Together

If your primary goal is prediction or understanding relationships between variables, use regression.

If you need to explore patterns or segment data without predefined categories, clustering is your best choice.

If your data is time-based and you need to analyze trends or make future projections, go with time series analysis.

By following this decision-making guide, you'll be able to choose the statistical method that best fits your data and analysis goals. Each technique offers unique insights and can drive impactful data-driven decisions when applied to the right type of data. As you continue to master these techniques, you'll gain the flexibility to select the optimal approach for any data analysis challenge, enhancing the depth and quality of your insights.

Case Study: Analyzing Customer Churn in a Subscription-Based Business

In this case study, we'll explore a mini-project focused on understanding customer churn in a subscription-based business. Customer churn— the rate at which customers stop using a service— is a critical metric for businesses with recurring revenue models. High churn can negatively impact revenue, so identifying the factors contributing to churn can help a company take proactive steps to retain customers.

The goal of this project is to:

1. Retrieve customer and subscription data from a SQL database.
2. Process and clean the data in Python or R.
3. Use logistic regression to model churn and identify key factors associated with customers leaving the service.

Step 1: Retrieve Data from a SQL Database

The database contains two tables:

- **Customers**: Information about each customer, including CustomerID, SignupDate, Country, Age, and Gender.
- **Subscriptions**: Information about each subscription, including SubscriptionID, CustomerID, SubscriptionDate, Churned (Yes/No), and MonthlySpend.

Our goal is to retrieve data that allows us to explore customer demographics and subscription details to identify churn patterns.

SQL Query to Extract Data

We'll start by joining the **Customers** and **Subscriptions** tables on the CustomerID, filtering for customers who have had at least six months of subscription history. This helps us avoid including new customers who might not have been with the service long enough to decide if they want to stay or leave.

SQL Query for Data Extraction

Let's start by constructing our SQL query to bring together customer demographics and subscription details. Here, we join the Customers and Subscriptions tables on CustomerID to combine these insights. Additionally, we use the DATEDIFF function to filter for customers who signed up at least six months ago. This query effectively prepares a dataset for further analysis by ensuring we only work with established customers.

Step 2: Load and Process the Data in Python or R

Once the query is ready, the next step is loading this data into either Python or R, where we can process it further.

In **Python**, we connect to the database using the SQLAlchemy library, run the SQL query, and load the results into a DataFrame. This makes the data readily accessible for cleaning and analysis.

In **R**, we use DBI and RSQLite to connect, execute the query, and load the results into a DataFrame. After finishing, we disconnect from the database. With our data now in a DataFrame called df, we're ready to start the cleaning and transformation process.

Step 3: Data Cleaning and Feature Engineering

Now that we have our dataset, it's time to clean and prepare it for analysis. Here's a breakdown of the main steps:

1. **Convert Date Columns**
   We convert the SignupDate and SubscriptionDate columns into datetime formats to make date-based calculations easier.
2. **Calculate Subscription Duration**
   Next, we calculate the number of months since each customer signed up, giving us

an idea of how long each has been with the service.

3. **Encode Categorical Variables**
Finally, we convert categorical variables like Country and Gender into numerical values, using one-hot encoding in Python or binary encoding in R. This step is essential for running predictive models effectively.

Data Cleaning and Feature Engineering in Python

In Python, we use Pandas to convert date columns, calculate subscription duration, and apply one-hot encoding to categorical variables. These transformations help make the dataset model-ready.

Data Cleaning and Feature Engineering in R

In R, we achieve the same results using lubridate for date transformations and dplyr for data manipulation. The mutate function helps us create new features, while one-hot encoding allows us to handle categorical data.

Step 4: Apply Logistic Regression to Model Churn

With our cleaned and transformed data, we're ready to apply logistic regression. This model is ideal for predicting binary outcomes, like whether a customer will churn (1) or stay (0).

Logistic Regression in Python

In Python, we use scikit-learn to split our data into training and testing sets, train a logistic regression model, and evaluate its performance. By defining features and the target variable, we can train the model on one part of the data and test its predictions on another. Metrics like accuracy and classification reports give insight into the model's effectiveness.

Logistic Regression in R

In R, we use caret to split the data, train a logistic regression model, and evaluate its predictions. After fitting the model, we use the predict function to generate predictions, setting a threshold to classify results. Finally, a confusion matrix provides an accuracy measure, helping us understand the model's predictive power.

Through these steps, we've taken raw data, prepared it for analysis, and used logistic regression to predict customer churn. This process not only aids in customer retention strategies but also demonstrates how SQL,

Python, and R can work together to turn data into actionable insights.

Step 5: Interpret and Analyze the Results

After running the logistic regression, you can analyze the output to understand which features significantly impact customer churn.

- **Feature Importance**: By examining the coefficients in the logistic regression model, you can identify the factors most associated with churn. For example, a higher SubscriptionDuration might indicate a reduced likelihood of churn, while customers with higher MonthlySpend may have a lower risk of leaving.
- **Model Accuracy**: Assess the model's accuracy to determine how well it predicts churn. You can use metrics like accuracy score, precision, recall, and F1-score to evaluate performance.
- **Recommendations**: Based on the insights, you might recommend targeted retention strategies. For instance, customers with shorter subscription durations might benefit from engagement campaigns, while those with lower monthly spending might respond to upsell opportunities.

Conclusion: Applying Advanced Statistical Techniques to Business Challenges

This case study demonstrates how to integrate SQL, Python or R, and logistic regression to analyze customer churn. By retrieving data from a database, processing it in a programming environment, and applying statistical modeling, you gain valuable insights into customer behavior that can directly inform business strategy. Through this hands-on project, you've learned how to leverage data analytics tools to solve real-world business problems—an essential skill set for any intermediate data analyst.

Integrating Skills for Real-World Data Analysis

Connecting Theory to Practice: Real-World Scenarios Requiring Databases, Programming, and Statistics

As data analytics evolves, so does the need for multifaceted skill sets that can address complex problems. In the real world, data analysts often work with massive datasets stored in databases, transform and analyze these data using programming, and apply statistical models to uncover insights that drive decision-making. This section explores real-world scenarios across various industries where the combined use of databases, programming, and statistics is essential for effective data analysis.

By understanding how these skills interact, you'll be better prepared to bridge the gap between theory and practice, turning your technical knowledge into actionable insights that can solve business challenges.

1. E-commerce: Customer Lifetime Value Analysis

In e-commerce, understanding customer lifetime value (CLV) is crucial for optimizing marketing spend, personalizing promotions, and forecasting revenue. Calculating CLV requires the integration of databases, programming, and statistical methods.

Step-by-Step Application

- **Databases**: CLV analysis begins with retrieving data on customer transactions, demographics, and purchase history from a database. This may involve joining multiple tables (such as customers, orders, and products) to get a comprehensive view of each customer's purchase behavior.
- **Programming**: After extracting data, programming languages like Python or R are used to clean, transform, and analyze the data. Using libraries such as Pandas in Python, analysts can calculate the total amount spent per customer, purchase frequency, and recency of purchases.

- **Statistics**: Finally, statistical techniques such as regression analysis or predictive modeling can forecast the CLV based on historical purchase behavior. For instance, logistic regression might be used to model the probability of repeat purchases, while a predictive model can estimate the future spending of each customer.

Real-World Impact

This integrated approach allows e-commerce businesses to predict which customers are likely to bring high value over time. With these insights, companies can create targeted marketing strategies, allocate resources efficiently, and enhance customer retention.

2. Healthcare: Predicting Patient Readmissions

In healthcare, hospitals and clinics strive to reduce patient readmissions, which can indicate issues with patient care quality and increase operational costs. Predicting patient readmissions requires combining data from electronic health records (EHR), programming skills to process this data, and statistical models to predict readmission risks.

Step-by-Step Application

- **Databases**: Patient data, including demographic information, medical history, treatment details, and previous admissions, is stored in EHR databases. SQL is typically used to retrieve relevant data, joining tables with patient records, admissions, and treatment codes.
- **Programming**: Python or R is used to preprocess the data. This might involve handling missing values, encoding categorical variables (e.g., treatment types), and calculating derived features (e.g., the time since the last admission). Libraries like Pandas in Python and dplyr in R make it easier to transform data into a format suitable for analysis.
- **Statistics**: Predictive models, such as logistic regression or machine learning classifiers, can help predict the likelihood of readmission based on historical data. These models may use variables like patient age, diagnosis, length of stay, and treatment plan to assess readmission risks.

Real-World Impact

By identifying patients at high risk of readmission, healthcare providers can take preventive measures, such as personalized follow-ups or improved discharge planning, to reduce readmission rates. This not only improves patient care but also reduces healthcare costs and enhances hospital efficiency.

3. Retail: Inventory Optimization and Demand Forecasting

Inventory optimization is a common challenge in retail, where businesses need to balance stock levels to meet demand without overstocking. Demand forecasting requires integrating databases (for sales data), programming (for data processing), and statistical methods (for trend and seasonality analysis).

Step-by-Step Application

- **Databases**: Inventory and sales data are typically stored in relational databases. Using SQL, analysts can retrieve historical sales data by product, location, and date. They might also pull data on seasonal promotions, discounts, and stock levels.
- **Programming**: Python or R is used to clean and prepare the data for forecasting. Data transformations might include calculating moving averages, smoothing fluctuations, and normalizing sales figures. Python libraries like Pandas and NumPy, or R packages like dplyr, make it easier to handle these operations.
- **Statistics**: Time series analysis, using methods such as ARIMA (Autoregressive

Integrated Moving Average) or exponential smoothing, can forecast future demand based on historical sales patterns. These models help identify trends and seasonality, which are crucial for optimizing inventory.

Real-World Impact

Accurate demand forecasting enables retailers to maintain optimal inventory levels, ensuring that popular items are available when needed while minimizing excess stock. This reduces storage costs, improves cash flow, and enhances customer satisfaction by preventing stockouts.

4. Finance: Credit Risk Assessment

In finance, credit risk assessment is vital for determining the likelihood that a borrower will default on a loan. Financial institutions rely on data-driven insights to make lending decisions, requiring the integration of databases, programming, and statistical modeling.

Step-by-Step Application

- **Databases**: Credit history, transaction data, and borrower demographics are stored in financial databases. SQL queries can be used to retrieve relevant data, such as income, employment history, credit score, and existing debt, from various tables.

- **Programming**: After extracting the data, Python or R is used to preprocess it. This might include handling missing values, transforming variables (e.g., normalizing income levels), and generating new features, such as debt-to-income ratio. Programming also allows for exploratory data analysis to better understand patterns in credit behavior.
- **Statistics**: Logistic regression or machine learning models, such as decision trees or random forests, are used to predict the probability of default. These models use multiple predictors—such as credit score, income, and past defaults—to estimate risk levels and assign a risk score to each borrower.

Real-World Impact

By accurately assessing credit risk, financial institutions can make more informed lending decisions, reduce the risk of loan defaults, and optimize interest rates. This ensures a healthier loan portfolio and minimizes financial losses.

5. Marketing: Campaign Performance Analysis and Customer Segmentation

Marketing teams often analyze campaign performance and segment customers to deliver personalized experiences. This analysis requires data from multiple sources, programming for data transformation, and statistical techniques for segmentation and performance measurement.

Step-by-Step Application

- **Databases**: Data on customer demographics, interactions, and purchases is stored in marketing databases. SQL is used to pull together relevant data from multiple tables, such as customer profiles, campaign touchpoints, and purchase history.
- **Programming**: Python or R is used to preprocess the data, which may include aggregating metrics (e.g., total purchases by customer) and calculating engagement scores (e.g., email opens or website visits). One-hot encoding can be applied to categorical variables like customer preferences.
- **Statistics**: Clustering techniques, such as K-means clustering, are used to segment customers based on characteristics like age, spending habits, and engagement. Additionally, A/B testing or statistical tests like chi-square tests can evaluate the effectiveness of different campaign strategies.

Real-World Impact

Customer segmentation allows marketers to create targeted campaigns, ensuring that messaging resonates with specific customer groups. Campaign performance analysis helps optimize future marketing spend, resulting in higher engagement, conversion rates, and customer satisfaction.

6. Public Health: Disease Outbreak Prediction and Control

In public health, predicting and managing disease outbreaks is essential to prevent the spread of infectious diseases. This requires analyzing data from health records, using programming for data processing, and applying statistical models to forecast trends and hotspots.

Step-by-Step Application

- **Databases**: Data on patient cases, demographics, and geographical locations is stored in health databases. SQL is used to extract relevant data on reported cases, including the time and location of each case, as well as demographic details.
- **Programming**: Python or R is used to clean the data, calculate the rate of new cases, and create derived features, such as population density in affected areas.

Spatial data processing can also be performed to link case data with geographical information.

- **Statistics**: Time series analysis or predictive models, such as logistic regression, can forecast future case counts and identify hotspots. These models may take into account seasonality and environmental factors (e.g., temperature or humidity) that influence disease spread.

Real-World Impact

Disease outbreak prediction helps public health officials allocate resources efficiently, inform the public, and implement control measures, such as vaccination campaigns or travel restrictions, to mitigate the spread of disease.

Conclusion: The Power of Integrating Databases, Programming, and Statistics

In each of these scenarios, the combined use of databases, programming, and statistics allows data analysts to tackle real-world challenges effectively. By integrating data retrieval (SQL), data transformation (Python or R), and statistical modeling, analysts can uncover actionable insights that directly impact decision-making.

As you continue to develop these skills, you'll be better prepared to handle complex data projects and drive meaningful results in various industries. This integration of skills empowers you to move beyond theory, applying data analytics to solve practical, impactful problems in the real world.

Practice Exercise: Customer Purchase Behavior Analysis

In this structured practice exercise, you will assume the role of a data analyst for an online retail company. Your task is to analyze customer purchasing behavior to help the marketing team understand spending patterns, identify high-value customers, and explore potential insights for targeted marketing. This exercise will guide you through retrieving data from a SQL database, cleaning and transforming it using Python or R, and presenting your findings in a professional report.

By the end of this exercise, you will have a synthesized view of how databases, programming, and statistical techniques can be combined for real-world data analysis.

Scenario Overview

The online retail company wants to gain insights into customer purchase behavior to enhance customer loyalty and improve marketing strategies. They are particularly interested in understanding:

1. Which customers spend the most on the platform.
2. How customer demographics (e.g., age and location) relate to spending patterns.
3. Seasonal trends in purchasing behavior.

The dataset you'll work with consists of two tables in a SQL database:

1. **Customers**: Contains information on each customer, including CustomerID, Name, Age, Country, and SignupDate.
2. **Orders**: Contains details on each order, including OrderID, CustomerID, OrderDate, and TotalAmount.

Instructions

Step 1: Retrieve Data from the SQL Database

Your first task is to connect to the SQL database and retrieve relevant data from the **Customers** and **Orders** tables. You'll need to perform a join to merge customer demographics with their order history.

SQL Query to Retrieve Data

First, we'll write an SQL query to pull key information about customers and their orders. We want to retrieve the CustomerID, Name, Age, Country, and SignupDate from the Customers table, along with the OrderID, OrderDate, and TotalAmount from the Orders table. We'll focus only on customers who have made at least one purchase by joining these tables on the CustomerID. This query gives us a combined dataset of customer demographics and order details, ready for deeper analysis.

Step 2: Load Data into Python or R

Once the data is retrieved, the next step is loading it into either Python or R for further manipulation.

In **Python**, use pandas and SQLAlchemy to connect to the database, run the query, and load the results into a DataFrame. This DataFrame will serve as the foundation for further analysis.

In **R**, connect with the DBI and dplyr libraries, execute the SQL query, and load the results into a DataFrame. After that, disconnect from the database. Now, our data is in a DataFrame called df in both Python and R, making it accessible for cleaning and transformation.

Step 3: Data Cleaning and Transformation

With the data in place, let's clean and prepare it to make it analysis-ready:

1. **Handle Missing Values**
   First, check for any missing values. Decide whether to fill these gaps (perhaps with averages) or remove them to ensure consistent data quality.

2. **Convert Date Columns**
   Convert OrderDate and SignupDate into date formats, which allows you to extract useful information like the year and month for time-based analysis.

3. **Calculate Total Spending per Customer**
   Group the data by CustomerID and calculate the total spending for each customer, then add this as a new column, TotalSpent.

4. **Create Age Groups**
   To understand spending by demographics, categorize customers into age groups (like 18-25, 26-35, etc.).

Data Cleaning and Transformation in Python

In Python, use Pandas to check for missing values, convert dates, calculate total spending, and create age groups. This setup allows for easy analysis on customer behavior.

Data Cleaning and Transformation in R

In R, use dplyr and lubridate for similar transformations. With mutate, you can create age groups and add calculated columns, ensuring the data is ready for further insights.

Step 4: Analysis

With the cleaned data, we're ready to perform some meaningful analyses:

1. **Top 10 High-Value Customers**
   Identify the top 10 customers based on total spending. This list provides insight into your most valuable customers by showing their CustomerID, Name, and TotalSpent.
2. **Spending by Age Group**
   Calculate the average total spent by each age group. This helps pinpoint which demographics contribute most to revenue.
3. **Monthly Sales Trend**
   Analyze monthly sales by aggregating TotalAmount by OrderDate, grouped by year and month. This allows you to identify seasonal trends in purchasing behavior, which can inform marketing and inventory strategies.

Analysis in Python

In Python, use Pandas to identify top customers, calculate average spending by age group, and analyze monthly sales trends. This setup provides a structured way to view customer behavior and sales patterns.

Analysis in R

In R, use dplyr for grouping and summarizing data, and ggplot2 (if needed) for visualizing the monthly sales trend. This analysis brings clarity to customer spending habits and trends over time.

By following these steps, you'll gain valuable insights into customer behavior, age-based spending, and monthly sales trends, providing a solid foundation for data-driven decisions.

Step 5: Report Findings

Write a professional report that includes the following sections:

1. **Introduction**: Briefly describe the purpose of the analysis.
2. **Methodology**: Summarize how data was retrieved, cleaned, and analyzed.
3. **Findings**:
   o **Top 10 High-Value Customers**: List customer details and total spending.

- o **Spending by Age Group**: Describe which age groups are the most valuable.
- o **Monthly Sales Trend**: Show seasonal patterns or trends in customer spending.
4. **Conclusion**: Summarize insights and suggest potential actions, such as targeted marketing campaigns for high-value age groups or timing promotions during high-spending months.

Sample Report Excerpt

Introduction

This report analyzes customer purchasing behavior to provide insights into high-value customers, spending trends by age group, and monthly sales patterns. The purpose of this analysis is to support the marketing team in identifying target customer segments and optimizing promotional strategies.

Methodology

Data was retrieved from the company's SQL database, containing information on customer demographics and order details. The data was cleaned, transformed, and analyzed using Python/R, focusing on calculating total spending per customer, average spending by age group, and monthly sales trends.

Findings

- **Top 10 High-Value Customers**: The top 10 customers accounted for a significant portion of total revenue, with each spending an average of $X.
- **Spending by Age Group**: The 26-35 age group showed the highest average spending, indicating potential for targeted marketing.
- **Monthly Sales Trend**: Sales peaked in November and December, suggesting a seasonal trend tied to holiday shopping.

Conclusion

The analysis highlights the importance of targeting the 26-35 age group and planning marketing campaigns around high-spending months. Additional analysis could explore specific products purchased by high-value customers for more focused marketing.

This structured exercise combines database querying, data manipulation, statistical analysis, and report writing. It provides a complete workflow that synthesizes the skills covered in this chapter, giving you hands-on experience with real-world data analysis and preparing you for similar projects in a professional setting.

End-of-Chapter Summary and Key Takeaways

Recap Key Points

In this chapter, we delved into the essential components of intermediate data analytics, building on foundational knowledge to equip you with advanced skills. Here's a summary of the main techniques and concepts we explored, with an emphasis on how they go beyond beginner-level approaches:

1. **Databases as the Core of Data Storage and Retrieval**:
   - **Advanced SQL Queries**: We introduced complex SQL queries, including joins, subqueries, and window functions, that allow you to retrieve and manipulate data from multiple tables efficiently. These techniques are essential for handling relational data at scale, unlike basic SELECT queries that only retrieve simple data views.
2. **Programming for Data Manipulation and Analysis**:
   - **Key Libraries in Python and R**: We discussed intermediate libraries like Pandas and NumPy in Python, and dplyr and ggplot2 in R, which enable data manipulation and

visualization at a level of complexity beyond basic spreadsheets.

- **Data Transformation and Cleaning**: You learned how to apply functions and chains to filter, aggregate, and reshape data, preparing it for analysis. Unlike beginner approaches that rely on manual cleaning or limited tools, programming offers automation and efficiency for large datasets.

3. **Advanced Statistical Techniques for Insightful Analysis**:
   - **Regression, Clustering, and Time Series Analysis**: We explored statistical methods that enable deeper insights into data. Regression helps understand relationships and predict outcomes, clustering uncovers patterns within data, and time series analysis reveals trends over time. These techniques are crucial for identifying actionable insights, as opposed to basic descriptive statistics.

4. **Integrating Skills for Real-World Data Analysis**:
   - **Connecting Theory to Practice**: Through real-world scenarios and a structured practice exercise, you learned how to combine databases,

programming, and statistics for comprehensive data analysis. This integration prepares you for real-world projects where multiple skills are required to extract meaningful insights and communicate findings effectively.

Challenge Questions

To reinforce the concepts covered in this chapter, here are some thought-provoking questions designed to encourage critical thinking and practical application. Try to answer these questions based on the techniques you've learned, and consider how each approach would apply to real-world situations.

1. **Advanced SQL and Data Retrieval**
   o When analyzing a large dataset stored in multiple tables, how would you decide which type of join (INNER JOIN, LEFT JOIN, etc.) is most appropriate for your analysis? Can you think of a scenario where using a LEFT JOIN would provide insights that an INNER JOIN would miss?
   o Imagine you're tasked with retrieving the most recent purchase for each customer from a database.

What SQL techniques could you use to accomplish this efficiently?

2. **Programming for Data Manipulation**
   o When working with a dataset that includes missing values, how would you decide between removing the rows, filling them with averages, or applying other imputation techniques? What factors would influence your decision?
   o Suppose you have a dataset with thousands of rows and want to create a new feature based on multiple existing columns. What programming techniques could you use to streamline this process, and how would they improve efficiency compared to manual calculations?

3. **Statistical Techniques for Analysis**
   o If you're tasked with predicting customer churn for a subscription service, how would you decide whether regression or a clustering approach would be more appropriate? Under what conditions might you use both methods in the same project?
   o Imagine you are analyzing seasonal sales trends for a retailer. How would you decide whether to use a time series model (e.g., ARIMA) or

another approach like moving averages? What factors, such as seasonality or cyclic patterns, would you consider in your analysis?

4. **Integrating Skills for Real-World Data Analysis**

   o Consider a scenario where you're working with a SQL database, Python/R for data manipulation, and a statistical model for analysis. How would you organize your workflow to ensure data accuracy and maintain a smooth transition between each stage?

   o Reflecting on the practice exercise from this chapter, how would you communicate your findings to a non-technical audience, such as a marketing or business team? What elements would you focus on to make your analysis understandable and actionable?

5. **Practical Applications and Future Exploration**

   o How could you apply the techniques in this chapter to a field outside of business, such as public health, education, or environmental science? For instance, how might clustering or regression be used to solve problems unique to these fields?

- o Looking ahead, what additional skills or tools do you think would be useful to continue advancing in data analytics? Are there areas from this chapter you'd like to explore more deeply, such as machine learning techniques for predictive analysis or advanced SQL optimizations?

Final Thoughts

This chapter introduced you to intermediate data analytics techniques that go beyond basic analysis, equipping you with the skills to handle real-world data challenges. By combining databases, programming, and statistics, you're now better prepared to tackle complex datasets, extract valuable insights, and present your findings in a meaningful way.

As you move forward in your data analytics journey, continue practicing these techniques, experimenting with different approaches, and seeking opportunities to apply your skills in new contexts. With each project, you'll gain confidence in selecting the right tools, interpreting results accurately, and making data-driven decisions that can have a real impact.

Chapter 2: Advanced SQL Techniques for Data Analysts

Enhancing Data Retrieval Skills

Complex Joins and Nested Queries

In this section, we'll explore advanced SQL join techniques and nested queries. These techniques are essential for handling complex data retrieval tasks, where basic joins or single-layer queries won't suffice. We'll cover FULL OUTER JOIN, SELF JOIN, and nested queries, each with examples to help illustrate their usefulness.

By mastering these skills, you'll be able to combine data across multiple tables and extract multi-layered information, helping you answer detailed and complex questions from your database.

FULL OUTER JOIN

Let's start with the FULL OUTER JOIN. This type of join is useful when you want to retrieve all records from two tables, including any records that don't have matching rows in the other table. In a FULL OUTER JOIN, if there's no match in one table, the columns from that table will have NULL values for those rows.

Imagine you have two tables: **Customers** and **Orders**. The **Customers** table lists all your customers, and the **Orders** table shows each customer's orders. Now, if you want to see all customers along with their orders—even if some customers haven't placed any orders, and some orders don't have a matching customer ID—you'd use a FULL OUTER JOIN.

Here's how the SQL query works. In this example, we're selecting the CustomerID and Name from the Customers table, along with OrderID and OrderDate from the Orders table, using a FULL OUTER JOIN to bring in all rows from both tables. If a customer hasn't placed an order, their details will still appear, with NULL values in the order columns. Similarly, if there's an order without a matching customer, the customer details will show as NULL. Essentially, a FULL OUTER JOIN gives you a complete view of both tables, showing all data regardless of matches.

Now let's talk about the SELF JOIN. A SELF JOIN is simply when a table joins with itself. This is useful when you need to compare rows within the same table. Imagine you have a table called Employees with columns for EmployeeID, Name, and ManagerID, where ManagerID represents the ID of each employee's manager. To create a list that pairs each employee with their manager's name, you would use a SELF JOIN. In this query, we're using the Employees table twice with two different aliases—e1 for the employee and e2 for the manager. By joining e1.ManagerID with e2.EmployeeID, we can pair each employee with their manager, displaying both names. The SELF JOIN is a great tool when you need to relate rows within the same table, such as connecting employees to their managers.

Lastly, let's explore nested queries, or subqueries, which are queries within queries. They're ideal when you need to perform multiple steps to get the desired data. For example, suppose you want to find customers who have spent more than the average amount on their orders. To do this, you'd first calculate the average order amount, and then use that result in another query to filter customers. This is where a nested query comes in handy. Here, we're selecting CustomerID and Name from the Customers table, but only for customers whose total spending exceeds the average order amount.

Let's break this down. The **inner query** calculates the average order amount. Then, in the **middle query**, we group the orders by CustomerID and use **HAVING** to filter for customers whose total spending is above this average. Finally, the **outer query** selects the customer details for those customers.

Nested queries allow you to layer your logic, making it possible to perform complex filtering and calculations that wouldn't be possible with a single query alone.

Combining Techniques

Let's look at a quick example of how these techniques can be combined in a real-world scenario.

Imagine you're analyzing sales data for a retail company. You want to:

1. Retrieve all customers and their orders.
2. List employees and their managers.
3. Find customers who have spent above average.

You could use a FULL OUTER JOIN to view all customers and orders, a SELF JOIN to list employees and their managers, and a nested query to find high-spending customers.

Together, these techniques give you powerful ways to handle complex data retrieval tasks, providing a comprehensive view of your data.

In this section, we covered some advanced SQL techniques for data retrieval, including FULL OUTER JOIN, SELF JOIN, and nested queries. These techniques expand your ability to work with data from multiple tables, perform self-referencing joins, and layer queries for complex filtering.

By mastering complex joins and nested queries, you'll be better prepared to handle sophisticated data requests and unlock deeper insights from your database. These skills will allow you to tackle real-world data challenges with confidence.

Window Functions for Statistical Analysis

In this section, we'll explore SQL window functions, powerful tools for performing calculations across sets of rows related to the current row. Unlike regular aggregate functions that summarize data and collapse rows, window functions keep each row in your result set intact while adding new insights alongside it.

We'll cover some of the most commonly used window functions—**ROW_NUMBER**, **RANK**, **LEAD**, and **LAG**—and provide practical examples of how to use them in real-world scenarios, like tracking trends and performing time-based analysis.

Understanding Window Functions

Window functions calculate values over a set of rows, known as the "window," that are related to the current row. The window can be based on partitions or specific orderings, allowing you to compare data across different segments or track changes over time. Window functions are valuable when you need to analyze data trends, rank data, or access values from previous or subsequent rows without collapsing the result set.

ROW_NUMBER: Assigning a Sequence to Each Row

Let's start with **ROW_NUMBER**. The **ROW_NUMBER** function assigns a unique number to each row within a partition. This is helpful when you want to create a sequence for rows within a certain group, like ranking orders by date for each customer.

Imagine you have an Orders table with columns for CustomerID, OrderID, and OrderDate, and you want to assign a row number to each order for every customer, sorted by the date of the order. You can use the ROW_NUMBER function to accomplish this. Here's how it works: by using PARTITION BY CustomerID, we create a unique numbering sequence for each customer, and ORDER BY OrderDate ensures the orders are arranged by date within each customer's sequence. This query will return each order with an additional column called OrderSequence, which numbers each order chronologically for every customer. This approach is especially helpful when you want to review each customer's order history in the sequence they made their purchases.

Now, let's look at the RANK function, which is similar to ROW_NUMBER but designed to handle ties. When multiple rows have the same value in the column used for ordering, RANK assigns the same rank to those rows and skips the following rank. For instance, imagine you're working with a table called EmployeeSales, which contains columns for EmployeeID, SalesAmount, and Department. You want to rank employees within each department based on their sales. Here, PARTITION BY Department divides the data by department, and ORDER BY SalesAmount DESC ranks employees in each department from the highest to the lowest sales. RANK is ideal when you need to consider ties in your ranking, providing a fair representation even when multiple employees have the same sales figures.

In this query:

- **PARTITION BY Department** creates separate rankings for each department.
- **ORDER BY SalesAmount DESC** ranks employees from highest to lowest sales within each department.

If two employees have the same sales amount, they'll receive the same rank. For example, if two employees have the highest sales in their department, they'll both be ranked 1, and the next employee will be ranked 3. **RANK** is useful when you need to handle ties, like ranking top performers in each department or identifying top products in each category.

LEAD and LAG: Accessing Next and Previous Rows

LEAD and **LAG** are window functions that allow you to look at the values in the next row or previous row within a specific window. These functions are extremely useful for time-based analysis, where you might want to compare a value with the previous or next period.

Imagine you're working with a **MonthlySales** table that includes **Month**, **ProductID**, and **SalesAmount**. You want to compare each month's sales with the sales from the previous month for each product. To do this, you can use **LAG** to access the previous month's sales amount.

Here's how the query works. We're selecting the Month, ProductID, and SalesAmount from the MonthlySales table, and we're adding a new column that shows the sales amount from the previous month for each product. By using the LAG function and setting it to partition by ProductID, we're able to look back at the previous month's sales for each individual product. This is especially useful for tracking month-to-month changes in sales, helping you easily compare each product's performance over time.

In this query:

- **PARTITION BY ProductID** ensures that the previous month's sales are only compared within each product.
- **ORDER BY Month** arranges the sales data chronologically for each product.

This query returns the sales amount for each month, along with the previous month's sales amount in a new column called **PreviousMonthSales**. This lets you calculate month-over-month changes directly in SQL, which is useful for identifying trends or drops in sales.

Similarly, **LEAD** works the same way, but instead of looking at the previous row, it looks at the next row. For example, if you wanted to compare each month's sales to the following month's sales, you could use **LEAD(SalesAmount)**.

Practical Scenarios for Using Window Functions

Let's look at some real-world scenarios to see how these window functions are applied.

1. **Customer Retention Analysis**: Use **ROW_NUMBER** to assign a sequence to

each customer's orders, helping you analyze retention by looking at repeat purchases over time.

2. **Top Performers by Department**: Use **RANK** to find the top-performing employees in each department based on sales or productivity, even when there are ties.

3. **Month-over-Month Sales Trends**: Use **LAG** to compare monthly sales for each product, identifying trends, growth, or declines over time.

4. **Customer Behavior Patterns**: Use **LEAD** to look at the next purchase date for each customer, helping you analyze the typical time between purchases.

In this section, we covered some powerful SQL window functions—**ROW_NUMBER, RANK, LEAD**, and **LAG**—and showed how they're used for statistical analysis and time-based comparisons. These functions allow you to perform complex calculations over specific sets of rows, giving you valuable insights without altering the structure of your result set.

By mastering these window functions, you'll be able to conduct sophisticated data analysis directly in SQL, making your work more efficient and insightful.

Data Cleaning and Transformation with SQL

Data Preprocessing with SQL

In this section, we'll cover methods to clean and transform raw data directly in SQL, allowing for immediate preprocessing at the database level. When working with large datasets, cleaning and transforming data at the source can save time and improve the efficiency of downstream analysis. We'll look at some commonly used SQL functions for data preprocessing, including **TRIM, CASE,** and **COALESCE**. These functions will help you clean up messy data, handle missing values, and create standardized outputs.

TRIM: Removing Extra Spaces

Let's start with **TRIM**. The TRIM function is used to remove unwanted spaces from the beginning and end of a string. Extra spaces are common in raw data and can cause issues, especially when matching or comparing values.

Imagine you have a **Customers** table with a **Name** column, but some names have extra spaces at the beginning or end. These spaces can create inconsistencies and make it difficult to search for specific names.

Here's how you would use the TRIM function to remove unwanted spaces in SQL.

SELECT CustomerID,
TRIM(Name) AS CleanedName
FROM Customers;

In this query:

- The **TRIM(Name)** function removes any leading and trailing spaces from each name in the Name column.
- Using **AS CleanedName** renames the output column to indicate that it's the cleaned version of the name.

If you only want to remove spaces from the beginning or end, SQL also offers **LTRIM** for removing spaces from the left and **RTRIM** for removing them from the right. To recap, TRIM is a simple yet powerful tool for ensuring consistent formatting by cleaning up unwanted spaces in text fields.

CASE: Creating Conditional Values

Next, let's look at the **CASE** statement. CASE is like an IF-THEN-ELSE statement in programming and is useful for creating new, conditional values based on existing data. You can use CASE to categorize data, handle exceptions, or create flag indicators.

Imagine an Orders table with an **OrderAmount** column, and you want to categorize orders into spending tiers: "Low," "Medium," and "High," based on the amount spent.

```
SELECT OrderID, OrderAmount,
CASE
WHEN OrderAmount < 50 THEN 'Low'
WHEN OrderAmount BETWEEN 50 AND
200 THEN 'Medium'
ELSE 'High'
END AS SpendingTier
FROM Orders;
```

In this query:

- **WHEN OrderAmount < 50 THEN 'Low'** assigns the category "Low" to orders with an amount less than 50.
- **WHEN OrderAmount BETWEEN 50 AND 200 THEN 'Medium'** categorizes orders between 50 and 200 as "Medium."
- **ELSE 'High'** assigns "High" to all other orders.

The CASE statement is versatile and allows you to create custom categories or classifications based on various conditions, which is especially helpful for organizing data for analysis.

COALESCE: Handling Missing Values

Now, let's talk about **COALESCE**. This function is essential for managing missing values. COALESCE returns the first non-NULL value in a list, so you can replace NULLs with default values.

Imagine a **Products** table with a **Discount** column. If some products don't have a discount value, the column shows NULL. To replace these NULLs with a default discount of 0, you'd use COALESCE.

SELECT ProductID, Price, COALESCE(Discount, 0) AS Discount FROM Products;

In this query:

- **COALESCE(Discount, 0)** replaces any NULL values in the Discount column with 0.
- **AS Discount** renames the output column, making it clear that this is the final discount value.

This function is particularly useful when you need to perform calculations on columns that may contain NULLs. By replacing NULLs with a default value, COALESCE ensures consistency and prevents errors in calculations.

To summarize, COALESCE helps manage missing data by providing fallback values, making your data cleaner and more reliable.

Practical Scenarios for Data Preprocessing with SQL

Let's go through a few real-world examples of how these functions can work together in data cleaning.

1. **Standardizing Customer Names:** Use TRIM to remove extra spaces, CASE to correct inconsistent capitalization or misspellings, and COALESCE to fill in missing values in optional fields like middle names.
2. **Categorizing Spending Levels:** Use CASE to create spending tiers, making it easy to segment customers or orders by their spending behavior.
3. **Handling Missing Values in Financial Data:** Use COALESCE to replace NULL values in columns like discounts, taxes, or fees, ensuring calculations aren't disrupted by missing data.

Conclusion

In this section, we've explored essential SQL functions for data preprocessing, including

TRIM, **CASE**, and **COALESCE**. These functions allow you to clean and transform raw data directly within the database, making it analysis-ready without needing to export it to another tool. Mastering these SQL functions enables you to handle messy data more effectively, ensuring consistency and quality in your datasets. These skills are foundational for data analysts, helping you deliver cleaner, more reliable insights.

Creating Temporary Tables and Views

Now, let's look at temporary tables and views in SQL. These structures are incredibly valuable for efficient data analysis, especially in real-time analytics. Temporary tables and views allow you to store the results of complex queries, making it easier to reuse data or build on previous calculations without rerunning the same code repeatedly. Let's start with temporary tables.

Temporary Tables: Storing Data for Short-Term Use

Temporary tables are tables created within your SQL session to store data temporarily. They're ideal for breaking down complex queries into manageable steps, making your analysis more efficient. Once your session ends or the temporary table is dropped, it's automatically deleted, so it doesn't take up permanent space in your database.

Imagine you're working with a large **Sales** table and want to calculate each customer's total spending. Instead of recalculating this every time, you can store the result in a temporary table and use it in multiple queries.

CREATE TEMPORARY TABLE CustomerSpending AS SELECT CustomerID, SUM(TotalAmount) AS TotalSpent FROM Sales GROUP BY CustomerID;

In this example:

- **CREATE TEMPORARY TABLE CustomerSpending** creates a new temporary table called CustomerSpending.
- **AS** defines the data you want to store in this table—in this case, the total spending for each customer.

Once created, you can use this temporary table in other queries as if it were a regular table. For example, you could join it with a Customers table to get more information about high-spending customers.

```
SELECT c.CustomerID, c.Name,
cs.TotalSpent
FROM Customers c
JOIN CustomerSpending cs ON
c.CustomerID = cs.CustomerID
WHERE cs.TotalSpent > 500;
```

This query joins the **CustomerSpending** temporary table with the **Customers** table, allowing you to identify customers who have spent more than 500 quickly. Temporary tables are especially useful for organizing intermediate results in complex analyses and help reduce the need to rerun time-consuming calculations.

Views: Creating Reusable Virtual Tables

Now, let's talk about views. A view is a virtual table that's based on the result of a query. Unlike temporary tables, views don't store data physically. Instead, they store a SQL query that's executed each time the view is referenced. This makes views great for creating reusable query structures without storing actual data.

Views are especially helpful when you have complex calculations or filters that you want to apply consistently across multiple analyses.

Imagine you have a Transactions table, and you want to create a view that shows only high-value transactions—those where the total is above 1,000.

```
CREATE VIEW HighValueTransactions
AS
SELECT TransactionID, CustomerID,
TransactionDate, TotalAmount
FROM Transactions
WHERE TotalAmount > 1000;
```

In this example:

- **CREATE VIEW HighValueTransactions** defines a new view called HighValueTransactions.
- The query inside the view selects only transactions where the TotalAmount is greater than 1,000.

Now, whenever you reference HighValueTransactions in a query, SQL will apply this filter automatically, saving you from having to rewrite the condition each time. For instance, you could join this view with a Customers table to retrieve names of customers who made high-value transactions:

```
SELECT c.Name, hvt.TotalAmount,
hvt.TransactionDate
FROM Customers c
JOIN HighValueTransactions hvt ON
c.CustomerID = hvt.CustomerID;
```

This query retrieves customer names alongside their high-value transactions, using the view to keep your SQL clean and concise.

Key Differences Between Temporary Tables and Views

To summarize the main differences:

- **Temporary Tables** physically store data for the duration of your session, making them ideal for intermediate steps in a multi-step analysis and avoiding recalculations.
- **Views** are virtual tables that don't store data but store a query instead, useful for creating reusable, simplified views of complex queries you need often.

Temporary tables and views are both powerful tools with distinct purposes: temporary tables for short-term storage and views for reusable query structures.

Practical Scenarios for Using Temporary Tables and Views

Here are a few real-world scenarios where temporary tables and views can simplify your work:

1. **Complex Data Transformation** – Use temporary tables to store intermediate

results, such as calculations or aggregations, for more efficient analysis without repeating calculations.

2. **Data Filtering for Analysis** – Create views to filter data, like high-value transactions or active customers, so you can reuse these filtered datasets in multiple queries without reapplying the filter each time.

3. **Organizing Multi-Step Queries** – Use both temporary tables and views in large, multi-step analyses. Temporary tables handle intermediate data, while views simplify repeated query structures.

Conclusion

In this section, we covered temporary tables and views, which allow you to preprocess, organize, and simplify data directly in SQL. Mastering these tools gives you the ability to handle complex queries in a structured, reusable way, providing greater flexibility and control in your data analysis tasks. These skills are essential for real-time analytics, where efficient data processing is key to delivering fast, reliable insights.

Optimization Tips

In this section, we'll cover essential optimization techniques that improve the performance of your

SQL queries, especially when working with large datasets. As a data analyst, efficient querying is key to managing large databases effectively. Slow queries can delay your analysis and consume unnecessary resources, so understanding optimization can make a big difference.

We'll look at three main areas: **Indexing**, **Query Optimization**, and **Best Practices**. By mastering these techniques, you'll be able to speed up your queries, reduce server load, and improve overall efficiency in your data analysis work.

Indexing: Making Data Retrieval Faster

Let's start with indexing. An **index** is a data structure that improves the speed of data retrieval on specific columns in a table. Think of an index like the index at the back of a book—it allows you to find information quickly without having to read every page. In SQL, indexing does the same for columns in your database tables.

For example, if you frequently search for customers by their **CustomerID** in a large **Customers** table, creating an index on **CustomerID** will make those searches much faster.

Imagine you have a Transactions table, and you want to create a view that shows only high-value transactions, specifically those where the total amount is over 1,000.

To do this, you'd write:

CREATE VIEW HighValueTransactions AS
SELECT TransactionID, CustomerID, TransactionDate, TotalAmount
FROM Transactions
WHERE TotalAmount > 1000;

In this example:

- **CREATE VIEW HighValueTransactions** creates a new view named HighValueTransactions.
- The query inside the view filters for transactions where the **TotalAmount** is greater than 1,000.

Now, whenever you reference HighValueTransactions in a query, SQL automatically applies this filter, saving you from having to rewrite the condition each time. For instance, you could join this view with a Customers table to get the names of customers who made high-value transactions.

Key Differences Between Temporary Tables and Views

To summarize, here's a quick comparison:

- **Temporary Tables** physically store data for your session and are ideal for multi-step analyses, letting you avoid recalculating results repeatedly.
- **Views** are virtual tables that store a query, not the data itself, allowing for simplified, reusable views of complex queries.

Both tools have unique advantages: temporary tables are perfect for temporary storage, while views are great for creating reusable query structures.

Practical Scenarios for Using Temporary Tables and Views

Let's look at a few real-world examples of how temporary tables and views can make your work more efficient:

1. **Complex Data Transformation:** Use temporary tables to store intermediate results, making your analysis more efficient without rerunning calculations.
2. **Data Filtering for Analysis:** Create views to filter data, like high-value transactions, so you can reuse these filtered datasets in multiple queries.
3. **Organizing Multi-Step Queries:** Use temporary tables for intermediate steps

and views for simplifying repeated query structures in large, multi-step analyses.

Conclusion

In this section, we covered the basics of temporary tables and views in SQL. These tools allow you to preprocess, organize, and simplify data, making your analysis more efficient and queries easier to manage. Mastering temporary tables and views will help you handle complex queries with structure and reusability, giving you greater flexibility in data analysis.

Building Reusable SQL Code

Stored Procedures and Functions

Now, let's move on to two powerful tools for building reusable SQL code: **stored procedures** and **functions**. These tools allow you to create repeatable workflows, saving time and reducing errors. With stored procedures and functions, you can automate tasks and standardize calculations, making your SQL code more efficient. Let's start by understanding the difference between stored procedures and functions.

Understanding Stored Procedures and Functions

Stored procedures and functions are both reusable blocks of code in SQL, but they serve slightly different purposes:

- **Stored Procedures**: Used to perform a series of SQL statements, often including conditional logic or loops. Procedures can accept parameters, making them ideal for automating complex workflows.
- **Functions**: Designed to perform calculations or return a single result. Unlike procedures, functions usually return a specific value and are commonly used within other queries.

Let's explore how to create each of these.

Creating a Stored Procedure

Imagine you work for a company that wants a monthly sales report for a specific region. Instead of running the same queries each month, you can create a stored procedure to automate the process.

```
CREATE PROCEDURE
GenerateMonthlySalesReport
@Region VARCHAR(50),
@StartDate DATE,
@EndDate DATE
AS
BEGIN
```

```
SELECT ProductID, SUM(TotalAmount)
AS MonthlySales
FROM Sales
WHERE Region = @Region
AND OrderDate BETWEEN @StartDate
AND @EndDate
GROUP BY ProductID;
END;
```

In this example:

- **CREATE PROCEDURE GenerateMonthlySalesReport** defines a new procedure.
- **@Region, @StartDate,** and **@EndDate** are parameters, allowing you to specify the region and date range.
- **AS** and **BEGIN...END** define the SQL statements within the procedure, calculating each product's total sales for a specified region and date range.

After creating this procedure, you can call it with different parameters for different regions or months.

EXEC GenerateMonthlySalesReport 'North', '2024-01-01', '2024-01-31';

This command runs the procedure for the "North" region, generating the sales report for January 2024. Stored procedures allow you to encapsulate complex logic into a single, reusable command, making workflows more efficient.

Creating a Function

Functions are generally used for calculations or transformations that you want to apply repeatedly in queries. Unlike stored procedures, functions return a single value, which can be directly used in SQL statements.

Imagine you need to apply a discount to prices in a Products table, with a frequently changing discount rate. Instead of recalculating it each time, you can create a function to apply the discount dynamically.

```
CREATE FUNCTION
CalculateDiscountedPrice (@Price
DECIMAL(10, 2), @DiscountRate
DECIMAL(5, 2))
RETURNS DECIMAL(10, 2)
AS
BEGIN
RETURN @Price * (1 - @DiscountRate /
100);
END;
```

In this example:

- **CREATE FUNCTION CalculateDiscountedPrice** defines a function called CalculateDiscountedPrice.
- **@Price** and **@DiscountRate** are input parameters for the original price and discount rate.
- **RETURNS DECIMAL(10, 2)** specifies that the function returns a decimal value with two decimal places.
- **RETURN @Price * (1 - @DiscountRate / 100)** calculates the discounted price.

Once created, you can use this function in other queries to calculate discounted prices on the fly.

SELECT ProductID, Price, dbo.CalculateDiscountedPrice(Price, 10) AS DiscountedPrice FROM Products;

This query selects each product's original price and applies a 10% discount using the CalculateDiscountedPrice function. With this function, you can easily adjust the discount rate across all products without rewriting the calculation.

Query Optimization: Writing Efficient SQL Code

Now, let's talk about query optimization—writing SQL in a way that minimizes database processing. Here are some key techniques:

1. **Avoid SELECT ***: Instead of retrieving all columns with SELECT *, specify only the columns you need. This reduces data retrieval time, especially in large tables.
2. **Use WHERE Clauses to Filter Data Early**: Adding a WHERE clause to filter data as soon as possible helps the database retrieve only relevant rows, speeding up queries.
3. **Avoid Functions on Indexed Columns in WHERE Clauses**: When using a function in a WHERE clause on an indexed column, it can disable the index. Use range conditions instead to keep the index effective.
4. **Optimize JOINs by Filtering First**: Filter tables before joining, if possible, to reduce the number of rows involved in the join.

Best Practices for Performance and Efficiency

1. **Use Aliases for Readability**: Short names for tables and columns make complex queries easier to read.

2. **Monitor Query Performance**: Use database tools like Query Analyzer or Execution Plans to review performance.

3. **Limit Subqueries**: Excessive subqueries can slow performance. Replace them with JOINs or temporary tables when possible.

4. **Periodically Update Statistics**: Databases use statistics for query optimization. Keep these updated to ensure accurate performance.

5. **Archive Old Data**: Large datasets can slow queries. Consider archiving data that's no longer needed for daily operations.

Conclusion

In this chapter, we covered indexing, query optimization, stored procedures, and functions. By applying these techniques, you can significantly improve the speed and efficiency of your queries, especially with large datasets. Optimizing SQL queries not only saves time but also reduces server load, making your data analysis more scalable.

These skills are essential for data analysts working with complex databases, helping you deliver fast, reliable insights.

End-of-Chapter Exercise: Real-World Application - Designing a Data Analytics Workflow

Imagine you're a data analyst for an online retail company aiming to monitor sales performance, track customer segments, and identify high-value products. This exercise will guide you through building a workflow that supports these goals, ensuring data quality, efficiency, and reusability.

Step 1: Data Cleaning and Transformation

Use SQL to:

1. **Remove Extra Spaces** in customer names with the TRIM function.
2. **Fill in Missing Values** in the TotalAmount column with COALESCE, replacing NULL with 0.
3. **Categorize Customers by Age Group** using the CASE statement.

Step 2: Creating Reusable Queries with Views and Temporary Tables

1. **Create a View for High-Value Orders** to filter orders with a TotalAmount over $500.

2. **Create a Temporary Table for Monthly Sales** to store monthly totals, which simplifies trend tracking.

Step 3: Generating Actionable Reports

1. **Monthly Sales Report by Product Category**: Track total monthly sales by category.
2. **Customer Segmentation Report**: Show total spending per customer by age group.
3. **Top Products Report**: Identify the top 5 products based on sales.

Step 4: Simulating a Live Analytics Environment

To handle daily updates, consider refreshing temporary tables and views regularly, and automate processes with stored procedures.

Conclusion

By completing this exercise, you've designed a complete SQL-based workflow for cleaning, organizing, and analyzing data. These skills are crucial for real-world data analysis tasks, helping you build efficient, reusable workflows and delivering insights directly from the database.

Chapter 3: Data Manipulation in Python and R for Intermediate Analysts

Exploring Data Frames for Complex Analysis

Advanced Data Frame Techniques

In this section, we'll dive into advanced techniques for working with data frames in Python and R. Data frames are the backbone of data manipulation in both languages, allowing analysts to store, organize, and transform data effectively. Here, we'll cover some intermediate-level techniques, including **multi-indexing in Pandas**, **merging large datasets**, and **handling missing data**.

These skills will help you manage and analyze complex datasets with greater precision, flexibility, and efficiency.

Multi-Indexing in Pandas (Python)

Multi-indexing allows you to use multiple levels of indexing in a data frame, making it easier to work with hierarchical or grouped data. This is especially useful when you have datasets with natural hierarchies, like sales data organized by region and product, or stock prices grouped by company and date.

Imagine you have a DataFrame called **sales_data** with columns like **Region**, **Product**, **Year**, and **Sales**. By setting up a multi-index in Python's Pandas, you can organize this data hierarchically, making it quicker to access and analyze at multiple levels.

Setting Up a Multi-Index

To create a multi-index in Pandas, you use the **set_index** function. Start by defining sample data with columns for **Region, Product, Year**, and **Sales**. Then, create a DataFrame and apply the **set_index** function with **Region** and **Product** as the index levels. This lets you access subsets of data based on these levels. For instance, to view sales data for the **North** region and **Product A**, you can specify these index levels directly.

Benefits of Multi-Indexing

Multi-indexing offers several advantages:

- It organizes data hierarchically, making it easy to perform grouped calculations.
- You can filter data efficiently by specifying levels in the index.
- It enables you to aggregate data at different levels, such as calculating total sales by region or product.

Merging Large Datasets in Python and R

Merging datasets is crucial for combining information from multiple sources. Both Python's Pandas and R's dplyr package provide efficient methods to merge large datasets.

Merging in Python (Pandas)

In Pandas, you can merge two datasets using the **merge** function. Suppose you have **customers** and **orders** DataFrames, where **customers** includes **CustomerID** and **Name**, and **orders** includes **CustomerID**, **OrderDate**, and **Amount**. Use **pd.merge** with the **on** parameter set to **CustomerID** to combine them based on matching IDs. Specifying **how='inner'** includes only matching rows. Other join types include **left**, **right**, and **outer**.

Merging in R (dplyr)

In R, the dplyr package provides **left_join**, **right_join**, **inner_join**, and **full_join** functions for merging. Suppose **customers** and **orders** are data frames with **CustomerID** as the shared column. Using **left_join(customers, orders, by = "CustomerID")** merges the two tables on **CustomerID**, retaining all rows from **customers** and matching rows from **orders**.

Handling Missing Data in Python and R

Dealing with missing data is essential for clean analysis. Both Python and R offer flexible methods to handle missing values.

Handling Missing Data in Python (Pandas)

In Pandas, you can identify missing values with **isnull().sum()** to get a count of missing values per column. To fill missing values with the column mean, use **fillna** on the column, specifying the mean as the replacement value. To remove rows with missing values, use **dropna**.

Handling Missing Data in R (dplyr)

In R, **is.na** can identify missing values in a column, and **sum(is.na(column))** provides the count. To fill missing values with the column mean, use **mutate** with **ifelse** to conditionally replace **NA** values. To remove rows with any missing values, use **drop_na** from dplyr.

Properly managing missing data ensures the integrity of your analysis.

Conclusion

This section covers advanced data handling techniques in Python and R, including multi-indexing, merging large datasets, and managing missing data. Mastering these techniques will equip you to handle complex datasets more effectively, making your analysis structured, accurate, and efficient.

Chapter 4: Advanced Statistical Methods: Beyond the Basics

Regression Analysis for Predictive Insights

Multiple and Logistic Regression

Regression analysis is a powerful tool for predictive modeling. It allows analysts to understand relationships between variables, make predictions, and gain insights from data. In this section, we'll dive into two advanced regression techniques: **Multiple Regression** and **Logistic Regression**. Each technique will be demonstrated with case studies to show how these methods can be used for customer segmentation and risk analysis.

Multiple regression is commonly used to predict a continuous outcome based on multiple independent variables, while logistic regression is suited for binary classification problems, such as predicting whether a customer will purchase a product or default on a loan.

Multiple Regression for Customer Segmentation

Overview

Multiple regression is an extension of simple linear regression that allows you to include multiple independent variables to predict a single continuous dependent variable. This method is particularly useful for understanding the factors that influence customer behavior, such as spending, satisfaction, or likelihood to purchase.

In this example, we'll use multiple regression to predict **Customer Spending** based on multiple predictors: **Age**, **Income**, and **Number of Visits** to the store.

Example Case Study: Predicting Customer Spending

Suppose you work for a retail company that wants to identify the factors influencing customer spending. By understanding these drivers, the company can target specific customer segments more effectively.

Step 1: Prepare the Data

Assume you have a dataset with the following columns:

- **CustomerID**: Unique identifier for each customer.
- **Age**: Age of the customer.
- **Income**: Annual income of the customer.
- **Visits**: Number of visits to the store in the past year.

- **Spending**: Total spending in the store over the past year.

To start analyzing this dataset, load it into Python or R. Begin by creating a small dataset with variables like **Age**, **Income**, **Visits**, and **Spending**. This allows you to simulate customer data for practice in building a regression model.

Step 2: Building the Multiple Regression Model

In Python, you can use the **statsmodels** library to create a multiple regression model, which will help identify the relationship between multiple factors (independent variables) and customer **Spending** (dependent variable). Define the dependent variable (**Spending**) and select independent variables like **Age**, **Income**, and **Visits**. Add a constant term for the intercept and then fit the model to the data. The model's summary will include important metrics, like coefficients, R-squared values, and p-values, all of which help you understand the impact of each factor on spending behavior.

- **Age**: A positive coefficient here would suggest that older customers tend to spend more.

- **Income**: If positive, it would indicate that higher-income customers spend more.
- **Visits**: A positive coefficient for **Visits** implies that more frequent visits correlate with increased spending.

Interpreting Multiple Regression Results

By examining the coefficients, you can interpret the impact of each factor on spending. For example, if **Income** has a strong positive effect, the retail company may decide to target high-income customers. This approach allows the company to refine its strategy based on customer segments that are likely to contribute more to revenue.

Logistic Regression for Risk Analysis

Logistic regression is ideal for binary classification tasks—predicting whether an outcome will be one of two categories, such as Yes/No or 0/1. It's widely used in risk analysis scenarios, such as estimating the likelihood of a customer making a purchase. This section walks through how to use logistic regression to predict a customer's purchase behavior based on various factors.

Example: Predicting Customer Purchase Likelihood

Consider an e-commerce company aiming to forecast if a customer will make a purchase. Variables include **CustomerID** (for unique identification), **Age, Income, Previous Purchases**, and a binary **Purchase** outcome (1 for Yes, 0 for No). With this data, you can develop a logistic regression model to predict which customers are more likely to buy, helping the company optimize marketing outreach.

Step 1: Preparing the Data

Simulate this dataset by including **Age, Income, Previous Purchases**, and **Purchase** as columns in a DataFrame.

Step 2: Building the Logistic Regression Model

Using **statsmodels** in Python, set **Purchase** as the dependent variable and **Age, Income**, and **Previous Purchases** as independent variables. Fit the model and check the summary output to evaluate the relationships.

By examining the coefficients, you'll gain insights into the predictors' impact on the likelihood of purchase. A positive coefficient for **Income**, for instance, would imply that higher-income customers are more likely to make a purchase. Similarly, a positive **Previous Purchases** coefficient would indicate that customers who bought previously have a higher chance of buying again.

Summary

Multiple regression helps identify how different factors influence spending, while logistic regression estimates the likelihood of specific outcomes, such as purchases. Using these models, a company can make data-driven decisions to focus on high-value customers and optimize marketing strategies for those likely to engage.

In this example:

- **y = data['Purchase']** sets the dependent variable to Purchase.
- **X = data[['Age', 'Income', 'PreviousPurchases']]** sets the independent variables.
- **sm.Logit(y, X).fit()** fits the logistic regression model.

The output shows the coefficients and p-values, helping you understand the significance of each variable.

Step 3: Interpret the Results

The coefficients represent the effect of each predictor on the log-odds of the outcome (whether the customer will purchase or not):

- **Age**: A positive coefficient suggests that older customers are more likely to purchase.
- **Income**: A positive coefficient indicates that higher income increases purchase likelihood.
- **PreviousPurchases**: A positive coefficient means that customers with more previous purchases are more likely to buy again.

Step 4: Predict and Evaluate the Model

After building the logistic regression model, it's time to put it to the test by making predictions and evaluating its accuracy.

Start by using the model to make predictions. These predictions will be probabilities that indicate the likelihood of each outcome. To turn these probabilities into clear "yes" or "no" (or "0" and "1") results, set a threshold—for instance, considering any probability above 0.5 as a "yes."

Once predictions are made, calculate the model's accuracy by comparing the predictions to the actual outcomes. This accuracy score tells you how often the model correctly predicted the outcome, giving you a quick look at its overall reliability.

In this example:

- If the calculated accuracy is 0.80, it means the model is correctly predicting outcomes 80% of the time.

Summary: Logistic regression provides insights into which factors influence purchase likelihood. The e-commerce company can use these insights to target customers more likely to buy, improving marketing efficiency.

Practical Applications of Multiple and Logistic Regression

1. **Customer Segmentation**: Multiple regression helps in understanding factors that influence customer spending, loyalty, and satisfaction, aiding in better segmentation and targeted marketing.
2. **Risk Analysis in Finance**: Logistic regression is valuable for predicting loan defaults, credit card fraud, or insurance claims, helping financial institutions manage risk.
3. **Healthcare Analysis**: Logistic regression is often used to predict patient outcomes (e.g., survival rates, disease

presence) based on multiple factors like age, blood pressure, and cholesterol levels.

4. **Employee Retention**: Multiple regression can be used to predict employee turnover by analyzing factors like salary, job satisfaction, and years of experience, helping companies address retention proactively.

Conclusion

In this section, we explored multiple regression and logistic regression, two essential tools for predictive modeling. Multiple regression allows for continuous outcome prediction based on several factors, while logistic regression enables binary classification, useful in risk analysis.

By mastering these regression techniques, you'll be able to gain predictive insights from your data, making informed decisions based on statistical analysis. Whether in customer segmentation, financial risk, or healthcare analysis, regression models are powerful tools for understanding complex relationships and predicting outcomes in real-world scenarios.

Interpreting Results in Real-World Contexts

When conducting regression analysis, interpreting the results is crucial to extracting meaningful insights that can inform real-world decisions. This section will explain how to understand the main components of a regression output—**coefficients**, **p-values**, and **R-squared values**—and what they imply in practical terms.

By learning to interpret these elements, you'll be able to draw actionable conclusions from your data, making your analysis more impactful and relevant.

Understanding Coefficients

What Are Coefficients?

In regression analysis, coefficients represent the relationship between each independent variable and the dependent variable. They tell you how much the dependent variable is expected to change when the independent variable changes by one unit, assuming all other variables are held constant.

- **Positive Coefficient**: If the coefficient is positive, the dependent variable increases as the independent variable increases.
- **Negative Coefficient**: If the coefficient is negative, the dependent variable decreases as the independent variable increases.

Interpreting Coefficients in Real-World Contexts

Example 1: Customer Spending

Suppose you're analyzing the impact of **Income** and **Age** on **Customer Spending** using multiple regression. Here's an example of what the output might look like:

Variable Coefficient

Income   0.02

Age   5.00

- **Income Coefficient (0.02)**: For every additional dollar in income, customer spending is expected to increase by $0.02, assuming age remains constant.
- **Age Coefficient (5.00)**: For each additional year in age, customer spending is expected to increase by $5, assuming income remains constant.

In practical terms, this suggests that both income and age positively influence spending, but age has a stronger impact. This insight might guide the company to focus on targeting older, higher-income customers for premium products or services.

Example 2: Predicting Loan Default

In a logistic regression model predicting **Loan Default** (yes/no), you might have coefficients for **Income** and **Debt-to-Income Ratio**.

Variable	Coefficient
Income	-0.03
Debt-to-Income Ratio	0.15

- **Income Coefficient (-0.03)**: A negative coefficient for income implies that higher income reduces the likelihood of loan default.
- **Debt-to-Income Ratio Coefficient (0.15)**: A positive coefficient for debt-to-income ratio indicates that higher ratios increase the probability of default.

In real-world terms, the bank might use this information to prioritize loan applicants with lower debt-to-income ratios and higher incomes, thereby reducing the risk of default.

Note: In logistic regression, coefficients represent the change in log-odds rather than direct change in the dependent variable. However, the direction and relative size of coefficients still provide insights into how each factor influences the outcome.

Understanding p-values

What Are p-values?

A p-value is a measure of statistical significance. It tells you whether the observed relationship between the independent variable and the dependent variable is likely to be real or just due to random chance.

- **Low p-value (< 0.05)**: A p-value below 0.05 typically indicates that the variable is statistically significant, meaning there's strong evidence to suggest a real relationship between the variable and the outcome.
- **High p-value (> 0.05)**: A high p-value suggests that the variable may not have a meaningful effect on the outcome.

Interpreting p-values in Real-World Contexts

Example: Evaluating Predictors for Customer Retention

Suppose you're analyzing factors that affect **Customer Retention** and find the following results:

Variable	Coefficient	p-value
Age	4.0	0.01
Annual Income	1.5	0.06
Engagement Rate	10.0	0.0005

- **Age (p-value = 0.01)**: Since the p-value is below 0.05, age is statistically significant, suggesting it has a real impact on customer retention.
- **Annual Income (p-value = 0.06)**: This p-value is slightly above 0.05, indicating that income might not significantly impact retention in this sample. However, if income is critical to your analysis, you might consider including it in further analysis with additional data.
- **Engagement Rate (p-value = 0.0005)**: The low p-value indicates that engagement rate is highly significant, suggesting a strong relationship with customer retention.

Real-World Takeaway: This analysis shows that engagement rate has the strongest impact on customer retention, followed by age. The company may choose to focus on increasing engagement to improve retention.

Example: Risk Analysis for Credit Score

In a logistic regression model to predict **Credit Score Risk** (low/high), you might find the following p-values:

Variable	Coefficient	p-value
Income	0.05	0.001

Variable	Coefficient	p-value
Debt-to-Income Ratio	0.20	0.02
Marital Status	-0.10	0.08

- **Income and Debt-to-Income Ratio** have p-values below 0.05, making them statistically significant predictors of credit risk.
- **Marital Status** has a p-value of 0.08, indicating it's not statistically significant and may not be a reliable predictor in this model.

Real-World Takeaway: Focusing on income and debt-to-income ratio may be more useful for predicting credit risk, while marital status can potentially be excluded from the model to simplify it without losing predictive accuracy.

Understanding R-squared Values

What is R-squared?

R-squared (R^2) is a measure of how well the independent variables explain the variability in the dependent variable. It ranges from 0 to 1, where:

- **Higher R-squared values** (closer to 1) indicate that a large proportion of the variability in the dependent variable is explained by the model.

- **Lower R-squared values** (closer to 0) suggest that the model does not explain much of the variability, and other factors might be influencing the dependent variable.

Note: R-squared is typically used with multiple regression (not logistic regression), as logistic regression uses other measures (e.g., pseudo-R-squared).

Interpreting R-squared in Real-World Contexts

Example: Sales Prediction Model

Suppose you create a multiple regression model to predict **Monthly Sales** based on factors like **Marketing Spend**, **Store Location**, and **Season**. Your model outputs an R-squared value of 0.85.

- **R-squared = 0.85**: This means that 85% of the variability in monthly sales is explained by the independent variables in the model. This high R-squared value suggests that the model is well-suited for predicting sales based on the input factors.

Real-World Takeaway: With a high R-squared, you can confidently use this model to make sales predictions and even identify key factors, like marketing spend, that could be optimized to boost sales.

Example: Employee Satisfaction Analysis

If you create a model to predict **Employee Satisfaction** based on variables like **Salary**, **Work Hours**, and **Manager Rating** and find an R-squared value of 0.40, this suggests that only 40% of the variability in satisfaction is explained by these factors.

Real-World Takeaway: In this case, the low R-squared indicates that other variables might be influencing employee satisfaction, such as work-life balance, benefits, or career development opportunities. This insight could encourage HR to gather additional data to improve the model.

Conclusion

Interpreting regression results is crucial for drawing actionable insights from your data. By understanding coefficients, p-values, and R-squared values, you can determine the importance and impact of each variable on the outcome in real-world terms. Whether you're predicting customer behavior, assessing risk, or analyzing sales performance, interpreting these measures helps ensure that your findings are relevant, reliable, and actionable.

Mastering the interpretation of regression outputs will empower you to make data-driven decisions and communicate your findings effectively to stakeholders in business, finance, healthcare, and beyond.

Clustering and Segmentation Techniques

K-Means and Hierarchical Clustering

Clustering is a powerful technique for identifying patterns and natural groupings in data. It's particularly useful for customer segmentation, where you want to group customers based on similar characteristics, behaviors, or preferences. In this section, we'll explore two popular clustering methods: **K-Means Clustering** and **Hierarchical Clustering**.

K-Means is known for its speed and efficiency in handling large datasets, while Hierarchical Clustering provides a more flexible approach to grouping data and visualizing relationships between clusters. Both techniques offer unique insights and can be applied in various domains, such as marketing, customer segmentation, and product categorization.

K-Means Clustering

Overview

K-Means is a partitional clustering algorithm that divides the dataset into a specified number of clusters, or **K** clusters. Each data point is assigned to the nearest cluster based on the Euclidean distance to the cluster's center (called the centroid). The goal is to minimize the distance between data points and their cluster centroids, making each cluster as cohesive as possible.

K-Means is widely used for its simplicity and speed, making it suitable for large datasets. However, it requires the number of clusters (K) to be specified in advance.

Steps of K-Means Clustering

1. **Choose the number of clusters (K)**.
2. **Initialize cluster centroids randomly**.
3. **Assign each data point to the nearest centroid**.
4. **Update centroids** based on the mean of the assigned points.
5. **Repeat** steps 3 and 4 until the centroids no longer change significantly or a maximum number of iterations is reached.

Example Case Study: Customer Segmentation with K-Means

Suppose you work for a retail company and want to segment your customers based on their annual spending and number of store visits. Segmenting customers can help target marketing campaigns and identify high-value customers.

Step 1: Prepare the Data

Assume you have a dataset with the following columns:

- **CustomerID**: Unique identifier for each customer.
- **Annual_Spending**: Amount spent by the customer in the past year.
- **Visits**: Number of visits to the store in the past year.

Here's how you can approach customer segmentation using Python and K-Means clustering:

Step 1: Load and Prepare the Data

Start by loading the data. In this example, we have customer data with CustomerID, Annual_Spending, and Visits. We'll drop CustomerID since it's not relevant for clustering, focusing instead on Annual_Spending and Visits.

Step 2: Determine the Optimal Number of Clusters

To decide on the best number of clusters (K), use the elbow method. This method involves running

K-Means for a range of cluster numbers and plotting each cluster's sum of squared distances. When plotted, the optimal K appears as an "elbow" where adding more clusters results in diminishing improvements.

Step 3: Apply K-Means Clustering

Once you have chosen the ideal number of clusters (suppose K=3), fit the K-Means model to the data. This will assign each data point (customer) to one of the clusters based on their spending and visit patterns.

Step 4: Interpret and Visualize the Clusters

Finally, visualize the clusters. Plot Annual_Spending against Visits, with each point colored by its cluster. This will help you see distinct customer segments based on their spending and visit frequency.

Each cluster represents a distinct customer segment. For example:

- **Cluster 0**: Low spenders with few visits.
- **Cluster 1**: Moderate spenders with moderate visits.
- **Cluster 2**: High spenders with frequent visits.

These insights allow the company to tailor its marketing strategy to each customer segment.

Hierarchical Clustering

Overview

Hierarchical clustering creates a tree-like structure (dendrogram) that shows how data points are grouped at various levels. It does not require specifying the number of clusters beforehand, making it useful for exploratory analysis.

There are two types of hierarchical clustering:

- **Agglomerative**: Starts with each data point as a separate cluster and merges them based on their similarity.
- **Divisive**: Starts with all data points in one cluster and splits them based on their dissimilarity.

Agglomerative clustering is more common and will be the focus here.

Steps of Hierarchical Clustering (Agglomerative)

1. **Calculate the distance** between every pair of data points.
2. **Merge the two closest clusters** to form a new cluster.

3. **Recalculate distances** between the new cluster and all other clusters.
4. **Repeat** steps 2 and 3 until only one cluster remains.

Example Case Study: Customer Segmentation with Hierarchical Clustering

Here's how you can use hierarchical clustering for customer segmentation, starting from the same customer data used in the K-Means example:

Step 1: Prepare the Data

Using the previously prepared data on customer spending and visits, select these features for clustering.

Step 2: Generate a Dendrogram

The dendrogram is a tree-like diagram that visually represents hierarchical clustering. It shows at which points data points merge into clusters and helps determine the optimal number of clusters by observing where to "cut" the tree. Using Python's scipy library, perform hierarchical clustering and calculate the dendrogram to see how clusters form at various levels.

Step 3: Apply Hierarchical Clustering

Once you have analyzed the dendrogram, you can decide on the number of clusters, for instance, three clusters. Use AgglomerativeClustering from scikit-learn to assign each customer to a cluster based on the hierarchical structure.

Step 4: Visualize and Interpret the Clusters

Finally, plot the clusters to interpret the results, similar to the K-Means method. Each cluster will represent a distinct customer segment based on spending and visit frequency. Hierarchical clustering offers a more visual approach to clustering, with the dendrogram providing a detailed view of how clusters group together at various levels.

Choosing Between K-Means and Hierarchical Clustering

- **K-Means Clustering**: Best for large datasets with well-defined clusters. It's computationally efficient and produces distinct clusters, making it suitable for applications where you know the number of clusters in advance.
- **Hierarchical Clustering**: Ideal for smaller datasets or when you're exploring the data and unsure of the optimal number of clusters. The dendrogram helps you

understand data structure and identify the natural groupings.

Real-World Applications of Clustering Techniques

1. **Customer Segmentation**: Group customers based on demographics, purchasing behavior, or engagement metrics to tailor marketing strategies for each segment.
2. **Product Categorization**: Identify similar products based on features, enabling e-commerce platforms to recommend similar items or group products in categories.
3. **Document Clustering**: Organize documents based on topics or content similarity, useful for organizing large datasets of text or for content recommendation.
4. **Anomaly Detection**: Spot outliers in datasets by identifying items that don't belong to any cluster, useful in fraud detection and quality control.

Conclusion

In this section, we covered two popular clustering methods: **K-Means** and **Hierarchical Clustering**. Both methods allow you to group data into meaningful clusters, revealing patterns and segments that aren't immediately visible in raw data.

K-Means is well-suited for large datasets where you know the number of clusters, while Hierarchical Clustering provides flexibility in exploring data structure without needing to predefine the number of clusters. By mastering these techniques, you'll be able to apply clustering for customer segmentation, product categorization, and other applications, gaining valuable insights that can drive business decisions and improve data-driven strategies.

Evaluating Cluster Quality

After performing clustering analysis, it's essential to evaluate the quality of the clusters to ensure that the results are meaningful and useful. A good clustering solution should have well-separated clusters with cohesive points. In this section, we'll discuss key methods for assessing cluster validity, including the **silhouette score**, **elbow method**, **Dunn index**, and **Davies-Bouldin index**.

By using these evaluation metrics, you can make informed decisions about the optimal number of clusters and the overall quality of your segmentation.

Silhouette Score

Overview

The silhouette score is a popular metric for evaluating clustering quality. It measures how similar each data point is to its assigned cluster compared to other clusters. The score ranges from -1 to 1, with:

- **Values close to 1** indicating that points are well-clustered and far from other clusters.
- **Values around 0** suggesting that points are on or near the boundary between clusters.
- **Negative values** indicating that points may have been assigned to the wrong cluster.

Here's an overview of using clustering metrics like the silhouette score, elbow method, and Dunn index to evaluate and interpret clustering solutions effectively:

Silhouette Score: Understanding Cluster Quality

The silhouette score measures how distinct each cluster is, helping determine the quality of clustering by evaluating how similar each point is to its own cluster versus others. This score is calculated for each data point and ranges between -1 and 1, where higher values indicate well-defined clusters, and lower values suggest that clusters might be overlapping.

To calculate the silhouette score:

1. Run K-Means clustering with different values of KKK (the number of clusters).
2. For each KKK, calculate the score and examine which value yields the highest score, indicating the best separation between clusters.

Each data point's score is based on:

- **Intra-cluster distance** (how close the point is to others within its cluster).
- **Inter-cluster distance** (the distance to points in the nearest neighboring cluster).

If you find the silhouette score drops when increasing KKK, it could suggest "over-clustering," where the data is split too finely into multiple clusters, losing meaningful structure.

Elbow Method: Finding the Ideal Number of Clusters

The elbow method is a visual technique to determine the optimal number of clusters by examining the sum of squared distances, or **inertia**, between data points and their assigned cluster centroids. It involves plotting the inertia for various values of KKK and finding the "elbow," or point of diminishing returns, which indicates the best KKK for clustering.

To use the elbow method:

1. Run K-Means clustering with different values of KKK, typically ranging from 1 to 10.
2. Plot the inertia for each value of KKK to observe the curve.
3. Identify the "elbow" point where adding more clusters no longer significantly reduces inertia.

The point at which the curve begins to flatten is considered the ideal number of clusters, as further increases in KKK add little value in minimizing distances within clusters.

Dunn Index: Assessing Cluster Separation and Compactness

The Dunn index is a metric used to evaluate clustering quality by comparing the **minimum inter-cluster distance** (distance between clusters) with the **maximum intra-cluster distance** (distance within a cluster). A higher Dunn index suggests well-separated, compact clusters. This metric is especially valuable when comparing different clustering algorithms or setups, as it emphasizes both separation and cohesion of clusters.

The Dunn index calculation involves:

1. Finding the smallest distance between any two clusters.
2. Finding the largest distance within a single cluster.

This ratio yields a value indicating clustering quality—higher values mean clusters are distinct and tightly grouped. However, keep in mind that the Dunn index can be sensitive to noise, so it's generally more effective with clearly distinct clusters.

Davies-Bouldin Index: Evaluating Cluster Quality

The Davies-Bouldin index is a measure used to assess clustering quality by calculating how similar each cluster is to its most similar neighboring cluster. In contrast to some other metrics, a **lower Davies-Bouldin index** indicates better clustering, as it suggests that clusters are more distinct and well-separated.

The formula for the Davies-Bouldin index is:

The formula for the Davies-Bouldin index is:

$$DB = \frac{1}{K} \sum_{i=1}^{K} \max_{j \neq i} \left(\frac{\sigma_i + \sigma_j}{d(c_i, c_j)} \right)$$

where:

- **KKK** is the number of clusters.
- **σi\sigma_iσi** is the average distance of points within cluster iii to its centroid.
- **d(ci,cj)d(c_i, c_j)d(ci,cj)** is the distance between the centroids of clusters iii and jjj.

In this formula, the index evaluates how compact and well-separated each cluster is from others. A lower value indicates that clusters are more compact and well-distanced from each other.

Using the Davies-Bouldin Index to Evaluate Clusters

To calculate the Davies-Bouldin index in Python, you can use the davies_bouldin_score function from the sklearn.metrics module. This is particularly useful for comparing the quality of different clustering solutions:

1. Apply clustering to your data with your chosen number of clusters, KKK.

2. Calculate the Davies-Bouldin index for the resulting cluster labels.
3. A lower score suggests better clustering performance.

For example, you can run K-Means clustering on a dataset with $K=3K=3K=3$ clusters and calculate the Davies-Bouldin index for the resulting clusters to evaluate how well-separated and compact the clusters are. The lower the index, the better the clustering outcome.

Interpretation: A lower Davies-Bouldin index indicates that clusters are well-separated and have minimal overlap. This metric is useful when comparing clustering solutions to find the one with the least similarity between clusters.

Choosing the Right Evaluation Metric

Each clustering metric has its strengths and weaknesses, and the choice of metric depends on the specific clustering task and dataset:

- **Silhouette Score** is ideal for quick evaluations and works well with K-Means, especially when clusters are well-defined.
- **Elbow Method** is a simple and effective way to choose the initial number of clusters for K-Means.
- **Dunn Index** is useful when you're seeking a strong separation between

clusters, though it can be sensitive to noise.

- **Davies-Bouldin Index** provides a more robust assessment of cluster separation and works well when comparing different clustering algorithms.

Using a combination of these metrics often provides the best insight into cluster quality, helping you make informed decisions about clustering parameters and validation.

Conclusion

Evaluating the quality of clusters is a critical step in clustering analysis. By understanding and applying metrics like the silhouette score, elbow method, Dunn index, and Davies-Bouldin index, you can assess the validity and cohesiveness of clusters in your data. These metrics allow you to refine your clustering model, ensuring that it captures meaningful patterns and segmentation.

Mastering cluster evaluation techniques will help you create reliable and actionable clustering models, whether you're segmenting customers, categorizing products, or identifying patterns in complex datasets.

Time Series Analysis for Trend Prediction

Understanding and Forecasting Trends

Time series analysis is a powerful tool for identifying patterns and predicting future values in data collected over time. It's commonly used in fields like finance, economics, sales forecasting, and supply chain management. This section introduces two popular time series forecasting techniques—**ARIMA** (Auto-Regressive Integrated Moving Average) and **Exponential Smoothing**—and explains how to use them to forecast trends and make data-driven predictions.

By the end of this section, you'll understand the fundamentals of these techniques, how to apply them, and their applications in real-world scenarios.

Time Series Fundamentals

Before diving into forecasting methods, let's review some basic concepts in time series analysis:

- **Trend**: The long-term upward or downward movement in a time series.
- **Seasonality**: Regular patterns that repeat over specific time intervals, such as daily, weekly, or yearly.
- **Noise**: Random fluctuations or irregularities in the data that do not follow a pattern.

- **Stationarity**: A time series is stationary if its statistical properties (mean, variance) are constant over time.

Most forecasting methods aim to model the trend and seasonality while accounting for noise to make accurate predictions.

ARIMA (Auto-Regressive Integrated Moving Average)

Overview

ARIMA is one of the most widely used models for time series forecasting. It combines three components:

1. **Auto-Regressive (AR)**: A model that uses past values to predict future values.
2. **Integrated (I)**: A differencing step to make the time series stationary, removing trends and seasonality.
3. **Moving Average (MA)**: A model that uses past forecast errors to improve predictions.

ARIMA models are defined by three parameters: **(p, d, q)**:

- **p**: The number of lag observations in the auto-regression model.
- **d**: The number of times differencing is applied to make the series stationary.

- **q**: The size of the moving average window.

Steps for Applying ARIMA

1. **Make the Series Stationary**: Use differencing if needed to remove trends or seasonality.
2. **Identify Optimal Parameters (p, d, q)**: Use methods like **autocorrelation** and **partial autocorrelation** plots, or try different combinations to find the best fit.
3. **Fit the Model**: Train the ARIMA model on your data.
4. **Forecast**: Use the model to make predictions and evaluate its performance.

Example: Sales Forecasting with ARIMA

Suppose you want to forecast monthly sales for the upcoming year based on historical sales data. Here's how you can use ARIMA to achieve this in Python.

Step-by-Step Guide for Time Series Forecasting with ARIMA and Exponential Smoothing

Step 1: Load and Visualize the Data

First, start by loading your dataset and visualizing it to get an initial sense of the data's trend and pattern over time. For example, if you're analyzing monthly sales data, you can use a line chart to see the fluctuations and any potential seasonality.

Step 2: Make the Series Stationary

Time series forecasting models like ARIMA work best when the data is stationary, meaning it has a consistent mean and variance over time. To achieve this, apply differencing if you detect a trend. Differencing essentially subtracts the previous data point from the current one, helping to stabilize the trend.

Step 3: Determine ARIMA Parameters

To configure an ARIMA model, you need three parameters:

- **p**: The number of lag observations included.
- **d**: The degree of differencing needed to make the series stationary.
- **q**: The size of the moving average window.

Using autocorrelation (ACF) and partial autocorrelation (PACF) plots helps to identify these values visually, but an automated tool like auto_arima can suggest optimal parameters for you, simplifying the setup.

Step 4: Fit the Model and Forecast

After identifying the best parameters, fit the ARIMA model. Then, use it to forecast future values. If, for example, you want a 12-month forecast, set your forecast steps to 12. Plotting both historical and forecasted values can visually validate the model's performance.

Applications

ARIMA is ideal for non-seasonal data with trends, widely used in economic and financial forecasting, sales predictions, and demand planning.

Exponential Smoothing: An Alternative Approach for Trend and Seasonality

Overview

Exponential Smoothing models are useful for time series with different components, such as level, trend, and seasonality. There are three main types:

1. **Simple Exponential Smoothing (SES)**: For data without trend or seasonality.
2. **Holt's Linear Trend Model**: For data with a trend but no seasonality.
3. **Holt-Winters Seasonal Model**: For data with both trend and seasonality.

Each type uses smoothing parameters to control the weight given to recent data points:

- **Alpha (α)**: Controls smoothing of the level.
- **Beta (β)**: Controls smoothing of the trend.
- **Gamma (γ)**: Controls smoothing of the seasonality.

Example: Forecasting Seasonal Sales with Holt-Winters

Suppose you're dealing with seasonal sales data and want to apply the Holt-Winters model. Here's how to proceed:

1. **Fit the Holt-Winters Model**: Using ExponentialSmoothing from Python's statsmodels library, you can specify both trend and seasonality as additive components if the pattern is additive.
2. **Set Seasonality Parameters**: For monthly data with annual seasonality, specify seasonal_periods=12.
3. **Visualize the Forecast**: As with ARIMA, visualize both the historical and forecasted data to evaluate the model's predictions.

Applications

Exponential Smoothing is ideal for data with seasonality and trends, making it useful for industries like retail, where sales and demand often follow seasonal patterns. It's also beneficial in inventory management and any scenario involving periodic time series data.

Choosing Between ARIMA and Exponential Smoothing

- **ARIMA** is suitable for time series with a trend and no seasonality, particularly when the data is stationary or can be made stationary through differencing.
- **Exponential Smoothing** (especially Holt-Winters) is ideal for data with trend and seasonality. It's often easier to interpret and implement, especially for seasonally varying data.

Practical Applications of Time Series Forecasting

1. **Sales Forecasting**: Predict monthly or quarterly sales based on historical patterns, helping companies optimize inventory and resource planning.
2. **Demand Planning**: Use forecasts to anticipate demand, reducing overstock and stockouts, which is crucial in retail, manufacturing, and supply chain management.

3. **Economic Forecasting**: Project future economic indicators, such as GDP or inflation, to inform government policy or business strategy.
4. **Financial Market Analysis**: Forecast stock prices or trading volumes, helping investors and analysts make informed decisions.
5. **Utility and Resource Forecasting**: Predict energy consumption or water demand based on past usage patterns, assisting utility companies in planning resource allocation.

Conclusion

In this section, we introduced time series forecasting techniques—**ARIMA** and **Exponential Smoothing**—which are essential tools for predicting trends in temporal data. Both methods offer unique advantages, with ARIMA suitable for stationary data with trends and Exponential Smoothing well-suited for seasonal data with trends.

By mastering these techniques, you can develop robust forecasting models for applications ranging from sales and demand forecasting to economic and financial analysis. Time series forecasting is a valuable skill that enables data analysts to extract actionable insights from historical data, empowering data-driven decision-making in various industries.

Case Study in Forecasting: Sales Prediction

Time series forecasting is widely used in business applications to predict future values based on historical data. In this case study, we'll walk through a real-world example of **sales forecasting** for a retail company. Using historical monthly sales data, we'll apply time series techniques—**ARIMA** and **Holt-Winters Exponential Smoothing**—to generate a forecast that can help the company anticipate future sales and make informed business decisions.

By following this case study, you'll gain a deeper understanding of how to apply these forecasting methods and interpret the results in a business context.

Business Scenario

Imagine a retail company that sells seasonal products. The company wants to forecast monthly sales for the next year to plan inventory, allocate resources, and optimize marketing strategies. They have collected monthly sales data for the past five years and want to use this historical data to predict sales trends.

Data Overview

The dataset contains:

- **Date**: The month and year for each data point.
- **Sales**: The total sales for each month (in dollars).

The goal is to analyze the time series data to understand the trend and seasonality, and then generate a forecast for the next 12 months.

Step 1: Data Exploration and Visualization

Start by loading the sales data and visualizing it to identify any overall trends, seasonal patterns, or recurring peaks. This step is essential to understand the general behavior of sales over time, which will guide the choice of forecasting method.

1. Load the data and plot the time series to observe monthly sales trends.
2. Look for key patterns, such as whether sales show a steady increase (upward trend) or if they peak seasonally, for example, during holiday periods.

In our example, let's assume that sales data shows a clear upward trend with predictable peaks around certain months, such as the holiday season.

Step 2: Applying ARIMA for Forecasting

ARIMA (AutoRegressive Integrated Moving Average) is effective for data with trends but limited seasonality.

Step 2.1: Make the Series Stationary

ARIMA models require the data to be stationary, meaning it has a constant mean and variance over time. Applying "differencing" helps remove trends and stabilize the data.

1. Perform differencing on the dataset to remove the trend.
2. Visualize the differenced data to confirm it is now stationary, showing less trend over time.

Step 2.2: Identify Optimal ARIMA Parameters

To configure ARIMA, three parameters are needed: **p** (auto-regression), **d** (degree of differencing), and **q** (moving average).

- Use the auto_arima function to automatically identify the best combination of these parameters.

Assume the model identifies the optimal configuration as ARIMA(1, 1, 1).

Step 2.3: Fit the ARIMA Model and Forecast

Using the identified parameters, fit the ARIMA model to the data and forecast future sales.

1. Fit the model with the chosen parameters.
2. Forecast the next 12 months to get an estimate of future sales trends.
3. Plot the historical sales alongside the forecasted values to visualize the predictions.

The ARIMA forecast projects sales based on past patterns, which is suitable if the data has a significant trend but limited seasonality.

Step 3: Applying Holt-Winters Exponential Smoothing

When the data exhibits both a trend and seasonality, the Holt-Winters (Exponential Smoothing) method is more appropriate. This approach accommodates patterns like seasonal peaks and trends over time, making it ideal for retail sales data.

Step 3.1: Fit the Holt-Winters Model

Using ExponentialSmoothing from the statsmodels library, fit the Holt-Winters model by setting both trend and seasonality as additive components, which is appropriate when these effects are consistent over time.

1. Fit the Holt-Winters model to the data, specifying both trend and seasonality settings.
2. Forecast the next 12 months.
3. Plot the historical data alongside the forecasted data to see how the model captures seasonal peaks and trends.

The Holt-Winters forecast accounts for both trend and seasonal variations, making it a strong option when you have data with regular, repeating seasonal patterns, such as holiday sales spikes.

Interpretation of Forecasts

- **ARIMA Forecast**: Suited for data with a clear trend but without strong seasonal fluctuations. It's useful for projecting future values in a straightforward trend scenario.

- **Holt-Winters Forecast**: Better for data with both trend and seasonal patterns, providing more precise predictions for cases where seasonal spikes are expected, such as during holidays.

Using these two approaches allows you to tailor forecasting based on the presence of trends and seasonality in your data, helping to create accurate, actionable sales projections.

Step 4: Comparing Forecast Results

By applying both ARIMA and Holt-Winters models, we can compare the forecasts and choose the one that best fits the historical data. In a business setting, it's essential to choose the model that captures the trend and seasonality accurately for optimal forecasting.

Comparison Points:

- **ARIMA**: Good for capturing trends but may miss seasonal peaks if they are irregular or vary in intensity.
- **Holt-Winters**: Ideal for data with consistent seasonal patterns, as it directly incorporates seasonality into the forecast.

In practice, plot both forecasts and compare them visually and quantitatively (using metrics like

Mean Absolute Error or **Root Mean Square Error**) to determine the best fit.

Step 5: Business Insights and Applications

With a reliable forecast, the retail company can leverage these predictions to make informed business decisions:

1. **Inventory Management**: By anticipating sales peaks, the company can stock up on products ahead of high-demand periods, reducing the risk of stockouts.
2. **Resource Allocation**: Knowing future sales trends helps the company allocate resources such as staffing, marketing budgets, and distribution efforts more effectively.
3. **Promotional Planning**: Forecasting sales allows the marketing team to plan promotions around anticipated dips, boosting sales during slow periods.
4. **Financial Planning**: Accurate sales predictions contribute to budgeting and financial forecasting, helping the company set realistic revenue targets and optimize cash flow.

For example, if the forecast indicates a sales peak during December, the company could ramp up holiday promotions in advance, adjust staffing levels, and increase product inventory to meet demand.

Conclusion

This case study demonstrates how to apply time series analysis to a practical business problem—forecasting monthly sales. By leveraging **ARIMA** and **Holt-Winters Exponential Smoothing**, the retail company can predict future sales trends and make data-driven decisions.

Mastering time series forecasting techniques enables data analysts to generate valuable insights in various domains, including finance, retail, and supply chain management. With accurate forecasts, businesses can optimize operations, improve customer satisfaction, and ultimately enhance profitability.

End-of-Chapter Data Project: Full Predictive Analytics Workflow

In this project, you'll apply your knowledge of regression, clustering, and forecasting to complete a full predictive analytics workflow. By using SQL, Python, and R, you'll gain practical experience in integrating multiple tools and techniques, mirroring the workflows used by data analysts and scientists in real-world projects.

This project will cover:

1. Data Extraction using SQL
2. Data Preprocessing and Regression Analysis using Python
3. Clustering and Segmentation using Python
4. Forecasting using R

Dataset Overview

For this project, imagine you're working for a retail company that wants to analyze and forecast customer purchasing behavior. You have access to a dataset containing transaction data with the following columns:

- **CustomerID**: Unique identifier for each customer.
- **Age**: Age of the customer.
- **Income**: Annual income of the customer.
- **Visits**: Number of store visits in the past year.
- **Spending**: Total spending by the customer in the past year.
- **OrderDate**: Date of each purchase made by the customer.

The dataset provides insights into customer demographics, purchasing behavior, and time-based purchase patterns.

Step 1: Data Extraction using SQL

Start by retrieving the data from a SQL database. Suppose the data is stored in two tables:

- **Customers**: Contains demographic information like CustomerID, Age, and Income.
- **Transactions**: Contains transaction details, including CustomerID, OrderDate, Visits, and Spending.

Step 1: SQL Query to Retrieve Customer Data

To start, retrieve the data for customers who made at least one purchase in the past year, including their demographics and transaction details.

In SQL, the query combines customer demographic data with their transaction history over the last year:

1. **Customer and Transaction Join**: This pulls in details for each customer and transaction.
2. **Filter by Date**: Only transactions from the past year are included.

Once retrieved, save this data as a CSV file to analyze in Python or R.

Step 2: Data Preprocessing and Regression Analysis in Python

Now, load the data in Python for preprocessing and perform regression analysis to understand which factors influence customer spending.

Step 2.1: Load and Explore the Data

Load the saved CSV file and preview the first few rows to get an initial look at the data's structure.

Step 2.2: Data Cleaning

Check for missing values, especially in key columns like income. Fill missing income values with the median, and convert any date fields to a date format.

Step 2.3: Regression Analysis

Using multiple regression, analyze how factors like age, income, and visits impact customer spending. Set spending as the dependent variable and age, income, and visits as the independent variables. After running the regression, review the model's coefficients and p-values to identify significant predictors of spending.

For instance, a strong positive coefficient for income would indicate that higher-income customers tend to spend more.

Step 3: Customer Segmentation with Clustering in Python

To understand different customer behaviors, segment customers based on demographics and spending habits using clustering.

Step 3.1: Prepare Data for Clustering

For clustering, select features like age, income, visits, and spending. Normalize these features so they have equal influence during clustering.

Step 3.2: K-Means Clustering

Using K-Means, find the optimal number of clusters with the Elbow Method, which involves plotting the sum of squared distances for different values of K. Suppose the Elbow Method indicates that three clusters are optimal.

Fit the K-Means model with three clusters and label each customer according to their cluster. These clusters represent distinct customer segments. For example, one cluster might represent high-income, high-spending customers, while another could represent low-income, low-spending ones. This segmentation can help in designing targeted marketing strategies.

Step 4: Forecasting Monthly Sales in R

Switch to R to forecast monthly sales for the next year, using the Holt-Winters Exponential

Smoothing method to capture both trend and seasonality.

Step 4.1: Aggregate Monthly Sales Data in Python

Before moving to R, aggregate sales by month to create a time series dataset suitable for forecasting. Save the monthly data as a CSV file for use in R.

Step 4.2: Forecasting in R with Holt-Winters

In R:

1. Load the monthly sales data and convert it to a time series format.
2. Apply the Holt-Winters Exponential Smoothing model, which accounts for trend and seasonality.
3. Forecast the next 12 months and plot the results, providing a visual representation of the expected monthly sales.

This approach helps predict future sales, making it easier to plan inventory and marketing efforts around expected seasonal trends.

Interpretation: The forecast provides expected monthly sales for the next year. This insight helps the retail company in planning inventory, budgeting, and optimizing marketing efforts for anticipated high-demand periods.

Project Summary

This project covers a complete predictive analytics workflow using SQL, Python, and R:

1. **Data Extraction**: Retrieve data from SQL and export it for analysis.
2. **Regression Analysis**: Use Python to analyze factors that influence spending.
3. **Clustering**: Segment customers into distinct groups based on behavior and demographics.
4. **Forecasting**: Use R to predict future sales based on historical patterns.

This end-to-end project showcases a multi-tool, multi-technique approach to predictive analytics, equipping you with practical skills for real-world data projects. By mastering this workflow, you'll be prepared to tackle complex data challenges and provide actionable insights across various business domains.

Chapter 5: Integrated Project: Building a Data Analytics Pipeline

Defining the Project Scope

End-to-End Analysis

Building a robust data analytics pipeline starts with a clear understanding of the project's objectives, data requirements, and analytical goals. Defining the scope of your project ensures that every step in the pipeline aligns with the intended outcomes, maximizing efficiency and relevance.

In this section, we'll guide you through the critical steps for defining the project scope, including:

1. Identifying the business objectives.
2. Determining data requirements and sources.
3. Outlining analytical goals and deliverables.

By carefully planning the scope, you'll set a strong foundation for the end-to-end analytics pipeline, enabling a streamlined approach to data analysis, from data gathering to reporting.

Step 1: Identify the Business Objectives

The first step in defining your project scope is to identify the overarching business objectives. This means understanding what problem the project aims to solve and what insights or decisions it will support. Clear objectives help narrow down the focus of the analysis, ensuring that the results are actionable and aligned with business needs.

Example: Retail Sales Forecasting

Imagine you're building a data analytics pipeline for a retail company that wants to improve its inventory management and sales performance. The company's primary objectives might include:

- **Accurate Sales Forecasting**: Predict monthly sales for the upcoming year to optimize stock levels and avoid overstock or stockouts.
- **Customer Segmentation**: Identify distinct customer groups to tailor marketing efforts and improve customer retention.
- **Product Performance Analysis**: Analyze sales by product category to identify best-selling items and underperforming products.

Each objective should be specific, measurable, and actionable. For instance, "predict monthly sales" is specific, and "optimize stock levels" is actionable based on the insights generated from the forecast.

Step 2: Determine Data Requirements and Sources

Once you've identified the objectives, determine what data is required to achieve these goals and where to obtain it. This step involves understanding the types of data, data sources, and data attributes necessary for the analysis.

Example: Required Data for Retail Analysis

For the retail sales forecasting project, the following data types and sources might be needed:

1. **Transaction Data**: Contains details of each sale, including:
   - **OrderDate**: Date of the transaction.
   - **ProductID**: Identifier for each product sold.
   - **Quantity**: Number of items sold.
   - **Price**: Sale price per unit.
   - **CustomerID**: Identifier for the customer who made the purchase.
   - **Source**: This data can be retrieved from the company's sales database.

2. **Customer Data**: Provides information on customer demographics and purchase behavior, including:
    o **Age**: Age of the customer.
    o **Income**: Annual income of the customer.
    o **Location**: Customer's location (e.g., city or region).
    o **CustomerID**: Identifier to link to transaction data.
    o **Source**: Typically available in the company's customer database or CRM system.
3. **Product Data**: Provides details about each product, including:
    o **ProductID**: Unique identifier for each product.
    o **Category**: Product category (e.g., electronics, apparel).
    o **Cost**: Cost price of the product.
    o **Source**: Available in the company's product catalog or inventory database.
4. **External Data** (Optional): For added context, consider incorporating external factors that might impact sales, such as:
    o **Weather Data**: Particularly useful for products that are weather-dependent (e.g., winter clothing).
    o **Economic Indicators**: Data like consumer spending trends, which may impact overall sales.

- Source: Public data sources, such as government databases or third-party data providers.

Step 3: Outline Analytical Goals and Deliverables

With the objectives and data sources defined, the next step is to outline the specific analytical goals, methods, and expected deliverables. This outline serves as a roadmap for the project, detailing each phase of the analysis and its intended output.

Example: Analytical Goals for Retail Project

For the retail sales forecasting project, here are some example analytical goals and deliverables:

1. **Data Cleaning and Preprocessing**
   - **Goal**: Clean and preprocess the data to ensure quality and consistency.
   - **Tasks**: Handle missing values, remove duplicates, and normalize data types.
   - **Deliverable**: A clean, standardized dataset ready for analysis.
2. **Descriptive Analytics**
   - **Goal**: Generate summary statistics to understand baseline metrics.

- Tasks: Calculate metrics such as average sales, customer demographics, and product performance.
- Deliverable: A report summarizing key metrics and descriptive insights.

3. **Customer Segmentation (Clustering)**
   - **Goal**: Segment customers based on demographics and purchasing behavior.
   - **Methods**: Use K-Means or hierarchical clustering to group customers.
   - **Deliverable**: Customer segments report with insights on each segment's characteristics and purchasing patterns.

4. **Product Performance Analysis**
   - **Goal**: Identify top-performing and underperforming products.
   - **Methods**: Analyze sales data by product category and calculate metrics such as total revenue, units sold, and profitability.
   - **Deliverable**: A dashboard showing product performance, enabling stakeholders to make data-driven decisions.

5. **Sales Forecasting**

- Goal: Predict monthly sales for the next year.
- Methods: Use time series forecasting techniques (e.g., ARIMA or Holt-Winters) to generate future sales projections.
- Deliverable: A forecast report or visualization that estimates future monthly sales.

6. **Actionable Insights and Recommendations**
   - Goal: Provide data-driven recommendations based on the analysis.
   - Tasks: Interpret the results of each analysis phase and suggest actionable steps for business improvement.
   - Deliverable: A final report with recommendations for inventory management, marketing strategies, and customer engagement.

Tips for Defining a Project Scope

1. **Align Objectives with Business Goals**: Ensure the objectives are relevant to the organization's strategic goals to increase the impact of the analysis.
2. **Define Clear Deliverables**: Outline specific, actionable deliverables to provide

clarity on the expected outcomes of each phase of the project.

3. **Specify Data Requirements Early**: Identifying data sources and requirements upfront can help prevent delays due to missing or incompatible data.

4. **Balance Scope with Resources**: Set realistic goals and timelines based on the resources, tools, and time available. This helps avoid overextending the scope and ensures that the project is achievable.

5. **Consider Data Privacy and Compliance**: When gathering and analyzing data, be mindful of data privacy and compliance requirements, especially for customer data.

Conclusion

Defining the project scope is a crucial first step in building a data analytics pipeline. By establishing clear objectives, gathering the necessary data, and outlining analytical goals, you set the stage for an organized and efficient pipeline. This foundational work ensures that every phase of the pipeline aligns with business needs and that the analysis provides actionable insights.

Through this process, you create a comprehensive roadmap for the entire analytics workflow, making it easier to navigate each step from data gathering to reporting. A well-defined scope is the cornerstone of a successful analytics project, leading to meaningful outcomes that drive business impact.

Data Collection and Storage with SQL

Data Ingestion and Database Structuring

Effective data ingestion and storage are critical to building a robust data analytics pipeline. By setting up a well-organized database and using SQL to clean and store data, you can ensure that data is accessible, accurate, and ready for analysis. In this section, we'll walk through the steps of setting up a database, cleaning incoming data, and storing it using advanced SQL techniques.

This process includes:

1. Creating a database and defining its structure.
2. Ingesting raw data and performing initial data cleaning.
3. Structuring and storing data in a way that optimizes accessibility and performance.

Step 1: Setting Up the Database

The first step in the data ingestion process is to create a relational database and define the structure that will support efficient storage and retrieval. In this example, we'll set up a database for a retail company that wants to analyze customer transactions, product details, and sales performance.

Step 1: Setting Up the Retail Analytics Database

Creating the Database
Begin by creating a database named **RetailAnalytics** to organize and store your data.

Next, define tables for each key entity— Customers, Products, and Transactions—with specific fields and primary keys to uniquely identify each record:

- **Customers**: Includes customer demographics like age, income, and location.
- **Products**: Contains details such as product name, category, price, and cost.
- **Transactions**: Records each transaction, connecting Customers and Products via foreign keys.

Step 2: Data Ingestion and Initial Cleaning

To ensure clean data, start by importing raw data into **staging tables**. These are temporary tables where initial cleaning occurs before data moves to the main tables.

Step 2.1: Create Staging Tables

Set up staging tables to hold raw data for customers, products, and transactions. This isolates the incoming data, protecting the core database from any potential quality issues.

Step 2.2: Load Data into Staging Tables

Using SQL commands, load data from CSV files into the staging tables. For example, use delimiter settings to handle CSV formatting and skip the header row.

Step 3: Data Cleaning and Transformation

With data in the staging tables, perform key cleaning steps to prepare it for loading into the main tables.

Step 3.1: Handle Missing and Invalid Values

Check for missing values in essential fields, like CustomerID and OrderDate, and address them accordingly. For example, remove rows with null CustomerID values to maintain data integrity.

Step 3.2: Remove Duplicates

Identify and remove duplicate records, particularly in the customer data, as duplicates can skew analysis results.

Step 3.3: Transform Data

Standardize values, such as converting product names to lowercase, and calculate any missing values, like TotalAmount, using quantity and price information.

Step 4: Load Clean Data into Main Tables

After cleaning, transfer the data from staging tables to the main tables in **RetailAnalytics**. This organized, high-quality data is now ready for analysis.

Step 5: Indexing for Optimized Performance

To speed up queries on large datasets, create indexes on commonly searched columns, like CustomerID, ProductID, and OrderDate. Indexing enhances query efficiency, making analytics faster and more effective.

Best Practices for Data Ingestion and Storage

- **Staging Tables**: Use staging tables to prevent low-quality data from impacting your main tables.
- **Automate Data Loading**: Automate data import processes for large datasets to ensure consistency.
- **Standardize and Clean Data**: Consistent data formats and cleaned fields enhance the accuracy of analysis.
- **Optimize Performance with Indexing**: For frequently queried columns, indexes can substantially improve query response times.

Data Processing and Analysis with Python/R

After setting up the database and ingesting data, you're ready to use Python and R for deeper data analysis.

Step 1: Data Extraction from SQL Database

Python: Using SQLAlchemy, connect to the **RetailAnalytics** database and load data into Pandas dataframes for further analysis.

R: Use the DBI and RMySQL packages to connect to the database and extract data into data frames.

Step 2: Data Transformation in Python and R

With data extracted, use Python or R to transform it:

- **Merging Tables**: Merge customer and transaction data on CustomerID.
- **Creating New Variables**: Calculate total spending per transaction and extract date components for time-based analysis.

Step 3: Regression Analysis to Explore Spending Drivers

Use multiple regression to examine factors influencing customer spending, with variables like age, income, and visits. The regression results reveal the relationship between each factor and spending, helping to identify which variables most impact customer purchases.

Step 4: Clustering for Customer Segmentation

Apply **K-Means clustering** to segment customers based on demographics and spending behavior. Use features like age, income, and total spending to group customers into distinct segments. These clusters reveal different customer types, supporting targeted marketing strategies.

Step 5: Sales Forecasting with Time Series Analysis

Use time series analysis to predict future sales patterns.

Python: Use Holt-Winters Exponential Smoothing to forecast sales over the next 12 months, capturing both trend and seasonality.

R: Similarly, apply Holt-Winters Exponential Smoothing to visualize forecasted sales, supporting business planning with reliable, data-driven projections.

This step-by-step process establishes a robust data pipeline from database setup and cleaning through to advanced analysis, making it easier to extract actionable insights from your data.

Interpretation:

- The forecasted values provide an estimate of sales for each month in the upcoming year, helping the business plan for future demand.

Conclusion

In this section, we covered the data transformation and analysis steps within a data analytics pipeline. By performing regression, clustering, and forecasting in Python and R, you can derive actionable insights from raw data. These techniques support informed decision-making, whether it's understanding factors that drive spending, identifying customer segments, or forecasting future sales.

This hands-on experience provides a comprehensive look at data processing and advanced analysis, preparing you for real-world applications in data analytics. With these skills, you're well-equipped to complete a full analytics pipeline, from data ingestion and transformation to insights generation and predictive modeling.

Visualization and Reporting

Visualizing Key Insights

Data visualization is the final step in a data analytics pipeline, where raw numbers are transformed into graphical insights that are easy to understand and interpret. Visualizations make complex data more accessible, highlight key insights, and facilitate informed decision-making. In this section, we'll cover how to use **Matplotlib** in Python and **ggplot2** in R to create dynamic and impactful visualizations.

By the end of this section, you'll know how to:

1. Visualize sales trends, customer segments, and forecasted data.
2. Customize visualizations to improve readability and aesthetics.
3. Use visualizations in reports to communicate key insights effectively.

Step 1: Sales Trend Visualization

Understanding historical sales trends is essential for tracking business performance over time. This example will show you how to create a time series plot to visualize monthly sales trends.

Step 1: Creating a Monthly Sales Trend Line Plot

To visualize monthly sales data trends, you can create a line plot using **Matplotlib** in Python:

1. **Python Line Plot**:
    - Load your sales data, then plot each month's sales, marking each data point for clarity.
    - This line plot gives an overview of monthly sales, showing upward or downward trends across months.
2. **R Line Plot with ggplot2**:
    - In R, using **ggplot2**, a similar line plot can be created, where geom_line forms the line and

geom_point highlights each sales point.

o This plot is both easy to read and visually appealing, helping to identify trends at a glance.

Step 2: Visualizing Customer Segments with Scatter Plots

For customer segmentation, scatter plots can be used to display each group's income and spending characteristics.

1. **Python Scatter Plot**:
   o Use **Matplotlib** to plot income against spending for each customer, color-coded by cluster.
   o This scatter plot provides a clear visual of customer groups, showing how clusters differ by income and spending patterns.
2. **R Scatter Plot with ggplot2**:
   o **ggplot2** in R also creates scatter plots, where each cluster is represented by different colors for easy identification.
   o This visualization helps in identifying distinct customer segments for personalized marketing or service strategies.

Step 3: Visualizing Forecasts Alongside Historical Sales Data

To illustrate forecasted sales alongside historical data, line plots provide an effective visual comparison.

1. **Python Forecast Plot**:
   - **Matplotlib** is used to plot historical and forecasted sales, with the forecasted data shown in a different color and a dashed line to distinguish it from historical data.
   - This type of chart is useful for spotting upcoming trends and planning based on predicted sales.
2. **R Forecast Plot with ggplot2**:
   - In R, **ggplot2** can plot both historical and forecasted data together, with color coding for easy differentiation.
   - This visualization highlights expected sales trends, helping businesses make data-driven decisions.

Each of these visualizations brings out specific data insights, from understanding monthly trends to segmenting customers and projecting future sales.

Explanation:

- **scale_color_manual()** customizes colors to differentiate historical and forecasted data.
- **geom_line()** and **geom_point()** plot lines and markers for each sales type.

Step 4: Putting It All Together in a Report

Once you've created the visualizations, compile them into a comprehensive report. Use tools like **Jupyter Notebooks** (Python), **R Markdown** (R), or a presentation software to organize your visualizations and add insights, observations, and recommendations based on your findings.

Key Components of the Report

1. **Introduction**: Describe the objectives and goals of the analysis.
2. **Data Summary**: Briefly summarize the data sources and any preprocessing performed.
3. **Key Insights and Visualizations**:
   - **Sales Trends**: Present the historical sales trend and any seasonal patterns.
   - **Customer Segmentation**: Show customer clusters and describe each segment's characteristics.
   - **Forecasts**: Display forecasted sales and explain projected trends.

4. **Recommendations**: Provide actionable insights and recommendations based on your analysis.
5. **Conclusion**: Summarize the findings and suggest potential next steps.

A well-structured report not only conveys data insights clearly but also provides a basis for informed decision-making, giving stakeholders the tools they need to act on the analysis.

Conclusion

In this section, you learned how to create dynamic visualizations using **Matplotlib** in Python and **ggplot2** in R. By visualizing key insights from your data, you can turn raw numbers into a compelling story that supports decision-making. Whether you're showcasing trends, customer segments, or forecasts, effective visualizations are a powerful tool in any data analyst's toolkit.

Mastering these visualization techniques will enable you to communicate insights more effectively, completing your data analytics pipeline and delivering impactful, data-driven reports.

Building an Analytics Dashboard

An analytics dashboard is a powerful way to present key insights and trends in a concise, interactive format. Dashboards allow stakeholders to quickly grasp essential metrics and drill down into specific areas of interest. In this section, we'll guide you through creating a simple dashboard to visualize and report findings from your data analytics pipeline.

You'll learn how to:

1. Select key metrics and visuals for your dashboard.
2. Build an interactive dashboard using Excel or a web-based tool like Tableau or Power BI.
3. Organize the dashboard for clear, effective communication.

Step 1: Define the Dashboard's Purpose and Key Metrics

Before diving into the creation of the dashboard, define the purpose of the dashboard and the key metrics it will display. This helps keep the dashboard focused and relevant to the business goals.

Example: Dashboard for Retail Sales Analytics

Suppose you're creating a dashboard for a retail company that wants insights into sales, customer behavior, and inventory. Key metrics might include:

- **Total Sales**: Monthly sales trend over time.
- **Top-Selling Products**: Products with the highest sales volume.
- **Customer Segments**: Clusters of customers based on spending behavior.
- **Sales Forecast**: Predicted sales for the next 6 or 12 months.

These metrics align with typical business goals in retail, such as understanding demand trends, optimizing inventory, and identifying valuable customer segments.

Step 2: Set Up the Dashboard in Excel

Excel is a versatile tool for creating interactive dashboards with charts, tables, and slicers. Here's a step-by-step guide to setting up a basic dashboard in Excel.

Step 2.1: Load and Organize Data

Import the cleaned and transformed data into Excel, and organize it in separate sheets or tables for each metric (e.g., sales data, customer segments, product sales).

1. **Monthly Sales Data**: Contains sales volume and revenue by month.

2. **Product Sales Data**: Lists products and their corresponding sales volumes.
3. **Customer Segmentation Data**: Shows customer clusters and average spending.

Step 2.2: Create Charts for Key Metrics

Use Excel's chart tools to create visualizations for each metric.

- **Monthly Sales Trend**: Select the monthly sales data, go to **Insert > Line Chart** to create a line chart showing the sales trend over time.
- **Top-Selling Products**: Use a **Bar Chart** to display the products with the highest sales volumes. Highlight the product names and sales data, then insert a bar chart.
- **Customer Segments**: Use a **Pie Chart** or **Bar Chart** to show the percentage of customers in each segment.
- **Sales Forecast**: Use a **Line Chart** to visualize forecasted sales data, adding it as a separate series to the monthly sales trend chart for comparison.

Step 2.3: Add Interactivity with Slicers

Slicers allow users to filter data by specific categories, such as month, product category, or customer segment. To add slicers:

1. Convert each data table to an Excel Table (Select data, then go to **Insert > Table**).
2. Go to **Insert > Slicer**, select the field you want to filter (e.g., Month or Product Category), and position the slicer on your dashboard.
3. Link each slicer to relevant charts, allowing users to filter the dashboard interactively.

Step 2.4: Arrange the Dashboard Layout

Organize the charts and slicers on a single worksheet to create a clean, user-friendly layout. Group similar metrics together (e.g., place sales charts on the left and customer-related charts on the right). Use text boxes to add titles and brief descriptions for each chart.

Step 3: Build a Web-Based Dashboard with Tableau or Power BI

Web-based tools like **Tableau** and **Power BI** offer powerful features for creating interactive, visually appealing dashboards. Here's a guide to creating a simple dashboard in these tools.

Step 3.1: Load Data into Tableau or Power BI

1. **Connect to Data**: Import your dataset into Tableau or Power BI by connecting to

your data source (e.g., Excel file, SQL database).

2. **Prepare Data**: Ensure that each dataset is cleaned and appropriately formatted, with relevant columns and metrics (e.g., Date, Sales, Customer Segment).

Step 3.2: Create Visualizations

Using Tableau or Power BI's drag-and-drop interface, build the individual visualizations:

1. **Monthly Sales Trend**: Drag the **Date** field to the X-axis and **Sales** to the Y-axis to create a line chart showing sales over time.
2. **Top-Selling Products**: Create a bar chart showing the top products by sales volume, using filters to display only the top 5 or 10 products.
3. **Customer Segments**: Use a pie chart or treemap to show the proportion of customers in each segment.
4. **Sales Forecast**: Combine historical sales data with forecasted values in a single line chart to display future sales trends.

Step 3.3: Add Interactivity with Filters and Slicers

In Tableau:

- Use **Filters** on the sidebar to enable filtering by specific categories, such as month or product category.
- Add **Dashboard Actions** to link multiple charts, so that selecting a specific segment on one chart filters other charts.

In Power BI:

- Use **Slicers** to enable interactive filtering. Insert slicers for fields like **Month**, **Product Category**, or **Customer Segment** to make the dashboard interactive.
- Configure **Cross-Filtering** to ensure that selecting an item in one visualization filters other relevant charts on the dashboard.

Step 3.4: Arrange the Dashboard Layout

Organize the charts and filters on the dashboard to create a clear, logical layout. Use titles, subtitles, and descriptions to label each section of the dashboard.

Dashboard Layout Example:

- **Top Left**: Monthly Sales Trend chart.
- **Top Right**: Sales Forecast chart.
- **Bottom Left**: Customer Segments chart.

- **Bottom Right**: Top-Selling Products chart.
- **Slicers**: Positioned along the side or top of the dashboard for easy access.

Step 4: Finalizing and Sharing the Dashboard

After creating the dashboard, review it for clarity and usability. Ensure each visualization is clearly labeled and that the layout is easy to navigate.

- **Test Interactivity**: Verify that filters and slicers work as expected.
- **Add Explanatory Text**: Include brief descriptions or insights for each metric to help users interpret the visualizations.
- **Export or Publish**:
  - In **Excel**, save the file as a dashboard template or export it as a PDF for sharing.
  - In **Tableau**, publish the dashboard to Tableau Public or Tableau Server for online access.
  - In **Power BI**, publish to the Power BI Service, where users can access and interact with the dashboard online.

Tips for Building an Effective Dashboard

1. **Keep It Simple**: Avoid clutter by focusing on essential metrics that align with the project objectives.
2. **Use Consistent Colors and Fonts**: Consistent styling makes the dashboard look professional and improves readability.
3. **Optimize for the Audience**: Tailor the dashboard to the end users' needs. For executives, focus on high-level KPIs; for analysts, include more detailed data.
4. **Test and Iterate**: Share the dashboard with stakeholders for feedback, and refine it based on their suggestions.

Conclusion

In this section, you learned how to create an analytics dashboard in **Excel**, **Tableau**, or **Power BI** to showcase key findings. Dashboards are a powerful way to present data insights in a visually appealing and interactive format, allowing stakeholders to explore and interpret the data easily.

Mastering the art of dashboard creation is an invaluable skill in data analytics, enabling you to communicate complex data insights effectively and support data-driven decision-making. With a well-designed dashboard, you can deliver actionable insights that have a tangible impact on business strategy and operations.

Conclusion

In this book, we've taken a journey through the stages of constructing an end-to-end data analytics pipeline, transforming raw data into meaningful insights that drive informed decision-making. We started with defining clear objectives, understanding the business context, and outlining analytical goals. This foundation enabled us to stay focused on delivering results that align with real-world needs.

From there, we explored the essential steps in data ingestion, storage, and preprocessing, learning how to use SQL to clean and structure data in a way that ensures consistency and accuracy. We saw how powerful data management practices help create a stable, reliable database that serves as the backbone of our analytics pipeline.

The next stages brought us into the heart of analysis and transformation, where we leveraged Python and R to apply advanced analytical techniques such as regression, clustering, and forecasting. These tools allowed us to derive insights from data patterns, uncover hidden trends, and generate predictions that enable proactive decision-making.

As we moved toward the final stages of the pipeline, we explored the importance of visualization and reporting. Through practical examples with Matplotlib, ggplot2, Excel, and web-based tools like Tableau and Power BI, we learned how to create compelling visuals and build interactive dashboards. These visualizations bring data to life, making complex insights easy to understand and act upon, and allowing stakeholders to explore the data in a dynamic, user-friendly format.

Throughout this journey, we emphasized a holistic approach to analytics—understanding not just the technical steps but also how each step fits into the larger goal of solving business challenges. This integrated view of data analytics allows you to tackle complex projects from start to finish, armed with a toolkit that combines SQL, Python, R, and visualization tools.

Final Thoughts

Data analytics is a rapidly evolving field, and mastering the pipeline covered in this book is just the beginning. The skills you've developed here will serve as a foundation for more advanced techniques and applications, from machine learning to real-time data processing. As you continue to grow as a data analyst, remember that the true power of analytics lies in its ability to solve problems and provide insights that make a real difference in the world.

By following this pipeline, you're equipped to handle diverse data challenges, drive data-driven decisions, and make an impact. As you put these skills into practice, continue exploring, experimenting, and honing your craft. The world of data is vast, and with this foundational knowledge, you're well-prepared to navigate it.

References

Below are some recommended references that provide further insights into the techniques, tools, and theories covered in this book on building a comprehensive data analytics pipeline. These references are a mix of foundational texts, technical manuals, and practical guides that can support continued learning.

1. **Data Analytics Fundamentals**
   - Provost, F., & Fawcett, T. (2013). *Data Science for Business: What You Need to Know About Data Mining and Data-Analytic Thinking.* O'Reilly Media.
   - McKinney, W. (2017). *Python for Data Analysis: Data Wrangling with Pandas, NumPy, and IPython* (2nd ed.). O'Reilly Media.
   - Wickham, H., & Grolemund, G. (2016). *R for Data Science: Import, Tidy, Transform, Visualize, and Model Data.* O'Reilly Media.

2. **SQL and Database Management**
   - Beaulieu, A. (2009). *Learning SQL: Master SQL Fundamentals* (2nd ed.). O'Reilly Media.
   - Oppel, A., & Riccardi, M. (2009). *Databases Demystified* (2nd ed.). McGraw-Hill Education.
   - Celko, J. (2009). *SQL for Smarties: Advanced SQL Programming* (4th ed.). Morgan Kaufmann.
3. **Python for Data Analysis and Machine Learning**
   - Géron, A. (2019). *Hands-On Machine Learning with Scikit-Learn, Keras, and TensorFlow* (2nd ed.). O'Reilly Media.
   - VanderPlas, J. (2016). *Python Data Science Handbook: Essential Tools for Working with Data.* O'Reilly Media.
   - Raschka, S., & Mirjalili, V. (2019). *Python Machine Learning: Machine Learning and Deep Learning with Python, scikit-learn, and TensorFlow 2* (3rd ed.). Packt Publishing.
4. **Data Transformation and Cleaning**
   - Wickham, H. (2014). *Tidy Data.* Journal of Statistical Software, 59(10), 1-23. doi:10.18637/jss.v059.i10

- Dasu, T., & Johnson, T. (2003). *Exploratory Data Mining and Data Cleaning*. Wiley-Interscience.
- Grus, J. (2019). *Data Science from Scratch: First Principles with Python* (2nd ed.). O'Reilly Media.

5. **Statistical Analysis and Modeling**
- Wooldridge, J. M. (2019). *Introductory Econometrics: A Modern Approach* (7th ed.). Cengage Learning.
- Montgomery, D. C., Peck, E. A., & Vining, G. G. (2012). *Introduction to Linear Regression Analysis* (5th ed.). Wiley.
- James, G., Witten, D., Hastie, T., & Tibshirani, R. (2013). *An Introduction to Statistical Learning: with Applications in R.* Springer.

6. **Data Visualization**
- Few, S. (2012). *Show Me the Numbers: Designing Tables and Graphs to Enlighten* (2nd ed.). Analytics Press.
- Cairo, A. (2013). *The Functional Art: An Introduction to Information Graphics and Visualization*. New Riders.
- Healy, K. (2018). *Data Visualization: A Practical*

Introduction. Princeton University Press.

7. **Time Series Analysis and Forecasting**
   - Hyndman, R. J., & Athanasopoulos, G. (2018). *Forecasting: Principles and Practice* (2nd ed.). OTexts. Available at: https://otexts.com/fpp2/
   - Box, G. E., Jenkins, G. M., Reinsel, G. C., & Ljung, G. M. (2015). *Time Series Analysis: Forecasting and Control* (5th ed.). Wiley.
   - Hamilton, J. D. (1994). *Time Series Analysis.* Princeton University Press.

8. **Building Dashboards and Reporting**
   - Kirk, A. (2016). *Data Visualisation: A Handbook for Data Driven Design.* SAGE Publications.
   - Tufte, E. R. (2001). *The Visual Display of Quantitative Information* (2nd ed.). Graphics Press.
   - Choudhury, S., & Tink, D. (2018). *Tableau 2019.x Cookbook: Over 115 Recipes to Build End-to-End Analytical Solutions Using Tableau* (2nd ed.). Packt Publishing.

9. **Machine Learning and Advanced Analytics**

- Bishop, C. M. (2006). *Pattern Recognition and Machine Learning*. Springer.
- Hastie, T., Tibshirani, R., & Friedman, J. (2009). *The Elements of Statistical Learning: Data Mining, Inference, and Prediction* (2nd ed.). Springer.
- Goodfellow, I., Bengio, Y., & Courville, A. (2016). *Deep Learning*. MIT Press.

10. **ETL and Data Engineering for Analytics Pipelines**

- Zalesskiy, M., & Wisniewski, M. (2021). *The Data Engineering Cookbook*. Self-published.
- White, T. (2015). *Hadoop: The Definitive Guide* (4th ed.). O'Reilly Media.
- Narkhede, N., Shapira, G., & Palino, T. (2017). *Kafka: The Definitive Guide: Real-Time Data and Stream Processing at Scale*. O'Reilly Media.

About the Author

Dr. Alex Harper is a dedicated data analyst, author, and educator with a passion for simplifying complex data concepts. Building on the success of their first book, *Essential Data Analytics*, they have continued to explore the intricacies of data science in this comprehensive follow-up, guiding readers through the full spectrum of data analytics pipelines. With extensive experience in the field, Dr. Alex Harper has helped professionals across industries harness the power of data to make informed, impactful decisions.

In this book, Dr. Alex Harper dives deeper into advanced techniques, expanding on foundational knowledge to equip readers with the skills needed to build end-to-end data solutions. Their clear, approachable style makes complex topics accessible, empowering readers to apply data-driven insights in real-world settings.

Disclaimer

The information contained in this book is intended to provide general guidance on data analytics practices, tools, and techniques. While every effort has been made to ensure accuracy, the author and publisher make no representations or warranties of any kind with respect to the contents of this book, including without limitation the accuracy, completeness, or suitability of the information, methods, and examples presented.

The examples, techniques, and code snippets provided in this book are for educational purposes only and may require modification to suit specific data, environments, or systems. Readers are encouraged to adapt the material to their own needs and should be aware that different software versions, datasets, or organizational requirements may produce varied results.

Neither the author nor the publisher shall be held liable for any direct, indirect, incidental, or consequential damages arising out of or in connection with the use or application of the information or software examples provided in this book. Readers are responsible for complying with all applicable data privacy laws, regulations, and organizational policies when collecting, storing, and analyzing data.

This book should not be considered a substitute for professional advice or technical consultation. If expert assistance is required, readers should seek the services of a qualified professional in the relevant field.

Copyright

Legal Notice

This book is provided "as-is" without any warranties of any kind, either expressed or implied, including but not limited to warranties of merchantability, fitness for a particular purpose, or non-infringement. The author and publisher make no representations or warranties regarding the accuracy, completeness, or suitability of the content, materials, or methods included in this book.

The author and publisher assume no liability for any loss or damage, including but not limited to incidental, consequential, or other damages, arising out of or in connection with the use, misuse, or interpretation of the information contained in this book. Readers are responsible for independently verifying any information or advice in this book before relying on it.

All product names, trademarks, and registered trademarks are the property of their respective owners. The mention of specific companies, products, or services in this book is for informational purposes only and does not imply endorsement or recommendation by the author or publisher.

Readers are advised to comply with all applicable laws, regulations, and policies when using or applying the techniques and practices discussed in this book. This book is not a substitute for professional advice, and readers should seek the services of qualified professionals when appropriate.

Any rights not expressly granted herein are reserved.

Book 3

Mastering Advance Data Analytics

Machine Learning, Data Mining and
Analytic Thinking

Dr. Alex Harper

Chapter 1: Introduction to Advanced Data Analytics and Analytic Thinking

Overview of Advanced Data Analytics and Its Role in Modern Business and Technology

In today's data-driven world, advanced data analytics stands at the intersection of innovation, strategic decision-making, and operational efficiency. Unlike basic analytics, which focuses on descriptive insights and surface-level trends, advanced data analytics delves into predictive and prescriptive analytics, uncovering the deeper insights and foresight needed for businesses to thrive in a competitive landscape. Through methods such as machine learning, data mining, and analytic thinking, advanced data analytics transforms raw data into actionable insights, driving value across every sector from finance and healthcare to retail and entertainment.

1. The Evolution of Data Analytics: From Descriptive to Advanced

Historically, data analytics began as a tool for reporting on past events. Descriptive analytics provided an understanding of what happened, and diagnostic analytics answered why it happened. However, as organizations amassed vast amounts of data and computational power increased, there emerged a need for predictive and prescriptive analytics, which allow businesses to anticipate future trends and optimize decision-making processes. Advanced data analytics leverages complex statistical methods, algorithms, and computational power to go beyond traditional analysis, enabling proactive decision-making that is essential for navigating today's fast-paced business world.

2. Why Advanced Data Analytics Matters in Modern Business

Advanced data analytics is essential in modern business for several reasons. First, it enables a competitive edge. Companies that effectively use data to drive insights can develop more accurate market strategies, create tailored customer experiences, and optimize operational efficiency, setting them apart from competitors. In addition, advanced data analytics empowers companies to better understand consumer behavior, predict demand fluctuations, and innovate new products and services that cater to evolving customer needs. Consider industries like finance, where predictive models assess credit risk, or healthcare, where machine learning algorithms predict patient outcomes. These applications save time, reduce costs, and improve service quality, exemplifying the crucial role of advanced data analytics in both business success and customer satisfaction.

3. The Components of Advanced Data Analytics

Advanced data analytics consists of several interconnected components that collectively generate deep, actionable insights. These components include:

- **Machine Learning (ML)**: ML algorithms learn from historical data to make predictions or decisions without explicit programming. From supervised and unsupervised learning to reinforcement learning, machine learning enables complex pattern recognition and automation in tasks like recommendation engines and predictive maintenance.
- **Data Mining**: Data mining identifies hidden patterns, correlations, and anomalies in large datasets, often leading to insights that inform strategic business decisions. Techniques like clustering, association rule mining, and anomaly detection are fundamental to uncovering valuable insights from data.
- **Analytic Thinking**: Analytic thinking involves a systematic approach to solving problems through data-driven decision-making. It requires breaking down complex challenges, hypothesizing potential solutions, testing with data, and refining insights. Analytic thinking forms the basis for a structured, hypothesis-driven approach to complex data analysis.

4. The Impact of Advanced Data Analytics on Technology and Innovation

With the rise of big data and advancements in computational power, advanced data analytics has fueled innovations in fields like artificial intelligence, automation, and IoT (Internet of Things). Data-driven technologies are reshaping industries, automating mundane tasks, and enhancing human capabilities. In the retail sector, for instance, data analytics personalizes the customer journey through targeted advertising and recommendation systems. Meanwhile, in manufacturing, predictive maintenance uses analytics to foresee equipment failures, preventing costly downtime.

Furthermore, advanced analytics plays a key role in the development of smart cities, autonomous vehicles, and medical diagnostics, marking an era where data-powered insights continuously push the boundaries of what technology can achieve.

5. Setting the Stage for a Data-Driven Culture

To harness the full potential of advanced data analytics, businesses must cultivate a data-driven culture. This entails aligning organizational goals with data-driven strategies, investing in talent and technology, and promoting analytic thinking at every level. Leaders play a pivotal role in fostering this culture by advocating for data-backed decision-making, encouraging continuous learning, and enabling cross-functional collaboration.

A data-driven culture not only enhances productivity but also fosters innovation, empowering employees to leverage data insights in creative, impactful ways. When every team member—from the C-suite to frontline employees—understands the value of data and analytics, businesses become more resilient and agile in adapting to change.

Conclusion

Advanced data analytics is transforming the way organizations operate, innovate, and compete. In an era where data is abundant and customer expectations are high, businesses that fail to leverage advanced analytics risk falling behind. By embracing machine learning, data mining, and analytic thinking, companies can navigate complexities, anticipate changes, and make informed decisions that drive lasting success. This chapter has introduced the foundational principles and significance of advanced data analytics, setting the stage for a deeper exploration of the techniques and methodologies that will define the future of data-driven decision-making.

Introduction to Machine Learning, Data Mining, and Analytic Thinking as Critical Skills for Data-Driven Decisions

In the modern landscape of business and technology, data is often referred to as "the new oil." However, data on its own is merely a raw resource; its true value is unlocked through the skills and techniques that transform it into actionable insights. Among these, machine learning, data mining, and analytic thinking stand out as foundational competencies that drive impactful, data-driven decisions. Each of these skills contributes uniquely to the analytics process, creating a robust framework that allows organizations to extract maximum value from their data.

1. Machine Learning: The Backbone of Predictive Analytics

Machine learning (ML) is a branch of artificial intelligence that enables computers to learn from and make predictions based on data without explicit programming for each task. Unlike traditional programming, where rules and logic are predefined, ML algorithms identify patterns and relationships within datasets and use these insights to make informed predictions or decisions. This capability makes machine learning a powerful tool for organizations that want to harness historical data to predict future trends and outcomes.

Machine learning's applications span a variety of industries. In finance, for instance, ML models assess credit risks and detect fraudulent transactions. In healthcare, they predict patient outcomes and optimize treatment plans. In retail, they personalize product recommendations and forecast demand. As a critical skill, machine learning empowers data analysts and decision-makers to move beyond descriptive statistics to predictive analytics, where they can anticipate what is likely to happen and make proactive adjustments.

Key components of machine learning that are vital for data-driven decisions include:

- **Supervised Learning**: Algorithms learn from labeled data, making it ideal for classification and regression tasks, such as predicting sales or categorizing customer feedback.
- **Unsupervised Learning**: Algorithms work with unlabeled data to uncover hidden patterns, such as customer segmentation through clustering.
- **Reinforcement Learning**: The algorithm learns by interacting with an environment, making it suitable for dynamic applications like robotics and game theory.

2. Data Mining: Uncovering Hidden Patterns and Relationships

Data mining is the process of exploring large datasets to identify hidden patterns, correlations, and anomalies. It provides a powerful way to transform raw data into valuable insights, allowing businesses to understand not just what happened but also why it happened. This deeper understanding supports the development of informed, strategic decisions.

The process of data mining involves several techniques:

- **Clustering**: Grouping data points with similar characteristics, often used for customer segmentation and market analysis.
- **Association**: Finding relationships between variables, frequently applied in market

basket analysis to determine product co-purchase patterns.

- **Anomaly Detection**: Identifying unusual patterns or outliers, which is useful for fraud detection, network security, and quality control.

By mastering data mining techniques, analysts can unlock insights that may not be immediately apparent. For example, a retailer could analyze purchase patterns to understand which products are often bought together, enabling targeted promotions and increasing revenue. In healthcare, data mining helps identify patterns in patient records, which can lead to better diagnostic methods and treatment protocols.

Data mining equips organizations with the ability to delve deeper into their data, making it an essential skill for anyone involved in advanced analytics.

3. Analytic Thinking: The Foundation of Insightful Decision-Making

While machine learning and data mining provide powerful technical tools, analytic thinking is the mindset that makes these tools effective. Analytic thinking involves a systematic, logical approach to problem-solving. It's about breaking down complex issues, hypothesizing solutions, testing with data, and refining conclusions based on evidence.

Analytic thinking goes beyond technical proficiency; it requires a curiosity-driven approach to understanding data and the stories it can tell. It enables data analysts to:

- **Ask the Right Questions**: Effective analytics begins with asking questions that data can answer. Analytic thinking helps frame questions that are specific, measurable, and aligned with business goals.
- **Identify Key Metrics**: By focusing on relevant metrics, analysts can avoid the trap of analysis paralysis and concentrate on data that drives actionable insights.
- **Connect Data to Business Goals**: Analytic thinking ensures that every data-driven decision is anchored in strategic business objectives, enhancing the impact of analytics on organizational success.

In practical terms, analytic thinking allows analysts to tackle problems creatively and adaptively. For example, if a company experiences a drop in customer satisfaction, an analytically minded data analyst might examine not only direct survey feedback but also indirect indicators, such as customer churn rates, purchase history, and social media sentiment. By connecting diverse data sources and developing a nuanced view of the problem, analytic thinking can reveal insights that might otherwise go unnoticed.

4. The Synergy of Machine Learning, Data Mining, and Analytic Thinking

Together, machine learning, data mining, and analytic thinking create a powerful framework for making data-driven decisions. Machine learning provides the predictive power, data mining uncovers hidden patterns, and analytic thinking ensures that insights are actionable and aligned with business objectives. When combined, these skills enable organizations to go beyond retrospective analysis and static reports, creating a proactive, responsive approach to analytics.

For instance, consider a telecommunications company aiming to reduce customer churn. Machine learning algorithms could predict which customers are likely to leave, data mining could reveal patterns and reasons behind customer dissatisfaction, and analytic thinking would guide the interpretation of these findings into strategic actions, such as personalized retention campaigns or product improvements.

Conclusion

Machine learning, data mining, and analytic thinking are indispensable skills for anyone looking to leverage advanced data analytics effectively. As critical components of the analytics toolbox, these skills empower professionals to uncover insights, predict trends, and make well-informed, data-driven decisions. Mastering these techniques is essential for individuals and organizations aiming to remain competitive in an increasingly data-centric world. In the following chapters, we will delve deeper into each of these areas, exploring practical applications, best practices, and real-world examples that demonstrate their transformative potential.

Differentiation from Basic Analytics and Setting the Foundation for Advanced Concepts

The journey from basic to advanced data analytics is a transformative leap that expands the scope and depth of insights that organizations can derive from their data. While basic analytics focuses on understanding past events and answering "what happened," advanced data analytics goes further, diving into "why it happened," "what is likely to happen next," and "what actions should be taken." This progression from descriptive to predictive and prescriptive insights provides organizations with the foresight and actionable recommendations necessary to stay competitive in an increasingly data-driven world.

1. Basic Analytics: The Foundation of Data Understanding

Basic analytics, also known as descriptive analytics, serves as the entry point for data analysis. It involves collecting, organizing, and summarizing historical data to gain a high-level understanding of trends and patterns. Techniques such as basic statistics, charts, and reports allow organizations to monitor key performance indicators (KPIs), track past performance, and identify areas of concern or opportunity.

However, while basic analytics provides valuable hindsight, it has limitations:

- **Limited to Past Insights**: Basic analytics can only describe past events, offering little in the way of predictive power.
- **Lacks Depth**: By focusing on surface-level data, basic analytics may overlook the underlying causes of observed trends.
- **Static Insights**: Descriptive analytics doesn't adapt to new data in real-time, making it less dynamic for fast-paced decision-making.

For example, a retail store might use basic analytics to identify that sales increased by 15% in the last quarter. However, without understanding why this increase occurred, or whether it will continue, the insight remains limited in scope and impact.

2. Advanced Data Analytics: Moving from Insight to Action

Advanced data analytics builds upon the foundation of basic analytics by incorporating more sophisticated techniques, such as predictive modeling, machine learning, and prescriptive analytics. By leveraging these advanced methods, organizations can gain deeper insights, anticipate future trends, and make data-driven decisions that proactively shape outcomes. Advanced data analytics not only reveals "what" happened but also explains "why" it happened and "what might happen next."

Key differentiators of advanced data analytics include:

- **Predictive Power**: Advanced analytics uses statistical models and machine learning algorithms to forecast future outcomes, helping organizations anticipate trends and make informed decisions.
- **Root Cause Analysis**: Through techniques like data mining, advanced analytics uncovers the root causes of patterns, allowing companies to understand and address the factors influencing performance.
- **Actionable Insights**: Prescriptive analytics takes things a step further, offering recommendations for action, which is invaluable for strategic planning and operational optimization.

In our retail example, advanced analytics might use predictive models to forecast sales for the next quarter, taking into account seasonal trends, marketing campaigns, and customer behavior patterns. This foresight allows the store to plan its inventory, marketing, and staffing accordingly.

3. The Stages of Advanced Analytics: From Descriptive to Prescriptive

To understand the spectrum of data analytics, it's helpful to break it down into four progressive stages:

- **Descriptive Analytics**: The most basic level, focused on summarizing past data to identify what happened. It answers questions like, "What were our total sales last year?" or "How many customers did we acquire?"

- **Diagnostic Analytics**: Building upon descriptive analytics, diagnostic analytics aims to understand why events occurred. For instance, it might analyze why sales in a particular region declined by examining customer demographics, market conditions, or competitor actions.

- **Predictive Analytics**: This stage leverages statistical models and machine learning to forecast future outcomes. Predictive analytics answers questions like, "What will sales look like next quarter?" or "Which customers are most likely to churn?"

- **Prescriptive Analytics**: The most advanced stage, prescriptive analytics, provides actionable recommendations based on predictive insights. It answers questions such as, "What marketing strategies should we implement to increase customer retention?" or "How can we optimize our supply chain to reduce costs?"

By progressing through these stages, organizations move from simple reporting to dynamic, proactive decision-making, unlocking greater strategic value from their data.

4. Setting the Foundation for Advanced Concepts

Understanding the differentiation between basic and advanced analytics is the first step toward embracing the methodologies that drive advanced analytics. A strong foundation in basic analytics provides the necessary skills in data handling, visualization, and statistical analysis. However, to transition to advanced analytics, it is essential to build expertise in areas like machine learning, data mining, and statistical modeling.

Core areas to focus on when advancing in data analytics include:

- **Statistical Analysis and Machine Learning**: Mastering these techniques allows data analysts to build models that not only describe but also predict and optimize.
- **Data Mining and Pattern Recognition**: Identifying patterns, correlations, and anomalies within large datasets is critical for uncovering valuable insights.
- **Analytic Thinking and Strategy**: Beyond technical skills, analytic thinking enables professionals to align data initiatives with organizational goals, ensuring that insights are not only accurate but also relevant and actionable.

This shift toward advanced analytics represents a strategic evolution for organizations. While basic analytics allows companies to understand past events, advanced analytics empowers them to shape the future by making informed, proactive decisions based on data-driven insights.

Conclusion

The difference between basic and advanced analytics is profound, not just in the complexity of techniques but in the impact it can have on decision-making. As businesses navigate an increasingly competitive and data-saturated landscape, advanced data analytics provides the tools and frameworks necessary to stay ahead. This chapter has highlighted the importance of moving beyond descriptive insights and setting the foundation for advanced analytic techniques that will be explored in greater detail in subsequent chapters. By understanding this evolution, readers are now prepared to dive into the world of advanced analytics, unlocking the skills and strategies that lead to smarter, data-driven decisions.

Chapter 2: Data-Driven Mindset: From Analytic Thinking to Strategy

Developing an Analytic Mindset for Real-World Problem-Solving

In a data-rich environment, having the right tools and technologies is only part of the equation for effective problem-solving. The ability to apply data to real-world challenges requires an analytic mindset—a way of thinking that emphasizes curiosity, critical evaluation, and a strategic approach to finding solutions. An analytic mindset combines technical skills with a problem-solving framework, guiding decisions that are grounded in data but responsive to the complexities of real-world scenarios. This chapter explores the elements of an analytic mindset and how it can be developed to tackle both immediate and strategic challenges.

1. What is an Analytic Mindset?

An analytic mindset is an approach to thinking that prioritizes evidence, curiosity, and a structured approach to problem-solving. Unlike traditional decision-making, which may rely on intuition or personal experience, an analytic mindset seeks to ground each decision in data and objective reasoning. This mindset is vital in today's competitive landscape, where access to quality data can turn insight into a powerful advantage. Characteristics of an analytic mindset include:

- **Curiosity**: A desire to understand the "why" behind every event or observation, leading to deeper insights and comprehensive analysis.
- **Structured Thinking**: The ability to break down complex problems into manageable components, ensuring that each aspect of the issue is examined and understood.
- **Objectivity**: An emphasis on data and empirical evidence, reducing personal biases that may distort conclusions.
- **Strategic Focus**: Aligning analysis with broader organizational goals, ensuring that data-driven decisions support long-term strategy.

2. The Role of Analytic Thinking in Problem-Solving

Analytic thinking is the foundation of a data-driven mindset. It enables professionals to look beyond surface-level information and dive into the root causes of problems. By approaching challenges analytically, one can avoid knee-jerk reactions and instead develop a thoughtful, strategic response. Analytic thinking is particularly valuable in complex or high-stakes situations where data is abundant but not immediately clear.

The problem-solving process within an analytic mindset includes several key steps:

- **Defining the Problem**: An analytic mindset begins by clearly defining the problem to be solved, identifying specific questions that data can help answer.

- **Data Gathering and Assessment**: Collecting and critically evaluating data ensures that analysis is based on reliable, relevant information.
- **Hypothesis Formation**: Developing potential explanations or hypotheses guides the focus of the analysis, ensuring that the approach is logical and systematic.
- **Testing and Analysis**: Using data to test hypotheses, either confirming or refuting initial assumptions.
- **Interpretation and Application**: Translating findings into actionable insights that address the original problem, contributing to real-world decision-making.

For example, imagine a company experiencing a sudden drop in customer satisfaction scores. An analytic approach would involve defining potential causes (e.g., product quality, service issues, or external factors), gathering relevant data (e.g., customer feedback, service records), forming hypotheses, and analyzing results to identify specific actions to improve satisfaction.

3. Curiosity as the Catalyst for Insight

Curiosity drives the analytic mindset, pushing professionals to ask questions and dig deeper into data. A curious analyst doesn't just accept trends or findings at face value; they seek to understand the underlying causes, patterns, and anomalies.

Curiosity fuels exploration and discovery, often leading to insights that may not be immediately obvious.

Encouraging curiosity in a data-driven environment involves:

- **Questioning Assumptions**: Curiosity helps analysts avoid confirmation bias by challenging pre-existing assumptions and exploring alternative explanations.
- **Exploring "What If" Scenarios**: Curious analysts often conduct exploratory analyses to test different scenarios, such as how changing one factor affects the outcome.
- **Identifying Outliers**: Instead of dismissing outliers, curious analysts examine these data points to understand why they deviate, often revealing critical insights about unusual behaviors or market segments.

Curiosity is essential in problem-solving because it broadens the scope of analysis, leading to a more comprehensive understanding of the situation at hand.

4. Structured Thinking: The Framework for Solving Complex Problems

Structured thinking is the ability to break down complex problems into logical steps, making the analysis process more manageable and efficient. When faced with a complex challenge, structured thinking helps analysts approach the problem systematically, examining each component before moving on to the next.

A structured approach to problem-solving involves:

- **Decomposing the Problem**: Breaking down the main problem into smaller, more specific issues or questions.
- **Prioritizing Elements**: Identifying which aspects of the problem are most critical, focusing resources on areas with the greatest impact.
- **Step-by-Step Analysis**: Tackling each component systematically, ensuring that insights are built on a solid foundation.

Structured thinking is particularly valuable in high-stakes or time-sensitive situations, where clear, logical reasoning is essential. By following a structured framework, analysts can ensure that each stage of the analysis is methodical, leading to thorough and accurate conclusions.

5. Objectivity and Bias Reduction in Analysis

One of the greatest challenges in data-driven decision-making is ensuring objectivity. Personal biases, preconceived notions, and organizational pressures can all influence how data is interpreted. An analytic mindset includes a commitment to objectivity, striving to let the data speak for itself without undue influence from subjective factors. Ways to maintain objectivity include:

- **Data Validation**: Cross-referencing data sources and verifying accuracy to avoid errors that could mislead the analysis.

- **Avoiding Confirmation Bias**: Actively seeking evidence that contradicts initial hypotheses to ensure a balanced perspective.
- **Peer Review**: Sharing findings with colleagues for feedback, allowing others to challenge assumptions and provide alternative viewpoints.

By maintaining objectivity, analysts can make decisions based on factual evidence, reducing the risk of biased conclusions that could lead to poor strategic choices.

6. Aligning Analytics with Strategic Goals

An analytic mindset is not only about solving isolated problems but also about contributing to broader organizational objectives. Aligning analytics with strategy ensures that every data-driven insight supports the company's mission, vision, and goals.

To achieve strategic alignment, analysts should:

- **Understand the Business Context**: Familiarize themselves with organizational goals, industry trends, and competitive pressures.
- **Focus on High-Impact Analysis**: Prioritize analytics projects that have a clear, measurable impact on strategic objectives.
- **Communicate Insights Effectively**: Present findings in a way that resonates with decision-makers, translating data into

actionable recommendations that drive value.

Strategic alignment adds context and direction to data analysis, ensuring that insights are relevant and actionable at an organizational level.

Conclusion

Developing an analytic mindset for real-world problem-solving goes beyond mastering technical skills; it requires a mindset rooted in curiosity, structured thinking, objectivity, and strategic alignment. By cultivating these qualities, data professionals can tackle complex challenges with confidence, transforming data into meaningful insights that drive effective decision-making. This chapter has outlined the elements of an analytic mindset, setting the stage for advanced strategies and techniques that will be explored in the following chapters. With this foundation, readers are better equipped to approach data-driven problem-solving with purpose and precision.

Connecting Data Analytics to Strategic Goals and Long-Term Business Objectives

In a data-driven organization, analytics is more than a set of tools or techniques; it is a critical function that aligns with and supports the company's strategic goals and long-term objectives. Connecting analytics to broader business goals involves embedding data-driven thinking into every level of decision-making, ensuring that every insight contributes to the company's mission, vision, and competitive advantage. This chapter examines how to integrate data analytics with strategic goals, from identifying impactful metrics to fostering collaboration and creating a culture of data-driven decision-making.

1. The Role of Data Analytics in Shaping Business Strategy

In today's competitive landscape, strategic decisions cannot rely on intuition alone. Data analytics offers a way to make informed, evidence-based decisions that align with the company's long-term vision. By connecting analytics to strategy, organizations can:

- **Anticipate Market Trends**: Using data to analyze customer behavior, industry shifts, and economic conditions helps businesses stay ahead of market trends.
- **Identify Growth Opportunities**: Analytics reveals new revenue streams, customer segments, or market niches that may be untapped.
- **Optimize Operations**: Data-driven insights improve efficiency and productivity, driving cost savings and process improvements.
- **Enhance Customer Satisfaction**: Analytics can deepen understanding of customer needs and preferences, enabling tailored offerings and improved customer experiences.

When data analytics aligns with strategy, it enables organizations to operate more proactively, adapting quickly to changes and seizing new opportunities.

2. Identifying and Prioritizing Key Performance Indicators (KPIs)

A critical step in connecting analytics to strategic goals is selecting key performance indicators (KPIs) that reflect the organization's objectives. KPIs are quantifiable metrics that track progress toward specific goals, helping companies measure success and make adjustments as needed. The right KPIs enable organizations to monitor performance, make data-driven adjustments, and achieve strategic outcomes.

When selecting KPIs, consider the following:

- **Alignment with Strategic Goals**: KPIs should directly relate to the organization's objectives, such as increasing market share, improving customer retention, or enhancing operational efficiency.
- **Actionability**: KPIs should be actionable, meaning that tracking them leads to insights that inform decision-making and potential changes.
- **Relevance to Stakeholders**: Different departments and stakeholders may have unique KPIs, but all should contribute to overarching business goals.

For example, a company focused on customer satisfaction might track KPIs like Net Promoter

Score (NPS), customer retention rates, and average response time. In contrast, a company prioritizing growth might focus on KPIs like market share, customer acquisition cost, and revenue growth.

3. Embedding Analytics in Long-Term Planning

While short-term analytics projects can offer quick wins, the true value of data analytics emerges when it is embedded in long-term planning. This approach requires an understanding of how current analytics efforts impact future objectives, as well as how data-driven insights can shape strategic initiatives.

Ways to embed analytics in long-term planning include:

- **Forecasting and Trend Analysis**: Use predictive analytics to forecast future trends, market conditions, or customer preferences. Long-term forecasting supports planning around resources, investments, and strategic shifts.
- **Scenario Planning**: Scenario analysis helps organizations prepare for various outcomes by modeling different "what-if" scenarios. This approach enables companies to be more agile and responsive to market changes.
- **Continuous Learning and Adaptation**: Data analytics is not a one-time task; it requires regular updates and adjustments. Organizations that treat analytics as an ongoing process are better equipped to

adapt to emerging trends and refine strategies over time.

For example, a retail company could use trend analysis to predict seasonal demand fluctuations, planning inventory and staffing accordingly. By integrating this data into long-term plans, they not only improve efficiency but also enhance customer satisfaction through timely product availability.

4. Fostering Collaboration Between Analytics and Business Teams

To connect data analytics with strategic goals, there must be a bridge between analytics teams and business units. Collaboration ensures that analytics insights are relevant, actionable, and aligned with strategic objectives. Business leaders bring context and industry knowledge, while analysts provide the technical expertise needed to extract meaningful insights from data.

Strategies for fostering collaboration include:

- **Cross-Functional Teams**: Establish teams that include members from analytics, marketing, finance, and other departments. These teams work together on projects, ensuring that all perspectives are considered.
- **Regular Communication**: Encourage regular meetings between analytics teams and business units to discuss goals, review insights, and refine analytics projects.
- **Business Literacy for Analysts**: Equip analysts with a deep understanding of the

business and its goals, enabling them to focus on data insights that drive strategic value.

For instance, in a retail organization, analysts working closely with the marketing team might develop customer segmentation models that align with marketing strategies, allowing for more targeted and effective campaigns.

5. Cultivating a Culture of Data-Driven Decision-Making

A data-driven culture ensures that decisions at every level of the organization are guided by evidence and analysis. When data-driven thinking is a part of the company's DNA, employees are more likely to embrace analytics insights and incorporate them into their daily decision-making. Elements of a data-driven culture include:

- **Leadership Support**: Leaders should champion the use of data in decision-making, setting an example for others to follow.
- **Accessible Data**: Ensure that data is readily available and accessible to all departments, empowering employees to make data-informed decisions.
- **Training and Development**: Invest in data literacy training, helping employees understand and interpret data, even if they are not in analytics roles.
- **Celebrating Data Successes**: Highlight examples of data-driven success,

reinforcing the value of analytics in achieving business outcomes.

Creating a data-driven culture encourages employees to think analytically and base their actions on evidence, creating a unified approach to reaching strategic goals.

6. Measuring the Impact of Data Analytics on Strategic Goals

Measuring the impact of data analytics initiatives is essential for validating their contribution to strategic goals. By assessing the outcomes of analytics projects, organizations can identify areas of success, adjust their approaches, and optimize future efforts.

Ways to measure impact include:

- **Comparing KPIs Before and After Analytics Projects**: Analyze changes in key metrics, such as customer retention rates or cost savings, to gauge the effectiveness of data-driven decisions.
- **Calculating Return on Investment (ROI)**: Evaluate the financial return of analytics initiatives relative to their cost, providing a quantifiable measure of value.
- **Conducting Case Studies**: Documenting case studies of successful analytics projects offers insights into how analytics contributed to business objectives, serving as examples for future efforts.

For instance, a logistics company implementing predictive analytics to optimize delivery routes might measure the reduction in fuel costs and delivery times, demonstrating the tangible benefits of data-driven decision-making.

Conclusion

Connecting data analytics to strategic goals and long-term business objectives is essential for deriving true value from data. By aligning analytics initiatives with key performance indicators, embedding data-driven thinking into long-term planning, fostering cross-functional collaboration, and cultivating a data-driven culture, organizations can ensure that analytics efforts support the broader mission and vision of the company. This approach enables companies to not only react to immediate challenges but also proactively shape their future, ensuring sustained growth and success in an increasingly data-driven world. As you move forward, this foundation of aligning analytics with strategy will be critical for unlocking the full potential of data-driven insights and achieving meaningful impact.

Techniques for Aligning Analytics with Decision-Making to Drive Impact

Incorporating analytics into decision-making processes is a powerful way to enhance organizational performance, predict market changes, and make evidence-based choices that support strategic goals. However, simply having data and insights is not enough. To maximize the impact of analytics, it's essential to align these insights with decision-making frameworks that guide business actions. In this section, we'll explore proven techniques for integrating analytics into decision-making processes to ensure that insights are not only actionable but also impactful.

1. Translating Data into Actionable Insights

Raw data and even well-crafted reports mean little without a clear path to action. Translating data into actionable insights involves making complex data understandable and directly linking it to business goals. This process requires both technical skill and the ability to communicate insights effectively to decision-makers.

Steps to make data actionable include:

- **Summarizing Key Findings**: Distill data into clear, concise insights that are directly relevant to the decision at hand. Use visualization tools, dashboards, and summary reports to make complex data accessible.

- **Highlighting Trends and Patterns**: Point out trends that indicate emerging opportunities or risks, focusing on how these insights relate to business goals.

- **Providing Clear Recommendations**: Go beyond presenting data; suggest specific actions that decision-makers can take. When possible, offer a range of options, such as high-impact but resource-intensive actions alongside lower-cost alternatives.

For example, if an e-commerce business sees a trend of high cart abandonment rates, actionable insights might include identifying at which stage users drop off and recommending interventions like checkout simplification or targeted discount campaigns.

2. Embedding Analytics into Decision-Making Frameworks

To make analytics part of everyday decision-making, organizations should embed analytics into structured decision-making frameworks, such as SWOT analysis (Strengths, Weaknesses, Opportunities, Threats) or KPI-driven scorecards. This approach formalizes the use of data in evaluating options and making choices.

Embedding analytics in decision-making frameworks can involve:

- **Integrating KPIs and Benchmarks**: Use relevant KPIs and industry benchmarks as metrics in decision-making frameworks. For instance, during a SWOT analysis, quantitative metrics can highlight strengths and weaknesses in specific areas, such as customer satisfaction or operational efficiency.
- **Creating Data-Driven Scorecards**: Scorecards provide a structured way to evaluate decisions based on performance metrics. By incorporating analytics directly into these scorecards, leaders can objectively assess options.
- **Developing Data-Driven Business Cases**: Whenever possible, support major

decisions with data-driven business cases that show potential ROI, projected impact, and alignment with long-term goals.

For instance, a healthcare organization using a data-driven SWOT analysis could evaluate a new patient management system. They might assess "strengths" by examining improved patient outcomes from similar systems, "weaknesses" by identifying costs, "opportunities" through expected efficiencies, and "threats" by anticipating implementation challenges.

3. Prioritizing High-Impact Analytics Projects

Not all analytics projects have the same potential for impact. Prioritizing projects that are most likely to influence critical business outcomes ensures that resources are allocated effectively and results are maximized.

Techniques for prioritizing high-impact analytics projects include:

- **Impact vs. Effort Matrix**: An impact-effort matrix helps determine which analytics projects offer the most value relative to their difficulty. Projects that are high-impact but low-effort should be prioritized, while high-effort, low-impact projects may be deferred.

- **Focus on Business Objectives**: Evaluate each project based on how well it supports key business goals, such as increasing market share, improving customer satisfaction, or reducing operational costs.

- **Quick Wins and Long-Term Investments**: Identify quick-win projects that can deliver immediate value alongside longer-term projects that support strategic growth. This balance allows analytics teams to show results quickly while working on high-impact initiatives.

For example, a financial institution might prioritize analytics projects that focus on fraud detection (high impact, quick win) while also investing in a longer-term project to improve predictive models for customer retention.

4. Scenario Analysis and Forecasting to Inform Decision-Making

Scenario analysis and forecasting enable organizations to evaluate potential future conditions and make proactive decisions. By modeling different scenarios, decision-makers can anticipate how various factors, such as economic shifts or competitive pressures, might impact the organization. This foresight allows companies to adapt more quickly and make informed decisions even in uncertain environments.

To leverage scenario analysis and forecasting:

- **Develop Multiple Scenarios**: Create best-case, worst-case, and most likely scenarios based on available data. This approach helps decision-makers consider a range of possibilities.
- **Identify Key Drivers**: Focus on key factors that influence outcomes, such as customer

demand, market conditions, or supply chain stability. Understanding these drivers enables more accurate forecasts.

- **Test Decisions Against Scenarios**: Evaluate potential actions against each scenario to see how they would perform under different conditions. This exercise can reveal both risks and opportunities, allowing leaders to make more resilient decisions.

For example, a logistics company might use scenario analysis to model the impact of fuel price fluctuations on delivery costs. This insight allows them to plan for contingencies, such as adjusting routes or partnering with alternative suppliers.

5. Establishing Feedback Loops for Continuous Improvement

Continuous improvement is essential for maximizing the impact of analytics on decision-making. By establishing feedback loops, organizations can monitor the outcomes of data-driven decisions, learn from results, and refine their approaches over time.

Key components of effective feedback loops include:

- **Performance Monitoring**: Track KPIs and other metrics that indicate whether a decision is achieving the desired outcomes. Regular monitoring helps identify areas that need adjustment.

- **Iterative Testing**: For decisions with multiple potential actions, consider A/B testing or pilot programs to evaluate effectiveness. This iterative approach allows organizations to learn and adapt before full-scale implementation.
- **Learning and Adaptation**: Use insights from feedback loops to refine analytics processes, improve accuracy, and enhance alignment with strategic goals.

For instance, an online retailer implementing a new recommendation engine could monitor customer engagement metrics like click-through rates and purchase frequency. This data helps them adjust recommendations over time, enhancing both customer experience and revenue.

6. Communicating Analytics Insights Effectively to Drive Decision-Making

The value of analytics insights depends not only on their accuracy but also on how effectively they are communicated to decision-makers. Communicating insights in a clear, compelling manner is crucial for driving impact, ensuring that leaders understand the data and its implications. Techniques for effective communication include:

- **Tailoring the Message to the Audience**: Customize the presentation of insights based on the audience's knowledge level and needs. Executives may need a high-level summary, while technical teams benefit from detailed analysis.

- **Using Data Visualization**: Visual aids, such as charts and graphs, make complex data more accessible, highlighting key trends and insights.
- **Storytelling with Data**: Frame data insights as part of a broader story, connecting insights to business goals and real-world implications. Data storytelling helps decision-makers see the relevance of insights and envision their impact.

For example, a data analyst presenting to the executive team might use a combination of high-level dashboards and storytelling to show how a new customer segmentation strategy could improve market penetration and customer loyalty.

Conclusion

Aligning analytics with decision-making is essential for organizations seeking to leverage data for strategic impact. By translating data into actionable insights, embedding analytics into decision-making frameworks, prioritizing high-impact projects, using scenario analysis, establishing feedback loops, and communicating effectively, companies can maximize the value of analytics in achieving business objectives. These techniques create a systematic approach to incorporating analytics into decision-making, empowering organizations to not only understand what the data says but also to act on it decisively and strategically. As we proceed through the book, each chapter will build on these foundational techniques, exploring advanced strategies for integrating analytics with organizational decision-making.

Chapter 3: Machine Learning Fundamentals for Advanced Analysts

Introduction to Essential Machine Learning Algorithms and When to Use Each

Machine learning has become a cornerstone of data-driven decision-making, enabling organizations to make predictions, automate processes, and uncover patterns that might otherwise go unnoticed. However, the power of machine learning depends on choosing the right algorithm for the task. Each algorithm is designed to tackle specific types of problems, from classification and regression to clustering and anomaly detection. This chapter provides an overview of essential machine learning algorithms, explaining when to use each and the types of problems they are best suited to solve.

1. Supervised Learning: Leveraging Labeled Data for Prediction

Supervised learning algorithms are trained on labeled data, meaning that each input in the training dataset is paired with the correct output. These algorithms are commonly used for tasks where the goal is to predict an outcome based on input data, such as classifying an email as spam or non-spam, predicting stock prices, or identifying fraudulent transactions.

Key supervised learning algorithms include:

- **Linear Regression**: Linear regression is a foundational algorithm used for predicting continuous values, such as sales forecasts or pricing trends. It assumes a linear relationship between the input variables and the output, making it simple but effective for many real-world applications.
  - ○ **When to Use**: Use linear regression when the relationship between variables is approximately linear, and the goal is to predict a continuous outcome.
- **Logistic Regression**: Despite its name, logistic regression is used for classification tasks. It is particularly useful for binary classification, such as determining whether a customer will make a purchase (yes/no) or if a patient has a certain disease (yes/no).
  - ○ **When to Use**: Choose logistic regression when you have a binary classification problem and need interpretable results.
- **Decision Trees**: Decision trees are versatile algorithms that can be used for both classification and regression tasks. They split data into subsets based on feature values, forming a tree structure that is easy to interpret.
  - ○ **When to Use**: Decision trees are ideal for cases where interpretability is important, such as in credit scoring

or medical diagnosis. They work well with both categorical and continuous data.

- **Random Forest**: Random forest is an ensemble algorithm that combines multiple decision trees to improve accuracy and reduce overfitting. By averaging the predictions of several trees, random forests achieve more robust results than individual decision trees.

    o **When to Use**: Random forest is suitable for complex classification and regression problems where accuracy is prioritized over interpretability.

- **Support Vector Machines (SVM)**: SVMs are powerful algorithms used for classification and regression, particularly effective in cases where the data is not linearly separable. SVMs create a hyperplane to separate data into different classes, maximizing the margin between them.

    o **When to Use**: Use SVM when you have high-dimensional data or non-linear relationships, such as in image recognition or text classification.

- **k-Nearest Neighbors (k-NN)**: k-NN is a simple algorithm that classifies data points based on the majority class of their nearest neighbors. It works well with smaller datasets and requires little training, as it stores all training data and calculates similarities during classification.

- **When to Use**: k-NN is useful for classification tasks in smaller datasets or when interpretability is essential. It's often used in recommendation systems and anomaly detection.

2. Unsupervised Learning: Discovering Patterns Without Labeled Data

Unsupervised learning algorithms work with unlabeled data, focusing on discovering patterns, structures, or clusters within the dataset. These algorithms are ideal for tasks like customer segmentation, anomaly detection, and dimensionality reduction.

Key unsupervised learning algorithms include:

- **k-Means Clustering**: k-Means is a popular clustering algorithm that partitions data into a specified number of clusters (k) based on similarity. Each data point is assigned to the nearest cluster centroid, creating distinct groups within the data.
  - **When to Use**: k-Means is suitable for clustering tasks where the number of clusters is known or can be estimated, such as customer segmentation.
- **Hierarchical Clustering**: Hierarchical clustering creates a tree of clusters,

organizing data into a hierarchy of nested groups. Unlike k-means, it does not require the number of clusters to be specified in advance.

- When to Use: Use hierarchical clustering when you need a hierarchy of clusters or are uncertain about the optimal number of clusters, such as in gene expression analysis.

- **Principal Component Analysis (PCA)**: PCA is a dimensionality reduction technique that transforms data into a lower-dimensional space while preserving variance. It is used for simplifying datasets with many features, reducing computational complexity, and avoiding overfitting.

  - When to Use: PCA is useful for data visualization, noise reduction, and when working with high-dimensional datasets in applications like image compression or exploratory data analysis.

- **Anomaly Detection (e.g., Isolation Forest)**: Anomaly detection algorithms are used to identify unusual data points or outliers within a dataset. Isolation forests are commonly used for detecting anomalies in large datasets by isolating data points in a tree structure.

- When to Use: Use anomaly detection algorithms when identifying rare or unusual events, such as fraud detection or network intrusion.

3. Semi-Supervised Learning: Combining Labeled and Unlabeled Data

Semi-supervised learning algorithms work with a mix of labeled and unlabeled data, which is useful in cases where labeled data is limited but unlabeled data is abundant. These algorithms use the labeled data to inform their understanding of the unlabeled data, achieving better performance than unsupervised learning alone.

- **Self-Training and Co-Training Algorithms**: Self-training and co-training are approaches where the model iteratively labels the unlabeled data based on predictions made by the labeled data. Self-training uses one model, while co-training employs multiple models to improve label accuracy.
  - When to Use: Semi-supervised learning is useful when labeling data is expensive or time-consuming, such as in medical imaging or speech recognition.

4. Reinforcement Learning: Decision-Making Through Trial and Error

Reinforcement learning (RL) involves training an agent to make decisions by interacting with an environment. Through a system of rewards and penalties, the agent learns to take actions that maximize cumulative rewards. RL is commonly used in applications that require dynamic decision-making and long-term planning.

- **Q-Learning**: Q-Learning is a popular RL algorithm where the agent learns a Q-function, which estimates the expected utility of actions in given states. It's suitable for discrete action spaces.
    - o **When to Use**: Q-Learning is ideal for problems with well-defined states and actions, such as games or robotic pathfinding.
- **Deep Q-Networks (DQN)**: DQN combines deep learning with Q-learning, enabling it to handle high-dimensional input spaces, such as image-based environments.
    - o **When to Use**: DQN is useful for complex environments where actions are continuous or involve large state spaces, like autonomous driving or advanced gaming applications.

5. Ensemble Methods: Combining Models for Improved Performance

Ensemble methods combine multiple algorithms to improve overall model accuracy and robustness. By aggregating the predictions of several models, ensembles reduce the risk of overfitting and improve generalization.

- **Bagging (Bootstrap Aggregating)**: Bagging trains multiple models independently on different subsets of the data, then aggregates their predictions. Random forest is a common example.
    - ○ **When to Use**: Use bagging to reduce variance in high-variance models, especially in noisy datasets.
- **Boosting**: Boosting trains multiple models sequentially, where each model attempts to correct the errors of the previous one. Algorithms like AdaBoost and Gradient Boosting are popular in this category.
    - ○ **When to Use**: Boosting is ideal for reducing bias and increasing accuracy, particularly in complex datasets with nonlinear relationships.

6. Neural Networks and Deep Learning: Handling High-Complexity Data

Neural networks are highly flexible algorithms inspired by the human brain, capable of handling complex data like images, text, and sound. Deep learning extends neural networks to multiple layers, allowing for more sophisticated modeling of high-dimensional data.

- **Convolutional Neural Networks (CNNs)**: CNNs are specialized for image data, using convolutional layers to capture spatial features and patterns.

- **When to Use**: Use CNNs for image recognition, object detection, and visual processing tasks.

- **Recurrent Neural Networks (RNNs)**: RNNs are suited for sequential data, as they maintain memory of previous inputs. They are commonly used in natural language processing and time-series analysis.
  - **When to Use**: RNNs are ideal for language translation, speech recognition, and financial forecasting.

Conclusion

Understanding the essential machine learning algorithms and their applications is critical for any advanced analyst. Each algorithm has strengths and limitations, making it suitable for specific tasks within supervised, unsupervised, semi-supervised, reinforcement learning, ensemble methods, and deep learning. By choosing the right algorithm for each problem, analysts can leverage the power of machine learning to deliver actionable insights, automate decision-making, and drive strategic impact. In the following chapters, we will explore practical examples and advanced techniques that will build upon this foundation, enabling you to apply these algorithms effectively in real-world analytics.

In-Depth Coverage of Supervised, Unsupervised, and Reinforcement Learning with Examples

Machine learning is built on three primary types of learning paradigms: supervised, unsupervised, and reinforcement learning. Each approach is designed to handle specific kinds of problems, data structures, and goals. This chapter dives deeply into each type, providing examples that illustrate their real-world applications, strengths, and best use cases.

1. Supervised Learning: Learning from Labeled Data

Supervised learning is a structured approach where models learn from labeled datasets. In this setting, each input has a corresponding output, allowing the algorithm to find patterns that link inputs to outputs. Supervised learning is used primarily for classification and regression tasks where predicting known outcomes is essential.

Supervised Learning Algorithms

Some common supervised learning algorithms include:

- **Linear Regression**: Used to predict a continuous output based on input variables. Linear regression models a linear relationship between variables and is often used in pricing models or demand forecasting.

- **Logistic Regression**: Despite its name, logistic regression is used for classification. It outputs probabilities for binary outcomes, making it ideal for binary classification problems like predicting customer churn or whether an email is spam.
- **Decision Trees**: Decision trees are intuitive models that split data into branches based on decision rules. These rules allow decision trees to classify data based on known input characteristics.
- **Support Vector Machines (SVM)**: SVMs are powerful classifiers that find the best boundary (hyperplane) that separates classes, especially useful in high-dimensional spaces.

Example of Supervised Learning

Predicting Loan Default

Consider a bank that wants to predict whether a borrower will default on a loan. The bank can use historical data on previous borrowers, including labeled data indicating who defaulted and who repaid their loan. Using supervised learning, the bank trains a model (e.g., a decision tree) on this dataset, with features such as borrower income, credit score, and loan amount. Once trained, the model can predict whether a new borrower is likely to default based on similar features, helping the bank make more informed lending decisions.

2. Unsupervised Learning: Discovering Patterns in Unlabeled Data

Unsupervised learning works with datasets that lack labeled outputs. The goal is to uncover hidden patterns, clusters, or structures within the data. This type of learning is useful for tasks such as customer segmentation, anomaly detection, and feature reduction, where the goal is to make sense of data without predefined categories or classes.

Unsupervised Learning Algorithms

Popular unsupervised learning algorithms include:

- **k-Means Clustering**: A simple but effective algorithm that groups data into k clusters based on similarity. Each data point belongs to the nearest cluster centroid.
- **Hierarchical Clustering**: Builds a hierarchy of clusters, creating a tree-like structure where similar clusters are nested within larger ones. It's useful for discovering hierarchical relationships within data.
- **Principal Component Analysis (PCA)**: A dimensionality reduction technique that reduces the number of features in a dataset while preserving the most important information, making it useful for simplifying high-dimensional data.
- **Anomaly Detection (Isolation Forest, One-Class SVM)**: These algorithms identify unusual or rare patterns, commonly used in fraud detection or quality control.

Example of Unsupervised Learning

Customer Segmentation for E-commerce

An e-commerce company wants to segment its customers based on their purchasing behavior to create targeted marketing strategies. Since there is no predefined label for "type of customer," the company uses an unsupervised algorithm like k-means clustering. The model analyzes purchase frequency, average spending, and product preferences, grouping customers into segments based on these patterns. Each segment represents a group with similar behaviors, such as "frequent buyers" or "price-sensitive shoppers," allowing the company to tailor its marketing to each group's preferences.

3. Reinforcement Learning: Learning Through Trial and Error

Reinforcement learning (RL) is a unique approach where an agent learns to make decisions by interacting with an environment and receiving feedback in the form of rewards or penalties. Unlike supervised and unsupervised learning, RL focuses on sequential decision-making, where actions taken in the present influence outcomes in the future. This trial-and-error approach allows the agent to learn strategies that maximize long-term rewards.

Reinforcement Learning Algorithms

Common reinforcement learning algorithms include:

- **Q-Learning**: A model-free algorithm that uses a Q-table to estimate the expected rewards of actions in given states. The agent updates its Q-values as it learns, seeking actions that maximize rewards.

- **Deep Q-Networks (DQN)**: Combines Q-learning with deep learning to handle complex environments with high-dimensional state spaces, such as image-based inputs. DQNs enable RL in scenarios where a simple Q-table would be insufficient.
- **Policy Gradient Methods**: These algorithms, like REINFORCE or Actor-Critic methods, learn policies directly, optimizing the probability of taking actions that yield high rewards. They are suitable for continuous action spaces.

Example of Reinforcement Learning

Autonomous Driving

An example of reinforcement learning in action is autonomous driving. Here, an RL agent (the car) interacts with the environment (the road and traffic) and receives feedback based on its actions, such as staying within lanes, avoiding collisions, or obeying traffic signals. The agent receives positive rewards for safe driving behaviors and penalties for dangerous actions. Over time, the RL agent learns an optimal driving policy, adapting to different traffic scenarios and improving its ability to drive safely and efficiently.

In-Depth Analysis of Each Learning Paradigm

A. Supervised Learning: Advantages and Limitations

Supervised learning excels when there is a clear relationship between input features and the target variable. Its predictive power makes it valuable in scenarios where the goal is to classify or predict outcomes. However, it requires labeled data, which can be costly and time-consuming to obtain. Additionally, supervised learning may struggle with complex patterns if the relationship between inputs and outputs is not linear or straightforward.

Strengths:
- High accuracy with labeled data.
- Well-suited for predictive tasks with clear outcomes.

Limitations:
- Dependency on labeled data.
- Risk of overfitting in complex models with small datasets.

B. Unsupervised Learning: Flexibility and Challenges

Unsupervised learning is advantageous when data lacks labels or predefined categories, enabling analysts to explore and discover patterns organically. It is particularly useful for exploratory analysis, reducing dimensionality, and clustering. However, results may be harder to interpret, as unsupervised algorithms do not provide clear labels, and it can be challenging to validate the quality of clusters or groups.

Strengths:
- Useful for exploratory data analysis.
- Capable of identifying hidden structures.

Limitations:

- Lack of labeled data can make interpretation difficult.
- Clustering results may be sensitive to initial parameter choices (e.g., number of clusters).

C. Reinforcement Learning: Dynamic Decision-Making with High Complexity

Reinforcement learning is unique in its ability to optimize actions over time, making it ideal for dynamic environments where decision-making is ongoing. RL's feedback-based system enables agents to learn complex behaviors in interactive settings. However, RL models are computationally intensive and require large amounts of training data, especially in complex environments with high-dimensional states or continuous action spaces.

Strengths:

- Effective for complex, interactive environments.
- Optimizes long-term strategies.

Limitations:

- High computational cost and training time.
- Requires well-defined rewards and penalties.

Conclusion

Supervised, unsupervised, and reinforcement learning represent the three pillars of machine learning, each tailored to specific types of tasks and challenges. Supervised learning excels at prediction with labeled data, unsupervised learning reveals patterns in unlabeled data, and reinforcement learning is ideal for interactive, dynamic environments. By understanding when and how to use each learning paradigm, advanced analysts can apply machine learning to a wide array of real-world problems, creating robust solutions that drive value across industries. As we continue, we will explore more complex applications and techniques, building upon this foundation to tackle sophisticated analytics challenges.

Chapter 4: Data Mining Techniques: Uncovering Hidden Patterns and Trends

Comprehensive Exploration of Clustering, Association Rules, Anomaly Detection, and More

Data mining is the process of discovering meaningful patterns, relationships, and trends within large datasets. By identifying these hidden insights, organizations can make data-driven decisions, optimize operations, and reveal opportunities that would otherwise go unnoticed. This chapter explores essential data mining techniques, including clustering, association rules, anomaly detection, and others, providing a comprehensive toolkit for uncovering hidden patterns in data.

1. Clustering: Grouping Data into Meaningful Segments

Clustering is an unsupervised learning technique that groups data points into clusters based on similarity. Unlike classification, clustering does not rely on labeled data. Instead, it discovers natural groupings within the data, making it useful for customer segmentation, image processing, and identifying similar patterns.

Popular Clustering Algorithms

- **k-Means Clustering**: The k-means algorithm partitions data into k clusters, where each data point belongs to the nearest cluster centroid. The algorithm iteratively adjusts the centroids to minimize variance within each cluster.

- o **Application**: k-means is widely used for customer segmentation, where it groups customers with similar purchasing behavior, enabling personalized marketing campaigns.
- **Hierarchical Clustering**: This algorithm creates a hierarchy of clusters, using either a top-down (divisive) or bottom-up (agglomerative) approach. The result is a tree-like structure, or dendrogram, that reveals nested groupings.
  - o **Application**: Hierarchical clustering is useful for scenarios where relationships between clusters are important, such as in genetic research or text analysis.
- **DBSCAN (Density-Based Spatial Clustering of Applications with Noise)**: DBSCAN groups data points based on density, identifying clusters of varying shapes and sizes while marking outliers. Unlike k-means, it doesn't require specifying the number of clusters.
  - o **Application**: DBSCAN is used in geospatial analysis to identify clusters in satellite images or geographic data, especially when there is noise or varying cluster densities.

Example of Clustering
Customer Segmentation in Retail

A retail company wants to better understand its customer base to enhance marketing efforts. By applying k-means clustering on data like purchase history, age, and location, the company segments customers into clusters (e.g., "frequent buyers," "price-sensitive shoppers"). This insight allows them to tailor their marketing campaigns to different customer needs and improve engagement.

2. Association Rule Mining: Discovering Relationships Between Variables

Association rule mining uncovers relationships, or associations, between items in large datasets. The technique identifies rules that reveal how items or events are related, typically in the form of "if-then" statements. Association rules are frequently used in market basket analysis, where the goal is to find patterns in customer purchases.

Key Concepts in Association Rule Mining

- **Support**: The frequency of an itemset appearing in a dataset. High support indicates that a rule is common in the data.
- **Confidence**: The likelihood of an item appearing if another item is present. Confidence measures the strength of the association.
- **Lift**: The ratio of observed support to expected support if items were independent. Lift values greater than 1

indicate a positive association between items.

Algorithm for Association Rule Mining

- **Apriori Algorithm**: The Apriori algorithm generates frequent itemsets by identifying subsets with high support. It then calculates confidence and lift to generate association rules.
  - ○ **Application**: The Apriori algorithm is widely used in market basket analysis to identify which products are frequently purchased together, enabling strategies like cross-selling and product bundling.

Example of Association Rule Mining

Market Basket Analysis in E-commerce

An online retailer analyzes transaction data to discover associations between items frequently bought together. Using Apriori, they find that customers who purchase coffee makers also buy coffee filters. With this insight, the retailer can bundle these items or recommend them during checkout, boosting sales and customer satisfaction.

3. Anomaly Detection: Identifying Unusual Patterns in Data

Anomaly detection identifies rare, out-of-the-ordinary data points that differ significantly from the majority of the data. These anomalies, or outliers, can represent unusual events like fraud, equipment failures, or data errors. Anomaly detection is critical in industries where such events have significant consequences, such as finance, cybersecurity, and manufacturing.

Anomaly Detection Algorithms

- **Isolation Forest**: This algorithm isolates anomalies by randomly selecting features and splitting data points along feature values. Anomalies are easier to isolate, requiring fewer splits. Isolation forests are fast and work well with large datasets.

    o **Application**: Isolation forests are commonly used in fraud detection, where they identify suspicious transactions that deviate from typical patterns.

- **One-Class SVM**: The One-Class Support Vector Machine (SVM) is a supervised anomaly detection algorithm that finds a boundary around normal data points, treating any point outside this boundary as an anomaly.

    o **Application**: One-Class SVM is suitable for network security, identifying unusual activity that might indicate unauthorized access.

- **Autoencoders**: In deep learning, autoencoders are neural networks that learn to compress and reconstruct data. Anomalies are identified when data points cannot be accurately reconstructed, suggesting they deviate from the normal pattern.

o **Application**: Autoencoders are used in industries like manufacturing, where they detect machine faults by analyzing deviations in sensor data.

Example of Anomaly Detection

Fraud Detection in Banking

A bank uses anomaly detection to monitor transactions for unusual activity that may indicate fraud. By training an isolation forest on normal transaction patterns, the model can detect anomalies, such as unusually large withdrawals or international purchases, and flag these for further review. This proactive approach helps prevent financial losses due to fraud.

4. Dimensionality Reduction: Simplifying Complex Datasets

Dimensionality reduction reduces the number of features in a dataset while preserving essential information. It is particularly useful in high-dimensional datasets, where many features can make analysis slow, complex, or prone to overfitting. Techniques like PCA and t-SNE (t-distributed stochastic neighbor embedding) are commonly used for dimensionality reduction.

Dimensionality Reduction Techniques

- **Principal Component Analysis (PCA)**: PCA transforms data into a lower-dimensional space by projecting it onto principal components, which capture the highest variance. PCA is widely used to simplify datasets for visualization and analysis.

- Application: PCA is applied in fields like image processing, where it reduces the dimensionality of images for faster computation without significant loss of information.
- **t-SNE**: This technique is primarily used for visualizing high-dimensional data by mapping it to a lower-dimensional space. t-SNE preserves local similarities, making it ideal for clustering visualizations.
  - Application: t-SNE is often used in bioinformatics to visualize gene expression data, revealing natural groupings and patterns.

Example of Dimensionality Reduction

Data Simplification in Marketing Analytics

A marketing analytics team analyzes customer behavior data with hundreds of features, from demographic data to online browsing habits. Using PCA, they reduce the dataset to a smaller number of principal components, making the data easier to visualize and analyze while still capturing key patterns. This reduced dataset helps the team identify broad customer trends without getting lost in excessive detail.

5. Text Mining: Extracting Insights from Unstructured Text

Text mining is a subfield of data mining that focuses on analyzing and extracting meaningful patterns from unstructured text data. With the rise of digital communication, text mining has become essential for analyzing customer feedback, social media, and reviews.

Text Mining Techniques

- **Natural Language Processing (NLP)**: NLP techniques enable computers to understand and analyze human language. NLP techniques include tokenization, stemming, sentiment analysis, and named entity recognition.
  - **Application**: NLP is used for sentiment analysis in social media monitoring, where companies analyze public sentiment toward their brand.
- **Topic Modeling (LDA)**: Latent Dirichlet Allocation (LDA) is a popular topic modeling technique that uncovers topics within a collection of documents, making it useful for organizing and summarizing large volumes of text.
  - **Application**: LDA is used in content recommendation systems, where it categorizes articles or products into relevant topics for users.

Example of Text Mining

Sentiment Analysis for Brand Monitoring

A company monitors customer sentiment across social media to gauge public perception of its brand. Using NLP techniques, the company identifies trends in sentiment, such as positive or negative feedback on new products. This analysis helps the company respond to customer needs and enhance brand reputation.

6. Time Series Analysis: Identifying Patterns Over Time

Time series analysis focuses on data points collected or recorded over time. This technique identifies trends, seasonality, and cyclic patterns within time-dependent data, making it ideal for forecasting and trend analysis.

Time Series Analysis Techniques

- **ARIMA (AutoRegressive Integrated Moving Average)**: ARIMA models time series data by combining autoregressive and moving average elements, making it useful for short-term forecasting.
  - **Application**: ARIMA is commonly used in finance for predicting stock prices and in sales forecasting.
- **Exponential Smoothing**: This technique smooths data by giving more weight to recent observations, helping identify trends and seasonality.
  - **Application**: Exponential smoothing is used for demand forecasting in supply chain management, where accurate predictions are essential for inventory planning.

Example of Time Series Analysis

Energy Consumption Forecasting

A utility company uses time series analysis to forecast energy consumption for the coming months. By analyzing historical energy usage data with ARIMA, the company identifies seasonal peaks and trends. This forecasting enables the company to prepare for periods of high demand, ensuring reliable service for customers.

Case Studies on Using Data Mining for Customer Segmentation, Fraud Detection, and Recommendation Engines

Data mining provides powerful techniques for extracting valuable insights from large datasets, transforming raw information into actionable strategies across industries. In this chapter, we'll delve into real-world case studies that demonstrate how companies leverage data mining to address key challenges such as customer segmentation, fraud detection, and personalized recommendations. These examples illustrate the process, techniques, and impact of data mining in driving business success.

1. Customer Segmentation in Retail: Targeted Marketing and Personalization

Customer segmentation is a critical application of data mining that allows companies to understand and target different groups within their customer base. By grouping customers based on shared characteristics, businesses can tailor their marketing efforts, improve customer satisfaction, and increase sales.

Case Study: Retail Store's Data-Driven Marketing Strategy

A large retail chain sought to improve the effectiveness of its marketing campaigns by identifying distinct customer segments based on shopping behavior and demographics. Using k-means clustering, the company analyzed data from thousands of customers, including purchase history, average spend, frequency of visits, and demographic factors such as age and income.

Data Mining Process

1. **Data Collection**: The company collected data from loyalty programs, in-store transactions, and online purchase histories.

2. **Feature Selection**: Key features included frequency of purchase, average transaction value, preferred product categories, and customer demographics.

3. **Clustering with k-Means**: By applying the k-means clustering algorithm, the company segmented customers into four primary clusters: high-frequency buyers, seasonal shoppers, bargain hunters, and high-spend loyalists.

Results and Impact

Each cluster revealed unique behaviors and preferences. For example, high-frequency buyers showed a preference for essential items, while seasonal shoppers were more responsive to holiday promotions. The company used these insights to create targeted marketing campaigns, offering personalized promotions to each segment. The result was a 20% increase in customer engagement and a 15% boost in campaign ROI, demonstrating the value of data mining in enhancing customer targeting and personalization.

2. Fraud Detection in Banking: Identifying Anomalous Transactions

Fraud detection is another crucial application of data mining, especially in sectors like finance where unauthorized transactions can lead to significant losses. By identifying anomalies in transaction patterns, financial institutions can flag suspicious activities for further investigation, protecting both their customers and their assets.

Case Study: A Bank's Approach to Transaction Anomaly Detection

A major bank faced increasing challenges in detecting fraudulent transactions due to the rise in digital banking. The bank decided to use anomaly detection techniques to identify suspicious transactions based on historical data. By training a model with isolation forest algorithms, the bank could pinpoint unusual patterns and flag potential fraud in real-time.

Data Mining Process

1. **Data Collection**: The bank analyzed millions of transactions, focusing on transaction amount, frequency, location, time, and device type.
2. **Feature Engineering**: The team created additional features, such as the average

transaction value for each customer, the distance between transaction locations, and the frequency of cross-border transactions.

3. **Anomaly Detection with Isolation Forest**: Using isolation forests, the model could isolate rare, unusual transactions that deviated significantly from a customer's typical behavior.

Results and Impact

The anomaly detection model flagged transactions that showed unusual patterns, such as high-value purchases in foreign locations or rapid transactions from different locations. The bank's fraud team reviewed these transactions, confirming a significant number of cases as fraudulent. By implementing this system, the bank reduced fraud losses by 30% within the first six months and improved its fraud detection rate by 40%, providing a proactive solution that benefited both the bank and its customers.

3. Recommendation Engines in E-commerce: Personalized Shopping Experiences

Recommendation engines are a powerful data mining application in the e-commerce industry, enhancing user experience by suggesting products that align with a customer's preferences. These engines analyze user behavior and item characteristics to provide personalized recommendations, improving engagement and sales.

Case Study: E-commerce Platform's Personalized Recommendation System

A popular e-commerce platform aimed to increase sales by providing personalized recommendations to its users. The company implemented a recommendation engine using collaborative filtering and association rule mining to suggest items based on customer behavior and item relationships.

Data Mining Process

1. **Data Collection**: The platform collected data on user behavior, including clicks, purchase history, browsing patterns, and product ratings.

2. **Collaborative Filtering**: By analyzing similarities between users, collaborative filtering identified items that similar customers enjoyed. For example, customers with similar browsing histories or purchase behaviors were more likely to receive recommendations for similar products.

3. **Association Rule Mining**: The platform also used association rule mining (using the Apriori algorithm) to identify frequently co-purchased items, enabling effective cross-selling and bundling suggestions.

Results and Impact

The recommendation engine provided highly relevant product suggestions to users, leading to increased engagement and a higher average order value. The platform's personalized recommendations contributed to a 25% increase in customer conversion rates and a 30% boost in repeat purchases, proving the value of tailored shopping experiences. Additionally, the association rules allowed the platform to create product bundles, increasing cross-selling opportunities and further enhancing the shopping experience.

4. Predictive Maintenance in Manufacturing: Reducing Downtime and Costs

In manufacturing, data mining techniques can help predict equipment failures before they occur, allowing companies to schedule maintenance proactively and reduce costly downtime. Predictive maintenance leverages anomaly detection and time series analysis to monitor equipment health and detect signs of wear and tear.

Case Study: Industrial Plant's Predictive Maintenance Initiative

An industrial plant producing heavy machinery wanted to reduce unexpected equipment failures, which led to costly production stoppages. By implementing a predictive maintenance system, the company could analyze sensor data in real-time, using anomaly detection to identify early signs of equipment malfunction.

Data Mining Process

1. **Data Collection**: The plant collected sensor data, such as temperature, vibration, and pressure readings, from each machine in the facility.

2. **Time Series Analysis and Feature Engineering**: The team used time series analysis to track sensor readings over time and engineered features like rolling averages and moving variances to monitor equipment health.

3. **Anomaly Detection with Autoencoders**: An autoencoder, a neural network model, was used to learn typical sensor patterns. When sensor readings deviated significantly from the norm, the system flagged these anomalies as potential indicators of equipment failure.

Results and Impact

The predictive maintenance system successfully detected early signs of wear and tear, allowing the plant to schedule repairs before breakdowns occurred. Over the course of one year, the plant reduced unexpected downtime by 40% and maintenance costs by 25%. These improvements translated to millions in savings, demonstrating the value of data mining in industrial applications.

Conclusion

These case studies highlight the versatility and impact of data mining techniques in solving real-world problems across industries. By leveraging clustering, anomaly detection, association rules, and recommendation engines, organizations can drive insights that improve customer engagement, protect against fraud, enhance operational efficiency, and deliver tailored experiences. As we continue, this foundation in data mining techniques will support the development of more complex applications, empowering analysts to unlock the full potential of data and drive strategic impact in their fields.

Practical Tips for Translating Patterns into Actionable Insights

Data mining techniques enable organizations to uncover valuable patterns and trends within their datasets, but the real value lies in transforming these findings into actionable insights that can drive decision-making and strategy. Translating data mining patterns into meaningful business actions requires a mix of analytical skills, strategic thinking, and effective communication. This chapter provides practical tips to help analysts convert raw patterns into insights that inform decisions and create measurable impact.

1. Start with Clear Objectives and Business Questions

The foundation of actionable insights begins with a clear understanding of the problem and objectives. Before diving into data mining, ensure that you have a well-defined question or goal that aligns with business priorities. This clarity will guide the analysis and help determine which patterns are most relevant.

Practical Tips:

- **Identify Key Business Objectives**: Start by collaborating with stakeholders to clarify the goals, such as increasing sales, reducing churn, or improving operational efficiency.
- **Define Specific Questions**: Break down broad objectives into focused questions. For example, instead of a general goal like "improve customer satisfaction," ask, "What factors are most correlated with high customer satisfaction ratings?"
- **Set Success Metrics**: Define how you will measure the success of the insights. Metrics like ROI, customer retention rates, or time savings help quantify the impact of the findings.

2. Prioritize Patterns that Align with Strategic Goals

Not all patterns uncovered through data mining will be relevant. Prioritize patterns that directly support strategic goals or address immediate business needs. By focusing on high-impact patterns, you can ensure that insights lead to meaningful, actionable outcomes.

Practical Tips:

- **Evaluate Patterns Against Goals**: Assess each discovered pattern based on its relevance to the original business question. For example, if the goal is to increase sales, patterns indicating customer purchasing behavior or seasonal trends are more valuable than less relevant patterns.

- **Consider Business Impact**: Prioritize patterns with the highest potential impact. Use an impact-effort matrix to identify low-effort, high-impact insights that can be acted upon quickly.
- **Look for Quick Wins**: Identify "quick win" insights that require minimal resources to implement and can produce immediate benefits. For example, a pattern showing a spike in website traffic after a specific type of post could lead to content adjustments that drive further engagement.

3. Use Visualization to Highlight Key Insights

Data visualization is a powerful tool for making patterns more understandable and compelling. Visuals can transform complex data into clear, intuitive stories that decision-makers can grasp quickly, facilitating faster and more informed decision-making.

Practical Tips:

- **Choose the Right Chart Type**: Select a visualization format that best represents the pattern. Use bar charts for comparing categories, line charts for trends over time, and scatter plots to show relationships.
- **Focus on Key Takeaways**: Highlight essential insights within the visuals, such as peaks, trends, or outliers. Use annotations or color to draw attention to the most important elements.

- **Simplify Complex Data**: Break down complex datasets into digestible visuals. Avoid overcrowding charts with too many variables or data points, and present one main message per visual to maintain clarity.

4. Contextualize Patterns to Enhance Relevance

Patterns on their own may not be actionable until they are placed in context. Adding context—such as historical comparisons, industry benchmarks, or business cycles—helps translate patterns into insights that resonate with stakeholders and reflect real-world situations.

Practical Tips:

- **Use Comparative Benchmarks**: Compare patterns to historical data or industry benchmarks to assess their significance. For example, an increase in monthly sales may seem promising, but comparing it to industry growth rates could provide a clearer picture.
- **Consider External Factors**: Identify external influences that may affect the pattern, such as seasonal trends, economic shifts, or competitive changes. For example, an increase in retail sales during the holiday season may not indicate long-term growth.
- **Incorporate Business Cycles**: Align patterns with business cycles or known industry trends. Understanding the cyclical nature of certain patterns helps determine if

the pattern is likely to repeat or requires immediate action.

5. Translate Insights into Specific Recommendations

To make insights actionable, it's crucial to move beyond reporting patterns and offer specific, data-backed recommendations. Recommendations should provide a clear path for implementation, outlining the actions necessary to capitalize on or address the discovered patterns.

Practical Tips:

- **Be Clear and Specific**: Avoid vague suggestions. Instead of saying, "focus on customer retention," provide concrete steps, such as "implement a loyalty program targeting customers with high purchase frequency but low engagement."

- **Align with Available Resources**: Ensure recommendations are feasible, considering budget, personnel, and time constraints. Suggest phased implementation if a large-scale change isn't feasible all at once.

- **Provide a Range of Options**: Offer multiple actions when possible, such as low-cost and high-impact alternatives. This allows stakeholders to select solutions that best fit their current capabilities and priorities.

6. Test Insights with Small-Scale Pilots

Before rolling out major changes based on insights, consider implementing small-scale pilots to test the effectiveness of your recommendations. Pilots allow you to validate insights, refine approaches, and gather additional data, reducing the risk of full-scale implementation.

Practical Tips:

- **Choose a Representative Sample**: Run pilots in a subset of the business that represents the larger organization, such as testing a marketing campaign on a specific customer segment.
- **Define Pilot Success Metrics**: Set clear success metrics for the pilot, such as increased conversion rates or improved customer feedback scores. Metrics provide an objective basis for deciding whether to proceed with full-scale implementation.
- **Iterate Based on Results**: Use feedback and data from the pilot to fine-tune recommendations. This iterative approach helps ensure that final actions are well-informed and likely to succeed.

7. Communicate Insights Effectively to Stakeholders

Effective communication is essential for turning insights into action. Insights must be presented in a way that resonates with stakeholders, addressing their concerns, aligning with their goals, and explaining the potential impact on the organization.

Practical Tips:

- **Tailor Communication to the Audience**: Present insights differently depending on the audience. Executives may need high-level summaries focused on business impact, while technical teams may benefit from a more detailed analysis.

- **Focus on Benefits and ROI**: Highlight the business benefits and expected ROI of following the recommendations. Explain how the insights can help achieve specific goals, such as cost savings, increased revenue, or improved customer satisfaction.
- **Encourage Interactive Discussion**: Invite feedback and discussion to foster buy-in and address potential concerns. This approach ensures that stakeholders understand the insights and feel involved in the decision-making process.

8. Establish Feedback Loops to Monitor Results and Adapt

Actionable insights should be continuously monitored to measure their effectiveness and refine strategies over time. Establishing feedback loops allows teams to track the impact of their actions, adapt based on results, and evolve strategies as new patterns emerge.

Practical Tips:

- **Define Metrics for Success**: Clearly outline the metrics that will indicate the success of each action. For example, if the recommendation was to target customer retention, track metrics like churn rate, repeat purchases, and customer lifetime value.

- **Regularly Review Outcomes**: Schedule regular check-ins to assess the outcomes and make necessary adjustments. Use dashboards to provide real-time visibility into key metrics and progress.
- **Adapt Based on Findings**: Be prepared to iterate and improve actions based on feedback. If initial recommendations are not yielding the expected results, re-evaluate the data, refine insights, and try new approaches.

Conclusion

The process of translating patterns into actionable insights is as critical as the data mining itself. By following these practical steps—defining clear objectives, prioritizing high-impact patterns, using effective visualization, providing context, offering specific recommendations, testing with pilots, communicating insights, and establishing feedback loops—analysts can ensure that their findings are both relevant and impactful. These practices allow organizations to leverage data mining techniques not only to uncover hidden patterns but to drive tangible results that align with strategic objectives. As we move forward, these skills will serve as the foundation for more advanced data analysis and decision-making approaches.

Chapter 5: Feature Engineering and Selection for Machine Learning Success

Techniques for Crafting High-Impact Features and Reducing Dimensionality

Feature engineering and selection are essential steps in building high-performing machine learning models. High-quality features transform raw data into meaningful signals, boosting model accuracy, interpretability, and computational efficiency. This chapter covers key techniques for creating impactful features, reducing dimensionality, and selecting the best attributes to improve model success.

1. The Importance of Feature Engineering in Machine Learning

Feature engineering is the process of transforming raw data into features that better represent the underlying patterns needed for a machine learning model to make predictions. It involves creating, modifying, or combining variables to reveal valuable insights that are not immediately visible in the raw data. High-impact features can significantly improve model performance by providing clearer, more meaningful inputs.

Benefits of Effective Feature Engineering

- **Improved Model Accuracy**: Good features enhance a model's predictive accuracy by capturing essential patterns.

- **Reduced Complexity**: By transforming raw data, feature engineering simplifies complex relationships, making it easier for models to learn.
- **Enhanced Interpretability**: Well-crafted features offer clearer insights, helping users understand the patterns that drive predictions.

2. Techniques for Crafting High-Impact Features

Creating high-impact features requires an understanding of the data, domain knowledge, and creativity. Here are some essential feature engineering techniques used to extract valuable information:

a. Binning and Discretization

Binning involves grouping continuous values into intervals, converting them into categorical bins. Discretizing data can help simplify patterns and make relationships easier for the model to learn.

- **Example**: Age can be binned into categories like "18–25," "26–35," and so on. This approach is helpful when different age groups have distinct behaviors or trends.

b. Polynomial and Interaction Features

Generating polynomial and interaction terms allows the model to capture non-linear relationships between variables. Polynomial features involve raising variables to a power, while interaction features involve combining variables.

- **Example**: In predicting housing prices, interaction features such as "house age * square footage" might reveal relationships between house age and size that affect price.

c. Encoding Categorical Variables

Machine learning algorithms require numerical input, so categorical variables must be encoded. Common encoding methods include:

- **One-Hot Encoding**: Creates a new binary column for each category, where each column represents the presence (1) or absence (0) of a category.
- **Label Encoding**: Assigns each category a unique numerical value, useful for ordinal categories with an inherent order.

d. Time-Based Features

Time-based features are derived from date and time data. Extracting components such as day of the week, month, hour, or season helps capture trends and patterns related to time.

- **Example**: In retail data, creating features like "day of the week" and "holiday" may reveal trends in sales that vary with the calendar.

e. Aggregation and Statistical Features

Aggregation features provide summary statistics based on groups within the data, such as mean, sum, or count. These features help capture general trends across groups or time periods.

- **Example**: In customer data, the average purchase frequency or total spending over time can be an indicator of customer loyalty.

f. Text Features

For text data, features such as word counts, term frequency-inverse document frequency (TF-IDF), and sentiment scores help convert unstructured data into useful numeric representations.

- **Example**: Analyzing product reviews might involve creating features based on positive or negative sentiment scores to understand customer feedback.

3. Feature Selection: Choosing the Most Valuable Features

Feature selection is the process of identifying and retaining only the most relevant features from a dataset. Reducing dimensionality helps improve model performance, reduce overfitting, and enhance interpretability. Here are popular techniques for effective feature selection:

a. Filter Methods

Filter methods select features based on statistical properties, independently of the model. These methods assess features according to their correlation with the target variable.

- **Correlation Coefficients**: Calculate the correlation between each feature and the target, removing features with low correlation.
- **Chi-Square Test**: For categorical data, the chi-square test evaluates whether there's a

significant association between each feature and the target variable.

b. Wrapper Methods

Wrapper methods use iterative model-based evaluations to select features, considering the performance of subsets of features on a specific model. Techniques include:

- **Forward Selection**: Starts with no features and adds features one at a time, choosing those that improve model performance the most.
- **Backward Elimination**: Starts with all features and removes the least impactful features one at a time, observing the effect on performance.

c. Embedded Methods

Embedded methods perform feature selection within the training process of the model itself. Regularization techniques like Lasso and Ridge regression add a penalty to the model to reduce the importance of less impactful features.

- **Lasso (L1 Regularization)**: Adds a penalty equal to the absolute value of the feature coefficients, forcing some coefficients to zero, thus excluding irrelevant features.
- **Ridge (L2 Regularization)**: Adds a penalty equal to the square of the coefficients, reducing the influence of less important features without forcing them to zero.

d. Principal Component Analysis (PCA)

PCA is a dimensionality reduction technique that transforms features into a smaller set of components based on the variance in the data. PCA reduces complexity while retaining essential information.

- **Application**: PCA is useful in high-dimensional datasets where many features are correlated. By transforming features into principal components, PCA preserves variance and reduces redundancy.

e. Recursive Feature Elimination (RFE)

RFE is a recursive wrapper method that uses a model to rank features by importance and iteratively removes the least important features. It's a robust approach that can work with a variety of algorithms.

- **Application**: RFE is useful in datasets with many features where traditional filter methods may overlook complex relationships. It's often used with models like decision trees or support vector machines.

4. Reducing Dimensionality for Better Model Performance

High-dimensional data can be computationally expensive, complex, and prone to overfitting. Dimensionality reduction techniques help simplify the dataset while preserving essential information, leading to faster training and improved generalization.

a. Feature Scaling and Normalization

Scaling and normalizing data are essential steps when working with models sensitive to feature scales, such as K-nearest neighbors or SVM. Common methods include:

- **Standardization**: Scales features to have a mean of zero and a standard deviation of one, making them comparable.
- **Normalization**: Scales features to a range, typically between 0 and 1, reducing the impact of large feature values.

b. Selecting Principal Components with PCA

As discussed, PCA reduces dimensionality by converting features into a smaller set of principal components. PCA is valuable when dealing with correlated variables, as it combines them into uncorrelated components that retain most of the variance.

c. t-SNE for Visualization

Although t-SNE (t-distributed stochastic neighbor embedding) is primarily used for visualization, it reduces high-dimensional data into two or three dimensions, highlighting clusters and patterns. t-SNE is particularly helpful in visualizing the relationships in complex datasets.

Example of Dimensionality Reduction

Customer Churn Prediction in Telecommunications

A telecommunications company wants to predict customer churn using customer demographic and usage data, which includes dozens of features. By applying PCA, the company reduces the dataset to the principal components that explain most of the variance, streamlining the dataset without sacrificing valuable information. The resulting data improves model training time and accuracy, leading to a more effective churn prediction model.

5. Practical Tips for Effective Feature Engineering and Selection

To get the most out of feature engineering and selection, here are some best practices:

- **Experiment with Multiple Techniques**: Try different feature engineering methods (e.g., interaction terms, aggregations) and compare results to identify the most effective features.
- **Use Domain Knowledge**: Incorporate insights from the domain to create relevant features that align with business goals. For instance, using seasonality in retail data can improve predictions of sales cycles.
- **Avoid Data Leakage**: Ensure that features derived from future data are not included in the training set, as this can lead to artificially high accuracy.
- **Automate Feature Engineering with Tools**: Explore tools like FeatureTools or automated machine learning (AutoML) platforms, which assist in creating and testing features more efficiently.
- **Validate Results with Cross-Validation**: Use cross-validation to confirm that selected features generalize well across

different parts of the dataset, ensuring robustness.

Conclusion

Effective feature engineering and selection are the cornerstones of building successful machine learning models. By crafting high-impact features, reducing dimensionality, and selecting the most relevant variables, analysts can significantly improve model accuracy, reduce complexity, and ensure the model's ability to generalize. Mastering these techniques enables data scientists and analysts to leverage raw data more effectively, uncover hidden insights, and deliver powerful, predictive models that drive business impact. As we continue, we'll delve deeper into advanced techniques for model tuning and evaluation, building on the foundation of strong feature engineering and selection.

Detailed Walk-Throughs of Feature Engineering Techniques Like Encoding, Scaling, and Extraction

Feature engineering is a transformative process in machine learning, turning raw data into valuable input for models. Techniques like encoding, scaling, and extraction allow analysts to prepare data so that machine learning algorithms can understand, learn, and make accurate predictions. This chapter provides detailed, step-by-step walk-throughs of these essential techniques, offering practical guidance on how to apply them for optimal machine learning success.

1. Encoding Categorical Variables: Converting Categories to Numeric Values

Machine learning models require numerical input, so categorical data must be converted into numerical format. Encoding categorical variables allows models to capture patterns within categories and relationships among them.

Encoding Techniques

- **One-Hot Encoding**: One-hot encoding converts each category into a separate binary column (0 or 1), where each column represents the presence or absence of a category.
    - ○ **When to Use**: One-hot encoding is effective for nominal (unordered) categories, such as "city," "color," or "product type."
    - ○ **Example**: Suppose we have a "Color" column with categories "Red," "Green," and "Blue." One-hot encoding would create three binary columns—Color_Red, Color_Green, and Color_Blue—where each entry has a 1 in the column representing its color.
- **Label Encoding**: Label encoding assigns each category a unique integer, making it easy to interpret, but it can impose an unintended ordinal relationship.

- When to Use: Use label encoding for ordinal categories where there is an inherent order, like "low," "medium," and "high."
- Example: For an "Education" level column with values "High School," "Bachelor's," and "Master's," label encoding could map these values to 1, 2, and 3, respectively.
- **Target Encoding**: This technique replaces categories with the mean target variable value within each category, often used for high-cardinality categorical features.
  - When to Use: Target encoding is useful for reducing dimensionality in categorical data with many levels, such as "zipcode."
  - Example: For a "Region" feature predicting sales, target encoding might replace each region with its average sales.

Best Practices for Encoding
- **Avoid High Cardinality**: When possible, group categories with many unique values into broader categories to avoid excessive columns in one-hot encoding.
- **Beware of Data Leakage**: When using target encoding, ensure that you apply encoding on training data only, and not on test data, to prevent data leakage.

2. Scaling and Normalization: Standardizing Data Ranges

Scaling and normalization standardize feature values, making them comparable. These techniques are essential when working with algorithms that are sensitive to feature magnitudes, such as K-nearest neighbors (KNN) and support vector machines (SVM).

Scaling Techniques

- **Standardization (Z-score Normalization)**: Standardization transforms data to have a mean of zero and a standard deviation of one. It centers the data, making all features comparable without losing the original data distribution.

  - **When to Use**: Standardization is effective when features have different units or ranges, such as height (inches) and weight (pounds).

  - **Example**: For a dataset with income and age, standardizing both features ensures they are on the same scale, preventing income from disproportionately affecting the model.

- **Min-Max Normalization**: This method rescales data to a specified range, typically between 0 and 1. Min-max normalization is particularly helpful in cases where all values must be positive.

- When to Use: Use min-max scaling for algorithms where the range of features impacts performance, such as neural networks.
- Example: For a dataset of house prices ranging from $100,000 to $1,000,000, min-max normalization would scale each price between 0 and 1, preserving relative distances.

- **Robust Scaling**: Robust scaling scales data based on the interquartile range (IQR), reducing the influence of outliers. It's effective when datasets contain extreme values.
  - When to Use: Apply robust scaling when you suspect the presence of outliers that could skew the data.
  - Example: In income data where a few extreme values exist, robust scaling limits the effect of these outliers on the overall data distribution.

Practical Tips for Scaling

- **Apply Scaling After Train-Test Split**: Always split the dataset into training and testing sets before scaling to avoid data leakage.
- **Choose the Appropriate Scaling Method**: Select the scaling method based on the characteristics of the dataset and the algorithm's sensitivity to scale.

3. Feature Extraction: Reducing Complexity While Retaining Information

Feature extraction techniques help condense information from multiple features into a smaller set, capturing essential information while simplifying the dataset. This approach is particularly useful for high-dimensional datasets where many features are redundant.

Feature Extraction Techniques

- **Principal Component Analysis (PCA)**: PCA reduces dimensionality by transforming features into a smaller set of uncorrelated components, each representing a combination of the original features that capture maximum variance.
  - **When to Use**: PCA is ideal for high-dimensional data where features are correlated, such as gene expression or image data.
  - **Example**: In a customer dataset with dozens of demographic and behavioral features, PCA might reduce the data to a few principal components, making analysis more manageable while retaining critical information.
- **t-Distributed Stochastic Neighbor Embedding (t-SNE)**: Primarily used for data visualization, t-SNE maps high-dimensional data to two or three

dimensions, preserving local relationships to highlight clusters.

- o **When to Use**: t-SNE is useful for visualizing complex patterns, such as clusters in text or image data.
- o **Example**: For visualizing customer segments, t-SNE can reduce hundreds of features into a two-dimensional map, allowing analysts to identify clusters based on customer behaviors.
- **Feature Hashing**: Feature hashing converts high-cardinality categorical data into a fixed-size numeric representation, often used in text data and situations where dimensionality reduction is needed.
  - o **When to Use**: Apply feature hashing for large categorical data (e.g., product IDs or URLs) where traditional encoding methods would lead to high dimensionality.
  - o **Example**: For a large text dataset with thousands of unique words, feature hashing reduces the number of dimensions, making the model training process faster.
- **Text Vectorization (TF-IDF)**: Term Frequency-Inverse Document Frequency (TF-IDF) is a feature extraction method for text data, assigning weights to words based

on their frequency and uniqueness in a document.

- o **When to Use**: Use TF-IDF for text classification, sentiment analysis, or any task involving textual data.
- o **Example**: In sentiment analysis, TF-IDF transforms a review's words into numerical values, highlighting unique words while downplaying common ones, helping the model focus on meaningful terms.

Practical Tips for Feature Extraction

- **Combine with Feature Selection**: After feature extraction, use selection techniques to identify which extracted features are most predictive.
- **Interpret Principal Components Carefully**: PCA components are combinations of original features, which may make them harder to interpret. Use feature loadings to understand the contribution of each feature.
- **Optimize for Task Requirements**: Choose the extraction method based on the dataset's characteristics and the specific analysis goals (e.g., TF-IDF for text, PCA for high-dimensional data).

4. Creating Aggregation Features: Summarizing Data at Different Levels

Aggregation involves creating summary features based on groups within the data, providing insights across different levels of granularity. Aggregation features can capture underlying patterns that are not visible in raw data.

Types of Aggregation Features

- **Temporal Aggregates**: Summarize data over specific time periods, such as weekly averages, monthly totals, or year-to-date sums.
  - **Example**: In a sales dataset, aggregating monthly sales per store helps detect seasonal patterns and store performance.
- **Group-Level Aggregates**: Calculate statistics based on groups, such as averages, counts, or sums for each customer, product, or region.
  - **Example**: In customer data, calculating the average purchase value per customer or the total visits per customer reveals patterns in spending behavior.
- **Rolling Aggregates**: Compute moving averages or rolling sums over a fixed window, allowing for trend analysis.
  - **Example**: In financial data, a 7-day moving average of stock prices smooths out daily fluctuations, highlighting broader trends.

Practical Tips for Aggregation Features

- **Select Appropriate Time Windows**: Choose aggregation windows that reflect natural business cycles (e.g., weekly, monthly) to capture meaningful trends.

- **Avoid Data Leakage**: When creating time-based aggregates, ensure that future data is not included in calculations to prevent data leakage.
- **Experiment with Different Aggregations**: Test various types of aggregations to identify which ones enhance model performance the most.

5. Practical Example: End-to-End Feature Engineering Process

Scenario: Predicting Customer Churn for a Subscription Service

- **Encoding**: Convert the categorical "Subscription Type" column into one-hot encoding, creating binary columns for each subscription level.
- **Scaling**: Standardize numerical features like "Monthly Spend" and "Customer Age" to ensure they're on the same scale.
- **Feature Extraction**: Use PCA on behavioral data (e.g., weekly usage statistics) to reduce dimensions and focus on core usage patterns.
- **Aggregation**: Create temporal aggregates for "Total Usage Last 3 Months" and "Average Weekly Visits," capturing recent engagement trends.

- **Final Model Preparation**: Select the most predictive features, ensuring only the most impactful data remains for model training.

This end-to-end feature engineering process transforms raw customer data into a structured dataset ready for modeling, maximizing predictive power while reducing complexity.

Conclusion

Feature engineering and selection are integral to the success of any machine learning model. By understanding and applying techniques like encoding, scaling, and extraction, data professionals can optimize their datasets, enhancing both model performance and interpretability. Mastery of these techniques allows analysts to transform raw data into meaningful, actionable features that drive machine learning success. As we progress, these engineered features will serve as the foundation for building and evaluating robust models that deliver business value.

Practical Examples of Feature Selection Methods That Improve Model Accuracy and Efficiency

Feature selection is the process of identifying the most relevant features from a dataset to enhance model accuracy, reduce computational complexity, and improve interpretability. Selecting the right features eliminates noise, prevents overfitting, and often results in faster and more accurate models.

This chapter provides practical examples of commonly used feature selection methods, demonstrating how each approach contributes to building better-performing machine learning models.

1. Filter Methods: Ranking Features Based on Statistical Properties

Filter methods evaluate each feature independently of the model, ranking features based on statistical metrics like correlation or mutual information. These techniques are often the first step in feature selection, as they are fast and effective for high-dimensional datasets.

Example: Using Correlation Coefficient for Feature Selection in House Price Prediction

In a house price prediction model, we have numerous features like square footage, number of rooms, age, location, and proximity to schools. To identify the most relevant features, we calculate the correlation of each feature with the target variable (house price).

- **Process**: Calculate the Pearson correlation coefficient between each feature and house price. Features with high positive or negative correlations (e.g., square footage, location) are likely to have more predictive power.
- **Outcome**: By selecting features with a correlation coefficient above a chosen threshold (e.g., 0.3 or -0.3), we retain

features that are highly relevant while discarding weakly correlated features.

- **Impact**: Reducing the feature set to only those with strong correlations improves model interpretability and accuracy, as the model focuses on features that meaningfully affect house prices.

Best Practices for Filter Methods

- **Apply Before Model Training**: Use filter methods as an initial step to remove low-value features and reduce dimensionality quickly.
- **Consider Multicollinearity**: Avoid including highly correlated features simultaneously, as they add redundancy. In this example, if square footage and number of rooms are highly correlated, choose one to prevent multicollinearity.

2. Wrapper Methods: Iteratively Selecting Features Using Model Performance

Wrapper methods assess the predictive power of feature subsets by training the model multiple times. This approach can provide higher accuracy than filter methods, although it can be computationally intensive.

Example: Forward Selection in Customer Churn Prediction

For a customer churn prediction model, we start with a blank slate and iteratively add features based on their ability to improve model performance.

- **Process**: Begin with no features, add one feature at a time, and evaluate model performance (e.g., using accuracy or AUC score). Retain features that improve model performance and continue adding until there's no further improvement.
- **Outcome**: Forward selection might identify features such as "monthly usage," "contract type," and "customer tenure" as highly predictive, while excluding features that don't add value (e.g., minor demographic details).
- **Impact**: Focusing only on the features that drive predictive power increases model accuracy while reducing the risk of overfitting. This streamlined feature set also leads to faster training and prediction times.

Best Practices for Wrapper Methods

- **Be Aware of Computational Costs**: Wrapper methods require multiple model runs, so use with smaller datasets or fewer features, or apply after an initial filter.
- **Monitor Model Overfitting**: Wrapper methods can lead to overfitting if not properly cross-validated, especially on small datasets.

3. Embedded Methods: Selecting Features During Model Training

Embedded methods perform feature selection within the training process, allowing the model to decide which features are most predictive. These techniques integrate regularization, penalizing less impactful features, and can improve both accuracy and efficiency.

Example: Lasso (L1 Regularization) in Predicting Loan Default

In predicting loan default, a financial institution uses numerous features, such as income, credit score, employment history, and existing debt. By applying Lasso regression, we can automatically select impactful features while penalizing less important ones.

- **Process**: Train the model with Lasso regression, which adds an L1 penalty to the objective function, pushing the coefficients of less important features to zero.
- **Outcome**: Features with non-zero coefficients (e.g., income, credit score) are retained, while redundant features (e.g., zip code, minor loan details) are eliminated.
- **Impact**: This approach improves model interpretability by highlighting the most important features and reduces the risk of overfitting, as irrelevant features are effectively ignored.

Best Practices for Embedded Methods

- **Choose the Right Regularization Method**: Use L1 regularization (Lasso) for sparse data or when you expect only a few features to be highly predictive.
- **Optimize Regularization Parameter**: Adjust the regularization strength (lambda)

to balance feature elimination with model accuracy.

4. Principal Component Analysis (PCA): Reducing Dimensionality While Preserving Variance

PCA is a powerful dimensionality reduction technique that combines features into principal components based on variance, reducing complexity while retaining essential information. PCA is particularly effective for high-dimensional data where features are highly correlated.

Example: Dimensionality Reduction in Image Recognition

In an image recognition dataset with thousands of pixel features, training a model on every pixel is computationally prohibitive. PCA reduces the dataset to a manageable number of components.

- **Process**: Apply PCA to transform the pixel features into principal components, each representing a portion of the data variance. Select the top components that explain 95% of the variance.
- **Outcome**: The original dataset with thousands of features is reduced to a smaller set of components (e.g., the top 50 components), preserving most of the information.
- **Impact**: PCA reduces the training time and memory usage, while retaining the predictive power needed for accurate image recognition. This approach also helps

prevent overfitting by focusing on core patterns rather than noise.

Best Practices for PCA

- **Standardize Features Before Applying PCA**: Ensure features are standardized to have a mean of zero and a standard deviation of one for consistent component scaling.

- **Select the Number of Components Based on Variance**: Choose components that capture most of the variance (e.g., 95%), balancing dimensionality reduction with information retention.

5. Recursive Feature Elimination (RFE): Iterative Removal Based on Model Performance

RFE is an iterative wrapper method that ranks features by importance and removes the least important ones in each iteration until reaching a specified number of features. RFE works well with algorithms that can assign feature importance, like decision trees or support vector machines.

Example: Feature Selection in Sentiment Analysis

In a sentiment analysis model using thousands of text features (words), many terms may add little value. RFE helps identify the most impactful words while reducing noise.

- **Process**: Use a model (e.g., SVM or logistic regression) to rank features by importance, remove the least impactful features iteratively, and retain the top features based on accuracy.

- **Outcome**: RFE identifies the most relevant words, such as "excellent" and "poor," while removing common or less meaningful words like "the" or "and."
- **Impact**: The resulting feature set improves model accuracy by focusing on words that contribute to sentiment prediction, reducing dimensionality and making the model faster and more interpretable.

Best Practices for RFE

- **Use with Feature Importance-Estimating Models**: Apply RFE with models that calculate feature importance, such as decision trees, SVM, or linear models.
- **Cross-Validate Results**: Validate RFE-selected features across multiple folds to ensure robustness and avoid overfitting.

6. Mutual Information: Quantifying the Predictive Power of Categorical Features

Mutual information measures the dependency between features and the target variable, capturing both linear and non-linear relationships. It is particularly useful for feature selection in classification tasks with categorical data.

Example: Predicting Product Recommendations Based on User Behavior

In a product recommendation system, we analyze categorical features such as user device type, country, and past product interactions. Mutual information quantifies the importance of each feature in predicting the likelihood of a product purchase.

- **Process**: Calculate mutual information for each categorical feature relative to the target variable, selecting features with the highest scores.
- **Outcome**: Retain features like "past purchases" and "device type" that have high predictive power, while discarding features with low mutual information.
- **Impact**: By focusing on features with high mutual information, the recommendation system makes more accurate predictions, increasing customer engagement and conversion rates.

Best Practices for Mutual Information

- **Handle Continuous Variables Separately**: Mutual information is most effective with categorical features, so consider using other methods for continuous variables.
- **Combine with Other Methods**: Use mutual information alongside other feature selection techniques for a comprehensive approach.

Conclusion

Feature selection methods like filter methods, wrapper methods, embedded techniques, PCA, RFE, and mutual information are invaluable tools for improving model accuracy and efficiency. Each technique offers unique benefits depending on the dataset and task, and by understanding when and how to apply each method, data scientists can streamline feature sets to build faster, more interpretable, and more accurate machine learning models. This careful selection of features forms a solid foundation for model training, enabling machine learning models to achieve optimal performance and create real business value. As we continue, we'll explore advanced methods for model tuning and validation, building on this foundation of effective feature engineering and selection.

Chapter 6: Evaluating and Optimizing Models: Beyond the Basics

Advanced Techniques for Evaluating Model Performance, Including ROC-AUC, Precision-Recall, and More

Model evaluation is a critical step in machine learning, determining whether a model is reliable and ready for deployment. Beyond standard accuracy, advanced evaluation techniques like ROC-AUC, precision-recall, and F1-score provide deeper insights into model performance, especially when dealing with imbalanced classes or complex classification tasks. This chapter explores these advanced metrics and techniques to help analysts evaluate and optimize models effectively.

1. Importance of Choosing the Right Evaluation Metric

Selecting the right evaluation metric depends on the nature of the problem, the data distribution, and the business objective. While accuracy is often used as a baseline metric, it can be misleading in scenarios like imbalanced classification, where correctly identifying the minority class is critical.

Considerations for Selecting Evaluation Metrics

- **Imbalanced Datasets**: When classes are imbalanced, metrics like precision, recall, and F1-score become more important than accuracy.
- **Prediction Objective**: For tasks where false positives and false negatives carry different

costs, metrics like precision, recall, and ROC-AUC are critical.

- **Application Context**: In fields like healthcare and finance, where the cost of misclassification is high, careful metric selection is essential for risk mitigation.

2. Confusion Matrix: The Foundation of Classification Metrics

The confusion matrix is a table that summarizes model predictions by counting true positives (TP), true negatives (TN), false positives (FP), and false negatives (FN). From this matrix, other metrics are derived.

Example: Fraud Detection in Banking

In a fraud detection model, each prediction is categorized into one of four classes:

- **True Positive (TP)**: Correctly predicted fraudulent transaction.
- **True Negative (TN)**: Correctly predicted non-fraudulent transaction.
- **False Positive (FP)**: Incorrectly predicted fraudulent transaction (non-fraud flagged as fraud).
- **False Negative (FN)**: Incorrectly predicted non-fraudulent transaction (fraud not detected).

This breakdown allows for calculating metrics such as accuracy, precision, recall, and F1-score.

3. Precision and Recall: Balancing False Positives and False Negatives

Precision and recall are particularly useful for imbalanced classification tasks where the cost of false positives or false negatives varies.

- **Precision**: Precision, or positive predictive value, measures the proportion of true positives out of all positive predictions. A high precision indicates fewer false positives.
  - ○ **Formula**: Precision = TP / (TP + FP)
  - ○ **Example**: In fraud detection, high precision means that most transactions flagged as fraudulent are indeed fraud, reducing unnecessary investigations.
- **Recall**: Recall, or sensitivity, measures the proportion of true positives out of all actual positives. High recall means fewer false negatives.
  - ○ **Formula**: Recall = TP / (TP + FN)
  - ○ **Example**: In medical diagnosis, high recall ensures that most actual cases (e.g., disease presence) are correctly identified, minimizing missed cases.

F1-Score: Balancing Precision and Recall

The F1-score is the harmonic mean of precision and recall, providing a single metric to balance both. It is useful when both false positives and false negatives are costly.

- **Formula**: F1 = 2 * (Precision * Recall) / (Precision + Recall)

- **Example**: In email spam detection, a high F1-score indicates a good balance between identifying spam accurately and minimizing false positives (non-spam marked as spam).

Choosing Between Precision, Recall, and F1-Score

- Use **precision** when false positives carry a higher cost.
- Use **recall** when false negatives carry a higher cost.
- Use **F1-score** when both false positives and false negatives have similar costs.

4. ROC-AUC: Evaluating Classifier Performance Across Thresholds

The Receiver Operating Characteristic (ROC) curve plots the true positive rate (sensitivity) against the false positive rate (1-specificity) at various threshold levels. The Area Under the Curve (AUC) summarizes the ROC curve into a single value, indicating how well the model separates classes.

- **Interpreting ROC-AUC**: An AUC score of 0.5 indicates random performance, while 1.0 represents a perfect classifier. Higher AUC values indicate better model performance.
- **Example**: In customer churn prediction, ROC-AUC helps visualize how well the model discriminates between churners and non-churners, guiding decisions on the probability threshold for labeling churners.

Using ROC-AUC in Imbalanced Data

- ROC-AUC is not always ideal for highly imbalanced datasets, as it considers both true and false positives equally. In such cases, precision-recall curves provide more insight.

5. Precision-Recall Curve: Performance with Imbalanced Classes

The precision-recall (PR) curve plots precision against recall at different threshold settings, providing a clearer picture of model performance with imbalanced classes. The area under the PR curve (PR-AUC) summarizes the model's ability to balance precision and recall.

- **Interpreting the Precision-Recall Curve**: A high area under the PR curve indicates effective performance, particularly in detecting the minority class.
- **Example**: In fraud detection, the PR curve can show how the model balances identifying actual fraud cases while avoiding false positives. PR-AUC is more informative than ROC-AUC in this scenario.

When to Use Precision-Recall Curves

- Use PR curves in cases where true negatives are abundant and less relevant (e.g., fraud detection, disease diagnosis).
- PR curves provide better insight into model performance on the minority class, which is often the focus in imbalanced datasets.

6. Advanced Metrics for Regression Models

While classification metrics focus on true/false predictions, regression models require different evaluation metrics to assess prediction accuracy.

Common Regression Metrics

- **Mean Absolute Error (MAE)**: Measures the average magnitude of prediction errors, providing an intuitive interpretation of model accuracy.
  - **Formula**: MAE = (1/n) * Σ |Actual - Predicted|
  - **Example**: In forecasting housing prices, MAE gives an average dollar deviation from the true price.
- **Mean Squared Error (MSE) and Root Mean Squared Error (RMSE)**: MSE emphasizes larger errors by squaring them, while RMSE provides results in the same units as the target variable.
  - **Formula**: MSE = (1/n) * Σ (Actual - Predicted)^2, RMSE = √MSE
  - **Example**: RMSE is useful in time-series forecasting, where small prediction errors are acceptable but large errors need emphasis.
- **R-squared (R^2)**: Measures the proportion of variance explained by the model. Higher values indicate a better fit.
  - **Formula**: R^2 = 1 - (SS_residual / SS_total)
  - **Example**: In advertising spend vs. sales forecasting, a high R^2 value

shows that advertising spend explains a large portion of sales variation.

Choosing Regression Metrics

- Use **MAE** when you want a direct interpretation of error magnitude.
- Use **MSE** or **RMSE** to penalize larger errors.
- Use R^2 to understand how well the model explains the variance in the data.

7. Cross-Validation for Robust Model Evaluation

Cross-validation splits the dataset into multiple subsets, training and testing the model on each subset to ensure robustness. Common techniques include:

- **K-Fold Cross-Validation**: Divides the data into k subsets, trains on k-1 subsets, and tests on the remaining one. This process repeats k times, providing a robust performance estimate.
  - ○ **Example**: In image recognition, 10-fold cross-validation helps ensure model accuracy without overfitting to a single subset of data.
- **Leave-One-Out Cross-Validation (LOOCV)**: Each data point is used once as a test set while the rest form the training set. LOOCV is ideal for small datasets but can be computationally expensive.

- o **Example**: In medical datasets with limited samples, LOOCV maximizes the use of all available data.

Benefits of Cross-Validation

- Reduces the likelihood of overfitting and underfitting by validating performance across multiple data subsets.
- Provides a more accurate measure of model performance on unseen data.

8. Hyperparameter Tuning to Optimize Model Performance

Hyperparameter tuning optimizes model performance by selecting the best set of parameters for the algorithm. Techniques include:

- **Grid Search**: Tests all combinations of a predefined parameter grid to identify the best settings.
- **Random Search**: Randomly samples parameters from the grid, making it faster than grid search for large parameter spaces.
- **Bayesian Optimization**: Uses probabilistic models to estimate the best parameters, iteratively refining search space based on previous results.

Example: Tuning Hyperparameters in a Random Forest Model

In a random forest model for predicting loan defaults, hyperparameters like the number of trees, maximum depth, and minimum samples per leaf affect performance. Using grid search, we test combinations of these parameters to find the set that yields the highest cross-validation accuracy.

Tips for Effective Hyperparameter Tuning

- Use cross-validation during tuning to prevent overfitting.
- Limit grid size or use random search to reduce computation time on large datasets.

Conclusion

Evaluating and optimizing models requires more than just standard accuracy metrics. Advanced techniques like ROC-AUC, precision-recall curves, F1-score, and cross-validation provide a comprehensive view of model performance, allowing data scientists to choose the best metrics for their problem. Hyperparameter tuning further refines model parameters, optimizing for accuracy and efficiency. By applying these advanced techniques, machine learning practitioners can develop robust, high-performing models that meet specific business objectives and deliver meaningful insights. Moving forward, these evaluation and optimization methods will play a crucial role in ensuring models are ready for deployment and real-world application.

Guide to Hyperparameter Tuning, Cross-Validation, and Ensemble Methods for Boosting Performance

In machine learning, building an accurate model is only the beginning. To achieve the best performance, it's essential to refine and optimize the model through techniques like hyperparameter tuning, cross-validation, and ensemble methods. These techniques help extract maximum predictive power from the model, ensuring it generalizes well to new data. This chapter covers practical strategies for fine-tuning hyperparameters, validating models effectively, and using ensemble methods to boost performance.

1. Hyperparameter Tuning: Fine-Tuning Model Parameters for Optimal Performance

Hyperparameters are model parameters set before training that significantly influence performance. Unlike parameters learned from data (like weights in neural networks), hyperparameters control the training process itself, such as learning rate, maximum depth of trees, or regularization strength.

Hyperparameter Tuning Methods

- **Grid Search**: Grid search exhaustively tests all possible combinations within a specified set of hyperparameter values.
    - **Example**: In a support vector machine (SVM), grid search might test different values for the kernel type, regularization parameter (C), and gamma. Grid search identifies the combination that yields the best model performance on the validation set.
    - **Pros**: Comprehensive and ensures that every combination is tested.

- Cons: Computationally expensive, especially with large parameter grids.
- **Random Search**: Rather than testing all combinations, random search selects random hyperparameter combinations from a predefined range.
    - **Example**: For a random forest model, random search may randomly select values for the number of trees and maximum depth to find an effective combination.
    - **Pros**: Faster than grid search, especially when the hyperparameter space is large.
    - **Cons**: May miss the optimal combination but still finds reasonably good results.
- **Bayesian Optimization**: Uses probabilistic models to predict the best parameters based on previous results, refining the search over iterations.
    - **Example**: In a gradient boosting model, Bayesian optimization might adjust learning rate, number of estimators, and maximum depth iteratively to maximize accuracy.
    - **Pros**: Efficient and smart search, focusing on promising regions of the hyperparameter space.

- Cons: More complex to implement but often more computationally efficient than grid search.

Best Practices for Hyperparameter Tuning

- **Start with Random or Grid Search**: Use these methods to get a sense of the hyperparameter space before refining with Bayesian optimization.
- **Use Cross-Validation**: Perform hyperparameter tuning with cross-validation to ensure generalizability and avoid overfitting.
- **Track Results**: Use tools like logging frameworks or experiment tracking to monitor combinations and their outcomes for future reference.

2. Cross-Validation: Ensuring Robust Model Performance

Cross-validation divides the dataset into multiple subsets, iterating the model training and evaluation process to assess its stability and generalizability. Cross-validation provides a more accurate measure of model performance than a single train-test split, reducing the risk of overfitting or underfitting.

Common Cross-Validation Techniques

- **K-Fold Cross-Validation**: The dataset is divided into k subsets, and the model is trained on $k-1$ subsets while the remaining subset serves as the validation set. This process repeats k times, with each subset used once as the validation set.

- o **Example**: In a 5-fold cross-validation, the dataset is split into 5 subsets, and the model is trained and evaluated five times. The average performance across folds provides a robust estimate.
- o **Pros**: Effective and suitable for most datasets.
- o **Cons**: Can be computationally intensive with larger datasets or high k values.
- **Stratified K-Fold**: Ensures each fold has the same class distribution as the entire dataset, which is especially useful for imbalanced datasets.
  - o **Example**: In a binary classification task with 10% positives and 90% negatives, stratified K-fold maintains this ratio within each fold.
  - o **Pros**: Maintains class balance, improving reliability for imbalanced datasets.
  - o **Cons**: Similar computational requirements to standard K-fold.
- **Leave-One-Out Cross-Validation (LOOCV)**: Uses each individual data point as a validation set while training on the remaining points, repeating for every data point.

- **Example**: For a dataset with 100 samples, the model trains 99 samples each time and tests on the 1 remaining sample, repeating this process 100 times.
- **Pros**: Useful for small datasets, maximizes training data use.
- **Cons**: Computationally expensive, not practical for large datasets.

Best Practices for Cross-Validation

- **Choose the Right k-Value**: A higher k (e.g., 10) provides a more reliable performance estimate but increases computational cost. Select a balance based on dataset size.

- **Use Stratified K-Fold for Classification**: This ensures balanced class representation within each fold, especially helpful in imbalanced datasets.

- **Track Cross-Validation Scores**: Calculate and monitor the mean and standard deviation of cross-validation scores to assess model consistency.

3. Ensemble Methods: Combining Models for Enhanced Performance

Ensemble methods improve model accuracy and robustness by combining the predictions of multiple models. This approach reduces variance and bias, often resulting in better overall performance than individual models.

Popular Ensemble Techniques

- **Bagging (Bootstrap Aggregating)**: Trains multiple models on different subsets of the data and aggregates their predictions. Random forests, a popular bagging method, use multiple decision trees to increase stability and accuracy.
  - **Example**: In a random forest for credit scoring, each tree may assess customer risk differently, and the forest's final prediction averages these results.
  - **Pros**: Reduces overfitting and variance, ideal for high-variance models like decision trees.
  - **Cons**: Requires more computational power due to multiple model training.
- **Boosting**: Sequentially trains models, with each model correcting errors from the previous one. Common algorithms include AdaBoost, Gradient Boosting, and XGBoost.
  - **Example**: In predicting customer churn, boosting models focus on difficult-to-predict samples, gradually improving performance.
  - **Pros**: High accuracy, especially effective for weak learners.
  - **Cons**: Prone to overfitting if not carefully tuned, computationally intensive.

- **Stacking**: Combines different model types by training a "meta-model" on the predictions of base models. The meta-model learns how to best combine the base models' predictions for optimal results.
  - ○ **Example**: A stacking ensemble for housing price prediction might combine the outputs of a decision tree, a linear regression, and a neural network, using a meta-model to blend these predictions.
  - ○ **Pros**: Flexible and leverages strengths of diverse models.
  - ○ **Cons**: Complex to implement and requires careful tuning of base and meta-models.

Practical Example: Using XGBoost for Boosting Performance

In a loan default prediction model, XGBoost is used due to its flexibility and high accuracy. Hyperparameters like learning rate, max depth, and number of estimators are tuned using cross-validation to balance accuracy and prevent overfitting.

- **Step 1**: Perform grid search to find the optimal combination of learning rate and max depth.
- **Step 2**: Apply 5-fold cross-validation to validate performance.

- **Step 3**: Monitor feature importance scores in XGBoost, using only the most impactful features for final tuning.
- **Impact**: The tuned XGBoost model achieves higher precision and recall than single models, making it reliable for predicting defaults with minimal false positives and negatives.

Best Practices for Ensemble Methods

- **Optimize Individual Models**: Tune each base model individually before combining them in an ensemble.
- **Use Voting for Simplicity**: In classification, simple voting (majority for classification, average for regression) is effective when combining similar models.
- **Regularize Boosting Models**: Apply regularization techniques in boosting (e.g., shrinkage in gradient boosting) to avoid overfitting.

4. Practical Steps for Implementing a Comprehensive Evaluation and Optimization Workflow

To ensure robust model performance, a structured workflow is key. This workflow combines hyperparameter tuning, cross-validation, and ensemble methods for systematic model optimization.

Step-by-Step Workflow

1. **Initial Model Training**: Start with a simple model to establish a baseline for performance.
2. **Initial Hyperparameter Tuning**: Use grid search or random search to narrow down a reasonable hyperparameter range.
3. **Cross-Validation**: Validate model stability and reliability using K-fold cross-validation.
4. **Refine Hyperparameters with Bayesian Optimization**: Apply Bayesian optimization to fine-tune hyperparameters within the best-performing range.
5. **Apply Ensemble Methods**: Experiment with bagging (e.g., random forest), boosting (e.g., XGBoost), or stacking for further improvements.
6. **Evaluate with Advanced Metrics**: Use ROC-AUC, precision-recall curves, or F1-score for final evaluation, ensuring performance meets business needs.

Case Study Example: Fraud Detection Model in Banking

In a fraud detection model:

- **Step 1**: Random search is used to tune initial parameters for a random forest model.
- **Step 2**: 10-fold cross-validation assesses stability, ensuring performance across folds.
- **Step 3**: Bayesian optimization further tunes max depth and minimum sample splits.

- **Step 4**: A stacking ensemble combines the tuned random forest, logistic regression, and XGBoost for optimal performance.
- **Step 5**: The model is evaluated with ROC-AUC and PR curves, confirming high precision and recall in fraud detection.

Outcome: This structured process results in a robust, accurate fraud detection model that generalizes well, minimizes false positives, and meets regulatory standards.

Conclusion

Advanced techniques like hyperparameter tuning, cross-validation, and ensemble methods are essential for developing high-performing machine learning models. By following a structured workflow that includes these techniques, data scientists can build models that maximize accuracy, minimize overfitting, and generalize well to new data. Through systematic optimization, these models provide reliable predictions and insights, allowing businesses to make informed, data-driven decisions with confidence. As we proceed, these evaluation and optimization strategies will prove invaluable in preparing models for deployment and real-world impact.

Introducing Model Interpretability for Transparency in Decision-Making

As machine learning models play an increasingly significant role in critical decision-making processes across industries, understanding and explaining model behavior has become essential. Model interpretability enhances transparency, helping stakeholders understand how predictions are made and ensuring that models align with ethical standards, regulatory requirements, and organizational goals. This chapter introduces key interpretability techniques that make models more transparent, enabling data scientists to balance predictive power with the need for trustworthy, explainable decisions.

1. Importance of Model Interpretability in Machine Learning

Interpretability is vital for ensuring that models are not only accurate but also understandable and actionable. Transparent models help build trust among stakeholders and allow organizations to validate model fairness, avoid biases, and ensure that model predictions are in line with domain knowledge.

Why Interpretability Matters

- **Trust and Transparency**: Interpretable models help stakeholders understand and trust predictions, especially when models influence high-stakes decisions (e.g., medical diagnoses, financial credit approvals).
- **Bias and Fairness Detection**: Interpretable models enable analysts to detect and mitigate bias, ensuring that

model outcomes are fair across demographic groups.

- **Compliance with Regulations**: In highly regulated fields, such as finance and healthcare, organizations must meet transparency standards to comply with data protection and fairness laws.

Challenges in Interpretability

- **Complexity vs. Simplicity**: Highly accurate models like deep neural networks and ensemble methods are often complex, making them harder to interpret than simpler models like linear regression.
- **Need for Explanations**: Stakeholders require explanations that are both technically accurate and accessible, balancing depth with clarity.

2. Global vs. Local Interpretability: Understanding the Scope of Explanation

Model interpretability can be divided into two types: global interpretability, which explains the overall model behavior, and local interpretability, which focuses on individual predictions. Both are essential for providing a comprehensive view of model decisions.

- **Global Interpretability**: Provides insights into how the model generally works, such as which features are most influential across all predictions.
  - o **Example**: In a customer churn prediction model, global

interpretability might reveal that "contract length" and "monthly charges" are the most important factors for predicting churn.

- **Local Interpretability**: Focuses on explaining the decision-making process for a specific prediction, highlighting the contributions of each feature in that instance.

  o **Example**: In a healthcare model predicting disease risk, local interpretability explains why a specific patient is at high risk, detailing the influence of factors like age, blood pressure, and family history.

Choosing Between Global and Local Interpretability

- Use **global interpretability** for model insights, feature importance, and overall understanding.
- Use **local interpretability** to understand individual cases, particularly in applications requiring specific justifications (e.g., explaining why a loan application was rejected).

3. Feature Importance: Identifying Key Drivers of Model Predictions

Feature importance quantifies the contribution of each feature to the model's overall predictions, providing insights into the most influential factors driving model behavior.

Techniques for Measuring Feature Importance

- **Tree-Based Feature Importance**: Tree-based models, like random forests and gradient boosting, calculate feature importance by measuring the reduction in impurity each feature contributes across splits.

  - **Example**: In a random forest for loan default prediction, "income level" may have the highest importance score, indicating it's a key factor in predicting defaults.

- **Permutation Importance**: This technique measures the change in model performance when a feature's values are randomly shuffled. A significant drop in performance indicates that the feature is important.

  - **Example**: If shuffling "monthly spending" in a customer segmentation model significantly decreases accuracy, it suggests that this feature is critical for segmentation.

Best Practices for Feature Importance

- **Use Permutation for Consistency**: Since permutation importance is model-agnostic, it's helpful when feature importances from tree-based models differ from reality.

- **Compare Across Models**: Evaluate feature importance across multiple models to verify which features consistently influence predictions.

4. SHAP (SHapley Additive exPlanations): Explaining Individual Predictions

SHAP values provide a unified approach to interpret individual predictions across various models, inspired by Shapley values from cooperative game theory. SHAP quantifies the contribution of each feature to the prediction for a specific instance, offering both local and global interpretability.

How SHAP Works

- **Global Interpretability**: SHAP generates average feature importance values, revealing which features have the largest impact across predictions.
  - **Example**: In a model predicting customer loyalty, SHAP can show that "customer tenure" has the largest average impact on loyalty scores across the dataset.
- **Local Interpretability**: SHAP assigns values to each feature for a specific prediction, showing how each feature influences the outcome.
  - **Example**: For a customer predicted to churn, SHAP might show that "high monthly charges" and "lack of contract renewal" have the highest

positive SHAP values, driving the prediction.

Advantages of SHAP

- **Model-Agnostic**: SHAP can be used with any model, making it versatile for explaining predictions across diverse model types.
- **Consistent Interpretations**: SHAP values are based on fair distribution principles, ensuring that feature contributions add up to the model's prediction.

Best Practices for Using SHAP

- **Visualize SHAP Values**: Use SHAP summary plots to visualize feature importance globally, and waterfall plots for local interpretability of individual predictions.
- **Combine with Feature Importance**: Use SHAP in conjunction with traditional feature importance to validate insights and deepen understanding.

5. LIME (Local Interpretable Model-agnostic Explanations): Simplifying Complex Predictions

LIME explains individual predictions by training a simple, interpretable model (such as linear regression) locally around a specific instance. This approach approximates the complex model behavior locally, making it easier to understand specific predictions.

How LIME Works

- **Step 1**: For a given instance, LIME perturbs the data to create variations of the instance.
- **Step 2**: The model predicts outcomes for each variation.
- **Step 3**: LIME fits a simple interpretable model (e.g., linear) on these variations, identifying the features most responsible for the original instance's prediction.

Example of LIME in Practice

In a credit scoring model, LIME can explain why a particular applicant was denied a loan. By creating variations of this applicant's profile, LIME shows which factors, like "low income" or "high debt-to-income ratio," had the greatest influence on the denial decision.

Advantages of LIME

- **Model-Agnostic**: Works with any model, providing flexibility.
- **Local Interpretability**: Ideal for explaining specific predictions, helping stakeholders understand individual outcomes.

Best Practices for Using LIME

- **Use for Complex Models**: Apply LIME when explaining predictions from complex models like neural networks or ensemble methods.
- **Combine with SHAP for Completeness**: LIME and SHAP are complementary; use LIME for case-specific explanations and SHAP for a broader understanding.

6. Surrogate Models: Building Interpretable Proxies for Complex Models

A surrogate model is a simpler model trained to mimic the behavior of a more complex model, providing interpretable approximations of the original model's predictions. Surrogate models are helpful when the primary model is too complex to interpret directly.

Steps to Create a Surrogate Model

1. **Train the Complex Model**: Develop the primary model to achieve high accuracy.
2. **Generate Predictions**: Use the primary model to make predictions on the training or validation set.
3. **Train the Surrogate Model**: Train a simpler model (e.g., decision tree) to approximate the primary model's predictions.

Example of a Surrogate Model in Healthcare

In a healthcare setting, a complex deep learning model might predict patient risk, but its black-box nature complicates interpretation. Training a decision tree surrogate model based on the deep learning model's predictions provides a more understandable framework that identifies key risk factors.

Advantages of Surrogate Models

- **Simplified Explanations**: Surrogate models offer insights into complex models without compromising too much on accuracy.

- **Flexible Approach**: Applicable to any black-box model, from neural networks to ensemble methods.

Best Practices for Using Surrogate Models

- **Balance Accuracy and Interpretability**: Ensure the surrogate model captures the complex model's behavior reasonably well while maintaining simplicity.
- **Use for Auditing**: Surrogate models can validate that the primary model's predictions align with expected patterns, making them useful for compliance.

7. Interpreting Results with Counterfactual Explanations

Counterfactual explanations identify the minimum changes needed in feature values to alter a model's prediction. This technique is particularly useful in fields where stakeholders want to understand actionable changes that could influence outcomes.

Example of Counterfactual Explanation in Loan Approval

In a loan application model, a counterfactual explanation might reveal that increasing the applicant's income by $5,000 or reducing debt by $10,000 would lead to a loan approval. This approach provides applicants with actionable steps to potentially change the outcome.

Benefits of Counterfactual Explanations

- **Actionable Insights**: Counterfactuals show what changes are needed for a different prediction, making them useful for customer feedback or strategic adjustments.

- **Clear Communication**: By specifying required changes, counterfactuals make it easier for non-technical stakeholders to understand how they could impact predictions.

Best Practices for Using Counterfactuals

- **Limit Changes to Feasible Adjustments**: Focus on counterfactuals that involve realistic, actionable adjustments.
- **Validate for Fairness**: Ensure counterfactuals do not suggest biased or unreasonable changes, maintaining ethical standards.

Conclusion

Model interpretability is a cornerstone of responsible machine learning, allowing data scientists to create transparent, trustworthy models that stakeholders can understand and rely upon. Techniques like feature importance, SHAP, LIME, surrogate models, and counterfactual explanations offer various approaches to make models understandable, balancing complexity with clarity. By incorporating interpretability into the evaluation and optimization process, machine learning practitioners can ensure that their models not only perform well but also align with organizational, ethical, and regulatory standards. As we continue, these interpretability techniques will be essential for creating robust models that not only predict effectively but also empower data-driven, transparent decision-making.

Chapter 7: Deep Learning in Advanced Data Analytics

Practical Steps for Implementing Deep Learning Models for Tasks Like Image Classification and NLP

Deep learning empowers data analysts to handle complex tasks such as image classification and natural language processing, or NLP, achieving remarkable levels of accuracy and efficiency. However, implementing these models successfully requires an understanding of the right neural network structures, careful data preparation, and specialized tools. This chapter provides a step-by-step guide to building and deploying deep learning models for tasks like image classification and NLP.

Implementing Image Classification Models with Convolutional Neural Networks (CNNs)

Image classification is a popular application of deep learning, where Convolutional Neural Networks, or CNNs, are used to categorize images. CNNs are ideal for this task because they can capture spatial details and hierarchies in images.

Step-by-Step Guide for Image Classification

Step 1: Prepare the Dataset

1. **Gather Images**: Collect labeled images relevant to the classification task, with each label representing a category, like "cat" or "dog."

2. **Split the Dataset**: Divide the images into training, validation, and test sets, commonly splitting with 70% for training, 15% for validation, and 15% for testing.
3. **Data Augmentation**: Apply techniques such as rotation, flipping, and scaling to expand the training set and improve the model's ability to generalize.

Example: For a dataset with 5,000 labeled animal images, using data augmentation to create variations will strengthen model robustness.

Step 2: Design the CNN Architecture

1. **Input Layer**: Set the input layer to match the image size, such as 128 by 128 pixels for RGB images.
2. **Convolutional Layers**: Add multiple convolutional layers with filters, or kernels, to capture image features like edges and textures. Increase the number of filters in deeper layers to capture more complex patterns.
3. **Pooling Layers**: Insert pooling layers, such as max pooling, after convolutional layers to reduce dimensions while keeping essential features.
4. **Fully Connected Layers**: Flatten the output and add dense layers for classification.
5. **Output Layer**: Use a softmax output layer, with a node for each class, like "cat," "dog," and "rabbit."

Step 3: Compile and Train the Model

1. **Compile the Model**: Choose a loss function like categorical cross-entropy for multi-class classification and select an optimizer such as Adam.
2. **Train the Model**: Train the model on the training set while using the validation set to monitor its performance. Adjust batch size and epoch settings based on dataset size and hardware capacity.

Step 4: Evaluate the Model on the Test Set

1. **Accuracy and Loss**: Measure accuracy and loss on the test set to assess generalization capability.
2. **Confusion Matrix**: Use a confusion matrix to visualize classification accuracy across categories and identify areas for improvement.

Step 5: Deploy the Model

1. **Save the Model**: Export the trained model for deployment or integration into applications.
2. **Inference**: Set up code for real-time inference, allowing the model to classify new images as they come in.

Implementing Natural Language Processing (NLP) Models with Recurrent Neural Networks (RNNs)

Recurrent Neural Networks, or RNNs, are effective for natural language processing tasks, such as sentiment analysis, language translation, and text classification, thanks to their ability to capture sequential information.

Step-by-Step Guide for Text Classification Using RNNs

Step 1: Prepare the Text Dataset

1. **Gather Data**: Collect labeled text samples, such as customer reviews labeled as "positive" or "negative."
2. **Tokenize and Clean**: Tokenize text to convert words into numerical format and clean by removing stop words, punctuation, and special characters.
3. **Padding**: Use padding to ensure that all sequences are the same length, which allows for batch processing.

Step 2: Design the RNN Architecture

1. **Embedding Layer**: Use an embedding layer to convert words into dense vectors, capturing semantic meaning.
2. **Recurrent Layers**: Add recurrent layers, like Long Short-Term Memory (LSTM) or Gated Recurrent Units (GRU), to capture sequence dependencies.
3. **Fully Connected Layers**: Flatten the output and add dense layers for classification.

Step 3: Compile and Train the Model

1. **Compile the Model**: Choose a loss function, such as binary cross-entropy for binary classification, and an optimizer like Adam.

2. **Train the Model**: Train the model on the training set and validate on the validation set to ensure optimal performance.

Step 4: Evaluate the Model on the Test Set

1. **Performance Metrics**: Assess the model's accuracy, precision, recall, and F1-score.
2. **Confusion Matrix**: Visualize misclassifications using a confusion matrix to spot areas for potential improvement.

Step 5: Deploy the Model

1. **Save and Export**: Export the model for deployment.
2. **Inference**: Set up a real-time inference process to allow users to input text and receive predictions.

Practical Tips for Training Deep Learning Models

Training deep learning models can be challenging, but these tips can help maximize performance:

1. **Regularization Techniques**: Use dropout layers to reduce overfitting by randomly disabling neurons during training, particularly in large networks.
2. **Early Stopping**: Monitor validation performance and stop training when performance plateaus to prevent overfitting and save time.
3. **Data Augmentation**: Apply data augmentation to images to increase dataset size and variety, enhancing the model's ability to generalize.

4. **Hyperparameter Tuning**: Experiment with learning rate, batch size, and layer configuration to find the optimal model setup.

Real-World Applications of Image Classification and NLP in Analytics

Deep learning applications are widely used across industries, turning complex data into actionable insights.

Image Classification Applications

- **Healthcare**: CNNs are used to analyze medical images like X-rays and MRIs for disease detection.
- **Retail**: Image classification helps with product identification in inventory systems, improving catalog organization.

NLP Applications

- **Customer Sentiment Analysis**: NLP models can analyze customer feedback and social media posts to detect trends in sentiment, guiding marketing strategies.
- **Chatbots and Virtual Assistants**: RNN-based models allow chatbots to understand and respond to user questions, improving customer support.

Conclusion

Implementing deep learning models for tasks such as image classification and NLP requires selecting the appropriate neural network architectures, preparing data effectively, and using efficient training practices. Convolutional Neural Networks are particularly suited to image tasks, while Recurrent Neural Networks are optimal for processing sequential text data. By following these practical steps, data scientists can successfully build, evaluate, and deploy deep learning models that drive meaningful insights and solve real-world challenges. As we continue, developing these deep learning skills will be essential to unlocking the value of unstructured data and driving innovation in the data analytics space.

Real-World Scenarios Where Deep Learning Outperforms Traditional Machine Learning Models

Deep learning has gained prominence for its ability to process and learn from vast amounts of complex, unstructured data—something traditional machine learning models struggle with. By leveraging layered architectures like neural networks, Convolutional Neural Networks (CNNs), and Recurrent Neural Networks (RNNs), deep learning models can identify patterns and make predictions in scenarios where traditional models fall short. This chapter explores real-world scenarios across industries where deep learning significantly outperforms traditional machine learning models.

1. Image Recognition and Object Detection in Healthcare

In healthcare, deep learning's image recognition capabilities have transformed the analysis of medical images, such as X-rays, CT scans, and MRIs. Traditional machine learning models are limited in image analysis, as they rely on predefined features, while deep learning automatically extracts relevant features, capturing complex details in images.

Example: Disease Detection in Radiology

- **Traditional Model Limitations**: Traditional machine learning models require manual feature extraction, which depends heavily on expert knowledge and is time-consuming.

- **Deep Learning Advantage**: CNNs automatically identify features such as tumor shapes, densities, and textures in radiological images, detecting diseases like cancer, pneumonia, and fractures with high accuracy.

Real-World Impact: CNNs are used in diagnostic tools to assist radiologists by highlighting areas of concern, reducing diagnostic time and improving accuracy in early disease detection.

2. Natural Language Processing (NLP) for Sentiment Analysis and Language Translation

Natural Language Processing (NLP) tasks, such as sentiment analysis and language translation, are essential for applications like social media monitoring, customer service, and content localization. Traditional models, like Naive Bayes and Support Vector Machines (SVM), are limited in their ability to handle long-range dependencies and context in text.

Example: Sentiment Analysis in Social Media Monitoring

- **Traditional Model Limitations**: Machine learning models like logistic regression and Naive Bayes analyze sentiment at a basic level but struggle with nuanced language, sarcasm, and context.
- **Deep Learning Advantage**: Recurrent Neural Networks (RNNs), particularly Long Short-Term Memory (LSTM) networks, excel at capturing sequential dependencies, understanding context, and processing long text sequences, improving sentiment classification accuracy.

Real-World Impact: Deep learning NLP models provide more accurate sentiment insights, enabling companies to gauge customer sentiment accurately, react promptly to crises, and refine marketing strategies.

Example: Language Translation

- **Traditional Model Limitations**: Rule-based or statistical machine translation models are limited by vocabulary size and cannot capture complex grammatical rules and context.
- **Deep Learning Advantage**: Neural Machine Translation (NMT) with attention mechanisms allows deep learning models to translate text accurately, considering context, grammar, and linguistic nuances.

Real-World Impact: NMT powers applications like Google Translate, enabling real-time language translation and supporting communication across language barriers in education, travel, and international business.

3. Image Classification in Retail and E-commerce

In retail, visual search and product categorization are increasingly essential as companies seek to improve user experience and inventory management. Traditional models struggle with the complexity of high-dimensional image data, requiring manual feature engineering and extensive pre-processing.

Example: Product Image Classification and Tagging

- **Traditional Model Limitations**: Machine learning models require human intervention to select features such as color and texture, which can be labor-intensive and error-prone.
- **Deep Learning Advantage**: CNNs automatically extract and learn complex visual features, enabling accurate classification of products based on attributes like color, style, and brand.

Real-World Impact: Deep learning-powered visual search engines let customers search for products by uploading images, improving user experience and increasing conversion rates. Retailers can also tag products automatically, streamlining catalog organization and search functionality.

4. Fraud Detection in Finance

Fraud detection in financial transactions is a high-stakes application requiring sophisticated models that can identify fraudulent patterns in real time. Traditional machine learning models are often limited by their reliance on manually engineered features and their inability to detect complex, evolving patterns.

Example: Detecting Anomalous Transactions

- **Traditional Model Limitations**: Models like decision trees or logistic regression rely on pre-defined rules and engineered features, which can struggle to adapt to new, sophisticated fraud tactics.
- **Deep Learning Advantage**: Deep learning models, such as autoencoders and LSTMs, excel at anomaly detection, identifying subtle, evolving patterns that indicate fraud. By learning directly from transaction data, these models are better at detecting outliers and adapting to new fraudulent behaviors.

Real-World Impact: Banks and financial institutions use deep learning models for real-time fraud detection, reducing losses and protecting customers from fraud by automatically flagging suspicious transactions.

5. Autonomous Driving and Object Detection in Transportation

Autonomous driving requires accurate object detection, classification, and tracking of other vehicles, pedestrians, and road signs. Traditional machine learning models are limited by their inability to process complex, high-dimensional image and video data efficiently.

Example: Object Detection for Autonomous Vehicles

- **Traditional Model Limitations**: Conventional object detection models, like HOG-SVM, struggle to handle dynamic environments with multiple objects and varying lighting conditions.
- **Deep Learning Advantage**: CNNs and their advanced architectures (e.g., YOLO and Faster R-CNN) excel at processing high-dimensional visual data, detecting multiple objects in real-time and capturing complex spatial relationships between objects.

Real-World Impact: Deep learning is the backbone of autonomous vehicle perception systems, enabling vehicles to detect objects, recognize road signs, and make split-second decisions to ensure passenger and pedestrian safety.

6. Voice Recognition and Speech-to-Text in Consumer Technology

Voice recognition is a rapidly growing area in consumer technology, powering virtual assistants like Siri, Alexa, and Google Assistant. Traditional models for voice recognition struggle with accents, background noise, and continuous speech, making them less reliable.

Example: Speech-to-Text for Virtual Assistants

- **Traditional Model Limitations**: Traditional models, like Hidden Markov Models (HMMs), rely on phoneme matching and predefined dictionaries, which are inflexible and less accurate for diverse speech patterns.
- **Deep Learning Advantage**: Deep learning models, especially RNNs and transformers, handle complex audio patterns, processing contextual information and enabling continuous speech recognition.

Real-World Impact: Deep learning has vastly improved the accuracy of speech-to-text systems, allowing virtual assistants to understand voice commands more accurately, enhancing the user experience and enabling hands-free device control.

7. Predictive Maintenance in Manufacturing

Predictive maintenance uses data from sensors and machines to predict equipment failures before they occur. Traditional models often struggle to capture the complexities of high-dimensional sensor data and dependencies over time.

Example: Failure Prediction for Industrial Machinery

- **Traditional Model Limitations**: Machine learning models like logistic regression require extensive feature engineering to capture signals from sensor data, limiting their predictive power.

- **Deep Learning Advantage**: Deep learning models, particularly RNNs and LSTMs, excel at processing time-series data from sensors. They capture temporal patterns in sensor readings that indicate wear or malfunction, predicting failures more accurately.

Real-World Impact: Predictive maintenance systems powered by deep learning prevent costly downtime and extend the lifespan of industrial equipment, resulting in substantial savings for manufacturers.

8. Recommender Systems in E-commerce and Streaming Services

Recommender systems play a vital role in e-commerce, streaming services, and social media by personalizing content for users. Traditional collaborative filtering approaches can only capture basic user-item interactions and are limited in scalability.

Example: Content and Product Recommendations

- **Traditional Model Limitations**: Collaborative filtering models struggle with the "cold start" problem, where new users and items lack sufficient data, and cannot capture deep patterns in user preferences.
- **Deep Learning Advantage**: Neural Collaborative Filtering and deep learning-based recommendation engines combine

user behavior, content features, and context to provide personalized recommendations. They excel at capturing non-linear relationships and adapting to changes in user preferences.

Real-World Impact: Streaming services like Netflix and Spotify use deep learning for personalized recommendations, enhancing customer satisfaction by providing relevant content, increasing engagement, and reducing churn.

9. Weather Prediction and Climate Modeling

Weather prediction relies on processing large volumes of meteorological data, such as temperature, pressure, and satellite images. Traditional statistical models are limited in capturing the non-linear, interdependent relationships in weather patterns.

Example: Short-Term Weather Forecasting

- **Traditional Model Limitations**: Statistical models rely on past patterns, but they struggle with complex, multi-dimensional data and are less effective in dynamic weather conditions.
- **Deep Learning Advantage**: CNNs and RNNs process multi-dimensional, temporal data, making them well-suited for weather prediction. CNNs analyze satellite images, while RNNs model time-series data from sensors and past weather records.

Real-World Impact: Deep learning models enable more accurate and timely weather predictions, aiding in disaster preparedness and reducing economic losses from extreme weather events.

Conclusion

Deep learning significantly outperforms traditional machine learning models in scenarios involving complex, high-dimensional, and unstructured data, such as images, text, and time-series data. From healthcare diagnostics to personalized recommendations and autonomous driving, deep learning models provide advanced pattern recognition and predictive capabilities, driving innovation and insights across industries. Mastering these deep learning applications enables data scientists to tackle sophisticated problems, creating opportunities for transformative impact in advanced data analytics. As technology continues to evolve, deep learning will remain a cornerstone of data-driven decision-making, pushing the boundaries of what's possible in analytics.

Chapter 8: Time Series and Sequential Data Analysis

Techniques for Analyzing Time-Dependent Data, Forecasting Trends, and Recognizing Patterns

Time series and sequential data analysis are critical for uncovering trends and patterns over time. Whether you're forecasting stock prices, analyzing customer behavior, or monitoring sensor data, time-dependent data offers powerful insights for decision-making and planning. This chapter delves into key techniques for analyzing time series and sequential data, focusing on forecasting trends, recognizing patterns, and detecting anomalies.

1. Introduction to Time Series and Sequential Data

Time series data consists of sequential observations taken at regular time intervals, like daily, monthly, or yearly. In contrast, sequential data includes any ordered data, such as text sequences or clickstreams, where the sequence matters even if the time intervals vary.

Key Characteristics of Time Series Data

- **Trend**: The overall direction of the data—whether it's increasing, decreasing, or stable.
- **Seasonality**: Repeating patterns or cycles at regular intervals, such as daily, weekly, or annually.

- **Noise**: Random fluctuations that obscure trends and patterns.
- **Stationarity**: Indicates whether the statistical properties (like mean or variance) of the series remain constant over time. Many forecasting models require stationary data.

Applications of Time Series Analysis

- **Financial Markets**: Predicting stock prices and economic indicators.
- **Supply Chain**: Demand forecasting for inventory management.
- **Healthcare**: Monitoring patient vitals to detect patterns or anomalies.
- **Utilities**: Analyzing energy usage for demand forecasting and optimization.

2. Preparing Data for Time Series Analysis

Effective time series analysis begins with proper data preprocessing to handle missing values, reduce noise, and ensure the data is suitable for modeling.

Common Preprocessing Techniques

- **Handling Missing Data**: Use methods like interpolation or forward and backward filling to maintain continuity.
- **Smoothing**: Techniques like moving averages reduce noise, highlighting trends and patterns.
- **Differencing**: Subtract consecutive observations to remove trends and achieve

stationarity, which is crucial for certain models.

Example: A 7-day moving average smooths daily sales data, helping businesses identify weekly trends without being distracted by day-to-day fluctuations.

3. Analyzing Trends and Decomposing Time Series Data

Decomposing time series data into components— trend, seasonality, and residuals—helps isolate patterns and prepare for forecasting.

Decomposition Methods

- **Additive Decomposition**: Assumes the series is the sum of its components.
- **Multiplicative Decomposition**: Assumes the components multiply together, often used when seasonal variations grow with the trend.

Example: By decomposing a monthly sales dataset, businesses can identify long-term growth trends, seasonal peaks, and random fluctuations.

4. Time Series Forecasting Techniques

Forecasting is the primary goal of time series analysis. Different models cater to various data types and forecasting horizons.

4.1 ARIMA (Autoregressive Integrated Moving Average)

- Combines autoregression, differencing, and moving averages to model stationary data.
- Effective for capturing dependencies in data over time.

4.2 SARIMA (Seasonal ARIMA)

- Extends ARIMA by including seasonal components, making it ideal for data with repeating cycles, such as monthly sales peaks.

4.3 Exponential Smoothing (ETS)

- Models that use weighted averages to forecast trends and seasonality.
- Includes variants like Holt-Winters, which accounts for both trend and seasonality.

5. Machine Learning Approaches to Time Series Forecasting

Traditional methods like ARIMA work well for simpler patterns, but machine learning can handle complex datasets with additional variables.

5.1 Tree-Based Models

- **Random Forests** and **Gradient Boosting** capture non-linear relationships.
- Useful for combining time series features with external factors like weather or marketing campaigns.

5.2 Neural Networks

- **Recurrent Neural Networks (RNNs)** and **LSTMs** excel at learning long-term dependencies in sequential data.
- Often used in stock price prediction, where historical prices influence future trends.

6. Recognizing Patterns and Detecting Anomalies

Beyond forecasting, pattern recognition helps identify seasonal cycles and unexpected deviations.

Anomaly Detection

- **Moving Average with Control Limits**: Flags data points outside predefined limits as anomalies.
- **Isolation Forest**: Identifies outliers by isolating points that deviate from the main pattern.

Seasonal Pattern Detection

- Recognizing recurring patterns, like increased sales during holidays, allows businesses to plan proactively.

7. Evaluating Time Series Models

To ensure accuracy, use evaluation metrics designed for time-ordered data.

Common Metrics

- **Mean Absolute Error (MAE)**: Measures average prediction errors.
- **Root Mean Squared Error (RMSE)**: Penalizes larger errors more heavily than MAE.
- **Mean Absolute Percentage Error (MAPE)**: Expresses error as a percentage of actual values, enabling comparison across datasets.

Conclusion

Time series and sequential data analysis provide powerful tools for understanding and forecasting trends, identifying patterns, and making proactive decisions. By mastering techniques ranging from traditional models like ARIMA to advanced machine learning approaches like LSTMs, professionals can unlock valuable insights in fields ranging from finance to healthcare. These methods are essential for building accurate, actionable models that drive real-world results.

Applications in Finance, IoT, and Retail Analytics

Time series and sequential data analysis have broad applications across industries that rely on real-time and historical data to drive insights and decision-making. In finance, Internet of Things (IoT), and retail, analyzing time-dependent data is critical for forecasting trends, optimizing operations, and enhancing customer experiences. This chapter explores real-world applications of time series and sequential data analysis in these three sectors, demonstrating how organizations can leverage these techniques for actionable insights.

1. Time Series Analysis in Finance

In finance, time series analysis is essential for forecasting stock prices, assessing economic indicators, predicting market trends, and managing risk. Financial data are often highly volatile, seasonal, and impacted by external factors like economic events, making it a perfect fit for time series techniques that handle complex temporal patterns.

Key Applications in Finance

- **Stock Price Prediction**: Time series models such as ARIMA, LSTM, and SARIMA are widely used for stock price forecasting. They help traders and investors make informed decisions by analyzing historical stock prices, volumes, and economic indicators.
    - ○ **Example**: LSTM networks, which capture long-term dependencies in sequential data, are applied to predict stock prices by analyzing past prices, volume, and market sentiment.
- **Algorithmic Trading**: Algorithmic trading systems leverage high-frequency data and time series models to identify trading opportunities, making quick buy/sell decisions based on real-time data.
    - ○ **Example**: Gradient Boosting models can analyze high-frequency data, such as second-by-second price changes, to spot short-term trends and execute trades automatically.
- **Risk Management and Volatility Forecasting**: Financial institutions use time series models to assess risk by predicting market volatility. Models like GARCH (Generalized Autoregressive Conditional Heteroskedasticity) specifically model changing volatility patterns.

- Example: Banks use GARCH models to assess currency volatility, which informs foreign exchange strategies and mitigates risks from exchange rate fluctuations.
- **Credit Scoring and Loan Default Prediction**: Time series analysis of credit card usage and loan repayment histories helps predict loan default risks, assisting banks in credit risk assessment.
  - Example: Analyzing payment behavior over time, banks apply logistic regression or LSTM models to identify customers likely to default, enabling proactive risk management.

Real-World Impact: By forecasting stock trends, managing risk, and automating trades, financial institutions optimize decision-making, increase profitability, and manage risks effectively.

2. Time Series and Sequential Data in Internet of Things (IoT)

IoT devices generate continuous streams of time-stamped data from sensors and systems, often deployed in industries like manufacturing, healthcare, energy, and smart cities. Analyzing this data helps organizations monitor assets, perform predictive maintenance, optimize energy use, and enhance safety.

Key Applications in IoT

- **Predictive Maintenance in Manufacturing**: Time series analysis of sensor data from machines identifies early signs of wear or malfunction, allowing for maintenance before a failure occurs.
  - **Example**: LSTM and anomaly detection models monitor variables like temperature, vibration, and pressure in factory machines, predicting failures and reducing unplanned downtime.
- **Energy Usage Optimization in Smart Grids**: Utility companies analyze time series data on electricity consumption to balance supply and demand, prevent outages, and promote efficient energy use.
  - **Example**: Seasonal ARIMA models forecast energy consumption, enabling utilities to adjust power distribution during peak and off-peak hours and prevent grid overload.
- **Anomaly Detection in Smart Cities**: Time series analysis of IoT data from traffic sensors, CCTV, and environmental sensors helps detect anomalies, such as unusual traffic congestion or air quality issues.
  - **Example**: Anomaly detection models can identify unusual spikes in traffic flow, which can inform traffic

rerouting strategies and reduce congestion in real-time.

- **Health Monitoring in Wearable Devices**: Time series data from wearable devices, like heart rate and activity level, allow for continuous health monitoring, providing valuable insights into a person's health trends.
    - o **Example**: Anomaly detection and RNNs analyze heart rate data to detect irregular patterns, alerting users to potential health risks such as arrhythmias.

Real-World Impact: By leveraging time series analysis, IoT applications improve operational efficiency, enhance safety, reduce costs, and empower proactive decision-making.

3. Sequential Data Analysis in Retail Analytics

In retail, analyzing sequential data such as purchase history, customer visits, and transaction trends enables companies to personalize customer experiences, optimize inventory, and drive sales. Time series analysis is crucial for demand forecasting, customer behavior analysis, and supply chain management.

Key Applications in Retail Analytics

- **Demand Forecasting**: Retailers use time series models to forecast demand for products, helping with inventory management, replenishment planning, and minimizing stockouts or overstocking.

- Example: Seasonal ARIMA and Exponential Smoothing models predict seasonal peaks in demand (e.g., holiday shopping season), allowing retailers to stock appropriately.
- **Customer Behavior Analysis and Segmentation**: Sequential data analysis of customer interactions, such as transaction history, browsing behavior, and purchase patterns, provides insights into customer preferences.
  - Example: RNNs analyze purchase history sequences to identify loyal customers and segment them based on purchasing patterns, enabling personalized marketing and rewards.
- **Sales Trend Analysis**: Time series analysis of sales data helps identify long-term and seasonal sales trends, empowering retailers to adapt strategies and product offerings.
  - Example: Retailers use decomposition techniques to separate trends, seasonality, and noise in monthly sales data, identifying growth opportunities and areas for improvement.
- **Inventory and Supply Chain Optimization**: Time series analysis allows retailers to optimize their inventory by

predicting lead times and sales cycles, reducing costs and ensuring stock availability.

- o **Example**: SARIMA models forecast restocking needs for high-demand items, reducing the risk of stockouts and improving supply chain efficiency.

Real-World Impact: Time series and sequential data analysis in retail enhances demand forecasting, personalizes customer experiences, optimizes inventory, and ultimately boosts profitability.

4. Practical Example of Time Series Analysis in Finance, IoT, and Retail

To illustrate the application of time series analysis across these sectors, let's examine a practical example:

Case Study: Predicting and Managing Demand Peaks Across Finance, IoT, and Retail

A large retail chain with connected IoT-enabled warehouses and distribution centers wants to prepare for the holiday season. The goal is to accurately forecast product demand, optimize inventory across locations, and secure additional funding to support increased sales.

Finance Application: Stock Price and Risk Management

- The company uses LSTM models to analyze the seasonal patterns in its stock prices during past holiday seasons, forecasting the expected impact on its stock value and allowing it to manage investor expectations.

IoT Application: Inventory Optimization with Predictive Maintenance

- IoT devices on warehouse equipment (e.g., forklifts and conveyor belts) continuously monitor usage data. Anomaly detection models predict when machines are likely to require maintenance, reducing the chance of equipment failures during peak demand.

Retail Application: Demand Forecasting and Customer Behavior Analysis

- ARIMA and SARIMA models forecast holiday demand for top products, allowing the retailer to optimize stock levels. Additionally, analyzing customer transaction sequences using RNNs identifies which customer segments are likely to increase their purchases, enabling targeted marketing campaigns.

Outcome: By applying time series analysis across finance, IoT, and retail, the retailer can prepare for demand surges, maintain efficient operations, and enhance customer satisfaction, leading to a successful holiday season.

5. Choosing the Right Time Series Model for Industry Applications

Selecting the right model depends on the data characteristics, the application, and the business goals. Here is a summary of recommended models by application:

- **Finance**: Use ARIMA for traditional trend forecasting, LSTMs for stock price prediction and sequential dependencies, and GARCH for volatility analysis.
- **IoT**: Use Exponential Smoothing and SARIMA for demand patterns, LSTMs for time-dependent predictive maintenance, and anomaly detection models for real-time monitoring.
- **Retail**: Use SARIMA and Exponential Smoothing for seasonal demand forecasting, RNNs for customer purchase sequence analysis, and time series decomposition for sales trend analysis.

Conclusion

Time series and sequential data analysis play a transformative role in finance, IoT, and retail analytics. Each of these sectors benefits from leveraging historical and real-time data to make informed predictions, optimize operations, and enhance customer experiences. By using time series models like ARIMA, LSTMs, and Exponential Smoothing, organizations can forecast trends, detect anomalies, and adapt strategies to changing patterns. As we continue, these applications will become increasingly sophisticated, supporting data-driven decision-making and driving innovation in advanced data analytics.

Methods for Evaluating Time Series Models and Improving Forecast Accuracy

Time series forecasting models are essential tools for predicting future trends and enabling proactive planning. To be effective, these models need rigorous evaluation and regular improvements to their accuracy. In this chapter, we'll explore key metrics and methods for assessing time series model performance, along with techniques to refine forecast accuracy through model tuning, data preparation, and advanced modeling.

1. Evaluation Metrics for Time Series Forecasting

Choosing appropriate evaluation metrics is crucial for accurately measuring how well a time series model performs. Common metrics help quantify the difference between predicted values and actual values, providing insights into forecast quality.

- **Mean Absolute Error (MAE)**: This metric calculates the average of absolute differences between predicted values and actual values. It gives a straightforward interpretation of the average error magnitude. Lower MAE values indicate a better model fit, offering an easily understood measure of forecast accuracy.

- **Mean Squared Error (MSE) and Root Mean Squared Error (RMSE)**: MSE measures the average squared difference between predicted and actual values, while

RMSE takes the square root of MSE to keep results in the same unit as the original data. These metrics emphasize larger errors, making them useful when minimizing large deviations is important.

- **Mean Absolute Percentage Error (MAPE)**: This metric calculates the average percentage error, which is helpful when comparing forecast accuracy across different datasets. However, MAPE may not be ideal for series with values near zero.

- **Mean Absolute Scaled Error (MASE)**: MASE provides a standardized accuracy measure by comparing model errors to those from a naive benchmark model. Values below 1 indicate that the model performs better than the benchmark.

Choosing the Right Metric: Use MAE and RMSE when error magnitude is a priority, MAPE for comparisons across scales with non-zero values, and MASE for standardized comparisons across different time series.

2. Backtesting: Validating Time Series Models with Historical Data

Backtesting is the practice of testing a model's performance on historical data by splitting it into training and testing sets. This process helps evaluate how well the model generalizes to unseen data.

- **Fixed Origin Backtesting**: In this approach, you divide data into a single training and testing period. For example, in a dataset covering five years, the first four years can be used for training, and the last year for testing. This approach is suitable for one-time forecasts.

- **Rolling Window Backtesting**: This method involves training the model on a fixed window of past data, then shifting the window forward for each forecast. For example, you might use 12 months of sales data to predict the next month, repeating this for each new period. Rolling windows provide multiple validation points, testing how adaptable the model is over time.

- **Expanding Window Backtesting**: Similar to rolling windows, but here, the training set grows with each new forecast, adding more historical data over time. For example, start with six months of data, then add each subsequent month to the training set before forecasting.

Best Practices for Backtesting: Select a window that matches the forecast horizon, assess performance over multiple periods, and use both rolling and expanding windows as needed to understand the model's adaptability.

3. Techniques for Improving Forecast Accuracy
Improving forecast accuracy often involves optimizing data preparation, fine-tuning model parameters, and exploring advanced modeling techniques.

- **Data Preprocessing**:
  - ○ **Smoothing and Denoising**: Techniques like moving averages reduce random fluctuations, allowing the model to focus on meaningful patterns.
  - ○ **Differencing**: Differencing removes trends and seasonality to make the series stationary, which is often necessary for models like ARIMA.
  - ○ **Seasonal Adjustment**: For consistently seasonal data, remove seasonal components so the model can focus on underlying trends.
- **Hyperparameter Tuning**:
  - ○ **Grid Search**: This method tests different combinations of parameters exhaustively to find the best configuration.
  - ○ **Random Search**: Randomly selects parameter combinations, making it less exhaustive but faster than grid search.
  - ○ **Bayesian Optimization**: This approach uses a probabilistic model to balance exploration of new parameter values with exploitation of known values, improving efficiency.
- **Ensemble Methods**:

- Bagging: Creates multiple models from different data samples and averages their predictions to reduce variance.
- Boosting: Trains models sequentially, where each model learns from the errors of the previous one, boosting overall accuracy.
- Hybrid Models: Combines different model types, such as using ARIMA for long-term trends and LSTM for short-term fluctuations, to capture both stable and dynamic patterns.

4. Advanced Forecasting Techniques

For complex time series, advanced methods offer improved accuracy by capturing intricate relationships within the data.

- **Recurrent Neural Networks (RNNs) and Long Short-Term Memory (LSTM)**: These models excel at sequential data analysis, handling long-term dependencies in time series data, making them well-suited for stock prices, energy demand, and sales forecasting. Adjust model depth, dropout rate, and unit count to prevent overfitting.
- **Prophet**: Developed by Facebook, Prophet is ideal for time series with strong seasonal patterns. It handles missing data, outliers, and seasonal trends efficiently, making it a

good choice for business metrics like sales or web traffic.

- **Transfer Learning in Time Series**: Transfer learning applies knowledge from one domain to another, reducing the need for large amounts of data in each new setting. In time series, a model trained on data from one region or product can be fine-tuned for another, enhancing forecast performance while minimizing data requirements.

5. Model Monitoring and Continuous Improvement

Once deployed, a time series model requires regular monitoring to maintain accuracy in dynamic environments.

- **Drift Detection**: Use statistical tests to detect changes in data patterns over time, which may signal the need for model retraining.
- **Retraining**: Regularly update the model with the latest data to adapt to shifting patterns.
- **Continuous Backtesting**: Periodically re-evaluate the model on recent data to ensure that it continues to perform well over time.

Conclusion

Evaluating and refining time series models requires a mix of appropriate metrics, validation techniques, and continuous improvement strategies. By using data preprocessing, tuning, ensemble methods, and advanced techniques like LSTM and Prophet, analysts can build more accurate and reliable forecasts. Continuous model monitoring ensures relevance in changing environments, empowering organizations to make proactive and data-driven decisions. As time series modeling evolves, these techniques will be essential for creating robust, high-performing models that support strategic planning across industries.

Chapter 9: Data Ethics and Responsible Analytics

Understanding Ethical Implications in Data Analytics and AI

As data analytics and AI become increasingly embedded in everyday life, the need for ethical practices in handling data and making decisions based on analytics has never been more critical. Ethical data use ensures fairness, protects privacy, builds trust, and mitigates the risk of harmful consequences that could arise from biased algorithms, misuse of personal data, and lack of transparency. This chapter explores the core ethical considerations in data analytics and AI, providing a foundation for responsible practices that respect user rights and promote fairness.

1. The Importance of Data Ethics in Analytics and AI

Data ethics is a framework of principles guiding the responsible collection, processing, and use of data. Ethical practices in data analytics ensure that individuals' rights are respected, decisions are fair, and outcomes are transparent. Misuse of data can lead to reputational damage, loss of customer trust, and even legal consequences.

Key Principles of Data Ethics

- **Transparency**: Individuals should understand how their data is used, and organizations should be open about their data practices.

- **Fairness**: Models and algorithms should avoid bias and ensure equitable treatment across all demographic groups.
- **Privacy**: Data must be handled responsibly to protect personal information, ensuring compliance with data protection laws.
- **Accountability**: Organizations and data scientists should take responsibility for the consequences of their data practices, whether intended or unintended.

Case Example: Importance of Data Ethics in Healthcare

In healthcare, algorithms are used to allocate resources, diagnose diseases, and recommend treatments. Ethical lapses, such as biased algorithms that underdiagnose certain groups, could lead to inadequate care for those populations. Ethical practices ensure that healthcare data is used fairly, safely, and effectively, improving patient outcomes without discrimination.

2. Privacy and Data Protection: Ensuring User Consent and Control

Privacy is a fundamental right, and responsible analytics should prioritize safeguarding individuals' personal information. Privacy is particularly relevant in analytics since data is often collected from sources like social media, mobile apps, and IoT devices, sometimes without full user awareness.

Best Practices for Privacy Protection

- **Informed Consent**: Users must be informed about data collection practices and have the choice to opt in or out, as required by laws like GDPR and CCPA.
- **Data Minimization**: Only collect the data necessary for analysis, reducing exposure to sensitive information.
- **Anonymization and Pseudonymization**: Mask identifiable data where possible to protect individual privacy, especially when sharing datasets with third parties.
- **User Control**: Provide users with control over their data, including options to delete, review, or update personal information.

Example: GDPR Compliance in Data Analytics

Under the European Union's General Data Protection Regulation (GDPR), organizations are legally required to obtain clear consent for data collection and to provide users with access to their data. Non-compliance with GDPR can lead to substantial fines and loss of consumer trust, emphasizing the importance of privacy in analytics.

3. Avoiding Bias and Ensuring Fairness in Data Models

Bias in data or algorithms can lead to unfair treatment of certain groups, resulting in discrimination and unjust outcomes. Ethical analytics should prioritize fairness by identifying and mitigating bias throughout the modeling process, from data collection to model deployment.

Sources of Bias

- **Data Bias**: Historical data may reflect societal biases, such as underrepresentation of certain demographics, which can lead to skewed results.
- **Algorithmic Bias**: Some algorithms amplify bias by overfitting on majority group data or underweighting minority groups.
- **Human Bias**: Unintentional bias introduced during data labeling, model selection, or interpretation of results.

Strategies for Ensuring Fairness

- **Diverse Data Collection**: Ensure the dataset represents a diverse population, reducing the likelihood of underrepresented groups being marginalized.
- **Fairness Metrics**: Use metrics like demographic parity, equal opportunity, and equalized odds to measure and mitigate bias in models.
- **Bias Audits**: Conduct regular audits to check for bias, particularly when deploying models that impact sensitive areas like hiring, lending, and criminal justice.

Case Study: Bias in Credit Scoring Models

Credit scoring algorithms sometimes discriminate against minority groups due to biased historical data, limiting their access to loans and financial services. By implementing fairness metrics and auditing these models, financial institutions can work to ensure that their models make unbiased, fair lending decisions.

4. Transparency and Explainability: Building Trust in Analytics and AI

Transparency in data analytics means being open about how data is collected, processed, and used to make decisions. Explainability goes a step further, ensuring that model decisions are understandable to non-experts. Together, transparency and explainability help build trust with users, regulators, and other stakeholders.

Challenges in Transparency and Explainability

- **Complex Models**: Deep learning and ensemble methods are often considered "black boxes" due to their complexity, making it challenging to explain how decisions are made.
- **Interpretability vs. Accuracy Trade-off**: Simple models like linear regression are more interpretable but may lack accuracy compared to complex models. Organizations need to balance this trade-off.
- **Stakeholder Understanding**: Transparency is only effective if explanations are understandable to stakeholders, including those without technical expertise.

Tools and Techniques for Explainability

- **Model-Agnostic Tools**: Techniques like SHAP (SHapley Additive exPlanations) and LIME (Local Interpretable Model-Agnostic Explanations) provide insights into feature importance, making model predictions more interpretable.
- **Surrogate Models**: Create simpler, interpretable models to approximate complex models, helping explain predictions without compromising accuracy.
- **Documentation and Disclosure**: Provide clear documentation and user-friendly explanations of model functions and limitations.

Example: Explainability in Healthcare AI

AI models are increasingly used in healthcare for diagnostics and treatment recommendations. To build trust, doctors and patients need to understand how a model arrived at a particular decision, such as a diagnosis. Using SHAP values or LIME to highlight key factors influencing a model's diagnosis allows medical professionals to validate the AI's recommendations.

5. Accountability and the Role of Human Oversight

Accountability in analytics requires organizations and data professionals to take responsibility for their models' impact, acknowledging potential risks and implementing safeguards to prevent misuse or unintended harm. Human oversight is essential, especially when models are deployed in high-stakes settings.

Key Aspects of Accountability

- **Model Monitoring and Evaluation**: Continuously monitor model performance to ensure it remains fair, accurate, and aligned with ethical standards.

- **Human-in-the-Loop Systems**: Include human oversight in model decision-making, allowing experts to review or override automated decisions, particularly in sensitive areas like hiring and criminal justice.

- **Ethics Committees and Governance**: Establish committees to review and approve data practices, ensuring alignment with ethical standards and organizational values.

Example of Accountability: Human Oversight in Hiring Algorithms

Many companies use AI to screen job applications, but biased algorithms may unfairly disadvantage certain groups. Implementing a human-in-the-loop process enables recruiters to review and validate AI-based recommendations, preventing biased or discriminatory hiring decisions.

6. Responsible Data Collection and Use

Responsible analytics begins with ethical data collection and use practices, ensuring that data is collected fairly, used responsibly, and respects individuals' rights.

Principles of Responsible Data Collection

- **Purpose Limitation**: Only collect data relevant to the specific analysis, avoiding unrelated or excessive data collection.
- **Honest Communication**: Clearly explain why data is being collected and how it will be used, building trust with users.
- **Data Longevity and Disposal**: Retain data only as long as necessary, implementing secure disposal methods once data is no longer needed.

Example: Purpose Limitation in Retail Analytics

In retail, data is collected to understand customer preferences and optimize inventory. Using this data solely for those purposes, rather than for unrelated applications, respects user consent and privacy, aligning with ethical standards.

7. The Role of Regulations and Compliance in Ethical Analytics

Various regulations, such as the GDPR in the EU and the CCPA in California, mandate ethical data practices and protect individual rights. Compliance with these regulations is essential for responsible analytics.

Key Regulatory Considerations

- **GDPR**: Emphasizes user consent, data minimization, and the right to be forgotten, holding companies accountable for protecting personal data.
- **CCPA**: Grants California residents rights over their personal data, including the right

to opt-out of data sales and to know how data is used.

- **Industry-Specific Standards**: Some industries, such as healthcare and finance, have additional regulatory standards (e.g., HIPAA in healthcare), governing data handling and ethical practices.

Example of GDPR Compliance in Financial Analytics

Financial institutions must comply with GDPR by ensuring that personal data, such as transaction history and demographic information, is collected with consent and protected from misuse. GDPR also requires financial institutions to delete data upon request, promoting responsible data handling.

8. Implementing Ethical Frameworks and Best Practices

Ethical frameworks provide organizations with guidelines for implementing responsible analytics. These frameworks help ensure that data practices align with societal values and protect individual rights.

Elements of an Ethical Framework

- **Ethics Policies**: Establish clear policies on ethical data use, detailing acceptable and unacceptable practices.
- **Bias Mitigation Plans**: Outline processes for identifying, monitoring, and addressing bias in data and models.

- **Transparency and Accountability Guidelines**: Set standards for transparency and documentation, ensuring stakeholders can understand and question decisions.
- **Ethics Training**: Provide ongoing ethics training for data scientists, analysts, and other team members to ensure they understand ethical standards and practices.

Example: Building an Ethics Framework in E-commerce

An e-commerce company develops an ethics framework covering customer data collection, transparency in product recommendations, and fairness in personalized pricing. This framework promotes ethical practices that enhance customer trust and align with the company's values.

Conclusion

Data ethics and responsible analytics are foundational to creating trustworthy, fair, and transparent AI and data-driven solutions. By adopting principles like privacy protection, bias mitigation, transparency, and accountability, organizations can protect individual rights and ensure that their analytics practices benefit society. As data analytics and AI technologies continue to advance, ethical considerations will be essential for fostering public trust, promoting fairness, and driving innovation responsibly. Developing a strong ethical framework allows organizations to uphold these principles and responsibly navigate the complexities of data analytics.

Strategies for Ensuring Privacy, Fairness, and Transparency in Analytics Projects

With the growing role of data analytics in decision-making, it's essential to implement strategies that protect user privacy, ensure fairness, and maintain transparency. These strategies not only align with ethical standards but also help organizations build trust with users and meet regulatory requirements. This chapter outlines practical strategies for embedding privacy, fairness, and transparency into analytics projects, ensuring responsible and ethical data use.

1. Ensuring Privacy in Analytics Projects

Protecting privacy is a fundamental aspect of responsible analytics. Safeguarding individuals' personal data reduces the risk of misuse, builds trust, and ensures compliance with privacy regulations. Effective privacy strategies encompass informed consent, data minimization, and secure handling of sensitive information.

Key Privacy Strategies

- **Informed Consent and Data Transparency**: Users should know how their data will be collected, processed, and used, and have the ability to consent or opt out.
  - ○ **Implementation**: Provide clear and accessible privacy policies detailing data collection and usage. Include explanations of how data will be

used, and give users options to manage their data preferences.

- o **Example**: In an app collecting location data, users should see a prompt explaining why their location is needed (e.g., personalized recommendations) and be able to opt out if desired.

- **Data Minimization**: Collect only the data necessary for analysis, reducing exposure of sensitive information and limiting the risk of misuse.

  - o **Implementation**: Define specific project objectives and collect only data directly relevant to those goals. Avoid collecting excessive information that may not be essential for the analysis.

  - o **Example**: In a customer segmentation analysis, collect basic demographic and purchase data instead of including unnecessary personal details, like home addresses.

- **Anonymization and Pseudonymization**: Remove identifiable information from datasets to protect user identities, especially when sharing data with third parties or using it in analytics.

  - o **Implementation**: Use anonymization techniques to

completely strip data of identifiers, or pseudonymization to replace identifiers with anonymous tags, retaining the ability to re-identify individuals if necessary.

- o **Example**: In a healthcare project analyzing patient data, replace personal identifiers with randomized codes to protect patient privacy while allowing researchers to analyze trends.

- **Implement Data Retention Policies**: Retain data only as long as necessary and securely dispose of it afterward, limiting potential risks if data is breached or mishandled.

  - o **Implementation**: Set clear retention periods based on regulatory guidelines and project requirements. Automate data deletion processes to prevent unnecessary storage.
  - o **Example**: In marketing analytics, retain data for a limited period (e.g., one year) to analyze seasonal trends, then securely delete it to minimize privacy risks.

2. Promoting Fairness in Analytics

Fairness in analytics involves treating all groups equitably, avoiding biases that could lead to unfair treatment, and implementing processes to ensure balanced model outcomes. Unchecked bias can result in discriminatory outcomes, so promoting fairness is essential for ethical analytics, especially in sensitive applications like hiring, lending, and healthcare.

Key Fairness Strategies

- **Balanced Data Collection**: Ensure datasets represent diverse groups and avoid over-representing or under-representing certain demographics, as this can introduce bias into model outcomes.
  - **Implementation**: Analyze datasets to identify potential imbalances and actively seek out additional data to fill gaps. If certain groups are underrepresented, consider synthetic data generation to balance the dataset.
  - **Example**: In a hiring algorithm, ensure the dataset includes a balanced representation of applicants from various demographics to avoid bias toward majority groups.
- **Fairness-Aware Model Training**: Use fairness metrics and constraints during model training to ensure that the model does not favor one group over another.
  - **Implementation**: Integrate fairness metrics such as demographic parity, equal opportunity, and equalized odds into the model training process.

Adjust model parameters to achieve balanced outcomes.

- o **Example**: In credit scoring, adjust the model to ensure that approval rates for applicants from different demographics are comparable, addressing any significant disparities.

- **Bias Audits and Fairness Testing**: Regularly audit models for fairness by examining their impact on different groups and running fairness tests to identify any unintended biases.

  - o **Implementation**: Conduct pre- and post-deployment bias audits. Track fairness metrics over time to monitor if biases emerge or worsen as the model is used.

  - o **Example**: In a health insurance pricing model, conduct regular fairness testing to ensure pricing does not unfairly penalize any demographic group, such as gender or age groups.

- **Adjust for Historical Biases in Data**: Recognize and address biases in historical data that could carry over into the model, particularly if the data reflects biased decisions made in the past.

  - o **Implementation**: Analyze historical data for known biases, such as biased hiring or lending practices, and adjust weights or use debiasing techniques to counteract them.

- ○ **Example**: In a criminal justice model predicting recidivism, adjust for historical biases that may unfairly target certain groups by modifying data weights or excluding biased features.

3. Increasing Transparency in Analytics Projects

Transparency builds trust and understanding by clarifying how data is used, how models make decisions, and how those decisions impact users. Transparency is particularly important in high-stakes applications where users have a vested interest in understanding the basis of model predictions.

Key Transparency Strategies

- **Model Explainability**: Make models interpretable so that users and stakeholders can understand the factors that drive predictions. This is essential for building trust, particularly with complex models.
  - ○ **Implementation**: Use model-agnostic tools like SHAP (SHapley Additive exPlanations) and LIME (Local Interpretable Model-Agnostic Explanations) to interpret and explain individual predictions.

- Example: In a loan approval model, use SHAP values to highlight which factors (e.g., income, credit score, loan amount) contributed most to a specific approval or denial decision.
- **Clear Documentation and Disclosure**: Document how data is collected, processed, and used in the model. Disclose any assumptions, limitations, or known biases of the model.
  - **Implementation**: Provide clear documentation on data sources, preprocessing steps, model design choices, and assumptions. Share this documentation with stakeholders and users where possible.
  - **Example**: In a predictive policing model, include documentation detailing data sources, such as crime reports, and outline any limitations, such as possible data bias.
- **Interactive Transparency Tools**: Offer tools that allow users to interact with and better understand model predictions. This may include visualizations, feature importance graphs, or interactive dashboards.
  - **Implementation**: Develop dashboards or visualizations to help stakeholders explore model predictions, see how different

factors influence decisions, and understand model confidence.

- o **Example**: In a healthcare diagnosis model, provide an interactive tool for doctors to explore how changes in patient features (e.g., age, symptoms) affect the diagnosis prediction, enabling informed decision-making.

- **Engage Stakeholders in the Model Development Process**: Involve stakeholders early on, gathering feedback on model objectives, ethical concerns, and transparency needs. This helps ensure that the model aligns with user expectations and ethical standards.

  - o **Implementation**: Conduct workshops or interviews with stakeholders to gather input on the model's design, transparency requirements, and potential impact.
  - o **Example**: In a hiring model, involve HR personnel and diversity officers to gather feedback on the model's fairness, ensuring it aligns with the organization's diversity and inclusion goals.

4. Implementing Governance and Accountability Structures

Accountability ensures that data practices are held to high ethical standards and that organizations are responsible for any impact resulting from their analytics projects. Establishing clear governance structures helps maintain ethical standards, ensuring models align with organizational values and user expectations.

Key Accountability Strategies

- **Ethics Committees or Review Boards**: Create ethics committees to review analytics projects, assess ethical risks, and ensure alignment with data ethics standards.
  - ○ **Implementation**: Form a multidisciplinary ethics board, including data scientists, legal experts, and representatives from impacted groups. Regularly review projects and provide feedback.
  - ○ **Example**: In a university using AI to analyze student performance, an ethics board reviews the model to ensure that it supports student growth without unfairly penalizing any group.
- **Model Monitoring and Auditing**: Continuously monitor model performance, fairness, and compliance with ethical standards, especially for models in dynamic environments.
  - ○ **Implementation**: Set up periodic audits of model predictions, tracking fairness, accuracy, and impact

metrics. Adjust the model if issues are identified.

- ○ **Example**: In an insurance pricing model, conduct quarterly audits to ensure pricing fairness and compliance with regulations, making adjustments if certain groups are found to be unfairly impacted.
- **Human-in-the-Loop Oversight**: Include human oversight in the decision-making process, particularly in high-stakes applications like hiring, lending, and healthcare, where automated decisions should be subject to human review.
  - ○ **Implementation**: Create a system where humans review or override algorithmic decisions as needed, particularly in sensitive cases that may affect individuals' livelihoods or health.
  - ○ **Example**: In a recruitment system using AI to screen applications, allow recruiters to review AI recommendations, ensuring fairness and human oversight in hiring decisions.
- **Accountability Reporting**: Regularly report on the ethical and societal impact of analytics projects to foster transparency and accountability.

- o **Implementation**: Create public reports summarizing model performance, fairness, compliance, and any significant adjustments made to address ethical concerns.
- o **Example**: A retail company using AI for personalized marketing could publish an annual accountability report detailing how they protect customer privacy, maintain data security, and avoid discrimination.

Conclusion

Implementing strategies to ensure privacy, fairness, and transparency in analytics projects is essential for ethical, responsible data use. Privacy measures protect individuals' rights and data, fairness initiatives prevent biased outcomes, and transparency fosters trust by making data practices understandable and accountable. Establishing governance and accountability structures further strengthens responsible analytics, ensuring that organizations remain aligned with ethical standards and respond effectively to evolving expectations around data use. By embedding these strategies, data practitioners can make ethical considerations a core part of every analytics project, benefiting users, stakeholders, and society at large.

Best Practices for Building Trust with Stakeholders Through Responsible Data Handling

Trust is fundamental to the success of any analytics project, as stakeholders need to feel confident that their data is used responsibly, securely, and ethically. Building and maintaining this trust requires implementing best practices for data handling that emphasize transparency, accountability, privacy, and fairness. In this chapter, we explore practical ways to build trust with stakeholders through responsible data practices.

1. Prioritizing Transparency in Data Practices

Transparency is essential for earning and keeping stakeholder trust. By being clear and open about data collection, use, and decision-making processes, organizations can build trust with stakeholders who rely on their analytics for insights and decision-making.

Key Strategies for Transparency

- **Communicate Data Collection and Usage Policies**: Ensure stakeholders understand how and why their data is collected and used. Provide clear documentation detailing data collection methods, data sources, and intended uses.
    - **Example**: A fitness app that collects health data could include a user-friendly privacy policy that explains

why each type of data is collected (e.g., heart rate for tracking fitness progress) and how it will be used.

- **Provide Access to Model Explanations**: Make sure stakeholders can understand the factors driving model predictions, especially for high-stakes decisions in healthcare, finance, or hiring.
  - ○ **Example**: In a credit scoring model, share information on factors that affect credit scores (e.g., payment history, credit utilization) so customers understand the criteria influencing their scores.
- **Offer Interactive Dashboards and Reports**: Allow stakeholders to interact with data visualizations, explore model outputs, and gain insights into analytics processes. Interactive tools help stakeholders understand results, building confidence in the analysis.
  - ○ **Example**: A retail analytics dashboard could display visualizations of sales trends, allowing store managers to interact with the data, view predictions, and better plan inventory.

Benefits: Transparency in data practices fosters stakeholder understanding, reduces the risk of misunderstandings, and creates an environment where users feel comfortable sharing their data.

2. Ensuring Privacy and Data Security

Stakeholders need assurance that their data is handled securely and kept private. Robust data security and privacy practices protect against data breaches, unauthorized access, and misuse, which are essential for building trust.

Key Privacy and Security Practices

- **Implement Strong Data Encryption**: Use encryption to protect data at rest and in transit, ensuring that sensitive information remains secure.
    - ○ **Example**: In financial analytics, encrypt customer transaction data both in databases and during transmission, protecting it from unauthorized access.
- **Adopt Access Controls and Role-Based Permissions**: Limit data access to only those team members who need it for their work. This minimizes the risk of data misuse and improves accountability.
    - ○ **Example**: In healthcare, restrict access to patient data so that only authorized personnel, such as doctors and nurses, can view sensitive health information.
- **Anonymize and Aggregate Data Where Possible**: Use anonymization techniques to strip personally identifiable information (PII) from datasets, especially when analyzing or sharing data externally.

- o **Example**: In marketing analytics, anonymize customer data before sharing it with third-party advertisers, ensuring individual identities are protected.
- **Regular Security Audits and Compliance Checks**: Conduct frequent audits of data handling practices to identify vulnerabilities and ensure compliance with privacy regulations like GDPR and CCPA.
  - o **Example**: In an e-commerce platform, schedule annual data security audits to verify adherence to regulatory requirements and ensure the security of customer payment information.

Benefits: Effective data security and privacy practices protect against breaches and foster stakeholder confidence, assuring them that their data is safe and responsibly managed.

3. Promoting Fairness and Addressing Bias

Fairness is a cornerstone of ethical data handling. Stakeholders expect that data analytics and AI models will treat individuals and groups equitably. Ensuring fairness in analytics involves detecting and correcting biases that could result in unfair treatment.

Key Practices for Fairness

- **Conduct Regular Bias Audits**: Evaluate data and model outputs regularly for biases, particularly for high-impact applications like hiring, lending, or medical diagnostics.

- o **Example**: In a hiring model, conduct periodic bias audits to ensure that the model does not discriminate based on gender, age, or ethnicity.
- **Use Fairness Metrics and Adjust for Bias**: Incorporate fairness metrics into model evaluation to monitor the treatment of different demographic groups. Make adjustments as needed to achieve balanced outcomes.
  - o **Example**: In a loan approval model, check metrics like demographic parity to ensure that approval rates are equitable across racial or socioeconomic groups.
- **Diverse Data Collection and Feature Selection**: Ensure that datasets represent diverse populations and that selected features do not introduce discriminatory effects.
  - o **Example**: In healthcare, use diverse demographic data to train models for disease prediction, reducing the risk of biased recommendations for underrepresented groups.

Benefits: Fair and unbiased models contribute to equitable treatment, helping organizations maintain credibility and ethical standards.

Stakeholders feel assured that analytics will provide fair and accurate insights.

4. Fostering Accountability in Analytics

Accountability in data handling builds trust by assuring stakeholders that an organization is responsible for the outcomes of its analytics processes. Clear accountability practices ensure that data scientists, analysts, and management take ownership of data handling, model performance, and ethical considerations.

Key Accountability Strategies

- **Document Analytics Processes**: Maintain thorough documentation of data collection, preprocessing, modeling, and evaluation processes. This documentation serves as a record that can be reviewed if questions or concerns arise.
    - **Example**: In a retail analytics project, document how sales data is collected, cleaned, and used for forecasting, ensuring transparency about each step in the process.
- **Human Oversight in Critical Decisions**: Implement human-in-the-loop systems for high-stakes applications, ensuring that model outputs are reviewed and validated by qualified personnel.
    - **Example**: In a medical diagnostic model, require a healthcare professional to review AI-generated diagnoses, ensuring that human

expertise guides final patient recommendations.

- **Establish Clear Accountability for Model Outcomes**: Assign accountability to specific individuals or teams for monitoring model performance, addressing potential biases, and managing ethical risks.
  - ○ **Example**: In a credit scoring model, assign a data governance team to monitor accuracy, fairness, and compliance, ensuring accountability for the model's outcomes.
- **Stakeholder Engagement and Feedback Mechanisms**: Involve stakeholders in the model development process, seeking feedback on data use, ethical considerations, and model behavior. Regular feedback builds trust and fosters collaboration.
  - ○ **Example**: In customer analytics, create surveys or forums where customers can voice concerns about data use and provide feedback on how insights are used to personalize marketing.

Benefits: Accountability practices establish clear ownership of data processes, providing stakeholders with confidence that their data is used responsibly and that ethical standards are upheld.

5. Implementing Ethical Frameworks and Governance Policies

Ethical frameworks and governance policies create a structured approach to managing data responsibly, ensuring that ethical standards are consistently applied across analytics projects. This helps organizations make ethical data decisions and fosters trust among stakeholders.

Key Ethical Frameworks and Policies

- **Develop and Communicate an Ethics Charter**: Create an ethics charter outlining the organization's values, principles, and commitments to ethical data practices. Share this charter with stakeholders to clarify the organization's dedication to ethical standards.
    - o **Example**: In an AI-driven customer service system, develop a charter that emphasizes transparency, privacy, and respect for customer data, ensuring ethical data use aligns with corporate values.
- **Establish Data Governance Policies**: Implement data governance policies that specify how data is collected, stored, processed, and shared, including compliance with regulations.
    - o **Example**: In healthcare analytics, establish strict governance policies that control access to patient records, ensuring compliance with HIPAA and protecting patient confidentiality.

- **Create an Ethics Committee**: Form an ethics committee to review analytics projects, evaluate ethical risks, and approve models that align with responsible practices.
  - ○ **Example**: In a financial institution, set up an ethics committee that reviews loan approval algorithms for fairness and compliance with anti-discrimination laws.
- **Regular Ethics and Compliance Training**: Provide ongoing ethics training for data scientists, analysts, and other team members to ensure they understand ethical standards, compliance requirements, and best practices.
  - ○ **Example**: In a retail company, conduct quarterly training on data ethics, focusing on responsible handling of customer data and awareness of data protection laws.

Benefits: Ethical frameworks and governance policies establish a culture of responsibility, guiding teams to uphold high ethical standards and building trust with stakeholders by demonstrating a commitment to ethical practices.

6. Communicating Ethical Practices with Stakeholders

Clear communication about ethical practices in data handling is essential for building trust. Stakeholders need to know that ethical considerations are integrated into the organization's analytics processes and that data handling aligns with their values and expectations.

Effective Communication Strategies

- **Publish Transparency and Ethics Reports**: Provide stakeholders with regular reports detailing data usage, model performance, and efforts to ensure privacy, fairness, and transparency.

  o **Example**: In an e-commerce platform, publish an annual ethics report outlining customer data protection measures, transparency efforts, and model fairness assessments.

- **Host Open Forums or Webinars**: Create opportunities for stakeholders to ask questions and discuss ethical data practices. These forums demonstrate a commitment to accountability and foster open communication.

  o **Example**: In healthcare, host webinars for patients to explain how their data is used in predictive analytics and answer any privacy or security questions they may have.

- **Develop a Code of Conduct for Data Handling**: Outline a code of conduct that guides how data is handled responsibly, emphasizing privacy, fairness, and ethical considerations.

o **Example**: A financial institution could adopt a code of conduct for data analysts, specifying respectful and responsible treatment of sensitive customer information in analytics projects.

Benefits: Transparent communication about data handling practices reassures stakeholders that ethical standards are prioritized, building a foundation of trust that can strengthen stakeholder relationships over time.

Conclusion

Building trust with stakeholders requires implementing and communicating responsible data handling practices. Transparency, privacy, fairness, and accountability are the cornerstones of ethical data use, enabling organizations to foster trust through clear and responsible practices. Ethical frameworks and regular communication ensure that stakeholders understand how data is handled and that their values are reflected in analytics projects. By embedding these best practices into data workflows, organizations can establish and maintain strong, trustworthy relationships with stakeholders, setting a high standard for responsible data analytics.

Chapter 10: From Insights to Impact: Presenting Data-Driven Solutions

Techniques for Translating Complex Analytics into Actionable Insights

Data-driven insights are only valuable if they can be clearly communicated and lead to informed decisions. The ability to distill complex analytics into actionable insights is essential for maximizing the impact of data projects. This chapter explores techniques for translating analytics into clear, meaningful recommendations that drive strategic action, emphasizing storytelling, visualization, and effective communication.

1. Crafting a Data Narrative: Telling the Story Behind the Numbers

Data narratives transform raw data into a compelling story, helping stakeholders understand the insights and their implications. A well-crafted narrative places data in a relatable context, connecting insights to business goals and showing stakeholders why these insights matter.

Key Techniques for Building a Data Narrative

- **Define the Central Message**: Identify the core takeaway from your analysis— whether it's an emerging trend, a critical risk, or a new opportunity—and build the narrative around this main insight.
  - ○ **Example**: In a customer retention analysis, the central message could

be, "Customer churn is most influenced by subscription costs and lack of loyalty programs."

- **Use a Structured Story Flow**: Structure your story using a familiar framework (e.g., problem, solution, impact) to guide stakeholders through the analysis logically.
  - o **Example**: For a supply chain optimization project, start by defining the current problem (e.g., delays and inefficiencies), introduce the solution (e.g., predictive analytics for demand planning), and highlight the expected impact (e.g., reduced costs and improved fulfillment rates).
- **Include Real-World Examples and Context**: Connect data points to real-world scenarios, using anecdotes, case studies, or hypothetical examples to show how the insights apply to business situations.
  - o **Example**: In a retail sales analysis, illustrate how regional sales trends vary by linking them to specific promotional campaigns or local events that influenced sales performance.

Benefits: A strong data narrative makes complex analytics accessible, aligns stakeholders with the analysis, and provides a clear direction for action.

2. Visualizing Data Effectively: Choosing the Right Charts and Visuals

Visuals are essential for presenting complex data in a digestible format. Choosing the right type of visualization helps communicate insights effectively, enabling stakeholders to grasp patterns, trends, and relationships at a glance.

Guidelines for Effective Data Visualization

- **Match Visuals to Insights**: Use specific chart types to highlight different insights. Line charts are great for trends, bar charts for comparisons, scatter plots for correlations, and heatmaps for geographical data.
  - **Example**: In a sales forecast presentation, use a line chart to show monthly trends and a heatmap to display sales by region.
- **Focus on Clarity and Simplicity**: Avoid clutter and keep visuals clean, emphasizing essential data points and removing unnecessary labels, colors, or gridlines.
  - **Example**: For a customer segmentation analysis, use a simple bar chart to compare average spending across segments, highlighting only the relevant segment differences.
- **Use Colors and Annotations to Draw Attention**: Color can highlight critical information, and annotations can provide

explanations directly within visuals, helping stakeholders quickly identify key takeaways.

- o **Example**: In a risk assessment report, use red to indicate high-risk areas on a heatmap and annotate them with the potential impact on business operations.
- **Choose Visuals That Match Stakeholders' Needs**: Tailor visuals to the audience's familiarity with data. Executives may prefer high-level visuals (e.g., dashboards or summary charts), while analysts may appreciate more detailed charts and plots.
  - o **Example**: In a financial performance report, create an executive summary with high-level KPIs for leadership and a detailed breakdown for financial analysts.

Benefits: Effective data visualization brings clarity to complex data, enhancing stakeholder understanding and facilitating informed decision-making.

3. Using Dashboards for Real-Time and Ongoing Insights

Dashboards are powerful tools for delivering insights in real-time and providing ongoing access to key metrics. When designed thoughtfully, dashboards allow stakeholders to explore data interactively and gain quick access to critical information.

Dashboard Design Best Practices

- **Prioritize Key Metrics and KPIs**: Choose metrics that align with business goals and focus on KPIs that reflect performance, progress, or risks.
  - ○ **Example**: In a marketing dashboard, prioritize KPIs like customer acquisition cost, conversion rate, and lifetime value to monitor campaign performance.
- **Organize Information Intuitively**: Group related metrics and design the layout to follow a logical flow, making it easy for users to find relevant information.
  - ○ **Example**: For a sales dashboard, place overall revenue metrics at the top, followed by breakdowns by product, region, and sales team performance.
- **Incorporate Drill-Down and Filtering Options**: Enable users to filter data by dimensions (e.g., time period, location) or drill down into specific segments to uncover detailed insights.
  - ○ **Example**: In an HR analytics dashboard, allow users to filter employee metrics by department, location, or tenure to analyze workforce trends.
- **Provide Alerts and Notifications for Key Changes**: Set up automated alerts for

significant metric changes, enabling stakeholders to respond promptly to potential risks or opportunities.

- o **Example**: In a financial dashboard, configure alerts to notify finance teams when expenses exceed budget thresholds or revenue falls below targets.

Benefits: Dashboards offer a user-friendly interface for continuous monitoring, enabling stakeholders to track real-time performance, identify emerging trends, and make timely decisions.

4. Communicating Uncertainty and Confidence Levels

Communicating uncertainty is essential in data analysis, as forecasts and predictions inherently involve a level of risk. Clearly expressing uncertainty helps stakeholders make informed decisions and sets realistic expectations for the outcomes of data-driven strategies.

Techniques for Communicating Uncertainty

- **Include Confidence Intervals and Prediction Ranges**: Show the range within which outcomes are likely to fall, providing a visual representation of uncertainty.
  - o **Example**: In a sales forecast report, include a prediction range (e.g., 95% confidence interval) to show potential variability in forecasted figures.

- **Use Probabilistic Language**: Describe outcomes in terms of probabilities to clarify likelihoods, using terms like "likely," "possible," or "unlikely" to describe events.
  - Example: In a risk analysis, say "There's a 70% likelihood of an increase in costs due to supply chain delays," instead of presenting a single cost estimate.
- **Visualize Uncertainty with Shaded Areas or Error Bars**: Use shaded areas in line charts or error bars in bar charts to represent uncertainty, helping stakeholders understand the range of possible outcomes.
  - Example: In a climate forecast, use shaded areas around projected temperature lines to illustrate the range of potential temperature variations.
- **Explain Limitations and Assumptions**: Be transparent about model assumptions, data limitations, and factors that could impact the accuracy of predictions.
  - Example: In a market trend analysis, disclose assumptions about economic growth rates and customer behavior, explaining how deviations could affect results.

Benefits: Communicating uncertainty builds credibility by setting realistic expectations and providing a complete picture, empowering stakeholders to make well-informed decisions.

5. Providing Actionable Recommendations Based on Insights

Data-driven insights should ultimately lead to clear, actionable recommendations that stakeholders can implement. Transforming analytics into specific actions requires connecting findings to tangible business opportunities or process improvements.

Steps for Delivering Actionable Recommendations

- **Prioritize Findings by Business Impact**: Focus on the insights that have the most significant potential to improve performance, reduce costs, or mitigate risks.
  - ○ **Example**: In an inventory management report, highlight recommendations for reducing stock on low-demand items to save storage costs and free up space for high-demand products.
- **Connect Insights to Business Objectives**: Frame recommendations within the context of organizational goals to make them relevant and actionable.
  - ○ **Example**: In a customer segmentation analysis, suggest targeted marketing strategies for high-value segments that align with the company's revenue growth goals.

- **Provide Step-by-Step Implementation Plans**: Outline practical steps for stakeholders to act on insights, including timelines, resources needed, and potential challenges.
  - Example: In a customer retention report, propose a 3-month action plan for launching a loyalty program, specifying target metrics and steps for implementation.
- **Quantify Expected Outcomes Where Possible**: Estimate potential impact in terms of revenue, cost savings, or efficiency gains, providing stakeholders with a clear understanding of the benefits.
  - Example: In a process optimization analysis, quantify the time savings from automating a manual task, illustrating how this change could improve productivity.

Benefits: Actionable recommendations bridge the gap between insights and impact, equipping stakeholders with clear steps to act on analytics and drive business improvements.

6. Tailoring Presentations to Stakeholder Needs

Effective communication of data-driven insights requires understanding the unique needs and perspectives of different stakeholders. Tailoring presentations to the audience's knowledge level, priorities, and concerns ensures that insights are relevant and persuasive.

Strategies for Audience-Centric Presentations

- **Identify Stakeholder Goals and Concerns**: Customize presentations to address specific priorities, such as cost efficiency for finance teams or customer experience for marketing teams.
    - ○ **Example**: When presenting to marketing, focus on insights related to customer engagement and conversion rates, while emphasizing cost control and ROI for finance.
- **Use Appropriate Language and Detail Levels**: Avoid jargon and technical details for non-expert audiences, and provide more in-depth analysis for technical teams.
    - ○ **Example**: For executives, present high-level takeaways and impact summaries; for data scientists, dive into detailed methodologies and model performance.
- **Address Potential Questions and Objections**: Anticipate common questions or concerns and prepare answers to clarify points or address potential reservations.
    - ○ **Example**: In a customer experience analysis, anticipate questions about data sources and privacy, preparing to explain data collection methods and privacy safeguards.
- **Highlight Relevant Action Items for Each Audience**: Identify actions each

stakeholder group can take based on the insights, focusing on recommendations aligned with their responsibilities.

- o **Example**: In an HR turnover analysis, recommend retention strategies for managers (e.g., employee engagement programs) and budgeting considerations for finance (e.g., cost of recruitment).

Benefits: Tailoring presentations to audience needs ensures that insights are understandable, relevant, and actionable, maximizing the potential for data-driven impact.

Conclusion

Transforming complex analytics into actionable insights requires a combination of storytelling, effective visualization, and tailored communication. By building a clear data narrative, using targeted visualizations, addressing uncertainty, and providing actionable recommendations, data professionals can empower stakeholders to make informed decisions based on the insights derived from data. Tailoring presentations to specific audiences further enhances understanding and encourages action, ensuring that analytics drive meaningful impact across the organization. With these techniques, data practitioners can bridge the gap between data insights and real-world outcomes, turning information into impactful decisions.

Visualization Best Practices for Storytelling with Data

Effective storytelling with data involves more than presenting charts and graphs—it requires thoughtful design and narrative to highlight key insights and guide stakeholders through a clear, impactful story. Visualizations help translate complex data into understandable, memorable insights that prompt decision-making. In this chapter, we cover best practices for using visualization to tell compelling stories with data.

1. Choose the Right Visualization Type to Match the Story

The choice of visualization is foundational to communicating insights effectively. Each chart type has specific strengths and is suited to different types of data stories, so selecting the right format aligns the visual with the insight you want to convey.

Common Chart Types and Their Uses

- **Line Chart**: Ideal for showing trends over time. Use line charts to illustrate gradual changes, seasonal trends, or historical comparisons.
  - ○ **Example**: Use a line chart to show monthly sales growth over the last year, highlighting seasonal peaks and troughs.
- **Bar Chart**: Effective for comparing quantities across categories. Bar charts are

great for discrete comparisons, such as regional sales or customer demographics.

- o **Example**: Use a bar chart to compare annual revenue by product category, helping identify top-performing categories.
- **Pie Chart and Donut Chart**: Best for showing parts of a whole, though they should be used sparingly. They work well when illustrating the distribution of a few components.
  - o **Example**: A pie chart showing market share among top competitors, with clear labels on each section for clarity.
- **Scatter Plot**: Useful for showing relationships or correlations between two variables. Scatter plots are especially helpful in finding clusters or trends in datasets.
  - o **Example**: In a marketing analysis, use a scatter plot to show the correlation between advertising spend and conversion rates across campaigns.
- **Heatmap**: Ideal for displaying data density or intensity, often used with geospatial or matrix data. Heatmaps reveal patterns in data concentration.
  - o **Example**: Use a heatmap to show user activity on an e-commerce site

by hour and day, identifying peak usage times.

Benefits: Using the right visualization type enhances comprehension by aligning the visual with the insight, making it easier for stakeholders to interpret and remember key findings.

2. Simplify and Declutter Visuals for Clarity

A clear, uncluttered visualization ensures that the audience can focus on the most critical information without distraction. Avoid unnecessary elements that could make the visual complex or difficult to interpret.

Best Practices for Simplification

- **Remove Unnecessary Gridlines and Labels**: Gridlines, borders, and excessive labeling can distract viewers. Keep only the essential elements.
  - **Example**: In a line chart showing sales trends, remove minor gridlines and extraneous labels to keep the focus on the trend line.
- **Limit Colors to Highlight Key Data**: Use a limited color palette to avoid overwhelming the viewer. Reserve bold or contrasting colors to highlight essential data points or trends.
  - **Example**: In a revenue bar chart, use a single color for most bars and a contrasting color for the top-performing product line.

- **Use Clean Fonts and Legible Sizes**: Choose fonts that are clear and professional, and ensure text sizes are large enough to read easily without overwhelming the visual.
  - **Example**: In a dashboard, use a clear, sans-serif font for all text, with larger sizes for titles and key figures, and smaller sizes for supporting labels.
- **Keep Titles and Axis Labels Descriptive but Concise**: Titles and labels should clearly describe what's being shown, making it easier for viewers to understand the context at a glance.
  - **Example**: Instead of "Revenue," use "Quarterly Revenue (in Millions)" as the chart title to specify the time frame and scale.

Benefits: Simplifying visuals improves readability and ensures that the audience's attention is directed toward the most relevant insights, making the data story clearer and more impactful.

3. Use Color Strategically to Emphasize and Differentiate

Color is a powerful tool for highlighting important information, distinguishing between categories, and reinforcing the data narrative. Using color purposefully can help emphasize key insights and guide viewers through the story.

Best Practices for Using Color

- **Limit Color Usage**: Stick to a maximum of 3-5 colors to keep the visual clean and cohesive, using more intense colors to emphasize key data points.

  o **Example**: In a customer satisfaction report, use a single color for neutral ratings and different shades to highlight positive and negative ratings.

- **Apply Color to Show Trends or Categories**: Use gradients to illustrate intensity or change over time, and distinct colors to differentiate categories.

  o **Example**: In a temperature heatmap, apply a gradient from cool blue to warm red to show low to high values, making intensity changes intuitive.

- **Use Consistent Color Schemes Across Visuals**: Choose a standard color scheme for all visualizations within a presentation or dashboard to create a cohesive and professional look.

  o **Example**: For a quarterly business review, use blue for positive metrics, red for negative metrics, and gray for neutral figures across all visuals.

- **Consider Accessibility and Contrast**: Ensure colors have sufficient contrast to be readable, especially for color-blind viewers. Use color-blind-friendly palettes and avoid relying on color alone to convey information.

○ **Example**: In a profit and loss chart, use patterns or labels in addition to colors to differentiate between gains and losses, accommodating color-blind stakeholders.

Benefits: Strategic color use enhances the impact of key data points, makes complex visuals more digestible, and improves accessibility, allowing the audience to focus on what matters most.

4. Add Context with Annotations and Descriptive Labels

Annotations provide context within the visualization, helping viewers understand the significance of specific data points, trends, or anomalies. Well-placed annotations make it easier for stakeholders to grasp the meaning behind the numbers.

Effective Annotation Practices

- **Highlight Key Data Points**: Add labels or annotations directly on significant data points, such as peaks, troughs, or outliers, to draw attention to critical insights.
  - ○ **Example**: In a sales trend line chart, add a label to indicate the highest sales month, along with a short note on contributing factors (e.g., "Holiday Promotion Boost").
- **Explain Trends or Anomalies**: Use text boxes to clarify unexpected trends or anomalies, providing context for changes in the data.

- **Example**: In a stock price chart, annotate a sharp decline with an explanation, such as "Market Reaction to New Regulations," to give viewers immediate context.
- **Use Tooltips for Interactive Visuals**: In dashboards, incorporate tooltips that display additional information when users hover over data points, allowing them to explore details without cluttering the visual.
  - **Example**: In a customer demographics dashboard, add tooltips that show customer count and average spend per demographic group.
- **Avoid Over-Annotation**: Focus annotations on essential insights, avoiding excessive text that could overwhelm the viewer. Select only the most impactful points for annotation.
  - **Example**: In a cost analysis chart, annotate only the top three cost contributors, rather than every data point, to keep the visual clean.

Benefits: Thoughtful annotations provide essential context, making it easier for viewers to interpret data accurately and reinforcing the narrative with additional information.

5. Use Dynamic and Interactive Elements for Enhanced Engagement

Interactivity can deepen understanding by allowing stakeholders to explore data at their own pace, view specific segments, or drill down into details. Dynamic elements create a more engaging experience, transforming static data into actionable insights.

Best Practices for Interactive Visuals

- **Enable Filters and Drill-Down Options**: Allow viewers to filter by categories or drill down into data for deeper insights, making it easier to analyze specific segments.
    - Example: In a sales dashboard, include filters for region and product line, enabling managers to view performance in their specific areas of responsibility.
- **Incorporate Time-Sliders for Temporal Data**: Use time sliders to allow viewers to explore data across different periods, which is particularly helpful for analyzing trends over time.
    - Example: In a web traffic analysis dashboard, add a time slider to let users view daily, weekly, or monthly data trends, revealing patterns in user behavior.
- **Use Hover-Over Tooltips**: For crowded visuals, add hover-over tooltips that display details when users interact with specific data points, reducing visual clutter.

- Example: In a budget variance chart, use tooltips to show the percentage variance for each expense category, reducing the need for extensive labels.

- **Add Interactive Annotations for Key Insights**: Provide clickable annotations that reveal more information or link to related insights, encouraging exploration without cluttering the visual.
  - Example: In a customer satisfaction dashboard, add clickable icons over key metrics that reveal the survey questions or specific feedback contributing to the score.

Benefits: Interactive visuals engage stakeholders, allowing them to explore data insights in depth, personalize their analysis, and make better-informed decisions.

6. Tell a Cohesive Story Across Multiple Visuals

When presenting multiple visuals, ensure they work together to build a cohesive narrative. This involves ordering visuals logically, using consistent design elements, and linking insights across charts to guide viewers through the data story.

Techniques for Building a Cohesive Visual Story

- **Order Visuals Logically**: Arrange visuals in a sequence that reflects the narrative structure (e.g., overview, breakdown, recommendations), guiding viewers through the insights.

- Example: In a marketing report, begin with an overall performance summary, then present visuals on campaign performance, and end with customer behavior insights.
- **Maintain Consistent Design Elements**: Use the same color palette, font style, and chart types across visuals to create a professional and cohesive look.
  - Example: For a company performance dashboard, use the same color scheme for profit-related metrics across charts, reinforcing consistency.
- **Link Related Insights Across Visuals**: Connect insights across multiple visuals to reinforce key points and provide context for deeper analysis.
  - Example: In a product launch report, link a customer engagement chart with a sales growth chart to show how engagement impacted revenue.
- **Summarize Key Takeaways**: End with a summary visualization, such as a KPI dashboard or bullet points, to reinforce the most important insights from the data story.
  - Example: After presenting a series of charts on cost-saving initiatives, conclude with a summary dashboard highlighting overall savings and impact metrics.

Benefits: A cohesive visual story ensures that each visualization builds on the previous one, creating a seamless narrative that makes complex insights accessible and memorable.

Conclusion

Visualization best practices are essential for effectively communicating data-driven insights and guiding stakeholders through a compelling story. By selecting the right visualization types, simplifying visuals, using color strategically, adding context with annotations, incorporating interactivity, and building a cohesive narrative, data professionals can transform complex analytics into clear, impactful insights. These techniques ensure that data-driven stories resonate with stakeholders, enabling them to understand key findings and make informed, actionable decisions. With strong visual storytelling, data can drive real impact and facilitate better outcomes across organizations.

Methods for Influencing Decisions and Driving Change with Clear, Persuasive Analytics Presentations

Effectively presenting data-driven insights is key to influencing decisions and driving positive change. A well-crafted analytics presentation doesn't just inform—it persuades, aligning stakeholders around a common understanding and motivating action. This chapter explores methods for structuring and delivering analytics presentations that resonate with stakeholders, helping them make data-informed decisions with confidence.

1. Start with a Strong Executive Summary

The executive summary serves as the anchor of any analytics presentation. A clear, concise summary provides stakeholders with the main takeaways upfront, setting the stage for the detailed insights that follow.

Key Elements of a Strong Executive Summary

- **Highlight Key Findings**: Present the most critical insights right at the beginning, capturing the audience's attention and framing the presentation's purpose.
    - ○ **Example**: For a customer retention analysis, start with "Customer churn is 15% higher in the last quarter, largely influenced by reduced engagement in the 18-25 age group."
- **Summarize Recommendations**: Briefly state actionable recommendations based on the data insights, giving stakeholders a preview of the proposed actions.
    - ○ **Example**: "To improve retention, we recommend introducing loyalty incentives for younger customers and enhancing personalized engagement."
- **Use a Visual Overview of Key Metrics**: A snapshot of key metrics in a dashboard or infographic format can provide a quick, high-level view.

o **Example**: In a financial performance report, include a one-slide dashboard with revenue, profit margin, and expense breakdowns.

Benefits: A strong executive summary builds interest, aligns stakeholders on the presentation's purpose, and provides a reference point for the insights to come.

2. Structure the Presentation Around the Audience's Goals

Understanding the goals, interests, and concerns of your audience is critical to delivering an impactful presentation. By focusing on insights that matter most to them, you can create a narrative that directly addresses their needs and drives engagement.

Strategies for Audience-Centric Structuring

- **Identify Key Audience Concerns**: Start by addressing any specific challenges or objectives that stakeholders are focused on.
  - o **Example**: When presenting to marketing, focus on customer behavior insights and segmentation, while for finance, highlight metrics like ROI and cost efficiency.
- **Organize Insights by Relevance**: Structure the presentation so that high-priority insights appear first, followed by supporting data and less critical findings.
  - o **Example**: In a product launch analysis, begin with overall launch

performance, followed by segment-specific data, such as customer feedback and regional sales.

- **Relate Insights to Business Objectives**: Connect each insight back to the organization's strategic goals, helping stakeholders see the bigger picture.
  - o **Example**: In an employee engagement report, relate survey findings to organizational goals of improving productivity and reducing turnover.

Benefits: A well-structured, audience-focused presentation captures attention, addresses relevant concerns, and increases the likelihood of buy-in from key decision-makers.

3. Use Storytelling to Make Data More Relatable

Storytelling transforms data into a relatable narrative, helping stakeholders connect emotionally with the information and better understand its relevance. A compelling story can illustrate the implications of data-driven insights and motivate stakeholders to take action.

Best Practices for Data Storytelling

- **Introduce the Problem and Context**: Frame the data in terms of a problem or opportunity, making the story relatable and engaging.
  - o **Example**: "Our customer retention rates are declining, particularly

among younger users. Here's how we can reverse this trend."

- **Use Real-Life Examples or Case Studies**: Incorporate examples or case studies to illustrate how data insights apply to real-world scenarios.
    - ○ **Example**: In a customer satisfaction analysis, highlight a recent case where improved response time led to higher satisfaction scores, linking it to potential improvements.
- **Follow a Clear Narrative Arc**: Structure the story with a beginning (the current situation), middle (the analysis and findings), and end (the recommended actions and expected outcomes).
    - ○ **Example**: "Last quarter, we faced increased costs due to inefficient supply chain management. Here's what the data revealed, and how we can streamline operations."

Benefits: Storytelling engages stakeholders emotionally, making data more memorable and impactful, while helping stakeholders visualize how insights connect to their roles and objectives.

4. Support Insights with Visuals that Reinforce Key Points

Data visuals are powerful tools for communicating insights, but they are most effective when they reinforce the presentation's main message. Well-chosen visuals highlight patterns, simplify complex information, and enhance the clarity of the data story.

Best Practices for Supporting Insights with Visuals

- **Use Highlight Colors to Emphasize Important Data**: Draw attention to critical metrics or trends by using bold colors for key data points, while keeping other data in muted tones.
    - ○ **Example**: In a budget report, use a bold color to highlight expenses that exceeded the budget, while displaying other expenses in gray.
- **Leverage Comparison Charts for Decision-Making**: Use side-by-side bar charts, before-and-after visuals, or heatmaps to make it easy to compare performance or outcomes.
    - ○ **Example**: In a product performance review, show a bar chart comparing unit sales across product lines to highlight top and underperforming products.
- **Add Annotations for Key Takeaways**: Label specific data points or trends with short annotations, ensuring stakeholders can quickly interpret the visual's message.
    - ○ **Example**: In a quarterly sales growth chart, annotate each peak and dip with the factors contributing to

changes, such as "Holiday season surge" or "Supply chain delay."

Benefits: Well-designed visuals make data-driven insights more accessible, reinforcing key points and helping stakeholders quickly grasp the information.

5. Use Clear and Persuasive Language to Build Credibility

The language used in an analytics presentation significantly influences how insights are perceived. Clear, persuasive language enhances credibility and builds confidence in the analysis, while overly technical or ambiguous language can detract from the message.

Techniques for Clear and Persuasive Communication

- **Avoid Jargon and Technical Terms**: Use plain language to describe findings, making sure terms are understandable to all stakeholders.
  - **Example**: Instead of "statistically significant," say "a meaningful increase" when describing changes that are important for decision-making.
- **Highlight Certainty and Acknowledge Limitations**: Be transparent about the level of confidence in predictions and any limitations of the data or analysis.
  - **Example**: "We're confident that this trend will continue under current

conditions, though changes in market demand could impact results."

- **Use Action-Oriented Phrases**: Frame recommendations with action-oriented language to make next steps clear and actionable.
  - o **Example**: "Implement a loyalty program targeting repeat customers to increase retention by 20% over the next quarter."

Benefits: Clear, straightforward language enhances understanding, instills confidence in the findings, and encourages stakeholders to take action on the insights presented.

6. Anticipate Questions and Address Potential Objections

A persuasive presentation proactively addresses stakeholder questions and potential objections, demonstrating thorough analysis and understanding of different perspectives. Preparing for these questions shows credibility and builds trust in the data's accuracy.

Best Practices for Addressing Questions and Objections

- **Present Assumptions and Methodology Transparently**: Explain the assumptions, data sources, and methods used in the analysis, providing context for the insights.
  - o **Example**: In a sales forecast, clarify that projections assume a stable

economy and consistent product demand.

- **Anticipate and Prepare Responses to Common Objections**: Consider likely questions or pushbacks from stakeholders and prepare responses backed by data or additional context.
  - ○ **Example**: In a budget allocation analysis, be prepared to justify higher spending recommendations with evidence of expected ROI.
- **Include Backup Slides with Supporting Data**: Have extra slides with detailed data, charts, or technical information ready to address specific questions without overwhelming the main presentation.
  - ○ **Example**: For a staffing analysis, prepare a backup slide showing productivity metrics by department to explain recommended hiring increases.

Benefits: Anticipating questions and objections demonstrates thorough preparation, reduces the risk of misunderstandings, and strengthens stakeholder confidence in the analysis.

7. Conclude with a Compelling Call to Action

A strong call to action provides clear next steps and motivates stakeholders to act on the insights presented. This final step reinforces the presentation's message and ensures that insights translate into impactful decisions.

Key Elements of a Compelling Call to Action

- **Summarize Key Takeaways and Impact**: Recap the most critical insights and the anticipated impact of following the recommendations.
  - Example: "By implementing the proposed customer engagement initiatives, we can reduce churn by 15%, adding an estimated $1M in annual revenue."
- **Outline Specific Action Steps**: Provide a clear list of next steps, specifying who should act, what actions are needed, and when they should be completed.
  - Example: "1) Launch targeted campaigns for high-risk customers by next month; 2) Introduce loyalty incentives within Q3."
- **Quantify the Benefits**: Where possible, include concrete metrics or estimates that demonstrate the value of taking action on the insights.
  - Example: "Implementing automation in the billing process will save an estimated 500 work hours annually, reducing operational costs by 10%."
- **Encourage Immediate Follow-Up**: Suggest specific follow-up actions or meetings to review progress, ensuring momentum and accountability.

- ○ **Example**: "We recommend a follow-up meeting in two weeks to discuss progress on the loyalty program rollout and adjust strategies as needed."

Benefits: A clear, compelling call to action motivates stakeholders to implement data-driven recommendations, translating insights into concrete, impactful changes.

Conclusion

Presenting data-driven insights effectively requires more than just data—it involves crafting a persuasive narrative, supporting insights with visuals, using clear language, and addressing potential objections. By structuring presentations around stakeholder goals, using storytelling, and ending with a strong call to action, data professionals can drive meaningful change and inspire decision-making based on solid analytics. These techniques ensure that analytics presentations resonate with stakeholders, encourage buy-in, and lead to real-world impact from data insights.

Chapter 11: Future Trends in Data Analytics and Machine Learning

Exploration of Emerging Trends in AI, Including AutoML, Reinforcement Learning, and Generative AI

As data analytics and machine learning continue to advance, new trends and technologies are shaping the future of AI, creating exciting opportunities for automation, efficiency, and innovation. Emerging trends like AutoML, reinforcement learning, and generative AI are driving developments that expand the reach of machine learning and make it accessible to more organizations. This chapter explores these technologies, their applications, and the potential impact on the field of data analytics.

1. AutoML: Automating the Machine Learning Pipeline

AutoML (Automated Machine Learning) simplifies the process of building, selecting, and tuning machine learning models, enabling organizations to create powerful models without requiring extensive expertise in data science. AutoML automates various steps in the machine learning pipeline, including data preprocessing, feature selection, model selection, and hyperparameter tuning.

Key Features of AutoML

- **End-to-End Automation**: AutoML automates the workflow from data preprocessing to model deployment, enabling non-experts to build predictive models with minimal manual intervention.

- **Model Selection and Tuning**: AutoML selects and tunes the best algorithms based on the data, choosing from a range of models (e.g., decision trees, neural networks, ensemble methods) to optimize performance.
- **Explainability and Transparency**: Many AutoML tools include model interpretability features, making it easier to understand model decisions and maintain transparency.

Applications of AutoML

- **Business Forecasting**: AutoML is increasingly used for sales forecasting, demand prediction, and inventory management, providing accurate predictions with limited manual tuning.
- **Customer Segmentation**: AutoML can identify customer segments based on purchasing behavior, demographics, and engagement, allowing businesses to personalize marketing strategies.
- **Healthcare and Diagnostics**: In medical diagnostics, AutoML aids in building models that analyze patient data and predict health outcomes, accelerating the adoption of predictive analytics in healthcare.

Benefits of AutoML

AutoML democratizes machine learning, making it accessible to non-experts and allowing organizations to accelerate the deployment of machine learning models. By automating repetitive tasks, AutoML also frees data scientists to focus on more complex aspects of projects, driving efficiency and innovation.

2. Reinforcement Learning: Learning from Interaction and Feedback

Reinforcement learning (RL) is a type of machine learning where an agent learns to make decisions by interacting with an environment and receiving feedback in the form of rewards or penalties. RL is inspired by behavioral psychology and has applications in areas where decision-making unfolds over time, allowing the model to learn optimal actions to maximize cumulative rewards.

Key Concepts in Reinforcement Learning

- **Agents and Environments**: The agent is the learner or decision-maker, while the environment represents the context or system within which the agent operates.
- **Reward System**: The agent receives rewards (positive or negative) based on actions, guiding it to make decisions that maximize cumulative rewards over time.
- **Exploration vs. Exploitation**: RL involves a balance between exploring new actions to discover rewards and exploiting known actions to maximize rewards.

Applications of Reinforcement Learning

- **Autonomous Vehicles**: RL helps autonomous vehicles learn to navigate, avoid obstacles, and make complex driving decisions, improving safety and efficiency.

- **Robotics**: In robotics, RL enables robots to learn tasks through trial and error, from object manipulation to complex assembly line tasks.
- **Personalized Recommendations**: In streaming services and e-commerce, RL optimizes content recommendations by learning user preferences and adapting suggestions over time.
- **Dynamic Pricing and Resource Allocation**: RL is used in industries like retail and energy to set prices dynamically based on demand or allocate resources efficiently in real-time environments.

Benefits of Reinforcement Learning

Reinforcement learning allows machines to learn complex, sequential decision-making processes, making it suitable for real-world applications where actions have long-term consequences. Its ability to adapt and improve over time holds promise for fields requiring continual optimization, such as supply chain management, finance, and operations.

3. Generative AI: Creating New Data and Content

Generative AI refers to models that can create new content, such as images, text, audio, or video, based on patterns learned from existing data. These models, particularly generative adversarial networks (GANs) and transformer-based models, have transformed the creative landscape, allowing machines to generate realistic and original content.

Key Techniques in Generative AI

- **Generative Adversarial Networks (GANs)**: GANs use a generator and discriminator in a competitive setting to create highly realistic images, videos, and other content.
- **Transformer Models**: Models like GPT (Generative Pre-trained Transformer) and BERT (Bidirectional Encoder Representations from Transformers) use large amounts of text data to generate coherent text, answer questions, and engage in conversation.

Applications of Generative AI

- **Content Creation**: Generative AI is used in content creation for marketing, entertainment, and education, including automated article writing, image generation, and video editing.
- **Healthcare and Drug Discovery**: Generative AI models are used to create synthetic molecules or simulate protein structures, aiding drug discovery and medical research.
- **Virtual Assistants and Chatbots**: Generative AI powers advanced conversational agents, allowing them to

understand and generate human-like responses in real time.

- **Data Augmentation**: Generative models create synthetic data to augment training datasets, particularly useful for improving model accuracy in scenarios with limited data.

Benefits of Generative AI

Generative AI opens up new possibilities for innovation, particularly in creative industries, healthcare, and AI research. By generating new content and data, it enables businesses to enhance customer experiences, automate repetitive content creation tasks, and develop novel solutions.

4. Edge AI: Bringing AI to the Edge of Networks

Edge AI involves deploying machine learning models on devices at the network's edge (e.g., smartphones, IoT devices) rather than in centralized data centers. This trend addresses the need for real-time processing, reduced latency, and privacy by enabling devices to process data locally without sending it to the cloud.

Key Features of Edge AI

- **Real-Time Processing**: Edge AI performs computations directly on devices, enabling real-time analysis and decision-making.
- **Privacy and Security**: Processing data locally reduces the risk of data breaches and minimizes the need to transmit sensitive information.

- **Reduced Latency**: By processing data on-device, edge AI reduces latency, which is critical for applications requiring immediate feedback.

Applications of Edge AI

- **Smart Cities**: Edge AI supports real-time monitoring of traffic, public safety, and environmental conditions, enabling rapid response to changing conditions.
- **Healthcare and Wearables**: Edge AI enables health monitoring on devices like wearables, where data can be processed in real-time to alert users or medical professionals.
- **Industrial Automation**: In manufacturing, edge AI analyzes sensor data on machinery to detect anomalies and optimize maintenance without relying on remote servers.
- **Augmented Reality and Gaming**: Edge AI powers augmented reality applications and mobile gaming by delivering seamless experiences without cloud dependencies.

Benefits of Edge AI

Edge AI reduces dependency on cloud infrastructure, increases data privacy, and allows for real-time processing. It is particularly valuable in industries with strict data privacy requirements and applications that demand instant feedback, such as autonomous vehicles, healthcare, and industrial automation.

5. Explainable AI (XAI): Enhancing Transparency and Trust

As machine learning models become more complex, explainable AI (XAI) seeks to make them understandable to humans. XAI addresses the "black box" problem by providing insights into how and why a model makes specific predictions, fostering transparency, accountability, and trust in AI systems.

Key Concepts in Explainable AI

- **Interpretability**: XAI provides tools to explain model outputs, helping users understand which features or variables influenced a decision.
- **Model Transparency**: XAI techniques enhance transparency by making machine learning models, particularly deep learning models, more accessible to non-experts.
- **Feature Attribution**: Tools like SHAP (SHapley Additive exPlanations) and LIME (Local Interpretable Model-Agnostic Explanations) offer feature attribution, showing the influence of individual variables on predictions.

Applications of Explainable AI

- **Healthcare Diagnostics**: XAI helps healthcare professionals understand AI-based diagnostic recommendations, allowing them to validate and trust the model's output.

- **Finance and Credit Scoring**: Explainable AI allows financial institutions to justify credit decisions by clarifying how various factors, like credit history and income, influence approval.
- **Compliance and Regulatory Reporting**: In regulated industries, XAI assists in documenting AI decisions, supporting compliance with laws requiring transparency in automated decision-making.
- **Customer Support and Personalization**: XAI enables businesses to explain personalization recommendations (e.g., content recommendations) to users, increasing trust in automated systems.

Benefits of Explainable AI

Explainable AI improves model transparency and helps build trust with users by clarifying how decisions are made. This is especially important in industries with high-stakes applications like healthcare, finance, and legal, where decisions must be justifiable and understandable.

6. Federated Learning: Collaborative Learning Without Data Sharing

Federated learning is a method that allows machine learning models to be trained across multiple decentralized devices or servers without transferring raw data to a central location. This approach enhances data privacy and security while enabling collaborative learning.

Key Features of Federated Learning

- **Decentralized Training**: Instead of sending data to a central server, federated learning trains models locally on devices and only aggregates model updates.
- **Privacy Preservation**: Since raw data never leaves the local device, federated learning minimizes data exposure and aligns with privacy regulations.
- **Scalability**: Federated learning allows scalable model training across a vast number of devices

Implications of Advancements in Data Analytics and Machine Learning for Professionals

The rapid advancements in data analytics and machine learning are transforming how data professionals work, offering new tools, methodologies, and challenges. Emerging technologies like AutoML, reinforcement learning, generative AI, edge computing, and federated learning present both opportunities and demands, requiring data professionals to adapt and expand their skillsets. This chapter explores the implications of these advancements for data analytics professionals, highlighting the skills, responsibilities, and strategic adjustments needed to stay relevant in a dynamic field.

1. Expanding Skill Sets to Include New Technologies and Techniques

The emergence of advanced technologies such as AutoML, reinforcement learning, and generative AI requires data professionals to continually evolve their skillsets. Mastering these tools enables professionals to leverage new capabilities and gain competitive advantages in their work.

Key Skills in Demand

- **Automation and AutoML**: As AutoML becomes more widely used, professionals need to understand how to leverage these platforms to automate repetitive tasks while maintaining control over model quality and interpretability.
- **Reinforcement Learning and Advanced Algorithms**: Reinforcement learning opens up opportunities in industries like robotics, finance, and logistics, requiring professionals to learn new algorithms and how to apply them in real-world scenarios.
- **Generative AI and Content Creation**: Knowledge of generative models, such as GANs and transformer models, is increasingly valuable for professionals in marketing, media, and design who wish to create data-driven content.
- **Edge and Federated Learning**: Working with edge and federated learning requires familiarity with decentralized data processing, making these skills crucial for industries prioritizing real-time analytics and privacy, like healthcare and IoT.

Implications: The demand for new technical skills encourages data professionals to invest in continuous learning. Those who adapt to and adopt these emerging technologies can bring innovative solutions to their organizations, staying at the forefront of the industry.

2. Embracing Automation to Increase Efficiency and Focus on High-Impact Work

As automation tools like AutoML reduce the time spent on repetitive tasks, data professionals can shift their focus toward more strategic, high-impact work. Automation does not replace the need for human expertise; instead, it augments it, allowing professionals to focus on interpretation, problem-solving, and strategic recommendations.

Shifts in Focus Enabled by Automation

- **Greater Emphasis on Business Problem Definition**: With AutoML handling model selection and hyperparameter tuning, data professionals can dedicate more time to defining the problem, selecting the right data, and ensuring that the analysis aligns with business goals.
- **Enhanced Focus on Interpretation and Communication**: As AutoML simplifies the technical modeling process, professionals need to excel at interpreting results and communicating actionable insights to stakeholders.
- **Model Monitoring and Continuous Improvement**: AutoML and automation

make it easy to deploy models but also necessitate ongoing monitoring and adjustments, especially as business conditions or data drift.

Implications: Automation enables data professionals to prioritize higher-value activities, such as understanding business objectives, refining data strategies, and communicating insights. This shift enhances their strategic role in organizations and requires strong business acumen and communication skills.

3. Navigating the Ethical and Responsible Use of AI and Data

The increased complexity and power of machine learning models, such as reinforcement learning and generative AI, raise ethical questions that data professionals must address. As models become more sophisticated, so too do the challenges of ensuring fairness, transparency, and accountability in AI-driven decisions.

New Ethical Considerations

- **Explainability and Transparency**: Advanced models, particularly deep learning and generative models, often operate as "black boxes." Data professionals must advocate for explainable AI, using tools like SHAP and LIME to make models understandable to stakeholders.
- **Bias and Fairness**: As machine learning models increasingly impact hiring, lending, and healthcare, it is crucial to identify and

mitigate bias. Professionals are responsible for assessing model fairness and ensuring that predictions do not reinforce harmful stereotypes.

- **Privacy and Data Security in Federated Learning**: Federated learning and edge AI offer new opportunities to protect data privacy by keeping data decentralized. Data professionals must implement these models responsibly, safeguarding privacy while balancing analytical needs.

Implications: Data professionals will increasingly serve as stewards of ethical AI, responsible for maintaining fairness, transparency, and accountability. This role requires awareness of ethical frameworks, proficiency with interpretability tools, and a commitment to ongoing ethical training.

4. Adapting to Real-Time and Decentralized Analytics

Technologies like edge AI and federated learning push analytics beyond centralized data centers, requiring data professionals to adapt to real-time, decentralized data processing. In fields like healthcare, IoT, and autonomous systems, real-time decision-making has become essential, creating demand for skills in decentralized data processing and edge computing.

New Responsibilities with Decentralized Analytics

- **Understanding Edge Computing and Real-Time Data Processing**: Data professionals working with IoT or real-time applications must learn to handle data on distributed networks, enabling low-latency processing and fast responses.
- **Managing Data Privacy and Security in Distributed Environments**: Decentralized analytics demand strong data governance skills, as sensitive data is increasingly stored and processed across numerous devices.
- **Maintaining Data Quality Across Devices**: Professionals must address challenges in ensuring data consistency, accuracy, and quality across decentralized systems where data may be fragmented or noisy.

Implications: The shift toward real-time, decentralized analytics requires data professionals to develop skills in edge computing, data security, and quality control in distributed networks. This trend emphasizes the need for adaptability as data processing becomes more fragmented and immediate.

5. Enhancing Collaboration with Business Units through AI-Driven Insights

As advanced analytics become more integrated into business processes, data professionals are expected to work closely with non-technical departments, translating complex models into actionable insights. The role of data professionals as strategic partners to business units becomes more critical, and they must bridge the gap between technical insights and business strategy.

Key Collaboration Strategies

- **Communicating Data Insights to Non-Technical Teams**: Professionals must explain insights from complex models in simple terms, showing how data-driven insights align with business goals and operational needs.

- **Building User-Friendly Dashboards and Tools**: Creating interactive dashboards with AutoML and visualization tools allows non-technical stakeholders to explore data insights independently, enhancing engagement.

- **Providing Training and Support for AI Applications**: As AI-driven tools are deployed, data professionals may be called upon to train business users, ensuring they understand and trust automated recommendations.

Implications: As data professionals become increasingly embedded within business units, communication skills and the ability to translate insights for a non-technical audience are paramount. Success in this role requires building strong relationships, aligning analytics with organizational goals, and promoting a culture of data-driven decision-making.

6. Developing Specialized Expertise for High-Demand Applications

With the growing number of machine learning applications, specialization is becoming increasingly valuable in areas like healthcare analytics, autonomous systems, and natural language processing (NLP). By focusing on high-demand, domain-specific applications, data professionals can deepen their expertise and position themselves as valuable assets within their industries.

Areas of Specialized Expertise

- **Healthcare and Diagnostics**: Specialized knowledge in medical data analysis, federated learning for patient privacy, and explainable AI are critical in healthcare applications.

- **Autonomous Systems and Robotics**: Understanding reinforcement learning, real-time processing, and ethical considerations is essential for professionals working in autonomous systems.

- **Natural Language Processing (NLP)**: With generative AI transforming language models, NLP expertise is in demand for applications like chatbots, virtual assistants, and sentiment analysis.

- **Financial Analytics**: Expertise in XAI and reinforcement learning helps professionals address the complex decision-making needs of the finance sector, from credit scoring to fraud detection.

Implications: Developing specialized knowledge within a high-demand application area enables data professionals to create targeted, impactful solutions. Specialization enhances career prospects and allows professionals to drive innovation in their chosen fields.

7. Embracing Continuous Learning and Adaptation

With AI and machine learning technologies evolving rapidly, continuous learning is crucial for data professionals. To stay relevant, data professionals need to adapt to new tools, methodologies, and industry standards, ensuring they remain capable of leveraging cutting-edge advancements effectively.

Strategies for Continuous Learning

- **Enroll in Specialized Training and Certification Programs**: Courses on new technologies, such as AutoML, reinforcement learning, or edge AI, provide structured learning opportunities to master emerging skills.

- **Engage with the Data Science Community**: Participating in conferences, online forums, and communities allows professionals to stay informed about new trends, best practices, and tools.

- **Experiment with New Technologies**: Hands-on experimentation with new tools and platforms enables professionals to develop practical skills, staying agile as new solutions emerge.

- **Follow Industry Leaders and Research**: Keeping up with thought leaders, academic research, and industry publications provides insights into the future direction of data science and machine learning.

Implications: A commitment to continuous learning ensures that data professionals remain competitive and informed, able to harness the latest advancements in AI. Those who embrace adaptability and lifelong learning will be best positioned to drive innovation and create impact in a rapidly changing field.

Conclusion

Advancements in data analytics and machine learning are reshaping the responsibilities and skill requirements for data professionals. As AutoML, reinforcement learning, generative AI, edge computing, and other trends reshape the landscape, data professionals must adapt by expanding their technical skills, focusing on ethical considerations, and collaborating closely with business units. By embracing continuous learning, developing specialized expertise, and adopting a proactive approach to emerging technologies, data professionals can drive innovation and maintain their value in a dynamic field. The future of data analytics holds vast potential for those who are prepared to evolve and lead in a rapidly advancing digital world.

Preparation Tips for Staying Relevant and Leveraging New Technologies in Analytics

In an era of rapid technological change, data analytics professionals need to continually evolve to stay relevant and effectively leverage new technologies. Emerging fields like AutoML, reinforcement learning, edge AI, and generative AI demand updated skills, adaptive mindsets, and a commitment to lifelong learning. This chapter provides practical tips for preparing to work with these advancements, empowering data professionals to navigate an ever-evolving landscape.

1. Build a Strong Foundation in Core Data Skills

A solid foundation in core data skills remains essential, even as advanced tools automate parts of the machine learning pipeline. Key competencies in data wrangling, statistics, basic machine learning, and programming are prerequisites for mastering new technologies.

Essential Core Skills to Develop

- **Programming Proficiency**: Master programming languages like Python and SQL, which remain fundamental in data science and are widely supported in emerging technologies like AutoML and generative AI.
- **Statistical Knowledge**: Strong statistical knowledge helps in understanding model outputs, evaluating results, and detecting

biases—a skill set that becomes even more valuable with sophisticated models.

- **Data Cleaning and Preparation**: Effective data wrangling and preparation skills ensure clean, high-quality data, which is critical to the success of advanced AI models.
- **Machine Learning Fundamentals**: Understanding foundational machine learning concepts allows data professionals to make informed decisions when using automated tools and interpreting complex models.

Preparation Tips: Regularly refresh and build on these core skills through online courses, certifications, and hands-on projects, ensuring a solid foundation to tackle more advanced topics as they emerge.

2. Learn the Basics of Emerging Technologies

While specialization can be beneficial, having a foundational understanding of emerging technologies like AutoML, reinforcement learning, and generative AI is key to staying adaptable and open to new opportunities.

Foundational Knowledge Areas for Emerging Technologies

- **AutoML**: Familiarize yourself with popular AutoML platforms like Google AutoML, H2O.ai, and DataRobot. Understand what these platforms can (and cannot) automate to effectively leverage them in projects.

- **Reinforcement Learning**: Learn the basics of reinforcement learning through courses or tutorials, exploring core concepts like agents, rewards, and policies. Experiment with simple RL environments using libraries like OpenAI Gym.
- **Generative AI**: Develop an understanding of transformer models (like GPT and BERT) and GANs (generative adversarial networks), as these models are foundational to generative AI applications. Tools like Hugging Face and TensorFlow can help you explore these models.
- **Edge and Federated Learning**: Familiarize yourself with decentralized processing and federated learning through introductory resources, focusing on applications where privacy and real-time analytics are priorities.

Preparation Tips: Take introductory courses on each of these topics to gain foundational knowledge, then experiment with simple projects using platforms and libraries. Staying updated with basic knowledge will help you pivot when more in-depth expertise is needed.

3. Experiment with New Tools and Platforms

Hands-on experience with the latest tools and platforms is essential for mastering new technologies. Experimenting with these tools allows you to understand their practical applications, limitations, and potential impact.

Popular Tools for Experimentation

- **AutoML Platforms**: Try platforms like Google Cloud AutoML, Amazon SageMaker Autopilot, or H2O.ai to automate data preprocessing, model selection, and tuning.
- **Reinforcement Learning Libraries**: Experiment with RL libraries like OpenAI Gym, Stable Baselines, or TensorFlow-Agents to develop simple models and explore reinforcement learning.
- **Generative AI Frameworks**: Use libraries like Hugging Face Transformers for text-based generative AI or TensorFlow/Keras for implementing GANs, enabling you to create models for text, images, or audio.
- **Edge AI Development Kits**: For those interested in edge computing, explore edge AI hardware like NVIDIA Jetson or Google Coral, and software tools like TensorFlow Lite, which allow you to experiment with on-device AI.

Preparation Tips: Choose a specific tool or platform each month to explore, working on small projects that demonstrate core functionalities. This approach builds practical experience and confidence in using cutting-edge tools.

4. Engage in Continuous Learning and Stay Informed

With the rapid pace of change in AI and data science, continuous learning is a necessity. Following industry thought leaders, participating in online communities, and staying updated on research developments helps professionals remain competitive.

Methods for Continuous Learning

- **Online Courses and Certifications**: Platforms like Coursera, edX, and DataCamp offer specialized courses on emerging topics. Certifications in areas like machine learning, reinforcement learning, and data privacy can add value to your skillset.

- **Industry Conferences and Webinars**: Attend conferences like NeurIPS, ICML, and KDD, which provide insights into the latest research and developments. Online webinars and workshops from these events are also valuable for keeping up to date.

- **Follow Thought Leaders and Blogs**: Follow AI and data science thought leaders on LinkedIn, Twitter, or Medium. Blogs like Towards Data Science, Fast.ai, and OpenAI's blog provide accessible content on cutting-edge advancements.

- **Academic Journals and Research Papers**: For deeper insights, explore journals like the Journal of Machine Learning Research (JMLR) or the arXiv preprint repository. Reading research papers helps you understand upcoming trends and potential applications.

Preparation Tips: Set aside time each week for continuous learning, whether through articles, papers, or online courses. Aim to complete at least one new course or certification each quarter to stay ahead.

5. Develop Strong Data Ethics and Governance Knowledge

As machine learning technologies grow in complexity, understanding the ethical implications and governance requirements is critical. Data professionals should be prepared to address issues like data privacy, fairness, and transparency in their work.

Core Ethical and Governance Skills

- **Understanding Data Privacy Regulations**: Familiarize yourself with regulations such as GDPR and CCPA to ensure compliant data handling practices. This is particularly relevant for fields like federated learning, where data privacy is paramount.
- **Bias Detection and Fairness**: Learn to identify and mitigate biases in machine learning models. Tools like SHAP, LIME, and Fairness Indicators by Google can help assess model fairness and interpretability.
- **Transparency and Explainability**: Become proficient in using explainability tools, especially for complex models like deep learning and reinforcement learning, to build trust with stakeholders.
- **Data Security Best Practices**: Knowledge of data encryption, access controls, and

decentralized processing techniques is essential for safeguarding data in cloud and edge environments.

Preparation Tips: Take online courses on data ethics, privacy, and AI fairness. Regularly review case studies to understand real-world applications and develop frameworks for ethically implementing new technologies.

6. Develop Soft Skills for Enhanced Communication and Collaboration

As data analytics becomes increasingly embedded across organizations, professionals are expected to work closely with cross-functional teams and communicate complex insights effectively. Soft skills are crucial for bridging the gap between technical findings and business objectives.

Key Soft Skills for Success

- **Effective Communication**: Simplify technical findings and present them in a way that resonates with non-technical audiences. Practice explaining complex concepts without jargon, focusing on implications and actionable insights.
- **Storytelling with Data**: Develop storytelling skills to present data in a compelling narrative format. Use tools like PowerPoint or Tableau to build engaging presentations that guide stakeholders through insights.
- **Collaboration and Teamwork**: Data projects increasingly involve collaboration

with other departments, such as marketing, finance, and operations. Build rapport and foster productive working relationships to drive data-driven initiatives.

- **Critical Thinking and Problem-Solving**: As automation handles more repetitive tasks, data professionals must focus on identifying complex problems, asking the right questions, and developing creative solutions.

Preparation Tips: Join public speaking or data storytelling workshops, volunteer to present data findings within your team, and seek feedback to improve. Regular practice in communicating data insights helps build confidence and makes data professionals more effective in collaborative environments.

7. Take on Real-World Projects and Internships

Nothing accelerates learning like practical, hands-on experience. Real-world projects expose data professionals to the challenges of deploying analytics in business environments, allowing them to apply theoretical knowledge and gain a deeper understanding of advanced technologies.

Finding Real-World Learning Opportunities

- **Freelance or Consulting Projects**: Look for freelance projects or short-term consulting opportunities to apply data analytics in diverse industries, gaining exposure to practical business problems.

- **Participate in Kaggle Competitions**: Kaggle competitions offer real-world datasets and complex challenges, giving professionals a way to experiment with new techniques and learn from peers.
- **Internships and Part-Time Roles**: If possible, take internships or part-time roles that focus on areas like machine learning, data engineering, or AI, providing experience in real-world applications of analytics.
- **Collaborate with Open-Source Projects**: Contribute to open-source AI projects on platforms like GitHub to gain hands-on experience in building and deploying models in collaborative settings.

Preparation Tips: Regularly apply for small projects or collaborations and document your work in a portfolio. The hands-on experience gained from real-world projects is invaluable for building confidence and demonstrating practical expertise.

8. Create a Personal Learning Plan for Continued Growth

With so many emerging technologies and skills to master, creating a structured learning plan helps data professionals stay organized and focused. A personal learning plan can set milestones, track progress, and ensure steady development in targeted areas.

Steps to Create a Learning Plan

- **Identify Key Areas of Interest**: Based on career goals, identify areas of specialization, such as AutoML, edge AI, or generative AI, and set long-term learning goals.
- **Set Measurable Goals and Milestones**: Define specific, measurable objectives for each skill area, such as "Complete an AutoML course by Q1" or "Build a reinforcement learning model by Q2."
- **Allocate Time for Learning and Experimentation**: Dedicate regular time slots for learning, whether it's weekly online courses, monthly experiments, or quarterly certifications.
- **Review and Adjust Regularly**: Periodically assess your progress, update your plan to include new technologies, and adjust timelines as needed to ensure steady growth.

Preparation Tips: Break down learning objectives into manageable steps and celebrate small milestones to stay motivated. A learning plan keeps you focused and ensures continuous development in line with evolving trends.

Conclusion

Staying relevant and leveraging new technologies in data analytics requires a proactive approach to learning, experimentation, and skill development. By building a solid foundation, exploring emerging technologies, developing soft skills, and embracing hands-on projects, data professionals can position themselves at the forefront of an evolving field. A commitment to continuous learning, coupled with a structured personal learning plan, ensures that data professionals are well-prepared to harness new technologies, create meaningful impact, and remain competitive in a fast-paced, technology-driven world.

References for "Future of Data Analytics and Machine Learning"

1. **Aggarwal, C. C. (2018)**. *Machine Learning for Text*. Springer.
   - An in-depth resource covering machine learning techniques in text processing, including applications in natural language processing (NLP).
2. **Alpaydin, E. (2020)**. *Introduction to Machine Learning (4th ed.)*. MIT Press.
   - This book provides a comprehensive introduction to machine learning, from fundamental concepts to more advanced topics.
3. **Barredo Arrieta, A., et al. (2020)**. "Explainable Artificial Intelligence (XAI): Concepts, Taxonomies, Opportunities and Challenges toward Responsible AI." *Information Fusion*, 58, 82-115.
   - An article providing a detailed overview of explainable AI, addressing techniques for making machine learning models interpretable and transparent.
4. **Bengio, Y., Goodfellow, I., & Courville, A. (2016)**. *Deep Learning*. MIT Press.
   - A foundational book on deep learning, covering neural networks, generative adversarial networks

(GANs), and applications in various fields.

5. **Brownlee, J. (2021)**. *Automated Machine Learning (AutoML): The Next Wave of Machine Learning.* Machine Learning Mastery.
   - A guide on AutoML, discussing how automation is transforming the machine learning pipeline and making data science more accessible.

6. **Chollet, F. (2021)**. *Deep Learning with Python (2nd ed.).* Manning Publications.
   - An introduction to deep learning with practical examples in Python, including applications of generative AI and reinforcement learning.

7. **Das, A., & McAfee, R. (2021)**. *Machine Learning for Decision Makers: Cognitive Computing Fundamentals for Better Decision Making.* Packt Publishing.
   - This book bridges technical machine learning with strategic business insights, ideal for understanding the impact of AI on decision-making.

8. **Géron, A. (2019)**. *Hands-On Machine Learning with Scikit-Learn, Keras, and TensorFlow (2nd ed.).* O'Reilly Media.
   - A hands-on guide covering a wide array of machine learning and deep learning techniques, with practical examples in Python.

9. **Goodfellow, I., Pouget-Abadie, J., Mirza, M., et al. (2014)**. "Generative Adversarial Networks." *arXiv preprint arXiv:1406.2661.*

   - The foundational paper introducing GANs, explaining the competitive training between the generator and discriminator models.

10. **Hastie, T., Tibshirani, R., & Friedman, J. (2009)**. *The Elements of Statistical Learning: Data Mining, Inference, and Prediction (2nd ed.).* Springer.

    - A comprehensive guide on statistical learning and machine learning, suitable for data science and analytics professionals.

11. **Howard, J., & Gugger, S. (2020)**. *Deep Learning for Coders with Fastai and PyTorch.* O'Reilly Media.

    - A practical resource for building and deploying deep learning models, focusing on PyTorch and Fastai for real-world applications.

12. **Koller, D., & Friedman, N. (2009)**. *Probabilistic Graphical Models: Principles and Techniques.* MIT Press.

    - This book introduces graphical models, which are key in reinforcement learning and probabilistic approaches to machine learning.

13. **Li, J., & Chen, S. (2021)**. *AutoML: Concepts and Applications*. Springer.
    - An overview of automated machine learning, discussing its applications, benefits, and challenges in simplifying the machine learning pipeline.
14. **Ng, A. (2020)**. *Machine Learning Yearning*. DeepLearning.AI.
    - A guide focused on practical tips and strategies for building successful machine learning projects, including advice on data preparation and model iteration.
15. **O'Reilly, C. (2019)**. *Data Governance: Creating an Environment of Data Quality and Integrity*. Elsevier.
    - This book covers essential topics in data governance, including compliance, security, and the role of governance in AI and machine learning projects.
16. **OpenAI (2021)**. "Language Models are Few-Shot Learners." *arXiv preprint arXiv:2005.14165*.
    - The paper introducing GPT-3, explaining the transformer model architecture and its applications in generative AI.

17. **Raschka, S., & Mirjalili, V. (2019)**. *Python Machine Learning (3rd ed.).* Packt Publishing.

   o An accessible book covering practical machine learning applications in Python, from basic machine learning to advanced deep learning topics.

18. **Russell, S. J., & Norvig, P. (2020)**. *Artificial Intelligence: A Modern Approach (4th ed.).* Pearson.

   o A widely used textbook on AI, covering a broad range of topics including reinforcement learning, probabilistic reasoning, and ethical considerations.

19. **Sharma, H. (2022)**. *Explainable AI with Python: Understand Data-Driven Decisions through Explainability.* Packt Publishing.

   o A guide to implementing explainable AI techniques, with Python examples that make complex models interpretable and trustworthy.

20. **Silver, D., Sutton, R., & Barto, A. (2018)**. *Reinforcement Learning: An Introduction (2nd ed.).* MIT Press.

   o The primary textbook on reinforcement learning, introducing key concepts like Q-learning, policy gradients, and applications in dynamic environments.

21. **Vallabhaneni, V., & Srinivasa, N. (2021)**. *Edge AI: Convergence of Edge Computing and Artificial Intelligence*. Springer.
     - An exploration of edge AI, discussing how AI at the edge of networks is used in real-time analytics, IoT, and privacy-sensitive applications.
22. **Vapnik, V. (1998)**. *Statistical Learning Theory*. Wiley-Interscience.
     - A foundational text on statistical learning, offering insights into the theory behind machine learning models, including support vector machines.
23. **Zhou, Z. (2021)**. *Federated Learning: Collaborative Machine Learning without Centralized Training Data*. Springer.
     - An introduction to federated learning, explaining how decentralized models are trained to preserve privacy in data-sensitive applications.
24. **Zhou, Z.-H. (2022)**. *Machine Learning (2nd ed.)*. Springer.
     - An advanced yet accessible book on machine learning, covering both foundational concepts and modern applications like generative models and federated learning.

Online Resources and Communities

- **arXiv.org** – A repository of research papers in AI and machine learning, where professionals can stay updated on cutting-edge research.
- **Kaggle** – A platform offering datasets and competitions, providing hands-on practice with real-world data science problems.
- **Towards Data Science on Medium** – A blog covering tutorials, industry trends, and discussions on machine learning, data analytics, and AI.
- **Data Science Central** – An online resource offering articles, webinars, and community discussions on trends and tools in data science.
- **Coursera and edX** – Platforms offering online courses from top universities on machine learning, AutoML, reinforcement learning, and data ethics.

These resources provide a foundational understanding of data analytics and machine learning, essential for data professionals adapting to emerging trends and technologies.

About the Author

Dr, Alex Harper

Driven by a passion for data-driven insights and their transformative impact on business and technology, Dr. Alex Harper has dedicated their career to advancing data analytics and empowering professionals through accessible, practical knowledge. Building upon the foundations laid in their previous books, *Essential Data Analytics: Quick-Start Guide to Data Literacy for Beginners* and *Intermediate Data Analytic Skills: Databases, Programming, and Advanced Statistics*, they continue to explore complex data concepts with a clear, approachable style.

With over a decade of experience in the field, Dr. Alex Harper combines deep technical knowledge with a commitment to ethical data practices and a strong focus on real-world applications. Their expertise spans statistical analysis, machine learning, and advanced analytics, equipping readers with the skills necessary to thrive in an evolving data landscape. In this ongoing series, they expand into advanced topics, offering comprehensive guidance on machine learning, data mining, and analytic thinking to help readers at every stage of their data journey.

Beyond authoring, Dr. Alex Harper is a sought-after speaker and advisor in data literacy and analytics education, frequently collaborating with industry experts to bridge the gap between complex analytics concepts and their practical use. This dedication has earned them recognition as a leading voice in data analytics, inspiring a new generation of data-driven thinkers.

Disclaimer

This book is intended for informational and educational purposes only. The author and publisher have made every effort to ensure the accuracy and completeness of the information contained within; however, they assume no responsibility for errors, omissions, or changes to the data and methodologies discussed. The content of this book should not be interpreted as professional advice, and readers are encouraged to seek expert consultation for specific issues related to data analytics, machine learning, or any other technical topics covered herein.

The use of any tools, techniques, or recommendations provided in this book is at the reader's discretion and risk. The author and publisher are not liable for any damages, losses, or claims resulting from the application of information in this book, nor do they endorse any third-party products or services mentioned. All trademarks, product names, and company names mentioned in this book are the property of their respective owners and are used solely for identification purposes.

The reader is encouraged to verify current laws, regulations, and industry standards, as these may impact the application of data analytics techniques discussed in this book. This book is not a substitute for legal, regulatory, or technical expertise in the fields discussed.

Legal Notice

This book is provided "as is" without warranty of any kind, either express or implied, including but not limited to the implied warranties of merchantability, fitness for a particular purpose, or non-infringement. The author and publisher disclaim any liability, loss, or risk incurred as a consequence, directly or indirectly, of the use and application of any of the contents of this book.

The information contained in this book is intended for general informational purposes only and does not constitute professional, legal, or financial advice. The strategies and techniques discussed may not be suitable for every individual or situation, and readers should consult with a qualified professional before applying the information to their specific circumstances. The author and publisher make no representations or warranties with respect to the accuracy or completeness of the contents of this book and specifically disclaim any liability for any damages, losses, or risks, whether direct, indirect, incidental, or consequential, incurred as a result of the use or application of any of the information provided herein.

All trademarks, service marks, product names, or named features are the property of their respective owners, and no claim is made by the author or publisher to any such mark or other intellectual property. The inclusion of any organization, website, or product name does not imply endorsement or affiliation.

By reading this book, you agree to assume all risks associated with the use of the information provided and release the author and publisher from any and all claims, liabilities, or damages that may arise from such use.